Woman Lawyer

Woman Lawyer

THE TRIALS OF CLARA FOLTZ

Barbara Babcock

STANFORD UNIVERSITY PRESS

STANFORD, CALIFORNIA

Stanford University Press
Stanford, California

Special discounts for bulk quantities of Stanford Business Books are available to
corporations, professional associations, and other organizations. For details and discount
information, contact the special sales department of Stanford University Press.
Tel: (650) 736-1782, Fax: (650) 736-1784

Printed in the United States of America on acid-free, archival-quality paper

Library of Congress Cataloging-in-Publication Data

Babcock, Barbara Allen.
  The trials of Clara Foltz / Barbara Babcock.
    p. cm.
  Includes bibliographical references and index.
  ISBN 978-0-8047-4358-7 (cloth : alk. paper)
    1. Foltz, Clara Shortridge, 1849–1934. 2. Lawyers—California—Biography. 3. Women
lawyers—California—Biography. I. Title.
  KF368.F585B33 2011
  340.092—dc22
  [B]

2010037262

Typeset by Bruce Lundquist in 10.5/14 Adobe Garamond

For Tom Grey, bird photographer

They called me the "lady lawyer," a pretty soubriquet which did much for me, for . . . I was bound to maintain a dainty manner as I browbeat my way through the marshes of ignorance and prejudice which beset me on every hand.

Clara Foltz, *Struggles and Triumphs of a Woman Lawyer*, Oct. 1916

Contents

Preface

Clara Foltz was one of the first women lawyers in the United States, and for a time one of the most famous. From the day of her admission to the bar in 1878, she was often in the news—arguing to all-male juries, stumping in political campaigns, and working for woman suffrage, penal reform, and other causes. She had a large part in the adoption of the first guaranties of equal access to employment and education in U.S. constitutional history, pioneered the public defender movement, and practiced law continuously for fifty years. In everything she did, Foltz enjoyed remarkable celebrity, partly because of the human interest of her personal situation. She was a single mother of five children and became a lawyer in order to support them as well as to find personal fulfillment and advance women's rights.

Despite the lavish attention during her lifetime, however, Foltz was largely forgotten until recently. The revival of her reputation started with the rise of the second women's movement in the 1970s, which brought a surge in the number of women attending law school. Almost overnight, the percentage of female students rose from 3 to 20 percent, and today it is nearly 50 percent. When all at once they became a large part of this important profession, women found themselves without a history to guide and to inspire.

Clara Foltz was one of the first beneficiaries of the interest these students and their male allies took in finding models and perhaps heroines for the new generations of women lawyers. In 1976, almost one hundred years after she successfully sued California's first law school for refusing to admit women, its law review featured an article about her extraordinary life, coauthored by a male professor and two female law students (Mortimer D. Schwartz, Susan L. Brandt, and Patience Milrod, "Clara Shortridge Foltz: Pioneer in the Law," 27 *Hastings Law Journal* 545). In 2002, the revival of interest in this pioneer woman lawyer reached a new level, when the central criminal court building in Los Angeles was renamed the Clara Shortridge

Foltz Criminal Justice Center. Justice Sandra Day O'Connor was the lead speaker at the dedication ceremony, which honored the accomplishments of women lawyers, and Foltz as first among them. My pleasure on behalf of my subject was only slightly dimmed by the query in the *Los Angeles Times*: "Clara Who?" In this book, I try to answer that question, and to examine the full dimensions of her achievement.

Though Foltz's personal papers did not survive—a serious loss to a biographer—she left behind an extensive public record. Her story is in court records, her own publications, biographical indexes, and perhaps most of all in news accounts and interviews. Most of her publicity was favorable, largely because, long before public relations became a recognized occupation, Foltz was a genius at managing her image. With confidence in her abilities and belief in her destiny, she was a true western character: larger than life and prodigious in her enjoyment of the moment and in her ambitions for the future.

Her distinctive voice—optimistic, figurative, hyperbolic, elevated but humorous—comes through not only in interviews and profiles, but also in the twenty-eight magazine columns she wrote when she was in her sixties titled "The Struggles and Triumphs of a Woman Lawyer." Foltz took her title from the book *Struggles and Triumphs: The Recollections of P. T. Barnum* (1882). Like the famous circus impresario, she lived a life of great highs and considerable lows, and also like him, she was an open and tireless self-promoter.

Though often speaking of her sacrifices for women's causes, Foltz never quite fit the mold of selfless crusader. Unwilling to relinquish any possibility, she was determined to be an inspiring movement leader, a successful lawyer and legal reformer, a glamorous and socially prominent woman, an influential public thinker, and a good mother. The result of these often conflicting desires was a life so frantic and scattered that it resists a logical, well-formed narrative. Yet these very qualities make her biography particularly relevant now, both as cautionary and heroic tale.

In my research and writing about Clara Foltz, I have come to admire her courage and charisma. At the same time, I have confronted her flaws and mistakes in judgment, which I try to portray accurately and fully—to mix the hag with the hagiography. But in a sense, full detachment is not really possible; I have necessarily interpreted Foltz's life through my own experiences—as a trial lawyer, a public defender, a first woman, and a feminist. Though I cannot wholly follow her direction to her anticipated biographer to "let wreaths of triumph my temples twine," I think she would approve of what I have done here.

The book is published at a moment when women lawyers have made gains that would have seemed incredible to most people in the past. Not to Clara Foltz, however; she predicted that women would win an equal place in the legal profession—and even sooner than it has actually happened. Foltz also believed that women would change the profession for the better and hoped that her own busy career promoting constitutional rights for the criminally accused and civil rights for women would inspire and instruct. I hope so too.

Acknowledgments

So many people have contributed to this book that naming names puts me in fear of omitting someone. But I must risk it. In the past few months as I have been organizing and arranging old files, I have thought fondly of the long line of wonderful student research assistants who have been companions in reconstructing Clara Foltz's life. Our work began before the golden age of search engines, and my early helpers worked in library archives and courthouse basements, reading old newspapers on microfiche and yellowing legal documents: Judith Carrithers, Lucy Carter, Mary Erickson, Ilana Hollenberg, John Ingrassia, Linden Joesting, Lisa Lindalef, Kara Mikulich, Catherine Ruckelshaus, Frances Scibelli, Paula Solario, and Karen Zobell.

With the advent of the Internet, many assistants have been particularly skilled in its use, and many have also had a knack for organizing the ever-growing mass of Foltziana. In those categories fall Frances Cook, Melinda Evans, Joanna Grossman, Menaka Kalascar, Karie Lew, Maureen Lewis, Hilary Ley, Kate Mann, Kim Mueller, Thomas Nosewicz, Jessica Oats, Katerina Rakowsky, Lisa Sitkin, Lauren Willis, and Rae Woods.

Some students worked closely on particular aspects of the research and did a superb job of organizing wide-ranging sources. On Foltz's Los Angeles years, Katherine McCarron; on public defense, Michael Evans, Julie Loughran, Angela Schwartz, and Michael Subit. Samantha Barbas was a great help on the form and organization of the online notes and other documentation. As the book went to press, Jenny Kim, Jenna Sheldon-Sherman, and Laura Zapain joined in shepherding it there, and Maggie McKinley helped immensely with the supplemental website.

In addition to the Stanford law students listed above, a number of former students and friends have helped with specific areas and locales. Darrin Hostetler took time out from practicing law to delve into old San Diego real estate transactions. Genevieve Leavitt investigated the activities of Elias Shortridge in Arizona; and Janet Hoeffel, Joyce Sterling, and their students pursued Foltz's Colorado activities. Alan Simon, a former Los Angeles public defender, took an interest when the courthouse was dedicated to Foltz. Jill Knuth, a genealogist, was a great help in tracking down family members. Paul Herman brought the trained historian's skills to the search and turned up many valuable resources

The staff members of the Robert Crown Library at Stanford Law School have been critical in writing and producing the book. To Paul Lomio and to Erika Wayne I owe the women's legal history website, and both of them, with Alba Holgado, have maintained and improved it over the years. Erika has joined me at every step, especially in coteaching the seminar on women's legal history; she inspired and helped with the papers that give substance to the website. Alba has done artistic work on presenting and improving the images of Clara Foltz and other pioneer women lawyers. Rich Porter and Sonia Moss have been indefatigable on locating hard-to-find sources. Indeed, the whole library staff has contributed to the work, including temporary workers such as Cynthia Goehler and college students Katharine Loh, Rita Lomio, and Nicola Perlman. Barbara Adams was my earliest helper in organizing and digitizing the news stories and other material found in our initial researches and brought exceptional skills and patience to the job. After Barbara retired, I was very fortunate in having Donna Fung as my chief assistant on presenting and organizing the work. She, too, encouraged me by finding Foltz fascinating, as did Arline Wyler, who was also involved for a period.

A grant from the National Endowment for the Humanities allowed me to accept a fellowship from the Stanford Humanities Center where I first laid my research plans. Throughout, I have had the interest and support of many colleagues, especially Dean Paul Brest, who sometimes doubted the project but never doubted me. For almost a decade, Diane Middlebrook and I sponsored a "Biographer's Seminar" for those engaged in this kind of work. The help of colleagues from other disciplines, especially Estelle Freedman, and regular vetting of work in progress were useful features of the seminar. Philip Ethington, who was a doctoral student at Stanford University and writing about the same period when I first met him, offered many insights into the Gilded Age politics of San Francisco.

The presentations I have given on Clara Foltz and her work are too numerous to mention here, but many audiences have helped me maintain my sense that this subject was interesting and important. My seminar in Women's Legal History has been a special muse as I saw many students affirm in their own work the usefulness of studying individual lives closely. I came to know Jill Norgren as a fellow biographer of a pioneer woman lawyer (Belva Lockwood), and we have shared research, ideas, and inspirations as well as frustrations. Finally, Ticien Sassoubre was the first person to read the work all the way through and helped me immensely in seeing it as a whole. At Stanford University Press, Norris Pope was a model of patience and support; Carolyn Brown and Jessie Dolch delivered first-rate editorial assistance.

The book is dedicated to my husband, Tom Grey, whose generosity and tolerance have benefited both Clara Foltz and me over the years. He has been a faithful editor even when it required adverse criticism—a hard thing for him to do. And he has brought his cool intelligence and warm encouragement to the struggles and triumphs involved in writing and living this life.

Installation of portrait at the Clara Shortridge Foltz Criminal
Justice Center. Photograph by Susan Schwartzenberg, 2008.

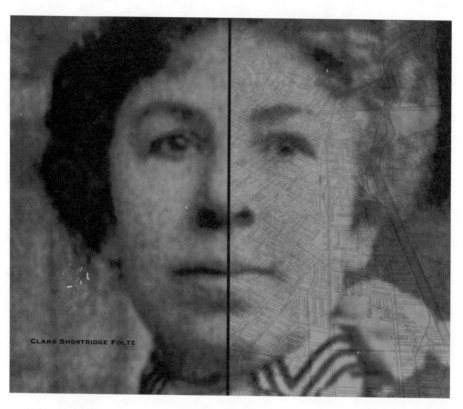

CLARA SHORTRIDGE FOLTZ

Portrait of Clara Shortridge Foltz as it appears over the courthouse entrance. Map detail is of Los Angeles where Foltz served as the first woman deputy district attorney and saw the enactment of the Foltz Defender Bill. Photograph by Susan Schwartzenberg, 2008.

Introduction

Clara Foltz was born Carrie Shortridge in Indiana in 1849 and grew up in a bucolic Iowa village. She eloped with a Union Army soldier at age fifteen, became a farm wife, and bore three children in five years. In any other period in history and place in the world, child-rearing and back-breaking labor would have been her permanent fate. Instead, Foltz left the farm and never looked back—like the United States itself. Within her lifetime the railroad, the steamship, the streetcar, the telegraph, the telephone, electrical lighting, the motor car, and the moving picture transformed America from a rural and parochial nation to one that was urban, industrial, and cosmopolitan. Foltz's personal story reflected what she called "the inventions of an active age." She thought of herself as unusually present to history, speaking of "startling points of contact with a world I seek to serve."[1]

Foltz found her main inspiration in the movement for women's rights, which had its official start at a meeting in Seneca Falls, New York, in 1848. Three hundred reformers gathered to consider the stark subordination of the female sex in the legal and political arenas. In most places in the United States, women could not own property after marriage, gain custody of their children upon divorce, attend institutions of higher learning, join the

professions, vote, or hold public office. As a girl, Carrie Shortridge heard
Lucy Stone, one of the best orators of the early women's movement, assail
the gender ideology that assigned females to the home while reserving public action exclusively to males. Into her old age, Foltz would describe this
speech as a life-altering event. But it took a while for Stone's words to have
their effect. On the political stage, the Civil War absorbed reformist energy;
women activists put aside their own demands for the duration of the conflict. They emerged from the war expecting to receive the vote along with
the former slaves whose cause many had linked with their own. Instead,
it would be a long battle for political equality. Like countless others, Foltz
spent most of her adult life petitioning, lobbying, leafleting, speaking, rallying, writing, pleading, and importuning for full rights as a citizen.

Paralleling the suffrage campaigns were women's efforts to enter the legal
profession. In some places, they were readily accepted and practiced in the
local fashion of most attorneys. But in California, Clara Foltz met tremendous resistance, and in overcoming it she became well-known within the
various reform movements and to the general public in the West and beyond. After joining the bar, she continued to make headlines both in her
suffrage activities and in her practice, especially her jury trials. At the same
time, Foltz established herself on the lecture circuit and became deeply involved in the raucous legislative and electoral politics of the day. She was a
paid orator in the presidential elections of the 1880s, speaking for hours to
huge crowds on subjects far removed from women's rights—the protective
tariff was one of her specialties, for instance. In her party affiliation, she followed family tradition (her father had been an early supporter of Abraham
Lincoln) and was a Republican for most of her life. For a time starting in
the late 1880s, she was a convert to the utopian socialism of Bellamy Nationalism, which enjoyed a short but stirring political moment before it
merged into the Populist (and ultimately the Progressive) movement.

The 1890s were the most important years of Foltz's public life. She
reached the high point of her career as a lawyer and law reformer by her
promotion of the public defender through speeches, writing, and lobbying
nationwide. In her last years, Foltz practiced law in Los Angeles, where she
began losing influence within the suffrage movement to a younger generation of college-educated women. Still, she played a significant role in the
final victory in California in 1911. Luckier than most of the pioneers, she
not only voted but experienced firsthand the achievement of virtually all
the goals set forth at Seneca Falls the year before she was born. She also saw

the initial success of her other major cause: the first public defender office in the nation was established in Los Angeles in 1913.

This book follows Foltz through four decades, as she worked for the liberation of women and due process for the criminally accused, while at the same time trying to raise her five children, enlarge her own celebrity, elevate the practice of law, influence public events, and strike it rich. The first four chapters give a chronological account, and the last three are thematic, examining her roles as "thinker" (or "public intellectual," in today's phrase), as a leader in the cause of women's rights, and as the founder of the public defender movement.

Focusing on Clara Foltz illuminates the history of her times. For instance, only a biographical interest would have uncovered the women's lobby at the 1879 California constitutional convention, which produced unprecedented guarantees of equal treatment (see Chapter 1). Similarly, the connection between public defense and women's rights that Foltz's life reveals has not been previously understood (see Chapter 7). The search for Clara Foltz also exposes the contributions of other largely forgotten figures, male allies especially. In her expansive social and professional lives, Foltz brought together all kinds of people: women activists joined with society ladies, and powerful men with poor, desperate people. Her cozy domestic circle melded with huge crowds cheering her "to the echo."

Foltz's story is also one of the precincts she could not enter, of disappointments and frustrated ambitions. No woman could be counsel to large corporate interests, hold high elective office, or even be a trusted legal advisor to those who did, though Foltz sought all these. She also longed to be a judge, but by the time a few women were elected or appointed to judgeships, she was well past her prime. The first female federal judge took office in 1934, the year that Foltz died.

If she had been a man, would Clara Foltz have won the lasting fame and large fortune she sought? She certainly thought so (and I tend the same way), but the answer is complicated. Much of the publicity and attention she received was on account of her sex as much as her brilliance and originality. Being an underdog and outsider sharpened her best gifts and enhanced her sympathies, as well as helping her to formulate her unique contribution: the idea of the public defender. In the women's movement, moreover, Foltz found companionship in her struggles and a cause that ennobled her efforts. She always said she was glad to be born female, and she proudly claimed the title of first woman.

Becoming a Lawyer, 1878–1880

Telling Her Own Story

Clara Foltz often had to explain why she became a lawyer—to justify an occupation that many people thought wrong and even unnatural for a woman.
In response to repeated questioning, she developed various accounts of "how
a sensitive conventional young woman" broke out of woman's accepted
"sphere."[1] Foltz's stories, related in interviews, lectures, and her autobiographical writings, provide much of what we can know about the events and
motives behind her dramatic entry into the California bar in 1878.

Foltz was born Carrie Shortridge in 1849 in Indiana, the middle child
between two older and two younger brothers. Her father, Elias Shortridge,
was a lawyer who apprenticed with Oliver Morton, subsequently the Civil
War governor of the state, an important Unionist, and an early supporter
of Abraham Lincoln. Shortridge left the law when, according to one of *his*
stories, he won an acquittal for a guilty murderer. He turned to itinerant
preaching in the "Campbellite" or "Christian" Church (today known as the
Disciples of Christ) and then during the war became head of its congregation at Mount Pleasant, Iowa. Though the town was small (thirty-five hun-

dred in 1860), it had a good road connecting it to Iowa Wesleyan University in Burlington and a railroad station that made it an agricultural and business center. Altogether, Mount Pleasant deserved its reputation as a prosperous and progressive community.[2]

Sometimes Foltz started with Mount Pleasant days when telling why she became a lawyer. Her father, she would say, "delighted in his only daughter's talent for abstruse thinking" and sighed: "Ah, if only you had been a boy, then I would have trained you for the law." Foltz remembered that she "did not like this opinion of my father's." Her mother was alarmed at how Clara might respond to such comments and warned against telling the girl such things, because, she said, "one of these days she will take it into her head to study law, and if she does, nobody on earth can stop her." "Indeed that was prophecy!" Foltz would add. As she later told it, the young Carrie thrived in the aptly named Mount Pleasant. She attended Howe's Academy there from 1860 to 1863 and loved school. Years later, her teachers remembered her as "a bright, ambitious, hard-toiling girl," and Foltz herself recalled with pride that she mastered the first *two* books of Latin by the age of twelve.[3]

The academy's founder (in 1841) and principal, Samuel L. Howe, was a classic mid-nineteenth-century reformer, of a kind often found in the small towns settled by idealistic believers in education and equality throughout the Midwest. He was an abolitionist, and his home was a station on the underground railroad for escaping slaves coming over the border from Missouri. A suffragist, he also believed in equal rights for men and women. Though coeducation was not widely practiced at the time, both Howe's Academy and nearby Iowa Wesleyan admitted women from their founding.

In the atmosphere of such a town, it seemed at least possible for a girl to think she might do great things. Another young woman from Mount Pleasant, Arabella Mansfield, who also attended Howe's Academy, would become the first woman lawyer in the United States. Years later, the two women from the same small community would meet at the Chicago World's Fair, both on the program at the first-ever nationwide meeting of female attorneys.[4]

But by 1869, when Mansfield broke the sex barrier for the American legal profession, Carrie Shortridge had taken steps that would seem to have forever foreclosed any such pioneering role for herself. She had become Clara Foltz, was bearing children every two years, and was running a farm household. The story of her marriage was not one Foltz often told, though early in her career she shared it with at least two sympathetic interviewers.[5] As she "drifted into young lady-hood," Foltz said, she shifted her ambitions from fame and glory to the traditional feminine dream of "a handsome, noble husband, who would cherish her and keep her sheltered from the unknown world in a happy little home. Against her parents' wishes and without their knowledge," she eloped with twenty-five-year-old Jeremiah Foltz, a good-looking Union Army soldier. Carrie Shortridge was fifteen.[6]

Before she eloped with Jeremiah, however, Carrie left Howe's Academy and became a schoolteacher herself for almost a year in Keithsburg, Illinois. She never explained this move, though she often spoke with regret of her interrupted and "imperfect" education. Throughout her long career, it would both fuel and bedevil her aspirations to be a serious jurisprudential thinker and a successful practitioner.

Leaving the academy was probably connected with her father's expulsion from the Mount Pleasant church for heresy—which Foltz never mentioned either. Elias Shortridge apparently started preaching the doctrine of "soul-sleep," which holds that the spirit does not go directly to God upon death but has no conscious existence until the resurrection of the body at the Last Judgment. These views are heterodox according to most Protestant denominations as well as Roman Catholics. Since Shortridge "was a preacher of much more than ordinary ability, numbers were carried away by the strange doctrine," according to church history.[7]

After being removed from the congregation, Foltz's father returned to his previous camp meeting and revival preaching, and the family moved to Keithsburg, Illinois. There, perhaps volunteering in a hospital near where she taught, the young girl met Jeremiah Foltz, who had left the Union Army because lumbago had disabled him. In her one extended account of her elopement, Foltz said that when she realized "the gravity of her course," she sorrowed most at disappointing her parents, for whom she held "childlike devotion." Nonetheless, at age fifteen, she became a woman "resolved to bend all the energies of her young being to marital happiness" and told herself, "I will be a perfect wife, as near as in me lies, and then all will be well." Foltz passed quickly over the eight years she spent on farms in Illinois and Iowa with Jeremiah, and the "little ones that came so fast."[8]

Her firstborn was Trella Evelyn in 1866, then Samuel Cortland in 1868, followed by Bertha May in 1870. In 1871, David Milton was born and Jeremiah left for Oregon. He may have been intending to desert his family, but if that was so, he failed this time. An observer in Portland later wrote about

Clara Foltz's arrival "in search of her husband" with "three little children tugging at her skirts and a babe in arms."[9] Her parents and younger brothers migrated with her, and they were settled in Salem, the state capital, by 1872. There, Jeremiah sold feed and farm machinery, and Clara sewed dresses and made hats. She also took in boarders. When the legislature was in session, many of the members would stay with Clara Foltz because her table was lively and afforded, some said, the best talk in the state. To keep everything running, Foltz rose before dawn to care for a house full of men and children. Then she spent hours cleaning and washing, sewing and cooking.

At the end of one such day, as she sat mending by the fire, a boarder made her a costly present—the four volumes of James Kent's *Commentaries on American Law*, the American equivalent of William Blackstone's famous exposition of English law. "I wish you would take these and read them: I think you would make a good lawyer," he said. Foltz often told this tale about her first professional recognition when she explained why she had taken up the study of law.[10]

In an 1882 interview, she related less pleasant personal experiences in Oregon that also drew her to the law. When the sheriff seized her sewing machine to pay Jeremiah's debts, a lawyer friend recovered it by arguing that the machine was a basic household good (like a cookstove) and thus not subject to attachment. When the same thing happened again, Foltz represented herself and added the argument that her sewing machine was a "workman's" tool used to support the family—a separate statutory exemption.[11]

In other versions of the story of how she became a lawyer, Foltz would skip the girlhood dreams, the Iowa farm, the Oregon boardinghouse and go straight to San Jose, California, where the Shortridges and the Foltzes moved around 1874, and where in 1876, Foltz delivered her last child, Virginia Knox. They had a neighbor who kept "a fine Jersey cow" in the backyard adjacent to theirs. "The heavy rains of winter had softened the rich deep soil and the cow waded in mud to its knees," Foltz later wrote. She felt that these unsanitary conditions jeopardized "my children's health, as also that of my neighbor." When neighborly requests failed, Foltz looked up the law and learned that a cow maintained in these conditions was an illegal nuisance. She called in the health department, which sent an officer "forthwith to lead the cow over to the common and stake her fast." As Foltz told it, the story revealed both the power of the law and its limitations. "In vain I sought to renew the former pleasant relations with the neighbor" (and the milk donations for the children), "but she was obdurate and unforgiving."[12]

Foltz also sometimes said she became a lawyer in order to help other women protect their families "when the shadow of death falls upon the head of the household." This followed from a life-altering experience of her own—Jeremiah's successful desertion in 1878, which left her at age twenty-nine a single mother of five children aged two to eleven. He moved to Portland, apparently for another woman. In 1879, Clara divorced him. She did not depict herself as abandoned and divorced, however, but said she was widowed by Jeremiah's sudden death.[13]

"Keeping boarders, dress-making and millinery are the first refuge of women so situated; and so she fell into line behind the army of women who preceded her," wrote an interviewer.[14] Unable to make enough to support her children, the story continued, Foltz saw that she must do something different or lose her family. Not from ambition and defiance of the norms of womanly conduct, but out of desperation, she decided to become a lawyer. Depicting herself as forced onto a path she would not have chosen made her move more acceptable, especially to the men whose help she needed. And no doubt economic need was part of the story of why Clara Foltz decided to become a lawyer.

But she framed her decision as if she had gone down the checklist of traditional alternatives facing a woman suddenly required to support herself and her children: try school teaching, try dressmaking, try taking in boarders, and, if those don't do the trick, then take your last resort and become a lawyer. This was a deliberate concealment, made for good strategic reasons, of the world-altering boldness of her choice. Many women had tried dress-making, many had taken in boarders; no woman in Clara Foltz's situation had ever decided to be a lawyer. In 1878, fewer than fifty women practiced as lawyers in the United States, and none of these was a single head of a family with five young children. None lived in California, either, where a section in the Code of Civil Procedure provided that only a "white male citizen" could apply to the bar.[15]

It was far against the odds that the young mother of five would be able to bring her daring choice to fruition. How she did it is a story with a large cast of characters—women suffragists and their male allies, helpful and hateful lawyers, judges and politicians, an attentive and, on the whole, admiring press. And the story's setting is California in the midst of an economic depression and on the verge of class and race war. During this perilous period, Clara Foltz and her movement comrades lobbied through a bill allowing women to become lawyers, then won two unprecedented clauses

Clara Foltz when she joined the bar in 1878. From Toland family scrapbook.

in the state constitution guaranteeing women the right to equal employment and public education. At the same time, she brought a court challenge to the exclusion of women from the state's first law school. For the rest of her life Foltz would call this her greatest case, and becoming a lawyer her best story.

Fearful Times for California

"The times are fearful; never so hard in California within the memory of the oldest inhabitant," wrote Clara Foltz in 1877. She and Jeremiah and their children, with her parents and two younger brothers, had settled in San Jose, a pleasant agricultural town of about sixteen thousand—some fifty miles from San Francisco and connected to it and to Sacramento (the state capital) by rail. Like so many of the midwesterners who went there, Clara Foltz took to California immediately; its people were "cosmopolitan," its landscape an "Eden of loveliness . . . exceeding in beauty the far-famed valley of the Nile!"[16]

Attractive though its orchards and surrounding mountains were, San Jose was a hard place to make a living in the decade called "the terrible seventies." The Shortridges and Foltzes had probably moved, as many did, because they thought the recently completed transcontinental railroad was about to transform the California economy. But it soon became clear that no boom was in sight. Instead, an economic depression in the East had propelled an army of workers across the continent only to find that the completion of the railroad had released thousands of laborers, many Chinese, into the market. Adding to the labor glut were drought and crop failures, ruinous gambling in silver stocks, banking collapses, and flamboyantly manipulative and dishonest plutocrats and politicians. "Capital threatened labor and labor menaced capital," as Foltz told the story many times, also noting "corruption in high places, malfeasance in office, immorality everywhere."[17]

Speaking of the subsidy-enriched railroad magnates and the corruption of the land office for allocating public property among settlers, Foltz complained of "vast landed estates [which] were the exclusive holdings of three or four men, technically acquired by law but really nothing short of the methods of highwaymen who take because they dare." Karl Marx, writing from London, used the California crisis as an object lesson: "nowhere else has the upheaval most shamelessly caused by capitalist concentration taken place with such speed."[18]

The political scene was set for the entrance of a demagogue, and Denis Kearney, an Irish drayman, assumed the part. In the summer of 1877, just when Foltz wrote to her friends about the "fearful times," Kearney started speaking on the sandlots in front of San Francisco's unfinished city hall. Thousands of unemployed workers, who became known as "sandlotters" or "Kearneyites," gathered there every day. Foltz remembered that their "forbidding presence in such vast numbers struck amazement if not fear in the breasts" of those who "terrorized the state with their lavish vulgar show of wealth." Kearney denounced the newly rich as "shoddy aristocrats" (soon shortened to "shoddies") and "bloated bondholders" and called for justice from "Judge Lynch," summoning from his followers roars of "Hemp, Hemp, Hemp." But the conclusion of every Kearney speech was not "Down with the Bosses" but "The Chinese Must Go."[19]

Driving out the Asian workers remaining in the West after the completion of the railroad was the founding principle of the Workingmen's Party of California (WPC). The Chinese immigrants were an easy target because most were single men who lived in segregated Chinatowns, spoke no English, and did not attempt to assimilate. It was with a racial rather than a class appeal that Kearney originally won control of the sandlots from the national Workingmen's Party, which had called on its followers to "direct their struggles against the ruling class, *not against* their victims, the Chinese."[20]

Employers argued that the Chinese were filling jobs no one else wanted, but many Californians believed they were depressing the wages of all workers. Moreover, so soon after the Civil War, the system of indenture under which some Chinese labored to pay for their passage to America appeared to be another form of slavery. Their presence also reprised the sentiments of those who had objected to the spread of slavery more because it brought the Negro to "white man's country" than on humanitarian grounds.

Denis Kearney and the WPC were particularly virulent in their anti-Chinese rhetoric, but they were hardly alone. A respectable reformer like the socialist Henry George, for instance, could write of the "servile and debased workers," "alien serfs" to the rich, who threatened to "crush" the white working class. Clara Foltz fell in with the pervasive sentiment among white Californians and included the Chinese among "the swindlers, land-grabbers and vulgar rich" who were ruining the state.[21]

From today's perspective, Foltz's anti-Chinese views seem to conflict with her lifelong devotion to outsiders and underdogs. Nor were they consistent with her stance toward the former slaves whose full citizenship she supported. An assessment of her position must await the account of her overall political ideology in the context of the larger women's movement (see Chapter 6). Suffice it to say here that the anti-Chinese position was widely held by Californians of otherwise progressive views and that Foltz deployed the point only in the context of the assumed tendency of Chinese labor to undercut the wages of white working-class citizens.

The WPC soon expanded its appeal beyond the moblike gatherings of unemployed men on the sandlots. Within a year of Kearney's first speeches, it was organizing in ward clubs and holding rallies in lecture halls where "Judge Lynch" was replaced by the call for working men to use the ballot to elect "their friends." Through electoral politics, the WPC would not only expel Chinese workers from California, but also regulate railroads and other corporations, guarantee the eight-hour workday, and provide for free public education. This moderated message brought white- and blue-collar workers, lawyers, teachers, and doctors into the party. At an organizational meeting for the WPC in San Jose, Elias Shortridge appeared on the same platform as Denis Kearney. Clara Foltz later portrayed Kearney as the "intrepid representative of the weak as against the mighty" who helped bring about a "new order" and thereby prevented "a result most awful to contemplate"—the very class warfare Kearney had been fomenting in his early speeches.[22]

The rise of the moderated WPC coincided with the passage of a referendum calling for a constitutional convention to replace the hurriedly constructed document with which California entered the union in 1850. Though the WPC had not organized the movement for a new constitution, Kearney seized on the occasion to urge the use of votes to transform the society. After whipping his crowds into revolutionary frenzy, he urged them to "cast their ballots aright" in the coming election. And he went on to indicate that if "ballots" failed, people must turn to "bullets." The two words not only sounded similar but were sometimes transposable in Kearney's speeches. Nevertheless, his main message was that voting could produce the needed change, and the possibilities of the constitutional referendum, followed by the election of delegates to the convention, made the claim plausible. The English political writer James Bryce, in his classic work *The American Commonwealth* (1888), noted the connection between constitution-making and direct democracy: delegates "go straight from the election to their work, have not time to forget or to devise means of evading their pledges, are less liable to be 'got at' by the capitalists. . . . The rarity and importance of the occasion fixes public attention."[23]

In his account of late-nineteenth-century U.S. political life, Bryce devoted a whole chapter to Kearneyism in California. His treatment, based on contemporary newspapers and personal interviews, captures the broad appeal of the WPC attack on the new rich of California. In a decade of hard times, they flaunted their wealth in what Foltz called vulgar and lavish shows. These millionaires "excited irritation," Bryce said, because their wealth flowed from luck rather than talent, and they failed to devote any share to "useful public objects."[24]

As insightful and informed as many of Bryce's observations were, he was mistaken in writing that "good citizens" had failed to see "the danger of framing a new Constitution at a time of such excitement."[25] In fact, many of the "good citizens" were as focused as any WPC member on the prospect of adopting sweeping reforms through a constitutional convention. These included middle-class Republican reformers; farmers, some organized in the Grange; and Democrats, including those who had supported the Confederacy and saw the convention as a potential path to the power they had lost when California backed the Union.

Suffragists, whose cause was to give women the full privileges of citizenship, saw their best opportunity in the constitutional convention. Just three years had passed since the Fifteenth Amendment to the U.S. Constitution had guaranteed the vote to "citizens"—not "men" or "male citizens"—without regard to "race, color, or previous condition of servitude." In California, the force of women's just claims as citizens was joined to widespread fears that the amendment's wording might also someday enfranchise races other than blacks—as it already had done for a few Chinese born in the United States. White women's votes could serve as an offset for those who saw this as a threat.

Feeding the prevalent unrest was a peculiarly Californian sense of loss—of great objects grown dim—that gave the move for a new constitution the tone of a moral crusade. All kinds of people with many motivations had apocalyptic hopes for transformation and regeneration through constitution-making. "I tell you the good God, Majority, means mischief," warned the state's chief curmudgeon, the writer Ambrose Bierce, on the eve of the delegate election.[26]

Fearful Times for Clara Foltz

In the midst of this social unrest and economic depression, Foltz's personal life, as she approached the age of thirty, was also in fearful shape. Jeremiah, on the verge of desertion, was making frequent trips to Portland. She had to think of what she would do if he left for good. Usually, women in such situations broke up their families, parceling the children out to relatives and friends, but Foltz was determined to keep them all with her and somehow support them.

From years of boarding, sewing, and teaching, she knew that "women's work" would not provide enough income. So in 1877, at the same time Denis Kearney started speaking on the sandlots, Clara Foltz turned to public lecturing while she read law and prepared to join the bar. Before she could even think of practicing law, however, she had to get the California Code limiting bar membership to white men changed or interpreted in her favor. Meanwhile, she would lecture for the suffrage cause and take contributions from her audiences. Though women lecturers were still a novelty, the social ban had ended before the Civil War when they spoke for the abolition of slavery and then for their own rights. As a girl, Foltz had heard Lucy Stone's radical teachings about women's place. Now she would put those lessons into practice.

Clara Foltz had no financial or political resources, but she brought remarkable personal qualities to the task before her. Physically, she was strong and exceptionally energetic—the latter a trait mentioned by many interviewers over the years. Though she was regularly photographed and described, the images are so various that it is hard to pinpoint what she looked like in person. Certainly, she was tall, had a good complexion, large hazel eyes, and blonde hair in her youth—with shadings of red in some accounts—and she was always dressed in the height of the current fashion. Mentally, she was quick and possessed a near-photographic memory. As unlikely as it seems, given her life situation, Foltz was also a true intellectual, thinking about large philosophical and public issues, forming and expressing often original opinions. Despite her meager formal education, she had tremendous self-confidence and certainty about her ideas. Added to the mix was an ebullient optimism that, even when unjustified, could still be overpowering.

The Shortridge family was another asset. As much as they disapproved of her elopement, Foltz's parents had continued to give support, and indeed had moved twice, first to Oregon and then to San Jose, along with Clara, Jeremiah, and the children. Without her mother's help, Clara Foltz could never have made her bold move into the public sphere. "My precious mother!" she would exclaim in this part of her story. "[A] wonderful housekeeper, who relieved me of many duties. How may I ever express my gratitude for her uniform faith in me, her great patience, her ready soothing words."[27]

Elias Shortridge, who, having left the ministry, was practicing law in San Jose, was able to guide his daughter's legal studies. The reputation of the Shortridges as a family of oratorical bent was a comforting thought as she prepared for her first lecture. From her father also, Foltz had learned about the power of words. She had seen him convert people to new beliefs and baptize them on the spot. Shortridge's greatest gift to his daughter, though, was his interest in her opinions and his belief in women's rights. She would need all the support her family could offer in the coming struggle.[28]

Leaving the Domestic Sphere: A Public Lecturer

San Jose was a welcoming venue for Foltz's maiden lecture. She was already well-known in the town because of a campaign she had waged soon after her arrival to replace the volunteer fire department with a professional one. "All the houses in town might burn up while the boys were getting out of bed and into their clothes," she said of the volunteers. By letter writing and lobbying, Foltz had succeeded in persuading the city council to install full-time firefighters. "My first public effort, gloriously successful," Foltz concluded.[29]

Votes for women was the subject of her first lecture. Foltz had heard the arguments since girlhood, and she could count on a good audience because the suffrage movement was strong in San Jose. "A number of the clergymen are suffragists," wrote a visitor in the 1870s, "and all the principal men of the city are signers to the petition for the [Woman Suffrage] Amendment." Foltz had connected with the local suffrage society during her first week in town, attending a meeting at the home of its president, Sarah Knox, and later describing her as "a widow of commanding personal appearance, an abundance of bank stock and a wealth of common sense." Knox's first husband was a successful businessman and California legislator who had supported women's rights. In 1879, she was married a second time to an architect, also wealthy and also "fully in sympathy with all of her progressive views" and subsequently called herself Knox-Goodrich.[30]

The two women became instant comrades despite a fifteen-year difference in their ages, and Knox-Goodrich would serve as both mentor and financial backer to Foltz. "My earliest appreciative friend," Foltz said of her.[31] From the first, they shared a spirit of fun and a sense of occasion, qualities sometimes in short supply among the reformers. For the Centennial Fourth of July celebration, Knox decorated her palatial home with militant and sarcastic suffragist placards that "hundreds of people stood and read." She rented "the fanciest turn-out in town" for the parade, and "at the center was a little daughter of Mrs. Clara Foltz . . . dressed in red, white and blue . . . carrying a white banner with silver fringe . . . and in letters large enough to be seen at some distance the one word 'Hope.'" Knox demanded a place toward the back of the parade, meant to show women's actual position—behind the Negroes, whose men had just been enfranchised by the Fifteenth Amendment. But the organizers insisted that she ride up front with the other leading citizens.[32]

Sarah Knox-Goodrich had not only wealth and social standing but also courage and confidence. In answer to the standard argument that women should not vote because they could not fight, she said "we can fire a gun and hit a mark about as well as the average man." Even before it was adopted as a widespread suffrage tactic (the "New Departure"), Knox-Goodrich went to the polls and tried to vote. She also wrote of the "pioneer mothers . . . who had transformed the howling wilderness into a garden of beauty" and deserved equality as a result. Of her role in the western movement, the *History of Woman Suffrage* observed, "she has nerved the weak and encouraged the timid by her example of unflinching devotion."[33]

Another prominent San Jose suffragist was J. J. Owen, editor of the leading newspaper, the *Mercury*. Foltz thought him a "gentleman" and "a fine writer," and he returned the admiration, printing detailed and favorable accounts of her activities. On February 7, 1877, he introduced Foltz for her first public lecture. Rather ominously, Owen warned the audience: "No class ever freely shares power. Rights must be demanded, and sometimes won at the point of a bayonet across a bloody chasm." Most women were apathetic and indifferent, said Owen, so it was critical to support one like Foltz, a warrior ready for battle. "Mrs. Foltz then stepped forward and began the delivery of her lecture," said the next day's paper—marking the exact moment in which she became a suffrage leader and public woman. In this first lecture, Foltz began to develop the arguments and rhetorical devices she would put to frequent use in the years to come.[34]

She pictured women in the basement of the temple of liberty, for instance, and rehearsed the lives of those who had taken great public roles: Deborah who judged Israel, Joan who freed France, Elizabeth who ruled England. Closer to home for Americans was Barbara Frietchie, who had stared down the British Army when they demanded that she remove the stars and stripes from her window. Of course, Foltz paused to quote John Greenleaf Whittier: "'Shoot, if you must, this old gray head / But spare your country's flag,' she said."

Foltz's speech was peppered with signs of her law study. To the standard suffrage argument against taxation without representation, she added evidence taken from the courthouse records about the actual amounts and percentages women paid locally in taxes. As for the existing legal barriers against woman suffrage, Foltz claimed that these were contrary to the laws of nature and cited Blackstone for the proposition that this rendered them void. The *Mercury* report concluded by noting that the "audience applauded throughout. . . . Mrs. Foltz appears perfectly at home on the rostrum," her gestures "easy and graceful."

Lecture invitations poured in over the next few months; Foltz delivered her talk, which she titled "Impartial Suffrage," a dozen times, refining as she went and adding new stories based on her accumulating experience. She told of speaking at a church in Gilroy, where the minister warned his flock to stay away because suffragists were "free lovers, poor mothers, dissatisfied wives and spinsters seeking annuities." Foltz said that this "volley of unjust accusations wounded the intelligent and highly cultured suffragists," and they turned out for her "a congregation larger than the minister had ever seen on the premises."[35]

After the Gilroy lecture, Foltz took a carriage ride around the countryside and dropped by the local newspaper office to enhance the chances of extensive and favorable coverage. It was a practice she would cultivate with increasing skill and energy over the years. This time, though, Foltz remembered feeling pressed: "I had left the little ones in dear good mother's care so there was no occasion for being uneasy, but as this was the first time I had ever been away from them, I was extremely anxious to return, having been gone a day and a night from my baby."[36]

Her early "gilt-edged reviews" compared Foltz favorably to other lady lecturers who had been in the same town, and later ones to famous lady lecturers generally. Nine months into her new career, the *Oakland Transcript* joined Foltz's name to that of a renowned male orator: Wendell Phillips. She had his "art of concealing art," the paper said. "Her elocution is faultless, except, perhaps, a too great precipitancy in the more passionate passages, though every word is clearly distinct. Her voice is full, musical and feminine, and her action [gestures] is singularly natural, graceful and appropriate, and although intensely dramatic at times, is entirely without affectation."[37]

While making the rounds with "Impartial Suffrage," Foltz was working on a second lecture for return engagements at the same nearby towns. Ultimately, she needed a repertoire so she could give a series of lectures in each venue, rather than being confined to single appearances. As with the religious revivals her father once ran, each lecture could generate a greater audience for the next; meanwhile, she would save on the trouble and expense of travel and arranging accommodations.

Her lecturing was an instant success in making more money than she could take in by traditional women's work. And it gave her something to fall back on if she failed in her more improbable and ambitious dream of becoming a lawyer. When she remembered these years, Foltz said, "in retrospect, everything seems weird, phantasmal and unreal." She recalled her minute planning, "regulating my life by the dial of a clock. Everything moved slowly, too slowly for my impetuous spirit." A friend said, "If she lives, she will prove that a woman can do some things as well as others."[38]

Studying Law

Foltz was fortunate to start her public career with some success at lecturing, because she encountered tough opposition as she took her first steps toward being a lawyer by seeking an apprenticeship. Starting in the right law office was important, especially in California, where there was no law school to credential aspiring attorneys. Of course the sponsorship of a prestigious mentor would matter even more for the potential first and only woman practicing on the Pacific Coast.

Everyone knew that Francis Spencer was the best lawyer in town, and Foltz applied by letter to study in his "big, fine offices," signing herself with a flourish on the z. She would always remember how "patiently, and I confess confidently . . . I waited for the answer. . . . My mother shook her head with a sigh as day after day I ran to meet the letter carrier, but my spirit was undaunted. At last I stood looking at the envelope which evidently contained the message—and somehow, without knowing its contents, I felt a sort of sinking feeling, as though—well, 'Coming events cast their shadows before.'"[39]

Forty years after the events, Foltz reproduced the rejection letter in an autobiographical column:

> My dear young friend:
> Excuse my delay in answering your letter asking permission to enter my law office as a student. My high regard for your parents and for you, who seem to have no right understanding of what you say you want to undertake, forbid encouraging you in so foolish a pursuit,—wherein you would invite nothing but ridicule if not contempt.

A woman's place is at home, unless it is as a teacher. If you would like a position in our public schools, I will be glad to recommend you, for I think you are well qualified.[40]

Though these views were common enough, Foltz was shocked to hear them from Spencer: "All my preconceived notions of his liberality and nobility of mind paled, and in proportion all men sank in my estimation. A woman's place is at home! Grant it, but must she necessarily be confined forever within its four walls!" She articulated her response in a fiery new public lecture, "Equality of Sex": "Woman must be either man's equal or his slave. There is no middle ground. The flag of our Union floats not over one free woman in all this broad land. Every inch gained by her in the last half century has been contested, and every inch gained has only subjected her to fresh demands." Yet, Foltz told her audience, woman's struggle had "strengthened and developed her, brought out her latent powers and embodied her, so that she is no longer merely spirit, but stands forth ready to conquer new fields, ready to receive the responsibilities of liberty."[41]

Rejected by the bar leader, Foltz instead studied with her father and his partner in the more modest offices of Stephens and Shortridge. Like Elias Shortridge, C. C. Stephens was a male ally in the battle for women's rights—the author of a pamphlet protesting against women's exclusion from "the learned pathways of the law."[42] A good man and a loyal friend, he was not especially prominent or influential in the legal world.

While Foltz was studying law, she hoped to join the local club for aspiring attorneys, which met weekly in a real courtroom and staged moot arguments. In a state without a law school, these legal clubs were important professional outlets. Moot courting was also something lawyers did for fun. All attorneys, judges, and students were said to be welcome, so one night in mid-December 1877, Shortridge and his daughter appeared and applied for membership. Debate flared up instantly over whether women should be admitted. Opponents pointed out that the practice of law was confined to "any white male citizen" by statute. Supporters argued that the code also provided that females were included whenever a statute used the word *male* or the male pronoun. The supreme court of the state had not, moreover, ever ruled on whether women might be admitted to the bar. In the "spirited discussion," the argument was not confined to its legal points. One opponent even quoted the notorious passage about African Americans from Chief Justice Roger B. Taney's *Dred Scott* opinion and said that women had "'no rights that a white man is bound to respect.'" But, the *Mercury* reported, "the better sense of the Club prevailed," and Foltz and her father were admitted, and she was even assigned to argue a case "involving many nice legal points" the next week.[43]

It was a new mode of public speaking for Foltz, requiring that she replace popular appeal with precise argument and ardor with analysis. When the night came, she pinned on a corsage of roses (her favorite flower, which blooms all year in San Jose) and on the arm of her father entered the domed court-house, with its Latin inscription "Justicia Dedicata" ("dedicated to justice") over its portals. But before her case was even called, her opponents renewed the dispute about her admission. One man compared women "to educated animals, such as dogs, cats, horses and monkeys, which can be trained to perform certain acts that they could never conceive or execute on their own." Many years later, Foltz remembered sitting in the back of the room "thinking, thinking how all the world is open to men, how every opportunity for service and for personal achievement is theirs" and resenting "the sneers and jeers" of the "prigs whose female relations generally are footing the bills for their legal education." Being treated with "such mean contempt" by young men whose equal at least she was in "birth and breeding" was infuriating.[44]

When the chair, a supporter, asked her to respond, Foltz had her first chance to speak in a courtroom. "I stand before you blameless. Who I am, what I am, what I have done, is an open book. Yet I stand here reproached and rebuked for being born a woman. . . . What follows from that? Nothing that touches on my right to practice law, or indeed to pursue any honorable calling of which I am capable. I propose to be a lawyer to earn an honest living for myself and my family. I already have a record of serious law study, which even those who deny my rights should accord some gentlemanly rec-ognition."[45] The debate resumed until finally the chair ruled in Foltz's favor. But when she tried to deliver her argument, the law student playing judge (anti-Foltz in the debate) rapped his gavel, declaring that only legitimate club members could argue. Others refused to play their parts if Mrs. Foltz was treated so meanly, and the San Jose legal club adjourned in confusion.

The next week there was a large audience for the moot court, almost half of them women there to support Foltz. But the student judge again ruled that only men could speak. "Call a doctor," said one man, "he is the only one who can settle the question of sex." Boos and hisses came from the audience, and the meeting finally broke up before the arguments in the moot case had been reached. Foltz crossed the courtroom to join her father for the walk home: "now it was my turn to show just how much of a real lawyer (afraid of nobody) I could be." She presented her corsage of roses to her main opponent, "congratulating him in the most gracious words at my command on his judicial performance." As she told the story later, the other young men gathered around, and invitations "to be one of them after all came thick and fast. That was my last thought! Never again would I invade the presence of the Moot court."[46]

A few weeks later, the papers reported that the club had disbanded as a result of the fight over Foltz's admission. She never had the chance to develop her advocacy skills in practice argument with other law students. The lost opportunity increased her desire to attend Hastings Law School when it was established a year later in 1879. Once again, however, she would be refused because of her sex. These early rejections lived in Foltz's self-presentation as vivid stories for the rest of her life.

Making Law

THE WOMAN LAWYER'S BILL

As a new state born in a gold rush, California had needed lawyers. The code made it very easy for a "white male citizen" "of good moral character" to join the bar.[47] Only six months of residence in the state was required, and there were no rules about the amount or content of legal study. Lawyers admitted in other places simply presented their credentials to the court in which they wished to practice.

The usual path for a new lawyer was to apply to the local trial court after some time of apprenticing in an established office. The judge, joined by several practitioners, would examine the applicant orally, and if he passed, other trial courts would generally accept the certification. A lawyer who wanted to appeal a case (or perhaps just add a prestigious credential) would apply to join the California Supreme Court bar, which held its own, more rigorous, but still oral, examination.

Clara Foltz had of course been concerned about the code's restriction to white males even before it came up at the legal club hullabaloo. She knew about Nellie Tator, a suffragist from nearby Santa Cruz, who had passed the bar in 1872 but was refused admission because of the code. Tator had even drafted a Woman Lawyer's Bill to overcome the objection, but it had died in the Senate. She did not appeal the adverse court ruling, however, so there was no definitive supreme court decision against women lawyers in California.[48]

Foltz probably considered going through the courts to gain the right to practice. Undoubtedly, she was familiar with the case of Arabella Mansfield, who had been admitted by an Iowa court in the face of a statute that restricted admission to men. Yet nearly a decade after Mansfield's success in 1869, there were few similar rulings in appellate courts. The precedents the other way had started the next year when the well-qualified Myra Bradwell, editor of the *Chicago Legal News*, was rejected by the highest court in Illinois. The main argument against her, however, was not the words of the code, but the idea that a married woman was incapable of making contracts on her own (including contracts for employment as a lawyer) and was not ultimately liable for her debts. Bradwell appealed to the U.S. Supreme Court, arguing that free choice of occupation was one of the "privileges or immunities of citizens of the United States" guaranteed by the newly enacted Fourteenth Amendment. But the Court disagreed and left it to each state to decide whether to admit women. For its own bar, the Court turned down the application of Belva Lockwood in 1876, and state courts tended to follow the High Court's example.[49]

Going through the courts first could mean at least a year before a final decision, and Foltz might lose and need to seek a bill anyway. Unwilling to risk defeat and delay, she decided to proceed straight to the 1878 session of the legislature for a bill to eliminate the statutory exclusion of women from law practice. She could count on the help of the suffragists, who had learned how to lobby by this time. Indeed, they had achieved their first success, a statute making women eligible to serve on school boards, shortly before Foltz arrived in San Jose. Sarah Knox had journeyed to Sacramento, "remaining there for weeks, urging the measure." Foltz was soon to follow her friend's method in lobbying for a Woman Lawyer's Bill.[50]

She drafted the measure simply, replacing the words "any white male citizen" with "any citizen or person" and otherwise leaving the code section unchanged.[51] No one remarked on the omission of the "white" qualification for bar membership. Perhaps it was generally recognized as unconstitutional under the Fourteenth Amendment, passed a decade earlier. Leaving in the qualification of whites only would, moreover, be inconsistent with the woman suffrage demand and create a situation in which black men would be able to vote but not practice law, white women could practice law but not vote, and black women could do neither. Though the wording of Foltz's bill opened the possibility of a multiracial bar, the debate was all about women as equals in public life.

LOBBYING THE LEGISLATURE

Soon after the legislature convened in 1878, the senator from San Jose, a friend of Foltz's, introduced the Woman Lawyer's Bill in the upper house. Barney Murphy was a first-generation native son of California and a graduate of Santa Clara University. A wealthy banker and a town favorite, he wryly described himself as "short but exceedingly good looking." According to Foltz, Murphy was "beloved by everybody because of his big warm Irish heart." When he was mayor of San Jose, she had worked with him on professionalizing the fire department.[52]

The *Sacramento Bee* called the Woman Lawyer's Bill an acceptable concession to sex equality that would affect only a few, since most women would prefer "to marry and be supported by their husbands." This tepid endorsement was the only press notice the bill received at first; it was one among hundreds flooding into the hopper. A record fifteen hundred bills would be submitted before the ending date of April 1 mandated by law. It was the busiest session in state history as a result of the approaching constitutional convention, which would replace the next session of the legislature in 1879. Lobbyists were pouring into Sacramento while they could still locate the levers of power, knowing that they would not have another chance for two years. The *Sacramento Record-Union* said no legislature in California history had been subject to such lobbying and depicted the swarm "circulating through halls and chambers, whispering in corners, closeted in alcoves, consulting in knots, buzzing in groups, bending over legislators at their desks, buttonholing, counseling, advising, plotting, working every plan, pulling every wire, bringing to bear every influence."[53]

Sometimes this influence was in the shape of bribes or wining, dining, and women. So conspicuous were the excesses that the new California constitution would actually ban lobbying.[54] Critics of the women's lobby implied that, though not actually corrupt, their one-on-one "still hunts" circumvented open debate, and in any case were unsuitable for ladies. The personal nature of Clara Foltz's entreaties for a chance to support her children only added to the vague air of impropriety around her lobbying.

"I coaxed, I entreated, I almost went down on my knees before them, asking for the pitiful privilege of an equal chance to earn an honest living in a noble profession!" Foltz wrote later. Bitterly, she added: "I would have reasoned had they been reasonable men. But I had to beg—not for a living, but to be allowed to earn a living." For the first two weeks of January, Foltz stayed in Sacramento, "living on next to nothing, eking out in every possible manner," cooking her food on "a tiny alcohol lamp." These details of her "desperate struggle" became a permanent part of the autobiography she would construct in dozens of interviews over the years.[55]

Her pleas won support in the Senate. A male admirer wrote, "I never knew before how much pluck and energy there was in a woman—how they could urge their claims, plead for the privilege of making the battle of life—for such Mrs. Foltz did, gently and eloquently."[56] Yet try as she did to paint the Woman Lawyer's Bill as a widow's relief act, she found her personal entreaties hopelessly enmeshed with arguments about woman's nature and her proper sphere. In the very act of lobbying, women became public actors defining their own interests; the effect was magnified when they lobbied to be lawyers.

Supporters and opponents alike saw Foltz's personal cause as part of the larger women's movement, which included demands for access to the professions as well as suffrage. The suffragists, including Sarah Knox, were at her side in lobbying for the Woman Lawyer's Bill. This was the point when Foltz met her most notable ally, Laura Gordon, who had made the first suffrage speech in California in 1868 and who also wanted to be a lawyer. Recently, Gordon had been publishing a newspaper but was discouraged by the constant financial uncertainties of such an endeavor. She thought law practice would provide both a better income and a fine platform for her equal rights advocacy.[57]

There were few women anywhere like Clara Foltz and Laura Gordon, yet they were very like each other. In addition to their shared ambitions, both were talented orators. Both had had unhappy marriages and were now on their own. Though childless, Gordon had a number of dependents— her parents and at times her sisters—whom she maintained on a farm in Lodi. Recently divorced (on the grounds of her husband's adultery) after twenty years of marriage, Gordon spoke privately of the anguish of losing one "nearer and dearer than life."[58] She sometimes called herself a widow, as Foltz would do consistently after her divorce; both saw widowhood as a more acceptable explanation than divorce for their lack of male protection.

As similar as they were in their beliefs and their life situations, the two women were quite different in appearance and style. Gordon was dark-haired and down-to-earth; her speaking style was earnest and at her best so plain and powerful that reviews called her "Websterian." Foltz was fair and her speech was elevated, at the same time that she projected warmth and womanly appeal. Their styles were complementary both on the platform and in the lobbying context. Over the next few years, the two were so closely associated that their individual achievements were interconnected, leading both at various points to claim top billing as California's most important woman lawyer.

THE OPPOSITION ARGUMENTS:
UNSEXED WOMEN AND FREE LOVERS

Though Foltz's suffrage alliance was beneficial and necessary, it also had its downsides. There was a well-developed opposition to women voting, and the arguments carried over to bar admission. For instance, opponents predicted that as voters women would select the best-looking politician and that as lawyers they would seduce male juries into acquitting the guilty and rewarding the undeserving. The only solution, ironically proposed, would be to place women (immune from each other's charms) on juries. But women jurors would skew the process by voting for the handsomest lawyer, and jury service would expose them to degrading testimony in court and unsuitable intimacy with men during deliberations.[59]

Another antisuffrage argument improbably extrapolated to women as lawyers had to do with the unwilling woman voter. It went this way: most good women do not want to vote; but good women are also good citizens; good citizens vote; thus, woman suffrage will force women to vote against their will. In the context of bar admission, according to Foltz in telling the story, opponents spoke about "the great wrong to the women of California who do not desire to enter upon the law as a profession to thrust such a duty upon them." How many times, she wondered, must she explain to Captain M. or Colonel S. that his wife or daughter so handsomely provided for would not be compelled to practice law? Her opponents, she said, "grew as red as turkey gobblers mouthing their ignorance against the bill. . . . Home and mother and prattling babes and cooing doves were dished up and handed forth as arguments" by "staid old grangers who had never been in a courthouse."[60]

Most dire was the charge that being a lawyer or a voter would change women themselves—"unsexing" them. Lines published in a popular humor magazine at the moment Foltz and her friends were lobbying the legislature for a Woman Lawyer's Bill captured this argument. "Shame unto womanhood!" it starts, and refers to women's "shallow tale of fancied wrongs."

> Mothers and wives are cast not in this mold.
> Rather, such are meet
> To herd with them whose love is bought and sold
> . . .

For these have hearts as empty and as cold
And all their lives are like them: incomplete
Unfruitful and unbeautiful and bold.[61]

Suffragists were attacked not only as unsexed but as oversexed. More than once in her early career, Foltz was accused of being a proponent of "free love." The charge originated from the connection of suffrage with Spiritualism, a movement with many female adherents that did preach free love, but not of the sort critics implied. Spiritualism's main message was that unlike animals, humans have a life extending beyond physical being, and thus beyond the grave. To this familiar Christian doctrine, Spiritualists added a belief in the possibility of communication with the physically dead through mediums. Especially during and after the Civil War, when so many families lost members with no chance for parting words, Spiritualism gained adherents in all walks of life.[62]

Suffragists were especially drawn to it because Spiritualism elevated women through the stress on spiritual power and concomitant deemphasis of men's superior bodily strength. Women were thought to have special access to the spirit world, and most mediums were female. In practice, moreover, Spiritualism approved of women's public speech, albeit in the voice of others. Laura Gordon, for instance, had started her lecture career as a Spiritualist trance speaker.

Free love was a doctrine that reflected Spiritualism's special concern for women's well-being. The idea was that marital relations should be an act of love freely given, so that it could be rightly refused—the flesh should not be subject where the spirit was unwilling. Though it applied to both marriage partners, the doctrine was designed for the benefit of women.

Spiritualism and suffrage were mutually beneficial and reinforcing to each other until the early 1870s, when Victoria Woodhull revised the ideal of free love in a way that gave both movements a bad name. Exceptionally attractive, Woodhull was a medium who deployed alleged tips from otherworld contacts, and the intimate relationship of her sister with the tycoon Cornelius Vanderbilt, to gain fame for both sisters as the first women stockbrokers on Wall Street. From her entrance on the public scene, Woodhull spoke for women's rights, and at the beginning Elizabeth Cady Stanton and Susan B. Anthony welcomed her to the suffrage cause.[63]

Then came the "free-love" fiasco. In a sensational 1871 lecture, Woodhull transformed the slogan for women's right to have only consensual sex within marriage into the very different meaning it has had ever since. She proclaimed: "I am a free lover! I have an inalienable, constitutional, and natural right to love whom I may, to love for as long or as short a period as I can, to change that love every day if I please!" After that speech, one newspaper headline read, "Died of Free Love—the Woman Suffrage Movement."[64]

Though Woodhull was well off the suffrage scene by 1878 when Foltz was trying to join the bar, her name and her scandalous conception of free love still came up whenever women wanted to be voters or lawyers or jurors. The idea that women's rights included free love in the Woodhullian sense meant that women risked their reputations by pursuing movement goals like equal access to the professions. Very few were brave enough to try.

Passage of the Woman Lawyer's Bill

The Woman Lawyer's Bill passed the California Senate in mid-January 1878. Though the debate was extended, the women's lobby, plus the backing of the popular Murphy, and supportive petitions from many prominent lawyers won the day. Moreover, many of the Senate's attorney members were for it, doing credit, one paper said, "alike to head and heart." Lulled by this clear success, Clara Foltz left for a six-week lecture tour in Oregon. She had three speeches ready for new audiences and needed the money. Also, Jeremiah had been in Portland for months, and she intended to see him. As she departed with Trella, her oldest daughter, to attend to her failing marriage and lecture to new audiences, Foltz thought everything was set for final passage in the State Assembly.[65]

Laura Gordon was in daily touch because she was covering the legislature for her own paper and several others and had a press desk on the Assembly floor. Foltz had already lobbied the members she could reach personally. Most reassuring, Grove L. Johnson, the influential assemblyman from Sacramento, promised her that the bill would pass. Johnson, a lawyer and the father of future Progressive governor Hiram Johnson, was serving his first term in the Assembly. Already, however, he was showing the ability that would make him a powerful political figure in the state for many years. Though he would later become one of the railroad's men, Johnson started out as a champion of the underdog. His first speech, "the most eloquent ever heard in the chamber," according to one newspaper, opposed a gag law directed at the WPC and Denis Kearney.[66] Johnson also supported women's rights across the board. Originally from New York, he had been a schoolteacher and school superintendent there. His wife was a suffragist, though the care of five small children was her chief activity. The Johnson children matched Foltz's exactly in age and sex, which may have added to his sympathy for her situation.

"Grove L," as everyone called him, stood out among his western peers in the fastidiousness of his dress and person. (It was a matter for comment that he bathed completely and washed his hair and full beard daily!) On business days, he arrayed himself in striped pants and a frock coat, fine leather boots to the knee, and a broad-brimmed black hat. In his lapel was a fresh nosegay watered from a small vial sewn into his jackets. But Grove L was much more than a dapper little dandy. An omnivorous reader, he filled his speeches with classical allusions and delivered them in a distinctive anguished voice that was said to fall like a physical assault on his opponents. His fierce demeanor, perhaps compensating for his small size, was remarked in contemporary descriptions. "Always Johnson's mind is on the leap, like a greyhound after a hare. He is terrible in sudden repartee, and it is hardly safe to provoke him," said an admirer.[67] "Belligerent" and "ferocious" were the usual adjectives applied to him by friend and foe—a good man to have on your side, everyone agreed.

In late February, while Foltz was still away in Oregon, Johnson entered the Assembly determined to pass the Woman Lawyer's Bill. Mr. William B. May of San Francisco, another supporter, opened by calling for "an end to all class distinctions." Immediately, three opponents launched into the standard rebuttal based on the ordained sphere for women. One claimed to be "a friend of the fair sex," who praised women's work and implied they should stay at it. Mr. May responded that no man would ever choose so-called women's work: "hewers of wood and drawers of water"—slaves in biblical terms.[68]

Johnson demanded of the opponents "what law of God or man has given you the right to fix the sphere of woman? God alone ordains her sphere and men such as you have no right to circumscribe it. Name a single instance," he roared, "where a woman attempting a position in life has not acquitted herself well."[69] No one stepped into his trap and attacked a specific woman. But the easy victory in the Senate could not be repeated; the bill lost by the painfully close margin of three votes. The quick-thinking Johnson switched his vote from yea to nay, making him a member of the majority, eligible to move for reconsideration. But the next day, with only a month before adjournment, the motion for reconsideration was put off indefinitely. Clara Foltz returned from Oregon to learn that her bill was probably dead.

She set out on another of her "night journeys to Sacramento in the caboose of a cattle train, without a dollar in her pocket, and a little bag of biscuits and boiled eggs for her refreshment"—details she would often repeat.[70] As the session wound down, the struggle for scarce floor time grew savage. With three days left before adjournment, the Assembly agreed that beginning on Friday, they would proceed alphabetically through the eighty members, with each allowed to bring one bill to a vote. The governor had until midnight on Sunday to sign or veto any measure that passed.

Late on Friday afternoon, the letter *J* was reached; Grove L. Johnson used his precious one shot to renew his motion for reconsideration of the Woman Lawyer's Bill. Foltz was on the floor of the Assembly with her sons, Sammy, age nine, and Davey, age seven, offering a living illustration that a woman might be a lawyer and a mother at the same time. In later years she recalled the moment: standing silently, with her boys nearby while echoing around her she heard all "the prejudices and preconceived ideas of the male superiority over the female, beginning with the barnyard and from there on to the forests and the wild beasts therein, all, all!" She would also remember that when one man "declared in stentorian tones" that the bill was a product of free lovers and childless women, Rush McComas, a friend from San Jose, rose in protest. He "pronounced such a eulogy upon me and upon all women who sought to qualify themselves for useful careers as made my heart ache with gratitude."[71] Old Father McComas, as he was known, had eight children and many daughters. The final vote was thirty-seven to thirty-five in favor of the bill, a crucial five-vote switch.

One step and two days remained before the legal profession could be open to Clara Foltz; the governor had to sign the bill. Governor William Irwin was a Democrat, the first elected to high office in California since the Civil War, and though an "uncompromising" partisan, contemporaries found him "entirely free from that strong animosity that sometimes characterizes men of his party." Also a Democrat, Laura Gordon "asserted her claims to some recognition," especially as editor of a loyal Democratic paper, and ultimately took credit for obtaining the signature.[72]

Foltz told a different and more theatrical story, which she polished over the years, compressing the action—and leaving out Gordon. Though she was a Republican (along with key supporter Grove Johnson) and thus had no party leverage, Foltz decided to make a last-minute plea to the governor.

"The closing day of the session of that memorable legislature had come. Midnight was drawing near and a huge hopeful mob filled the halls outside the Executive Chamber, waiting to hear the fate of the bills as yet unsigned." As Foltz mingled with the rest, an opponent emerged from the chamber and announced that the Woman Lawyer's Bill was dead. "'Very well then, only the good are raised from the dead.' And with that bit of Scriptural warning, I made a break through the solid ranks of men for the door of the chamber." Moving rapidly, Foltz pushed her way to the governor's side. About him were gathered the attorney general and many prominent members of the Senate and the Assembly. "The chandeliers shone fiercely, the oil paintings on the walls seemed to frown upon me," and for what seemed an age, no one spoke to the young woman or took any notice of her at all. "Undaunted, though hesitatingly, I said: 'Governor, won't you please sign the Woman Lawyer's bill?' He gazed at me for a moment and then turning to the large stack of bills unsigned he asked for the number and I gave it. Several of the men who ignored me at first now exchanged glances of concern." Finally, the bill was fished out from among the discarded ones, and was laid "all but dead before him. The Governor reached for a pen and dipped it into the ink-well." While Foltz "stood trembling before him," he declared: "This bill to entitle women to practice law is wise and just and I take great pleasure in signing it." And right then, as Foltz told it, "the clock struck twelve."[73]

Making History

THE PORTIA OF THE PACIFIC

Admission to the Bar

The Woman Lawyer's Act stands as a landmark in the history of women's professional progress. It was one of the earliest American statutes allowing women to practice law and probably the first to emerge entirely from the legislative process (rather than being a response to a court refusal of bar admission). Foltz often spoke of the "bliss" she felt in its passage. But, she usually added, the bliss was "of shorter duration than I would have my listeners know." Immediately, she turned to hard study for the bar exam at the next court term—just four months away. Wrestling with the body of the law, Blackstone's and Kent's commentaries and the California Code, she read "by a smoky coal lamp amidst the cries of my populous nursery." Despite the strain and uncertainty, however, she still managed to enjoy herself. "If I knew I should never be permitted to practice I should still make the law my study till I had mastered it," she said. "I do so love it." In interviews, she spoke of the "vein of fun in my nature" that lightened all her tasks.[74]

In San Jose, the judge appointed a three-person board of examiners to sit with him and question the applicants. One of these examiners was customarily the candidate's mentor. Thus, C. C. Stephens was on Foltz's board, along with D. W. Herrington, a good friend, and Francis Spencer, the lawyer who had refused to accept her as an apprentice and said she would invite "ridicule if not contempt" by studying law. Aware that the admission of a woman was an historic occasion, the panel questioned Foltz for three hours, twice as long as was customary. She reported not only passing but receiving many "highly colored compliments" on her legal acumen and the readiness of her responses.[75] The examination took place in the same courtroom where the legal club once met and rejected her as a member, and Foltz noted with glee that several of the men who scorned her had failed their examinations.

On the the day after she passed, September 5, 1878, Judge David Belden administered the oath making Clara Foltz the first woman lawyer on the Pacific Coast. To the happy story of acceptance she often added the rude encounter that followed as she left the courtroom. Another lawyer, apparently intending it as a friendly joke, called to her: "Now, Mrs. Foltz, a woman can't keep a secret, and for that reason if no other I doubt if anybody will ever consult a woman lawyer." Since she had just sworn to hold inviolate the confidences of her clients, the comment was insulting. The prejudice it reflected, moreover, would be an obstacle to acquiring clients for Foltz's whole career. "I made no reply but down deep in my heart I resented the remark," she said.[76]

First all over the West, then all over the country, newspapers printed the tale of the courageous mother-lawyer. "Without education or learning, burdened with the cares of a large family, and against the prejudice of sex," she had stepped from "cradleside into the ranks of one of the profoundest professions," said the *Mercury* in later summing up her achievement. A Chicago paper advised "young men who moan and groan because they have not the means to acquire an education that it is not money they need—it is the pluck and energy of a woman like Mrs. Foltz."[77]

Many of the accounts stressed that she "attended to her family and did her own housework" while she studied for the bar. The *New York World* compared Foltz to the famous English barrister Lord Thomas Erskine, who turned to the law because he needed a living. In his first case he obtained renown for assailing a great lord. When asked how he had such nerve, Erskine replied, "I felt my little children tugging at my stuff robe and whispering, 'Now is the time to get us bread.'"[78]

Foltz's fame even reached beyond the United States. In Turin, Italy, "a young signorina of proper qualifications, except for her sex, argued for admission to practice by citing the case of Signora Foltz who had been able to maintain five children of tender age with the fruits of her professional labors." The Italian procurator-general sneered that the case of Mrs. Foltz had occurred in the savage western wilderness of North America "and the lovely signorina was denied the privilege of becoming an advocate."[79]

Foltz and her mother laughed over the clippings, recalling how as a girl Foltz "often wondered whether my name would go down on the page of history for some personal achievement."[80] They started the first of many scrapbooks she would keep of her professional life. Virtually every article was favorable, reflecting a skill at handling the press that Foltz would demonstrate throughout her career.

First Cases

Foltz rented what she called a "bijou" of an office from her friend in the Knox Block of San Jose and ordered stationery with "Clara Shortridge Foltz, Attorney at Law" set in feminine type as the letterhead. The scent of fresh flowers replaced the usual tobacco and leather (and often whiskey) smell of a typical lawyer's office, and she decorated the premises with pictures of her "beautiful children," her usual designation for them. By the end of September 1878, Clara Foltz was a practicing attorney.

Her first specialty was "seized baggage" cases. When the employers of a "high-spirited German girl" took her trunk to pay for broken dishes, Foltz showed that the damage was caused "in the ordinary course of things" and regained the luggage. Next, she represented a "young English woman" whose husband deserted her when their train stopped in San Jose. Collapsing from shock, the woman was revived by a physician, who then appropriated her baggage for his fee. Foltz sued for its return with damages, "severely handling" the doctor and the officer who confiscated the luggage. Both of these cases were in the justice, or lower, trial courts.[81]

By the end of October, she had her first case in the more prestigious district court. The *San Francisco Chronicle* reported that "the bar was thronged with its best talent, all intently watching her" and that she was "calm and dignified, and seemed not in the least out of place." In another matter, Foltz noted enthusiastically that she had instigated "proceedings to set aside a fraudulent survey" in which her old nemesis, Francis Spencer, was her opponent. "It is an intricate and important case, but I feel master of it and am satisfied I am going to win it," she told a reporter.[82]

The Spencer matter aside, most of her early clients were unprotected women and poor people charged with crime whose cases did not command much in the way of fees or require great legal learning to resolve. Foltz's favorite story from this period showed her raconteur's eye for human interest and comedy, if not her love of the intricacies of legal doctrine. The story opened in San Jose soon after she passed the bar.[83]

Sitting at her "diminutive rolltop desk" anxiously awaiting clients, Foltz greeted a young lady, "a pretty dainty bit of Dresden," who "poured forth acts of cruelty and base ingratitude on the part of her husband." A man in her position, Foltz joked, would have gone right out and horsewhipped the husband, but "being just a woman and a lawyer at that, with almost insufferable dignity to support in this trying moment of my brief career, I decided to let the law punish this mean cruel husband." Foltz turned the client's tale into a legal complaint.[84] "Loading it down with descriptive adjectives," she assured her client that it was necessary "if she really wanted a divorce" to "blazon forth" all the "secrets of her sad heart." Lawyer Foltz and her lady client then set out together for the courthouse. "This being my first experience with the County Clerk I felt a little nervous," Foltz admitted, but she successfully filed the complaint and handed the papers to the sheriff, "who jumped into a two-horse rig, cracked his whip," and rode off to serve them on the unsuspecting husband.[85]

Disquieting thoughts, "wholly at variance with my first idea of the joy I would take in the practice of law," plagued Foltz as she hurried home. "Somehow I felt guilty. . . . But, brushing aside my unease, I reassured myself that . . . I acted just as any other lawyer would have done." (She was wrong in one respect: she had not taken, or even discussed taking, a fee in advance from her client.) Later, as she sat on her porch with her baby Virginia in her lap, "a trim, very respectable looking young man"—the husband—inquired for the "lawyer who lives here." But Foltz sent him away, thinking it would be false to her client even to speak with him. There followed a sleepless night "thinking of the clear-eyed handsome boy. . . . In my eagerness to be loyal to my client I had forgotten hospitality and consideration for those in trouble." Very early the next morning, the husband was again at Foltz's door with a well-phrased letter asking to see his wife.[86]

Modeling the Shakespearean comedies she loved, Foltz arranged for the husband and wife, unbeknownst to the other, to come to her office at the same time. High drama ensued, with the husband kneeling at his wife's feet, clasping her hands, kissing them repeatedly, and begging her to forgive him. Clara Foltz, whose own husband had recently deserted her, sat "calmly" at her desk "and almost breathlessly watched Love struggle back to life. . . . I decided that neither law nor lawyer had any proper place . . . and so—well, I forgot that I was a lawyer . . . —I cried."[87]

Then the three proceeded to the courthouse to dismiss the case, and Clara Foltz again confronted that great gatekeeper of the law, the county clerk: "'For whom do you appear, madam?' he said addressing me with the lofty official air usual at that time toward the one woman lawyer in the whole state. 'I—I appear for the defendant,' I stammered. The Clerk looked me straight in the eyes, pityingly if not contemptuously, and blurted out. 'You can't do it, madam. Your name appears here as attorney for the plaintiff.' 'Excuse me, Mr. Clerk, I mean I appear for both parties.' Again the Clerk glared at me and emphatically demanded, 'Don't you know that a lawyer can't appear for both parties?'" Collecting herself, Foltz said: "Now see here, we, myself, my client and the defendant, each of whom is standing here in your presence, request you to dismiss this case, and if you don't do it right now, I will apply to Judge Belden who will order you do so." One year later, "I attended the christening of their baby daughter—Clara, in honor of the lawyer who forgot which party she represented."[88]

If Foltz had continued with small cases like these first ones, she would never have become famous, though she eventually might have established a modestly viable local law business, as did some of the other early women lawyers. But she decided to expand her practice and improve her qualifications. In 1878, the legislature had accepted the gift of Serranus Clinton Hastings to establish a law school in the state. Foltz thought it appropriate that the first woman lawyer should attend the first law school.

Her only formal education had been a few years at Howe's Academy, which was below standard for the profession even in the day when many lawyers apprenticed rather than attending law school. Foltz felt that she needed to know more in order to properly represent her clients. Sarah Knox and several other suffrage friends gave her a "scholarship" to spend a semes-

ter at the new law college, so that she could "better go on with my practice."[89] But once again, just as had happened with the legal club and the
Woman Lawyer's Bill, Foltz was blindsided by the fury of the opposition.
In round three of *Clara Foltz v. the Male Legal Establishment*, her opponents
urged in effect that women might practice law but must not be allowed to
study it. The suffragists, led by Foltz and Gordon, countered by winning the
inclusion of both rights in the new California constitution.

THE CONSTITUTIONAL CONVENTION I

The Delegates

While Clara Foltz was joining the bar and starting her practice in the fall
of 1878, Laura Gordon put her own law studies aside to lobby the constitutional convention, which opened at the end of September. In a June
election, the men of California had chosen 152 convention delegates; most
were either white male lawyers (57) or white male farmers (39). The deeply
submerged majority of the population—Chinese, Mexicans, Indians, and
women—was absent altogether. Nevertheless, the convention delegates
were more representative than most legislative bodies of the time, as well
as being more diverse politically and personally than any previously elected
body in California. One-third of them represented the WPC and were determined to mold the new constitution into an anti-Chinese, anticorporate
document. The other two-thirds had mostly campaigned under the oxymo-
ronic flag of the Non-Partisan Party, whose main agenda was to stop the
WPC and save the state from their leader, Denis Kearney.

Brought together only by their opposition to the WPC, the Non-Partisan
delegates were not a unified bloc at the convention. Among their number
were many as militantly set on change as any Kearneyite. An astute observer
said of the majority of Non-Partisans: "If you would place these instinctive
radicals alone on a mountain to produce a constitution they would astound
the sandlots."[90]

David Terry, who would become both the de facto leader of the WPC
and a covert champion of women's rights at the convention, was one of these
so-called Non-Partisans. An able lawyer and a southerner of violent temperament, Terry was an extraordinary figure in western history—his life a series
of outlandish events, ending with his death at the hands of a bodyguard for
a U.S. Supreme Court justice. As a young man, Terry had served the Texas
Rangers during the Mexican–American War, read law in his uncle's office,

and joined the gold rush to California, arriving in 1849. He soon abandoned mining for practicing law, and in 1855 at the age of thirty-three, he was elected to the California Supreme Court. Four years later, having risen to chief justice, he killed David Broderick, the state's antislavery U.S. senator, in a famous duel. In the aftermath, Terry fled California for ten years. Returning in the early 1870s, he found a public short on historical recall and long on forgiveness.[91]

Running as a "Chivalry" or Copperhead Democrat—a supporter of the Confederacy during the Civil War—Terry was easily elected to the constitutional convention as a Non-Partisan. Most of the other "Chivs" were on the ticket of the WPC. One in particular, Charles Ringgold, was to become Terry's henchman and, illustrating the "strange bedfellows" nature of the politics of the convention and of California at the time, central to the passage of the clause assuring equal employment opportunity for women.

James Joseph Ayers was another "instinctive radical" among the Non-Partisans. A newspaperman who had followed the common route from printer to publisher, Ayers was the editor of the *Los Angeles Express*, a journal he said had "weight and character and . . . almost metropolitan influence." In its pages, Ayers attacked the railroads so harshly that they withdrew advertising. At the same time, he virulently inveighed against Chinese immigration.[92]

Ayers narrowly defeated a WPC candidate from whom he likely differed little in views and in lack of elective experience. Yet as a Non-Partisan, Ayers was able to obtain a hearing unavailable to most WPC members; he also showed a natural bent for oratory and parliamentary maneuvering. Women became the beneficiaries of both talents as Ayers led the major floor fight for suffrage and played a leading role in the adoption of the women's education and employment sections.

Just as their opponents had come together as Non-Partisans for the election, the WPC split into pro- and anti-Kearney factions. Frank Roney, a genuine Irish revolutionary, led the opposition. Though he was not a sandlot orator, Roney was a talented organizer and as a skilled iron molder had wage-labor credentials that Kearney, an employing drayman, or teamster, lacked. Ideologically much closer to the socialist Workingmen's Party of the United States, Roney had nevertheless joined the Kearneyites after they drove that party from the sandlots in 1877.[93]

The inevitable competition between the two forceful men erupted over the election of delegates to the convention. Roney wanted to serve and thought that other experienced leaders should be candidates as well. Kearney declared that no WPC officers should run, thus barring both himself and Roney. The reasons for Kearney's decree have never been clear, but the results were negative for winning delegates, and the schism contributed to the historical judgment that Kearney and his followers were unstable political fumblers. According to the standard story, the Kearney delegates were "utterly ignorant and inexperienced," as political economist Henry George wrote. James Bryce echoed this judgment in his chapter on Kearneyism in California in *The American Commonwealth*, and subsequent generations have largely and uncritically accepted the characterization. The only contemporary challenge came from the leader himself. After Bryce's book was published in 1888, Kearney protested, "Our delegates were equally divided among inteligent [sic] farmers, mechanics, merchants and lawyers."[94]

But George was hardly alone in reviling the WPC delegates. Typical was a cartoon in a popular magazine showing them as grotesque illiterates; comparisons were drawn to the Paris Communards of 1871. The historian Hubert Howe Bancroft called the Workingmen "more fit to clean legislative halls than to sit in them." "Vicious, idle foreign rogues" was a casual appellation from the weekly *Argonaut*.[95]

Twenty-three of the 51 WPC delegates were indeed immigrants from other countries (compared with just 5 of the remaining 152 delegates). But the charge of being foreign had less to do with birthplace than with harboring un-American ideas, and in this respect, it was misplaced. The foreign-born were often the most earnest in their individualistic Americanism. For instance, Alphonse Vacquerel, returning to his native Paris in 1857, found the government so "averse to his Americanized feelings" that he quickly went back to California "where he could express himself freely."[96] At the convention, he did exactly that—most cogently on the issue of suffrage for women.

Although their platform was unpolished and undermined by anti-Chinese rant, the actual proposals on which the WPC candidates ran included the regulation of banks and railroads, the equalization of taxes, the eight-hour workday, compulsory free public education, the direct election of U.S. senators, and equal pay to women for work of equal value. Most of the WPC delegates were also for woman suffrage—partly because they assumed that enfranchised women would oppose votes for the Chinese. Even if the Asians eventually won suffrage, moreover, there would be a lot more white women voters than there would be Chinese.

Early Suffrage Petitions and Debates

Though woman suffrage was not high on anyone's list of priorities, it seemed possible in the opening weeks of the convention that California might become the first state to give women the vote. (Wyoming Territory did it in 1869.) In addition to most of the WPC members, a number of Non-Partisans were also suffragists. For instance, soon after the convention started, a conservative lawyer advocated granting the vote to women property owners. Another Non-Partisan, James Shafter, urged impartial suffrage—no surprise to those who knew the late "Mrs. Judge Shafter," one of California's earliest suffragists. Old Father McComas from Santa Clara (who had praised Foltz on the Assembly floor a few months earlier) also presented a suffrage resolution during the convention's early weeks.[97]

Foltz and Gordon probably had a lot to do with the prosuffrage atmosphere at the convention's start. Their success in winning the Woman Lawyer's Act was still fresh, and in June they had campaigned together to elect Gordon as a delegate to the convention. In a whirlwind, ten-day tour, the two women had hit every town in San Joaquin County, piggybacking on the rallies of the male candidates wherever possible. They met "large," "delighted," and "respectful" audiences, according to all reports. Gordon received several hundred votes and said she had succeeded in her purpose to "scare the politicians and have some fun." More sedately, Foltz opined that their campaign did "great good and no harm" in establishing the right of women to participate in constitution-making.[98]

From the opening gavel of the convention, Laura Gordon was on hand, organizing the women's lobby and attending virtually every day. One evening early in the proceedings, the Committee on Suffrage sat in special session to hear her and others. The viewers' section was full in the cavernous Assembly chamber where the convention met by day, "more than half the audience being ladies." They came to confirm that women wanted the vote and their speakers sought "justice, not favor."[99] After this session, woman suffrage became the committee's main agenda item.

The press picked up on the fact that woman suffrage was under serious consideration and started featuring the issue in coverage of the convention, not always in agreeable terms. For instance, the *Wasp*, a popular illustrated weekly, showed a group of ugly women (two holding an umbrella—a token of militant spinsterhood) surrounding a speaker with clenched fists upraised. They cast a menacing androgynous shadow on the wall.[100]

In mid-November the committee issued its compromise proposal on suffrage for the new constitution. While confining the vote to men, it explicitly authorized the legislature to grant women suffrage at its discretion. If enacted by the convention, this "legislative proviso" would enable women to win the vote the same way they had won the right to practice law only a few months earlier—by persistent lobbying. James Caples, the sole dissenter from this compromise on the committee, pictured "the future legislative hall [as] a beleaguered fortress" subject to "the attack of crinoline and silk sophistry, and blandishments, smiles and tears." A Non-Partisan farmer from Sacramento, Caples was the women's chief opponent in the floor debates as well, where he continued to warn that women's lobbying would turn into "a standing vexation and impediment to business" of future legislatures. He railed against the "corrupting, degrading, demoralizing" suffrage lobby and implored each delegate to "bring it home. See what it looks like. Imagine your wife a candidate for the Legislature, stumping the county, your daughter locked up in the jury box all night." Continuing his fantasy, Caples had the wife elected, the husband at home with the babies. "You come up here and see a bevy of gallant gentlemen around your wife paying great attention to her." In pre-Freudian California, Caples could without embarrassment depict woman suffrage as "a yawning chasm, deep, dark, impenetrable into which man may be precipitated."[101]

Laura Gordon considered the clause with the legislative proviso a success and planned to continue lobbying until it was safely passed by the convention as a whole. She wrote about her need for more support to Sarah Knox, who passed the request on to Foltz. "I have just read your letter," Foltz responded to Gordon. "O how terribly awful it is that you are left alone in your good work and worse than all that not one dollar of your expenses are paid by the wealthy woman whose cause you so ably champion." She continued that she regretted her own lack of money because of "the expense of my great family of little ones" and added: "I have a notion to promise you I will run up one day next week and remain two or three days providing you will let me sleep with you. Do you not think this a brave proposition from a lawyer?"[102] Perhaps referring to herself as a lawyer was a little tactless on Foltz's part. While Gordon had been laboring at the convention, Foltz had captured forever the crown of first woman lawyer in the state. On the other hand, Gordon's appearance before the convention committee would, if suffrage were won, be an even greater achievement. Both could legitimately think the other had taken the better part.

Following on her offer, Foltz made the familiar run to Sacramento several times during the next month. Around mid-December the women retired from lobbying and petitioning the convention until the new year. They were home with their families on Christmas Eve when their opponents brought the suffrage clause to the floor in order to defeat it. Barely a quorum was stirring at the convention, yet the debate was a striking rehearsal of the later full dress performances.

Eli Blackmer led the woman suffrage cause for the WPC. Earlier he had presented a petition with a thousand signatures on it. A shop owner and former school superintendent, the Massachusetts-born Blackmer did not fit the WPC stereotype of an ignorant, unemployed rowdy from the sand-lots. Yet he identified himself as primarily a wage-earning music teacher and welcomed his association with the party. Though surprised by the attempt to debate suffrage on December 24, Blackmer was able to give the basic arguments in favor of votes for women. He then spoke of his mother, "whose steps are fast approaching the entrance of that 'low green tent whose curtain never outward swings.'" She had raised "ten sons and daughters to positions of honor and trust" and had been a schoolteacher herself. Yet, he said, "[i]n this convention gentlemen who wanted to find a figure of speech that was more contemptible than anything else, have [said] 'old woman' or a 'convention of old women.' I wonder if such gentlemen [remember] that she who bore them is a member of this despised class?"[103]

A few others urged the unfairness of taking up such an important question on Christmas Eve. Finally, a San Francisco Workingman spluttered the arguments from idealistic to instrumental in one long breath: "I believe that a woman who has to pay her taxes has as good a right to vote as a man. If we give Negroes and Chinamen and everything else a right to vote and proclaim the universal brotherhood of man and fatherhood of God, why in the name of God don't you give them equal rights?"[104]

The convention adjourned until the new year.

MOVING TO SAN FRANCISCO

Early in January 1879, Clara Foltz moved to San Francisco with Trella and her two boys, leaving the little girls, Bertha and Virginia, with her mother in San Jose. Rather than setting up a household, she rented rooms at one of the hotels near the Montgomery Block, a huge warren of a building housing many lawyers and a law library. She took an office in the block and planned to register at the newly opened Hastings College of the Law, also nearby, as soon as the second term began.

Foltz had never lived in a big city, and San Francisco was especially rough now because of the economic depression, with its accompanying political unrest and unemployed men in the streets. On her way there, she had a piece of luck so fortunate that even a less sanguine person would see it as a portent. As she traveled by train "with my noisy brood en route to my new scene of activity, there was a passenger by the name of DeWitt from Monterey County, on his way to the United Sates Land office" to defend a case contesting his ownership of property allocated to him as a settler. He spoke of his need for an attorney to the conductor, who pointed out "the young lady lawyer sitting in the rear of the car."[105]

DeWitt told Foltz about his case, and she said she knew nothing about Land Office practice, which involved appearing before an administrative agency in charge of awarding public lands and arbitrating disagreements about settlers' rights. He responded that he would rather trust her than any other lawyer and offered her $300 (more than $6,000 today) to take the case. "I almost fell from my seat at the bare mention of so enormous a fee!" Foltz later recalled. Revealing the lack of business instincts that would plague her whole career as a lawyer, she told her prospective client that he was offering too much. But he explained that his previous attempt to hire a lawyer had ended because the fee demanded was $1,000.

Arriving in San Francisco, Foltz "deposited the youngsters in a suite at the Lick House [a popular hotel] . . . and went at once to the Registrar [the administrator of the Land Office] and obtained a copy of the Rules and Regulations." Working through the night, she studied the procedures and prepared her client and his witnesses.[106] At the hearing the next day, her study, preparation, and courage paid off and she won her first case in the metropolis. "No one . . . regarded me as a novice—so intelligently and effectively did I guard the interests of my client." It was an auspicious start for Foltz's plan to try big-city practice while attending Hastings.

Years later she remembered the praise from "the ever-generous press of San Francisco" about her first case there. Newspapers were the chief source of information in the city, and with twenty-one dailies, San Francisco had one of the highest per capita circulation rates in the country. Almost everyone, from workers to millionaires, read at least one paper every day. Along with coverage of the astonishing number of assaults, murders, and lavish society parties, the papers carried full accounts of political meetings, complete texts of lectures, and serious essays on issues like the monetary standard and the tariff.[107]

The papers were also interested in news of a lady lawyer. A few weeks after Foltz's arrival, the most widely circulated daily, the *San Francisco Chronicle*, published a long, favorable profile of Foltz called "Woman at the Bar, The First Female Lawyer of the Pacific Coast"—the first of many like it throughout her career. In one of the standard tropes of the genre, the reporter wrote of his laborious quest for that exotic creature—a woman lawyer. After negotiating the maze of the Montgomery Block and climbing to the fourth floor, back in a small room at the end of the corridor he at last came upon his quarry, Mrs. Foltz. Not what he expected, she was "a bright, fair-haired, rosy-featured, cheerful, matronly woman neatly attired in a dress of dark material over which was worn a most non-judicial checkered apron." The apron was obviously an effective answer to the charge of being an "unsexed woman," and Foltz further charmed the reporter by saying she was tired of publicity, adding irresistibly: "Two other members of the city press have been up here to try it, and I sent them away." (From the amount of news she generated in a short time, this was hardly likely.) Disarmingly she continued: "There is nothing to be said of me. I originated from the cradle, the washtub, the sewing machine, and the cooking stove. I am now trying to earn a living for myself and my little ones by practicing law, and I mean to succeed, and that's all there is about me." Three thousand words later, the reporter, who clearly thought himself in charge of the interview, concluded by assuring his readers: "There is nothing indicative of the typical strong-minded woman about her. Her bearing is that of a brave, cheerful, enthusiastic little woman, modest, dignified and self-reliant."[108]

THREE DAYS AT LAW SCHOOL

At the time Foltz first left the supportive San Jose surroundings, she said it was to improve her practitioner's skills and to find a "larger field" for her legal talents.[109] Cobbling together a living out of seized baggage, divorce, and indigent criminal cases did not satisfy her ideal of law practice. Rather, she yearned to be learned in the law—to master its sources and its theoretical underpinnings, to argue great constitutional cases and to be a famous trial advocate. It would be a significant step toward all these goals if she could graduate from the first law school in the West.

However, Foltz did not anticipate the amount of opposition she would face. Even men who thought she should be allowed to earn a living for her children by practicing law balked at her attending the new law school. The founders and students of Hastings resented a woman's intrusion on their enterprise, feeling that her very presence made it less impressive. Others feared the competition, and some perhaps guessed correctly that women would draw all the public attention.

Though there were no formal admission requirements in the school's first years, other than payment of the ten-dollar tuition fee, the registrar hesitated to accept Foltz's money once he realized she was paying for herself. But he gave way, and she slipped into the back of the lecture hall. Any hopes that she would fit in easily were quickly disappointed. "The first day I had a bad cold and was forced to cough," she wrote later. "To my astonishment every young man in the class was seized with a violent fit of coughing. You would have thought the whooping cough was a raging epidemic among the little fellows. If I turned a leaf in my notebook, every student in the class did likewise. If I moved my chair—hitch went every chair in the room."[110]

Though she took the hazing bravely in public, that night she "stole into the room where my little ones slept and cried myself to sleep." At this point she would explain, "I often refreshed myself by a good cry, which a woman could enjoy without getting out of her sphere." Or, in a less sardonic mood, she would quote from *In Memoriam* by Alfred, Lord Tennyson:

I sometimes hold it half a sin
To put in words the grief I feel;
For words, like Nature, half reveal
And half conceal the Soul within.

The next day a janitor barred her entrance with the flat words: "This is a law school. I'm ordered not to let you come in here." Just then, "a half dozen or more students, fine young fellows they were too, came running up the steps, hurrying to reach their seats at 8 a.m. sharp. They eyed me pityingly, while my cheeks burned with indignation, and with humiliation."

She decided to appeal to Judge Serranus Hastings, the school's founder and first dean, and found him nearby in his law office. The old man gave her a note asking the professor to admit her until the Board of Directors decided what to do. If her presence proved distracting, Hastings proposed that some arrangement be devised for keeping Foltz out of sight. Later, the

Chronicle would have fun with this idea, suggesting "a gild-edged, golden-railed balcony, a pagoda with minarets, or perhaps a simple platform of Oregon pine."[111]

On the third day of classes, Laura Gordon joined Foltz at law school. They had probably made the plan on one of Foltz's fall trips to help lobby the constitutional convention. The two planned to support each other now in the law school effort and then to return to Sacramento when the suffrage clause came to the floor. Together they went to the lecture hall but did not dare go inside. Foltz asked the janitor to take Hastings's note to the professor. While they waited, she once more saw the young men "hurrying up the steps arm in arm, their faces aglow with enthusiasm—all the world open to them, law schools and colleges were built and endowed for men."[112] At last, after all the students had passed in and were seated, the janitor returned and allowed them to enter. The women sat at the rear and hurried out as soon as the lecture was over.

At the end of that day, her third in law school, Clara Foltz received a "Dear Madam" letter from the registrar: "I am instructed to inform you that at a meeting of the Directors, it was resolved not to admit women to the Law School." There was no written explanation for the exclusion, but Dean Hastings told her and Gordon that their presence, particularly their rustling skirts, was bothering the other scholars. Kindly, he offered to furnish them books from his private library to study on their own.[113]

But little did Serranus Hastings realize how resourceful and determined these two women were. First, they decided to approach the directors individually while continuing to audit the lectures. After several weeks, however, they came to class one day to find the men blocking their entrance, staring at them in silent hostility. Shaken, the women retreated and went to talk with the one man who could resolve their difficulties with a single word. Professor John Norton Pomeroy was the renowned legal scholar recruited from the East to design the curriculum and teach at the new law school. Though his eminence did not deter Foltz, the professor was a new type for her. She had no idea what might charm or persuade him, and started badly by trying to argue law. The "best legal minds," she told him, had assured her that she had a right to attend the college because it was part of the University of California, which was coeducational by law. Coldly, he replied: "You have no rights in the matter at all. If we have a mind to let you come, you can, but you have no right to do so." The interview went downhill from there.[114]

Clara Foltz in 1879 when she sued Hastings Law School.
From Oscar T. Shuck, *History of the Bench and Bar of California*, 1901.

When the women saw that all their efforts had failed, they sued the directors to require that they be admitted to Hastings Law School. Foltz later made an amusing lecture out of the case, but it was a serious matter and would result in one of the triumphs of her career. She never forgot or entirely displaced her anger at the obstinate and contemptuous resistance she faced in the suit. She thought the Hastings defense was "unworthy," inconsistent both with "the letter of the law" and "its intent and spirit."[115] The lady lawyer would bring the courts of California to agree with her.

TURNING TO THE COURTS

Throughout February 1879, Clara Foltz and Laura Gordon waged legal war against Hastings, trying to obtain admission before the semester ended. They had male allies and movement women on their side, but the state's most prestigious lawyers were against them. Before the case was over, it influenced the course of the constitutional convention, further raising the stakes of their personal battle and finally elevating the significance of their achievement.[116]

The women made Foltz's office in the Montgomery Block their headquarters. The bar library was there, and the librarians provided research advice and let Foltz use the books "long after the closing hours." Many other attorneys had offices near her, and Foltz said they ran "in and out all the time . . . some of them to assist and counsel, and others out of mere curiosity to see the first female lawyer in California."[117]

Preparing to bring suit, Clara Foltz moved in late January to join the San Francisco bar by presenting her San Jose certificate and asking for reciprocity. Without explanation, the presiding judge refused to honor her routine request. "Not particularly gallant to the lady, nor indicative of much respect for a sister court," said her hometown newspaper, the *San Jose Mercury*.[118] Foltz immediately demanded the appointment of a bar committee to test her qualifications. Another three-member board of eminent lawyers, this time from San Francisco, administered an unusually extensive oral examination, and, just as in San Jose, she passed with distinction.

Meanwhile, Foltz and Gordon were preparing their arguments in the Hastings case. Proudly, Foltz mentioned that David Terry was advising them on litigation strategy. Terry's motives, like his particular actions in the case and later at the convention, were hidden. He was not known as a crusader for women's rights by any means. On the other hand, he admired boldness and courage and was an old friend of Gordon's from Democratic politics in Stockton. Soon, he and Foltz became allies as well. Later she would write that Terry was the "gallant knight . . . [who] championed [the women's cause at the convention] in his incomparable manner."[119]

Terry may have advised an unusual step the women took in laying the groundwork for their suit, or they may have designed it themselves based on their suffrage lobbying experience. They proposed a constitutional amendment—the first in U.S. history explicitly guaranteeing equal civil rights to women. Their simple one-sentence clause read: "No person shall, on account of sex, be disqualified from entering upon or pursuing any lawful business, vocation or profession."[120] They thought passage of this clause could help their case against Hastings, and perhaps bring some practical benefits to women in general. At the least, it would prevent some future legislature from repealing the Woman Lawyer's Act.

Gordon sent it to Charles Ringgold, a WPC delegate from San Francisco. Although as a Chivalry Democrat, Ringgold was an incongruous ally in the battle for women's entry into the public sphere, he responded January 30 on convention stationery that he "heartily" endorsed their proposition and promised to introduce it at "the earliest opportunity."[121]

Their legal theory for the suit was clear. Hastings was a branch of the public university, which had been made coeducational by law. Whom, how, and where to sue were more complicated issues—which Foltz and Gordon had to get right or risk losing time arguing about procedure rather than substance. Every passing day saw Foltz's "scholarship" funds from Sarah Knox and other suffragists dwindling. Gordon, too, was financially pressed, having given up her newspaper business and not yet joined the bar.

They decided to sue the Board of Directors, a dauntingly prestigious group of defendants. Joseph Hoge, the president of the constitutional convention, was the chair of the board; his partner, Samuel Wilson, perhaps the most conservative and able man at the convention, served on the Hastings board as well. The remedy the women sought was mandamus—the extraordinary writ directing public officials (the Hastings board) to do their duty (admit qualified students).

Where to sue was the most delicate issue because of the time pressures; if they started in the trial court and won, Hastings could appeal, and the semester would end before they were admitted. Yet if they went directly to the California Supreme Court, it might send them back to make a record below, potentially causing even more delay. Covering both bases, the women brought actions simultaneously, Foltz in the trial court and Gordon in the high court. As soon as one woman obtained a hearing on the merits, the other would seek to join that lawsuit. A letter from Gordon to her parents on February 6 indicates that Terry may have advised this sophisticated strategy.[122]

On Monday, February 10, the women filed their virtually identical pleadings. The supreme court quickly rejected Gordon's suit, but the trial court ordered the board either to admit Foltz at once or to show cause why not. A hearing was set for February 14. Gordon wrote to her family in Lodi that she planned to stay and aid Mrs. Foltz: "I want to be there with her, tho it is not at all probable they will come to trial. They intend to make us all the trouble and delay possible, but I really believe we will win in the end."[123]

On the day set, the Hastings lawyers did indeed move to continue the case, and Judge Robert Morrison granted the delay, along with Gordon's motion to consolidate her petition with Foltz's. This was pretty dull stuff for the reporters, who were there in force; but they made do with lines like this from the *Chronicle*: "Mrs. Foltz, with yellow hair, crimped and plaited, and Mrs. Laura deForce Gordon with dark brown hair in Coke-upon-Lyttleton [the title of an English legal treatise] curls down her back sat at the bar table and the former evinced her knowledge of Court practice by answering, 'Ready.' However, an aged masculine attorney asked the Court that the hearing of the motion go over till next Friday."[124]

After another week of preparation and anxiety, Clara Foltz arrived in court on February 21. Again, Hastings counsel moved for a continuance. Eleven days had passed since filing; Foltz argued furiously that a mandamus action required speed, that the delay was purposeful, "ungentlemanly as it is unprofessional."[125] Desperate about her waning chances to attend Hastings, however the case might come out, she burst into tears for the first and last time in her long courtroom career. Perhaps moved, Judge Morrison set the case for hearing without fail on the following Monday.

THE ARGUMENT IN *FOLTZ V. HOGE*

Every seat in the courtroom was occupied February 24, 1879; the press, the lawyers, and women variously designated by the papers as "prominent adherents of woman suffrage" and "the aggressive female sex" were all there. The audience supported Foltz and Gordon. "A beam of pleasure seemed to float over the place when a point was made in favor of the ladies," wrote one sympathetic reporter.[126]

The reports made much of Foltz's elegant costume, less of Gordon's work-aday apparel, and recorded nothing at all about the men's dress. To argue her greatest case, Clara Foltz wore "a business suit of black silk, trimmed with velvet" and decorated with lace in the Piccadilly pattern. "At her throat was a modest gold brooch." One paper also commented on the "fringes of black silk, partially concealing hands not lacking in bone and muscle." These were the capable hands of a former farm wife. Of most interest to the reporters were the women's hats; would they remove them as men did in court? Both women did so, leading to observations about Foltz's "profuse hair done in braids" and its golden color. Gordon was said to have "curls enough to supply half the thin-haired ladies of San Francisco with respectable switches."

Two members of the Board of Directors, Thomas B. Bishop and Delos Lake, represented Hastings. Both men were well-known, successful lawyers and both former judges, referred to by that title throughout the proceedings. When Judge Morrison took the bench, he turned instinctively to them and said, "Proceed, Gentlemen." Bishop headed for the podium, but Clara Foltz was not going to let this happen. She was the petitioner, she bore the burden of persuasion, and she was going to speak first. Causing a ripple of laughter, Foltz edged past Bishop and seemed to sweep him aside, as she spread her papers and books over the podium. "Raising her lithe figure to its full proportions," the *Chronicle* reported, "she swept an eagle eye about the Courtroom, bestowed one earnest glance on the shrinking Judge, and plunged head foremost into her argument."

Foltz summarized her case simply and straightforwardly. She met the qualifications for entry to the law school. Hastings was a branch of the University of California, which by law was open to female students. In any event, admission decisions could not violate public policy, and discrimination against women did just that. Finally, given the recent passage of the Woman Lawyer's Bill, it would be, as the *Daily Alta* reported, "an anomaly to enact that women might practice in all the law courts of the state, and yet in the same session establish a law school from which they are excluded."

Arguing first for the law school, Bishop did not answer Foltz's points. Instead, he read word for word the Wisconsin Supreme Court's 1876 opinion denying Lavinia Goodell admission to the bar. He did not mention that the legislature had reversed the court immediately by passing a bill admitting women and that Goodell was currently practicing as a respected bar member. In any event, Goodell's case was an odd choice for oral rendition because its most salient passage was a miscellaneous catalog of the "filth and indecencies" that lawyers had to deal with and that were too awful for females to hear. Yet with Foltz and Gordon at counsel table, and the courtroom full of women, Bishop intoned the list: "sodomy, incest, rape, seduction, fornication, adultery, pregnancy [*sic*], bastardy, prostitution, lascivious cohabitation, abortion, infanticide, obscenity, libel and slander of sex, impotence, divorce."[127]

Trying to dissociate himself from Bishop's ridiculous performance, Delos Lake delivered a more reasoned version of the standard argument: "women are pure; law is dirty." The very goodness of women, he said, made them unfit for the advocate's role. Moreover, women would be "dangerous to justice, inasmuch as an impartial jury would be impossible were lovely woman to plead the case of the criminal." The women were familiar with this line; the opposition had used it repeatedly in debating the Woman Lawyer's Bill, which led some to suspect that the men feared women's competition most of all.

With a courtly bow to Foltz, Lake continued: "The case today is one of dry law, yet if this lady should go before a jury with as good a speech as she made on her own behalf, she would have an advantage of which the Bar might well complain." He went on to "caution Your Honor, whose well-known gallantry may succumb to such grace and beauty."

In rebuttal, Foltz repudiated his words, which were "intended to depreciate me and my efforts" though "spoken under the cloak of a honeyed compliment." She chided "learned and prolix counsel" for getting so far off the legal point. For Lake, Foltz had light sarcasm; for Bishop, heavy scorn. Though the antiwoman Wisconsin opinion that he read was only three years old, Foltz treated it with such contempt that the reporter for the *Call* wrote that the audience "quaked somewhat at the . . . sarcasm she heaped on the opinion of some ancient wearer of the ermine."

Finally, Foltz considered the central "separate spheres" argument. Deploring the notion that "broader education would make woman less womanly and would destroy our homes," she pleaded "that is not the legitimate effect of knowledge of any kind. Knowledge enlarges and improves people. Knowledge of the law particularly will make women better mothers, better wives, and better citizens." These were lines she would use for many years.

Laura Gordon then took the podium, representing herself by permission of the court. First, she said, she knew what the legislature intended when it set up the law school, because she was there as a newspaper reporter and lobbyist for the Woman Lawyer's Bill when they did it. Indeed, she had worked for both bills, which were connected because both would improve the caliber of the state bar. It was unlikely that the law school would even exist without the backing of the women's supporters. Invoking the anti-Chinese sentiment common among Californians, she pointed out that Hastings had admitted "a Chinaman, while respectable women were excluded, and she read from the rolls the name of Cain Mook Sow." Lake protested: "But he was afterwards excluded." Gordon retorted: "He remained long enough to get his name on the official books before he was bounced, anyway"—better than the women did.

In closing, Gordon focused on the relationship of the law college and the coeducational University of California and stressed again that Serranus Hastings sought this affiliation in making his gift. At the day's end, Delos Lake rose for the last word. "If," he said, "fair ladies were to be lawyers, he would rather have them as associates than as opponents." Jovially, Judge Morrison suggested a partnership.

As Foltz left the courtroom surrounded by admirers, a fellow lawyer called over to her: "A woman should be home with her children instead of arguing in court." Without missing a beat, Foltz retorted that a woman "would be better off most anywhere than home raising men like you." Her riposte became a staple among Foltz's stories and was widely repeated—not always admiringly.[128] Though clever and quick, the sharp answer was at odds with her constant efforts to present herself as no less a lady though a lawyer. Foltz's angry sarcasm was doubtless triggered by awareness that even if she won the legal argument, she was likely to lose the case. The semester was slipping away, and the judge had not announced a decision date or ordered Hastings to admit the women provisionally while he deliberated. It could be weeks before he ruled.

THE CONSTITUTIONAL CONVENTION II: SUFFRAGE FAILS, CLAUSES PASS

In mid-January, before the women filed suit and while they were still negotiating for admission to Hastings, female suffrage came to the convention floor for the second time. Foltz and Gordon took a few days off from auditing classes to attend the session, which lasted a full day and a half and reprised many of the arguments that had been raised in the previous debate on Christmas Eve.[129]

Again, the WPC delegates led the suffrage forces, some as idealistic egalitarians and others who saw women's votes as a defense against pro-Chinese legislation. They were joined by some of the Non-Partisans, who likewise included sincere supporters and those with mixed motives. One surprise source of at least mild support was Non-Partisan Volney Howard, like David Terry a former southerner who saw himself as a statesman at the convention. Howard proposed that the suffrage clause provide for a referendum of potential women voters to determine their wishes. He was pretty sure of the result, he said, because in his long life he had not met "even a dozen ladies or women who wanted to vote."[130] Hearing this from the spectator section, Foltz and Gordon must have sighed, since everyone knew that thousands of California women had petitioned for suffrage. Still, giving women a vote on whether to vote was better than nothing at all.

In the end, the idea for a women's referendum was defeated, as was the suffrage committee's compromise proposal granting the legislature discretion to allow woman suffrage in the future. The franchise was confined to male citizens in the clause sent forward for final convention action. Foltz and Gordon turned their energies back to the Hastings battle.

They were not in Sacramento in mid-February when the proposed male suffrage clause came to the floor for final approval. James J. Ayers, publisher of the *Los Angeles Express* and a nominal Non-Partisan sympathetic with WPC aims, stunned everyone by moving to reinstate the original committee report, empowering the legislature to adopt woman suffrage. In a passionate address, he said that "all the friends of female emancipation ask is that the door shall not be entirely shut." Anything less, he claimed, was "a wanton act of tyranny." Several eloquent WPC delegates made pleas from simple justice, and one entreated the convention to "[t]hrow no blocks in the way of the car of progress." On the legislative empowerment amendment, the vote was sixty-seven to fifty-five against the women. A handful of delegates "turned the scale and valiantly put the whole female sex to flight," said one commentator.[131]

At the least, though, these last two debates left many delegates with a sense of owing something to the ladies. As the convention moved toward its conclusion after 150 days, the women's friends maneuvered the passage of two favorable clauses. Both victories were helped along by the heavy publicity from the *Foltz v. Hoge* case. The first came right at the beginning of the suit when Hastings counsel asked for a continuance, indicating that they intended to fight the women. In a brilliant maneuver, Charles Ringgold saw to the passage of the employment clause sent to him by Laura Gordon: "No person shall, on account of sex, be disqualified to enter upon and pursue any lawful business, avocation, or profession." The women had drafted the provision in order to protect their hard-won right to practice law against the "caprice of future legislators."[132]

The historic occasion lacked a certain gravitas, however. President Hoge, a stern parliamentarian, was away, and the convention became like a school-room when the "master was absent and the pupils proceeded in singing songs, throwing books and turning hand springs over the benches." Out-side, it was early spring in California and the brown hills were turning a bright green and the acacia a startling yellow. All the beauty and balmy weather was "softening the delegates' brains," said one participant.[133]

Up for a vote was the Article on Miscellaneous Subjects, reported from the only committee with a majority of WPC members. Its many sections ranged from continuing Sacramento as the state capital to making mechan-ics' liens a constitutional right. One by one, the sections came up to be amended, eliminated, or accepted, and so on to the next. In an atmosphere that combined hilarity and hysteria, the day wore on through consideration of seventeen sections, with some unpredictably rousing opposition and oth-ers gliding by. Late in the afternoon, Section 18 was reached. Intended to prevent Chinese from acquiring property, its poor drafting made it virtu-ally incomprehensible. A delegate moved to strike the clause, and Ring-gold stepped in to "offer a new section," completely unrelated to what it replaced: the women's employment clause. It passed without comment.

"Ringgold caught Caples [the women's main opponent] off his guard," observed the San Francisco Post the next day and noted, "This is the one solitary victory for women." A few days later when the Article on Miscel-laneous Subjects, with its stowaway cargo, the women's employment clause, came to the floor for the vote of the whole convention, opponents were again distracted, this time by a tremendous battle over a section requiring an eight-hour day on public works. When they reached Section 18, disarm-ingly labeled "Disqualification," everyone was exhausted. Ringgold cut off debate by moving the previous question, and there was an affirmative vote without a call for recorded ayes and nays. He later wrote to Laura Gordon: "Your Section, presented by me, is preserved, thanks to the ignorance of many whom [sic] supported it not knowing the privileges [sic] it extends." Thus was adopted what in retrospect was a major landmark: the first provi-sion in any American constitution explicitly prohibiting discrimination on the basis of sex, and the first guaranteeing women equal opportunity in employment.[134]

Shortly after passage of the employment clause, Foltz and Gordon argued the Hastings case to exceptional publicity. The day after all the front-page stories, the convention was debating a section of the education article guaranteeing the state university's independence from political influence in admissions. Farmers in coalition with WPC members twice defeated the section and the clause because they feared the school would admit only the rich and privileged. A regent-delegate explained why a great university must be free to choose its students and pleaded for passage of the section without crippling amendments. At once, Ayers was on his feet offering this clause: "No person shall be debarred admission to any of the collegiate departments of the University on account of sex." Reassuringly, the regent responded that the university was already coeducational. To which Ayers snapped: "The gentleman intimates that there is no necessity for it. I think recent history points to the fact that there is a necessity for it." He referred of course to Gordon and Foltz's effort to attend Hastings, and to their pending lawsuit.[135]

With the women's education clause added, the section picked up enough WPC votes to pass the convention, though it was a close call at seventy votes to fifty-nine. The *Chronicle* noted: "Those who have charge of the law school at the University may be ungenerous and narrow enough in their views to wish to limit the sphere of women, but a majority of the members of the Constitutional Convention are not." One querulous delegate claimed that the women's education section was "a sop to the suffragists." If so, it was the last sop: when Ayers tried to bring suffrage up again, the votes were not there for it even to be considered.[136]

On the 157th day, the convention concluded, having produced what was said to be the longest constitution in the world. Despite the disorderly tone sometimes set by the WPC delegates, the final document was impressive in its direct response to the democratic desires to make the corporations and banks more responsible and accountable, to regulate railroads, to ease the tax burden on citizens, and, on the darker side, to prevent the employment of Chinese workers. "Amended beyond recognition of its framers" as Clara Foltz said in 1917 and even more so today, it still provides the governing structure of the state.[137]

The greatest accomplishment of the convention was not any particular article or clause, however, but its role in turning down the political heat. Californians fell to constitution-making instead of to race and class warfare. When the convention ended, they plunged with undiminished energy into the ratification campaign, which, if successful, would be followed by election of officers under the new constitution. Just as they had in the convention, the voteless women played a significant role.

From the perspective of history, the women's clauses prohibiting sex discrimination in entry to the professions and in the state university, as well as the near-miss on suffrage, were important achievements. Looking back on her early career, Foltz said the new constitution was "a light bearer" for women. It "furnished the first streak of dawn by which [their] awearied feet have been guided into larger fields of opportunity."[138] Even before ratification, for instance, the women's clauses were cited by Judge Morrison in his decision in the Hastings case.

NARROW VICTORIES

On March 5, two days after the convention closed, and ten days after the oral argument, Judge Morrison delivered his opinion in *Foltz v. Hoge, et. al.* He found for the women and ordered their admission. Twice he cited the Woman Lawyer's Act, which made it unnecessary for him to consider further the "many things which would disgust a woman" in law practice. The opinion also held that the constitutional convention's "intention was to put women on the same footing as men" in the practice of law.[139]

Though he granted Foltz and Gordon unequivocal relief, the opinion had a grudging quality. Modern trends made it necessary to accept women, the judge said, noting also the recent admission of Belva Lockwood to the U.S. Supreme Court bar after passage of legislation allowing women to practice in federal courts. Judge Morrison did not "believe in women lawyers," Foltz later wrote, but he "did believe I was right in the law."[140]

Against the wishes of founder Hastings, who thought the opinion correct, the directors decided to appeal. Judge Morrison stayed his order admitting the women pending the appellate outcome. The semester would be long over before the case could be briefed and argued in the supreme court. Judge Morrison knew that, just as he had earlier known that requiring Foltz to take another examination to be admitted to his court and twice continuing the case could be fatal to the female litigants' cause. In the end, his determination to give them only what could not be denied turned Foltz's courtroom victory into the defeat of her dream to achieve a formal legal education.

With her scholarship from her friends almost exhausted and only three days in the classroom for all her efforts, Foltz now faced writing her first appellate brief and preparing for another bar examination so she could argue her case in the California Supreme Court. Before returning to San Jose and taking up these tasks, Foltz stayed in San Francisco for a few days to enjoy the excitement of the ratification campaign. The referendum was scheduled for the first week in May, and the contest was intense. Thousands turned out to rallies on both sides. Much of the public debate was complex and detailed; speakers delivered and newspapers printed long discussions on tax theory and regulatory policy. In one of its last acts, the convention sent a copy of the lengthy constitution—all 223 sections—to every voter.

Generally speaking, opponents were the businessmen and bankers who would be subject to new regulations and taxes under the proposed constitution. Farmers and many middle-class progressives were for it, and so were Workingmen because of the anti-Chinese measures. The opposition poured huge sums into the campaign—and used new methods like providing ready-made stories to the rural press, and old tactics like threatening discharge of employees or withdrawal of advertising. Most of the press was also against ratification, with the notable exception of the *San Francisco Chronicle*. Both sides appealed to women's self-interest in trying to persuade them to use their influence over the male voters. Opponents argued that the fact that female suffrage was specifically debated and excluded would hurt the women's chances to win the vote for years to come.

Proponents gave serious attention to the women's employment and education clauses, which had been adopted with such little scrutiny in the closing days of the convention. The *Chronicle* identified the women's employment section as "an entirely new thing in California fundamental law. . . . The female brain and the female hand, for all professions and trades, meets the male brain and male hand on a dead level of equal rights before the law."[141]

The night before the ratification vote, Foltz wrote to Gordon, who was back home in Lodi. From January to May, the two women had spent most days together, litigating an unprecedented case, lobbying for suffrage at the convention, and basking in frequent and favorable press coverage. "I am all packed up ready to leave for home and away from the scene of so much storm and conflict," Foltz wrote. "I have been very happy in your society, my own sweet friend; and I have formed pleasant acquaintances that will be life long pleasure."[142]

Ninety percent of the mostly white and entirely male electorate voted the next day, ratifying the constitution by fewer than 11,000 of 145,093 votes cast. Immediately, everyone turned full attention to the election of new officers, scheduled for September. Back in San Jose, Foltz supported prosuffrage candidates, but mostly she practiced law, prepared to pass the California Supreme Court bar and argue her case, and with her friends planned a suffrage convention for the fall. "Worn and spent with the heavy cares of my growing children," she wrote of this period, "I studied night and day." In early December, she passed her third and most difficult bar examination, one which many applicants failed. The *Chronicle* favorably compared her performance before the supreme court with that of some male applicants who exhibited "a nervous, self-doubting manner that did not augur well for their future ability to handle witnesses and to blandly ask for heavy fees."[143]

A few weeks after passing the bar, she argued *Foltz v. Hoge* on appeal. Afterwards, the chief justice told her: "You are not only a good mother; you are a good lawyer. I have never heard a better argument for a first argument, made by anyone." The court decided the case speedily, ordering the admission of women to the law school at once and relying on the education and employment clauses—a double victory for the women. But it came too late for Foltz. The moment had forever passed for her to enjoy learning and reflection free of a client's demands and her own economic needs. Indeed, she was so hard-pressed financially at this time that she had pawned her only piece of good jewelry to pay the $10 admission fee to the supreme court—"the modest gold brooch" she had worn at the trial court argument of *Foltz v. Hoge*.[144]

Though she gained little for herself, Clara Foltz would always return to the Hastings lawsuit as the greatest moment of her public career. Of all victories, the first is the sweetest, but beyond that, she found in its memory the best images of herself: brave, idealistic, hopeful. In just two years, she had risen from obscure housewife to famous lady lawyer, "the Portia of the Pacific."[145]

Private Loss: Clara Foltz's Divorce

In the midst of lobbying for the Woman Lawyer's Bill, Clara Foltz had traveled to Portland, Oregon, to see her husband, who had been away for months. Upon returning, she listed herself as a widow and lecturer in the 1878 San Jose city directory. The final scenes of her marriage played out the next year in the middle of her case against Hastings.

Soon after Clara had moved to the city with the older children, Jeremiah came home to San Jose. In the weeks that followed, he could read about his wife in the news practically every day. She did not mention him

in interviews but said, "I have had troubles of which I do not like to speak."
A letter printed on the front page of the *Sacramento Record-Union* was the
only reference to his existence in all the coverage of Clara Foltz in 1879:
"Seven or eight years ago a young women with four children already under
her wings came to Oregon in search of her husband. She was twenty years
of age at that time, and was very self-possessed, besides being rather attractive." The writer continued that Jeremiah, who was clerking in a store, had
made himself unpopular by criticizing the virtue of the local women. "The
wife proved to be energetic and capable. She was a ready advocate of woman
suffrage. The husband was not of much force and whatever became of him
I cannot tell." The letter concluded that "Carrie" Foltz would be a success as
a lawyer because "she has no timidity or shrinking delicacy . . . and, on the
contrary, is a ready talker, sharp and quick witted."[146]

Jeremiah Foltz had married a girl of fifteen. Fifteen years later he had
a famous wife. His own story was never in the newspapers and is discern-
ible on the public record only in Civil War pension applications. These
show that he joined the Union Army in his home state of Ohio and then
within months of enlistment saw terrible action on the Tennessee front at
the battles of Fort Donelson and Shiloh. There, "from exposure and hard
marching," Foltz developed the severe lower back pain that would eventually paralyze him. He later served in an Illinois regiment, from which he was
discharged as disabled. The records describe him as being five feet, seven
inches to five feet, nine inches tall, with dark hair, fair skin, and blue eyes
and the occupations of carpenter, farmer, and clerk. This is about all we can
know about the man Carrie Shortridge married—this, and her recollection
that he had said she cooked better than "his dear old German mother."[147]

When Jeremiah returned to San Jose from Portland in the early months
of 1879, Foltz's friends feared that she would give up her ambitions, which
he thought wrong because no woman could be "a good wife, mother and
successful bread-winner at the same time." One suffragist wrote to Laura
Gordon: "I am sorry to hear that Mrs. Foltz's husband is here. She will rue
the day that she goes back to him as his submissive slave—for what does he
care about woman's freedom or personal liberty?"[148]

Foltz's grief over her situation was evident. Another suffrage woman
wrote to Gordon: "I am a little worried about our beloved Clara; others
will love her, whose love will not blight. Well be it if our gentle, magnetic
friend is poised against it all." Though Clara described "the bitter dregs of
heartache" mingled with the interest and excitement of the Hastings case,

she did not move back to San Jose when Jeremiah returned. After a few months, he left town, announcing his intention to "remove permanently" to Portland. Clara then sued for and was granted divorce on the grounds of desertion. Within a year of the decree, Jeremiah married again. In a few early interviews, Clara Foltz mentioned her divorce, but it soon dropped from the account entirely, replaced by a tragic tale in which her husband died, leaving her a very young widow with five children to support.[149]

At the outset of her career, Foltz said: "I don't believe in divorce. The legal partnership may be dissolved; but if there are children, the holier bond can never be broken. It exists forever." She may have been saying this strategically. Her endorsement of divorce could play into the charge that women attorneys endangered the home and supported free love (divorce enabled a change of partners). It might also prompt a closer look at her claim to be a widow. By the mid-1890s, however, Foltz had changed her publicly stated view. She no longer found "the sacredness of marriage . . . a sound argument against divorce. . . . When love is slain, the civil contract is but the husk and shell of marriage. Long before a divorce is sought love has ceased. All that is sacred is dead, and the civil court in a judgment of divorce only gives legal sanction to a decree that nature has already entered in their hearts."[150]

In the years between these conflicting statements, Foltz handled a number of divorce cases, mostly for wives, who were usually the plaintiffs. Some were charity cases, and others may have been contingency fee arrangements, allowed then but since barred as unethical because they give the lawyer a stake in marital dissolution. In still other divorce cases, the court might order a fee for the lawyer as part of the settlement between the parties. Under California's community property regime, moreover, both spouses were entitled to an equal share of what was acquired during marriage, which could give a wife the means to pay a divorce lawyer.

In this and other respects, California's divorce laws were the most liberal in the nation, with six capacious grounds for ending a marriage: adultery, cruelty (physical or mental), desertion, neglect, intemperance for two years, and felony conviction. Critics said these laws were undermining the family and made marriage "merely a legal partnership, virtually dissoluble at will." They blamed the women's movement for promoting easy divorce and lawyers who made their living "fattening on marital indecencies."[151] Foltz never seriously engaged in the divorce debate, perhaps prudently, given her secret personal history; her two public statements, spoken almost twenty years apart, were her only recorded utterances on the issue.

She did, however, lecture on marital discord—which she implied was the real threat to family life long before divorce was considered. Foltz told the story of her union with Jeremiah without revealing that she was speaking personally: "In the springtime of married life, they fly to each other's sides like steel and magnet. But as years go on indifference creeps over the pleasant surface of their lives, the tender courtesies begin to be forgotten. She is either engrossed with household cares or the gayeties of fashion, and he has a field of thought entirely foreign to either one or the other." In the sad denouement, the "society of each becomes irksome to the other and they long for different conditions all because there is no common ground between them."[152] In Foltz's case, of course, it was neither the "gayeties of fashion" nor "household cares" that engrossed her. Rather, she was occupied with becoming California's "first woman."

After the election of officers and legislators under the new constitution in October 1879, Foltz was named clerk to the Judiciary Committee of the California Assembly, the first woman to hold such a position in the state. Only two years after she had traveled to the capital to plead for the chance to earn a living, she returned as a full-fledged lawyer and, for all public purposes, as a widow.

"First Woman" at the Historic 1880 Legislature

The atmosphere was charged at the first legislature elected under the new constitution to implement its antimonopoly and anti-Chinese provisions. A third of the members were from the WPC, and most of the remaining majority were Republicans. (Votes for the WPC and other splinter parties had undermined the Democrats.) Many of the legislators were new to the work, though a few experienced hands survived the upheaval, including Foltz's supporters on the Woman Lawyer's Bill, Grove Johnson and William May. Among the new men were several avowed suffragists, one elected from San Jose.[153]

From her office as lawyer to the Judiciary Committee, Foltz promised "no peace until we sit side by side with our brothers in the council chambers of the nation." "Prepared for War" is the caption under her picture in a sketchbook of the historic legislature, and she carries a bullwhip. Foltz was backed by her suffrage friends; "all the strong-minded ladies of the state are present" said the *San Francisco Examiner*. A contemporary sourly noted that the women "continued their storming of the halls of legislation.[154]

The women's main goal was full and impartial suffrage; the fallback was voting on matters related to education (school board membership and local taxation). "School suffrage" had passed in several eastern states, and since children were directly involved, it was arguably within women's sphere. Proponents also urged that it would be a first step, preparing women to vote on larger issues. In California, moreover, women had previously won the right to serve on school boards, so it seemed right that they should be able to vote for these offices.

Foltz herself was not content with the half loaf of school suffrage. In a legal memorandum to the Judiciary Committee, she claimed that the new constitution empowered the legislature to enfranchise women. It was an audacious argument given that the convention had defeated that explicit provision and that the qualifier "male" appeared three times in the voting clause. Nevertheless, she wrote, the final suffrage clause specifically listed the people who could not vote (for instance, Chinese and people who were insane or incompetent). Since women were not listed, they could be granted suffrage. She summed the point in legal Latin—*Expressio Unius. Exclusio Alterius*—meaning that the expression of one thing excludes all others.[155]

Submitting a printed brief based on a technical legal argument was high-class lobbying. Foltz did plenty of the less elevated sort, also, buttonholing individuals in the anteroom and on the floor of the Assembly chamber when her official duties took her there. On three evenings during the session, woman suffrage was debated in the large chamber where the constitutional convention had lately met. This time, the women came in from the lobby and down from the gallery and spoke for themselves to the largest audience ever gathered at the capitol building. Among the women speakers, Laura Gordon and Clara Foltz were the stars by virtue of their recent victories in the Hastings case and at the convention. Foltz invoked an image of women irresistibly on the move: "No aristocracy of sex can check the swelling tide." The shackles "fall at our feet and we trample them in the dust."[156]

Newspaper coverage of the suffrage debates was extensive and generally sympathetic to the women. When one opponent produced a forty-foot-long fake petition from women who did not want the vote, a reporter for the *Examiner* observed that "the frowning gaze of Mrs. Gordon and the dignified but cold sarcastic glance of Mrs. Foltz will haunt him to his grave."[157]

The women won a majority for full suffrage in the Assembly but fell short of the two-thirds required to submit a constitutional amendment to the people. School suffrage as a fallback came within three votes of gaining the needed two-thirds. For the second time in as many years, the women almost won. The *Chronicle* said the suffragists came so close because of "complimentary and jocose votes" and warned that misplaced chivalry could lead the unwitting into "social and political revolution." Foltz declared that the names of their opponents would be "inscribed in a black book in letters of light" and that they would never again hold state office.[158]

Despite the defeat, Clara Foltz had a grand time in Sacramento after the strain of the previous few years. She enjoyed the lobbying, the speech-making, and the camaraderie with her suffrage friends, especially Laura Gordon, now the second woman lawyer in the state. Gordon traveled regularly from her home in Lodi to lobby and to debate, and she, too, submitted a printed brief on suffrage to the committee. It is not clear whether Foltz stayed in Sacramento for the whole legislative session or commuted home to San Jose on some weekends. She may have left the children with her mother or had at least the older ones with her part of the time.[159]

In the intense atmosphere of the session, Foltz also grew close to several people who had been only acquaintances before; one of these was Madge Morris, the postmistress to the legislature. Morris was a poet, later a very popular one, and in her published collection appears this ode to Clara Shortridge Foltz, describing her at the 1880 term:

> Thy voice has argued in debate
> In scathing satire sharply fell
> In forum and in hall of state
> Held listening thousands with its spell
> Then dropped its tones to softest keep
> And crooning sung a babe to sleep.
> . . .
> [T]hou hast proved that woman can—
> Who has the grace, and strength and will—
> Work in the wider field of man
> And be a glorious woman still.[160]

Another intimate personal connection Foltz made in these heady Sacramento days was with Charles, or "C.E.," as he signed himself, Gunn, chief clerk of the Assembly. At age twenty-seven (four years Foltz's junior), he had a young, eager face that he solemnized with a full beard. Like Foltz, he won an appointment at the legislature in the Republican sweep of the state, and like her, he was from San Jose. His hometown paper said that Gunn was "winning golden opinions for his admirable reading and for his dignified and courteous bearing."[161] Though Foltz and Gunn probably knew each other before they worked together in Sacramento, this is the period during which they became lifelong companions. From this time on, C. E. Gunn is present in Clara Foltz's story. He interviewed jurors after her trials; he testified when she sued a client for a fee; he bore the pall at her father's funeral. Gossip had it that they were lovers; in any case, they were certainly the closest of friends.

After the legislative term ended in the spring, Foltz returned to San Jose to take up her law practice. Though her finances were still shaky, she had made a name for herself, and California women seemed close to winning political equality. As she said after the Hastings argument, "the future seems just brighter than ever before and I can believe the good angels are shaping it all to suit themselves."[162]

Making a Living, 1880–1890

Political Orator, Prosecutor, Private Lobbyist, Public Lecturer

THE PATTERN OF HER PRACTICE

Clara Foltz had every reason for optimism as the 1880s began. In a short time, she had acquired a career, lobbying expertise, name recognition, a circle of friends and supporters, and had played a large part in the passage of constitutional clauses guaranteeing equal opportunity for women. Surely, political rights and professional distinction would now follow. The previous two years, during which she was often in the news influencing public events and arguing in court, had raised Foltz's expectations and ambitions about her new profession. She was not willing to settle back into local practice, defending poor people charged with crime and helping women write wills and obtain divorces. Instead, she wanted to be a famous jury lawyer and to accumulate great wealth through her own efforts.

She had models of the kind of attorney she aspired to be among her opponents in the Hastings case and friends at the San Francisco bar. But the lawyer she mainly admired was Edward Dickinson Baker, who became the subject of her most popular lecture in the 1880s. In giving it, she would both extol and imitate him as the master persuader of twelve men in the jury box.

Although Foltz achieved some reputation as a trial lawyer herself, she was never able to convert her superior skill into solid financial rewards. Indeed, merely making a living proved harder than she expected. Prejudice played a large part in her financial insecurity, but it was not the whole story, as many male lawyers also had trouble getting established in the profession. One reason was the lack of formal training and discipline for attorneys. To put "Esquire" after his name in California, a man need only live in the state and read law briefly, then answer a few questions from the bench. This meant that some certified lawyers were simply unqualified. But educated and talented men also failed if they had no stake or social and professional connections.

One way for lawyers to increase their assets and spread their risks was to practice together. And of course the best way to get started was to join an established partnership. This is why Foltz had originally sought to apprentice with the best office in San Jose, rather than to study with her father and C. C. Stephens. The advantages can be seen in the career of her brother, Sam Shortridge, who became a lawyer several years after Foltz. Though he was not nearly as intelligent and gifted as she, he became a partner to one of the best lawyers in the West, Delphin Delmas, and had none of the financial struggles Foltz faced. Surely she would have taken any similar opportunity, but instead she hung out her shingle and practiced alone for the best part of fifty years.

Some attorneys in her position supplemented their incomes through public offices such as notary public or district attorney, but women were ineligible for most of these because a person had to be an elector (that is, voter) to hold them. So Foltz followed another path that lawyers used to meet the overhead: political and platform lecturing. She also tried private lobbying and briefly took up newspaper editing.

Foltz was mostly unsuccessful at establishing a stable and lucrative practice without the necessity of outside employment. But she had other large goals at which she did much better. As an attorney, she became a political actor and reformer, a public thinker, suffrage leader, and founder of the public defender movement (see Chapters 5, 6, and 7). Her career would leave a lasting impression on the law.

LADY ORATOR OF THE REPUBLICANS

As she set out on her practice in the 1880s, without connections or financial backing, Foltz was fortunate that the publicity from her exploits led to her employment in several well-paid jobs in the public eye. The first of these was as a political orator. Soon after returning from her service as clerk to the legislature, the state Republican Party hired her to stump for James Garfield for president of the United States. In response, the Democrats enlisted Laura Gordon to speak for their candidate, Winfield Hancock. The assumption that it took a woman to counter a woman worked to the advantage of both Foltz and Gordon more than once.

Their employment as political orators was also a tribute to their ability to turn out large crowds, which they had demonstrated the previous year in Gordon's campaign for delegate to the constitutional convention. On election eve in Stockton, for instance, despite "the bonfires and intense excitement" of the WPC and Non-Partisan rallies, "the crowd adjourned and came over to hear the constitutional issues discussed from a woman's standpoint."[1] It was this kind of drawing power that the political parties hoped for in hiring the women orators.

Foltz spoke for Garfield about forty times throughout the state and was paid $3,000 (more than $60,000 today). Not since "the gifted Emma Hardinge" campaigned for Lincoln had a woman been so enmeshed in California politics, commented the *San Jose Mercury*. Hardinge had spoken as much on abolition and Spiritualism as on the presidential election, however, so Foltz and Gordon may have been the state's first purely political woman orators.[2]

In the 1880s, California, like the rest of the country, experienced a partial recovery from the depression of the "terrible seventies," but serious problems remained. The unregulated economy and widespread corruption of the government on every level contributed to cycles of boom and bust and to the growing gap between rich and poor that would continue for the rest of the century. Despite the new constitution's creation of a railroad commission in the state, the Southern Pacific Railroad continued its efficient domination of the entire governmental structure. Racism against the Chinese also persisted although Denis Kearney and the WPC were well off the scene by the mid-1880s and most of the WPC members returned to the Democratic Party.

Twenty years after the Civil War, the United States was still living out its aftermath. In her stump speeches, Foltz maintained party tradition and waved the bloody shirt, denouncing Winfield Hancock, a former Union Army general, for having a "copper head on a Union body" and "a rebel horde at his back." At the same time, she proclaimed that the Republicans were "the grandest party ever known, the child of the spirit of Freedom, embracing all the nobler thoughts and sentiments of the age."[3]

Though the war remained in the background of most politics, other issues separated the two major parties. Republicans were for protective tariffs and the Democrats for free trade, a carryover from antebellum divisions between North and South. Both parties espoused civil service reform and campaigned for its adoption, though neither practiced it much when in power. In late-nineteenth-century California, the Republicans were most closely associated with the political machine headed by the Southern Pacific Railroad, while the Democrats' preferred boss-dominated urban machine politics was centered in San Francisco.

Early in the decade, some splinter parties started arguing for inflated currency to benefit farmers and other debtors and to stimulate the economy. One of these was the Greenback Labor Party, which also supported woman suffrage. In 1881, Foltz backed its candidate for attorney general of the state—Marion Todd—who had spent a term at Hastings after Foltz had opened the doors to women and who had then been admitted to the bar. At a mass meeting in San Francisco, Foltz declared: "I am a Republican. All I know about Greenbacks is the absence of a circulating medium in my own pocket." But she did know that the employment clause of the new constitution opened all occupations to women. If elected, Todd could serve, in Foltz's legal opinion.[4]

The tactic of seeking elective office, though it could generate favorable publicity, was not approved by suffrage leaders in the East after Victoria Woodhull had made her largely symbolic campaign for president in 1871. In the West, Abigail Duniway of Oregon warned that running could lead a "captious public to give us the name of eccentricity."[5] Clara Foltz apparently did not agree with this assessment. She had stumped for Laura Gordon for delegate to the constitutional convention, and in 1884 she would support Belva Lockwood for president and in 1892 would herself run for city attorney on the People's Party ticket.

When she first started stump speaking, Foltz was frightened by the outdoor setting and the close, vocal, largely male crowds. Even when the rallies were held inside, the scene was much more intimidating than the platform lecturing in which she had achieved her early oratorical successes.

Stumping sometimes involved passionate personal solicitation and harsh partisan attacks, which respectable opinion regarded as especially unlady-like. Foltz would meet the same kind of objections when she argued to juries. But nerved by Laura Gordon, "the bravest woman in the west," as Foltz called her, she had quickly grown to enjoy stumping. Political oratory also helped pay the overhead for her law practice.[6] The Republicans employed Foltz again in 1884 when James G. Blaine lost to Grover Cleveland nationally but won in California. For these campaigns, Foltz relished her latest title: "Lady Orator of the Republicans."

SWITCH TO THE DEMOCRATS:
FIRST STATEWIDE OFFICE

In the 1886 gubernatorial election, Clara Foltz rather suddenly became the lady orator of the Democrats. Her switch ultimately led to her appointment to the Normal School Board, making her the first woman to hold statewide office in California. Exactly why she left the Republicans is not clear. Foltz said that a male leader "made a slurring remark about women in politics," but it doesn't seem likely that her party ties would slip over a single insult. Perhaps there were previous slights. Or perhaps, as Foltz's detractors claimed, the Republicans refused the high price she put on her services for this midterm election. At any rate, the Democrats signed her up for rallies statewide, from Siskyou to San Diego.[7]

The Democratic candidate was Washington Bartlett, the former mayor of San Francisco, who was running against John Swift for the Republicans. It may have been Swift himself who insulted Foltz. If so, she repaid him in her stump speeches, calling him "cold, bloodless, inhuman and barbarous" and "a political mountebank" who bought his nomination from the party that "peddled its highest office," among other things. Though the WPC had faded away by 1886, the election saw the rise of the American Party, which also maligned "revolutionary and incendiary foreign hordes." They were not talking about the Chinese, however, but about Irish and Jewish immigrants. This form of nativism had little appeal to Democrats, whose candidates and bosses frequently bore names like Sullivan, White, and Buckley.[8]

Initially, the American Party offered to endorse the Republican ticket. But in an open letter, its candidate Swift declined the support, writing that he believed "that Roman Catholics and Jews are as loyal to republican institutions . . . as Protestant Christians or people of any other faith." Foltz bluntly claimed that Swift was lying and that she was "credibly informed" of private correspondence showing his true anti-immigrant and anti-Catholic sentiments.[9]

Like her direct insults, such hard-hitting tactics were accepted political oratory. Yet a lady calling an opponent a liar carried added weight. Foltz was implicitly invoking her moral authority as a woman while speaking in a manner as bold and forceful as any man. To appear refined while delivering her rough remarks, she dressed in the latest fashion and often made her entrances on a gentleman's arm.

By late October, her stump speech perfected in dozens of appearances, Foltz was ready for the big city. A "vast audience," according to the papers, assembled at San Francisco's California Theater, which held five thousand people. Bonfires and rockets lit the night sky. Inside, every seat was taken, and as often happened when Foltz appeared, there was "an unusual number of ladies and their escorts."[10]

Foltz warmed up the audience with general banter about the difference between the two parties, finding money the inspiration of the Republicans and humanity the moving spirit of the Democrats. Especially, she said the Democrats were friends to working people, as shown by the eight-hour day on public projects, shorter hours for street-car drivers, and restrictions on convict labor—all measures she attributed to her current party. Soon, she turned to the part that the crowds liked best—lambasting Swift and lauding Washington Bartlett.

She focused on Bartlett as a friend to women during his two terms as mayor of San Francisco. "For a long time," she said, "my office has been a labor bureau for women, when I could do nothing else for them I would take them to [Bartlett] and he never failed to assist them." Generally, Foltz claimed that the Democratic Party "by its deeds" (there were very few words) showed a "more liberal" attitude toward her sex. "Frequently applauded," provoking "an almost continuous roar of laughter" by "her witty sallies," Foltz was "cheered to the echo" and presented with laurels tied in red, white, and blue.[11]

The Democrats won by fewer than seven hundred of the two hundred thousand votes cast, largely because the American Party siphoned off most of its eight thousand ballots from the Republicans. Clara Foltz could plausibly claim that in such a close election her efforts had been decisive and deserved recognition. Washington Bartlett apparently thought so too, appointing her as a trustee of the State Normal School (a teacher training institution) in 1887. Through her political oratory, long before women had the ballot, Foltz became the first woman to hold statewide office in California, and one of the few appointed to such a high post in the country.[12]

Though she remarked acerbically that "a woman may not hope [for] any position . . . when there is profit," but instead is given "places of trust where there is nothing but expense as in the Normal trusteeship," Foltz valued the post for its access to politicians in her new party.[13] Most notably, she had the chance to cultivate a relationship with Stephen White, also a Normal School trustee and the charismatic leader of the progressive wing of the Democrats. White was elected president of the state Senate in 1887 and became lieutenant governor the next year when Bartlett died in office. He was young and appeared to be inexperienced, but actually he had learned much about party leadership from his father. William White was an ardent Democrat, except for a brief fling as gubernatorial candidate for the WPC. The son took up where the father left off, transferring the WPC causes to the Democratic Party program.

In a few years, White would be the state's first native-born U.S. senator, known in Washington, D.C., as the "Little Giant of California." "Eloquent and learned," he "loved good liquor and good conversation," but most of all he loved politics behind and before the scenes. Though women's rights were not on his agenda, White was a good man to know and probably a help to Foltz in her career as political orator.[14]

STUMPING FOR THE DEMOCRATS
IN A NATIONAL ELECTION

As the 1888 presidential election approached, Stephen White was at the head of a state party severely divided between the antimonopoly and the anti-regulation factions. Yet the Democrats were hopeful because they had the best of the Chinese issue, which was still a potent political factor in California. The Republican nominee was Benjamin Harrison, who had a mildly pro-Chinese voting record in the U.S. Congress. Moreover, President Cleveland approved a further tightening of the 1882 Exclusion Act, which would virtually end Chinese immigration to the United States.

The California Democrats had promised Cleveland the state if he would sign the act, and when he did, they intensified their already vigorous campaign. Never "in the history of politics has [sic] there been so many Democratic speakers on the stand" in California, a friend wrote Harrison.[15] Every rally of any size had two speakers—one on the Chinese question and the other on the also hot issue of the protective tariff. In an unprecedented move, the Democrats fielded two well-paid lady orators: Laura Gordon on Chinese exclusion and Clara Foltz on the tariff.

Foltz had the harder job, trying to educate, persuade, and entertain large crowds on this dry subject, which many believed beyond the capacity of a woman to understand or to explain. She opened in Santa Barbara on August 25, the official first night of the campaign, and for the next two months she delivered increasingly effective versions of her arguments all over the state. By the sixth week of the campaign, her presentation was fully polished.[16] On a Saturday night in October, she took the platform at San Francisco's Metropolitan Temple. "Eloquent Mrs. Foltz" read the bold headline in the *Examiner*, recently taken over by William Randolph Hearst at the beginning of his extraordinary publishing career. To "one of the largest audiences ever assembled in the building" (it seated three thousand, and hundreds more could stand), Foltz spoke for two hours on the tariff issue.[17]

Though for the first time in a national election neither party raised the Civil War explicitly, it lurked in the background of the tariff debate. Foltz acknowledged that at one time a high tariff was necessary to fund the war, but now she said it produced "revenue far in excess of the need of government." To the argument that national growth depended on shielding industry, she responded, "After twenty years of coddling, capital can take care of itself." Foltz claimed that a lower tariff would reduce the cost of lumber for the workingman's house and of the wool for his shirt.

Her brother Sam was on the stump for the Republicans, arguing the opposite—that protected industries would be more profitable and so could pay higher wages. Foltz carried on an imaginary dialog with him, a rhetorical gambit that "aroused the liveliest interest in the minds of her audience." Smiling, she would start: "I would like to ask that imperturbable Republican orator, that beloved brother of mine, a few questions. Sam Shortridge, do you mean to say that because Andrew Carnegie gets 5 thousand a day that his laborer gets paid any higher wages?" Then she would draw herself up and drop her voice, imitating her brother's stentorian tones: "No indeed, Mr. Carnegie gets his labor as cheap as he can." "A number of similar interrogatories enlivened by genial humor and at times tinged with a gentle irony were propounded," reported the *Examiner*.

She had many examples of the tariff helping the rich and hurting the rest. "They remove the tax on bank capital but increase it on the ax and hammer, the poor man's capital. Diamond studs were taxed little but horseshoes much. Raw silk was free, raw wool taxed at 40 percent"; no tariff on "the playing cards of gamblers" but "20 percent on the Bible." Foltz's peroration was "a glowing tribute to the nation," in which she predicted that as a result of free trade "the year 1900 will find us the foremost commercial country in the world and our flag will float on every sea."

On the political platform, Foltz was fearless and effective. She spoke without notes or a podium and held her audiences "to the very end of her long address." Obviously, she enjoyed herself. "Mrs. Foltz was in her happiest mood," said the *Examiner* of a night in Oakland.[18] Almost everything about campaigning appealed to Foltz by this time: the real stakes, the bands and bunting, the bonfires, the fireworks, and the fired-up audiences.

Foltz's co-orator was one Major Venier Voldo, who was completely overshadowed. According to one press report, "A storm of applause followed the conclusion of her address, and then Major Venier Voldo was introduced. Major Voldo's address was mainly devoted to the Chinese question." Period, and end of story. Apparently, however, Voldo was not jealous of Foltz's success; he even wrote an adoring poem addressed to "Clara Shortridge Foltz, Jurist-Mother-Woman":

> The Forum's breath is hushed and still
> Pacific's Portia awes the scene!
> Invective, logic, wit, are here
> The patriot spirit of our laws
> And by her periods keen and clear
> The good are freed, the guilty fear
> The towering triumph of her cause.[19]

Though Foltz did not advocate women's rights in her campaign speeches, the propriety of her position on the platform was always a background issue. Her supporters and introducers stressed that she was a good woman as well as a great speaker. Her co-orator's poem, for instance, proclaimed:

> A kiss gave she for every blow,
> A smile she had where shadows vex;
> She was where ere her feet did go
> The swan-like Leda of her sex.

Some such references were needed on the unrefined campaign trail, though "swan-like Leda of her sex" may have been over the top even by the standards of Victorian rhetoric.

Foltz and Gordon were the only paid campaign orators in 1888, but women played a larger role in the election than ever before. Not only did they flock to rallies where the women orators spoke, but they decorated the halls, served huge banquets, and occasionally were invited to sit on the platform at rallies. In San Francisco, women organized their own slate of school board candidates in order to remove the office from the partisan patronage system.[20]

Women were also more present than usual on the national campaign scene; especially notable was Anna Dickinson, a big figure to Foltz from afar. Dubbed "The Joan of Arc of the Unionist Cause," she had been a major abolitionist speaker before and during the Civil War. Afterwards, Dickinson became a paid political orator as well as a celebrity on the lyceum circuit where she spoke on a variety of subjects, including women's and freedmen's rights. For awhile, she averaged 150 lectures and as much as $20,000 (more than $400,000 today) a season.[21]

Though her career was waning by 1888, Dickinson was hired by the Republicans to stump the Midwest for Harrison. Proving as partisan as ever, she assailed the Democrats as the party of war and denounced the prosaic Grover Cleveland as "the hangman of Buffalo" (a reference to his tenure as sheriff). As the campaign heated up, Foltz challenged Dickinson to debate her in Pacific Coast cities. Two women orators, both masters at rousing the passions of political audiences, would have been a real show and attracted nationwide publicity, much to Foltz's benefit. But nothing came of the challenge.[22]

Counting travel and preparation, Foltz spent several months in well-paid stumping. Though she continued to draw large crowds all over the state, the Democrats lost the election. Their platform had no appeal for the thousands of new voters in Southern California, who had come for a land boom after the completion of another transcontinental railroad and a rate war. These latest immigrants were mostly midwestern Republicans like Harrison of Indiana. They did not hate or fear the Chinese with the fervor of longtime Californians, and they also believed that the state's new industries, such as wine and wool, could use the protection of a high tariff.

Though Clara Foltz was on the losing side, people were still talking years later about her campaign oratory: "her skill, so marvelous that even the cold, dry subject of the tariff was clothed with new light and life. Her orations awakened the wildest enthusiasm."[23] Paid political stumping and her pay as legislative counsel were Foltz's financial mainstays during the early 1880s. But both took her away from daily law practice, and to settle into that, she must first decide where to live.

LOCATING HER HOUSEHOLD

Foltz vacillated between practicing in San Jose or moving to San Francisco where she had lived early in 1879 during the Hastings litigation. Initially, San Jose was an easier place to raise children because her mother was there to help. Foltz would always remember her morning routines: "my faithful, dear mother carried my baby away until after office hours, when she would bring her back to me as sweet as a new-blown rose. The larger children scampered away to school like baby birds, spilled from their nest. Ah me! I sigh as I think of that bevy of pretty ones."[24]

But in late 1880, Foltz had to face the desire of her mother to join Elias in Tucson, Arizona, where he had gone to mine silver the year before. This move was the last surprising act of a life full of sudden new directions for the former lawyer from Indiana and preacher from Iowa. The timing indicated that Elias Shortridge hoped to find a way to help support his daughter financially as she tried to make a living at the law. More immediately, however, it meant that Clara Foltz must manage career and family without her mother's aid.

Even if Foltz was on her own, the Garden City, as she called San Jose, had many advantages. She loved the "flower-laden, vine-covered homes" and the "surrounding gorgeous blooms of peach and prune and apricot." One of her favorite stories captured the charms of the valley town. Foltz described a spring day when "Judge Herrington, a prominent member of the local bar," invited her and the children for a picnic in the nearby town of Saratoga. She did not mention that Herrington was recently widowed or say directly that the occasion had some courting aspects. "We spread our luncheon beneath a century-old oak tree, and no happier bunch of youngsters, nor more hopeful young mother could have been found. The Judge relaxed his quiet manner and apparently was well pleased with his guests." While they were picnicking, a call came from Foltz's brother Charles in San Jose. It was her first experience with "the mystic telephone wire."[25]

The picnic story and the early divorce case in which she helped the couple reconcile represented the life Foltz could have in San Jose. But with her legislative counsel work, and her time on the road stumping, she had yet to establish a steady paying practice there. Indeed, at this period her only source of regular income was the $50 a month that Jeremiah owed in child support. But he had remarried soon after the divorce in 1879, and she knew she could not count on him.

By virtue of its size alone, San Francisco simply offered better chances for her to make money. With a population approaching three hundred thousand in 1880, it far eclipsed any other western city in size. Forty percent of San Franciscans were foreign-born, another third had at least one foreign parent. Most were also white, though three-fourths of the Chinese in the United States (fewer than one hundred thousand total) lived in northern California. There were still two men to every woman, but that was better than the eleven-to-one ratio of the gold rush days. And the saloons, one for every seventy-eight men, were beginning to be matched by the churches, fine houses, and hotels. A good number of respectable places of public entertainment welcomed women. The theater, which Foltz particularly enjoyed, had flourished from the city's earliest days, and literary and political lectures were well-attended. Speakers as varied as Ulysses Grant, Oscar Wilde, and Susan B. Anthony had found large audiences in San Francisco in the previous decade.[26]

Late in 1880 Foltz decided to move to the Pacific Metropolis, as she called San Francisco. She took rooms in the Dupont Hotel, respectable though not fashionable and near the Montgomery Block, where she rented a better office than the attic cubicle she had occupied during the Hastings litigation. Her plan was to practice while finishing the course at law school. Shortly after the move, Foltz would have read in the news about the latest shocking murder in the city—a case in which she was soon to be involved.

SPECIAL PROSECUTOR:

WHEELER, THE WOMAN SLAYER

The first news story about the murder appeared in October 1880: George Wheeler, respectably dressed and middle aged, voluntarily appeared at the police station to confess that he had killed Adelia Tillson and stuffed her body into a steamer trunk. He said that he and the victim had been lovers since his marriage to her sister and that Adelia wanted to die. Such facts provided a bonanza for the flamboyantly competitive San Francisco press.[27]

Reporters accompanied the police when they went to lift the trunk lid. One of them interviewed Wheeler and wrote that he killed the young woman at her request to deliver her from an unwanted suitor. Reporters broke the news of her death to the rival admirer and observed his "paroxysms of grief."[28] As a result of all the publicity, thousands viewed Adelia Tillson's body where it lay, practically in state, in the coroner's office.

Wheeler's lawyers laid the groundwork for an insanity defense with leaks about his lunatic relatives, a head injury he had suffered from a stampeding bull, and his strangely composed manner when surrendering. The defense of insanity, never very popular, was in especially bad odor with the press because of several recent acquittals, particularly one that involved the shooting of an unarmed newspaper editor as he sat at his desk. In that case, the defense had successfully argued that the paper's cruel exposé of the defendant's father (the mayor elected by the WPC) had driven the son temporarily mad.[29]

Press reports intimated that the susceptibility of local juries to the temporary insanity plea was making San Francisco a magnet for murderers. Indeed, Wheeler appeared to have come in from the country to commit his deed. Concerned about the insanity acquittal rate, the district attorney hired Clara Foltz, "an uncompromising exponent of the rights of women," to remind the jurymen of their duty to a female victim. It was not unusual in important cases to employ special counsel to prosecute, but Foltz was the first woman ever to serve in such a role.[30]

Her selection indicated that this prosecutor believed that she might have special persuasive powers with a jury—an argument made *against* her when Foltz was trying to become a lawyer. To offset the supposed advantage, the defense retained Laura Gordon. The anticipation of the state's first two women lawyers clashing in a dramatic murder case further inflamed the already intense coverage of the Wheeler spectacle. "[T]he two female barristers were formerly very intimate friends, sleeping in the same bed but [have now] bloomed out as rivals at the Bar and on the political stump," said the *Chronicle*. Their competition would add "zest" to the proceedings and "test

CLARA H. FOLTZ.   LAURA DE FORCE GORDON.

THE WHEELER MURDER TRIAL; SAN FRANCISCO, CAL.

A LIVELY COURT SCENE BETWEEN OPPOSING COUNSEL—MAKING THINGS MERRY FOR THE SPECTATORS.—[SKETCHED BY OUR SPECIAL ARTIST.

Clara Foltz and Laura Gordon in the Wheeler murder trial. *National Police Gazette*, 1881.

their respective abilities." Such a duel, the story continued, was the first "in the history of the country"; more likely, it was the first in the world.[31]

The "rivals at the Bar" line referred to Foltz's and Gordon's running competition for "first woman" titles; Foltz was the first lawyer, and the first legislative counsel, but Gordon had recently been first to argue to a jury. *People v. Saldez* was, like *People v. Wheeler*, a murder case; it arose from the local "disposition to carry arms and drink bad whiskey," according to the *Chronicle*.[32] The defendant was a seaman who had killed a ship's officer, and the prosecutor sought the death penalty to allay public concern about the city's dangerous waterfront.

Gordon received a lot of press coverage in *Saldez*, including sarcastic allusion to "woman's gallant struggle" to "vanquish the male oppressor in any field." The condescending tone changed to admiration, however, when, after an effective summation by the experienced public orator Laura Gordon, the jury acquitted with just thirty minutes of deliberation. Even with Gordon's presence, however, *Saldez* was a garden variety murder case in San Francisco. But *Wheeler*, with its white principals, woman victim, and two lady lawyers, was a cause célèbre.[33]

All of San Francisco was focused on the trial, and the huge crowd in the courtroom included many women, just as in the *Saldez* case. Their attendance in these sordid criminal matters was considered by many as different in kind, and far less appropriate, than the female turnout for the Hastings case, which did not involve a jury or racy testimony. In *Wheeler*, dozens of women heard about the ménage à trois among Wheeler and the two sisters and learned that Adelia had been "ruined by a missionary" at the age of fourteen. "A Lively Court Scene Between Opposing Counsel—Making Things Merry for the Spectators" was the caption on a large drawing of Foltz and Gordon at the trial in the *National Police Gazette*, a magazine published in New York that specialized in coverage of crime, boxing, and other sporting news. Found in saloons and barber shops, it easily reached a million readers a week—not usually including any respectable ladies.[34]

Before the trial, *Gazette* coverage headlined "Two Females Will Be Allowed to Wag Their Tongues to Their Hearts' Content." But the story of the actual trial was respectful, indeed flattering, to the two women lawyers from the West. Foltz was described as having a "fine figure, blond hair and honest brown eyes" and being "the mother of five children who depend on her for support" and "sympathetic, kind, generous and womanly though of a vigorous and energetic temperament." Gordon was said to be "very pleasing

in appearance with fine features, blue eyes and a face and manner quite fascinating. . . . She has remarkable self-possession, a logical mind and argues
in a strong masterly way."[35]

Despite all the press attention to their dress and appearance, the women
lawyers were not tokens or diversions at the trial but participated fully
and professionally. In her summation, Foltz "rapidly and easily ridiculed"
Wheeler's insanity defense and accused him of "coolly deciding to play
crazy" to save himself "the trouble of getting rid of the body of his victim."
Speaking for all women, she inquired "where are we to look for our own
safety" if a man could "calmly plan and deliberately commit an atrocious
murder and successfully plead insanity?"[36]

For the defense, Laura Gordon gave a powerful closing, pleading with the
jury to recognize that the very cold-bloodedness of the crime showed that
Wheeler was mad. She compared his mental illness to that exhibited in the
city and the courtroom itself, where "every man, woman and child seems
to be afflicted with homicidal mania, howling for a victim."[37] Some of the
women in the audience, unfamiliar with courtroom etiquette, applauded.

The jury, however, convicted, and after the verdict's return, an admiring
crowd gathered around Clara Foltz. Wheeler was sentenced to death, but
his conviction was reversed on appeal because a prosecutor (not Foltz) had
quoted from medical texts that were not in evidence. Later, he was retried
with a new cast of lawyers, convicted again, and publicly hanged in 1884.[38]

Despite Foltz's and Gordon's professional conduct in *Wheeler* and many
other trials over the rest of the 1880s (though not again against each other),
there was an undercurrent of censure just below the praise and attention they
received. Ultimately, the disapproval sprang from the advocate's relationship
to the jury—extending beyond rapport into a quest for love and commitment. It was one thing for women lawyers to draft wills and counsel others of their sex on property and family law issues; but it was another thing
entirely for them to make passionate pleas to all-male juries. Foltz sensed
the social disapproval that both dimmed her best successes and was a major
professional handicap in attracting clients. One of her responses was to try
to set up her own society. She dreamed of a lovely home where she would
receive the coming people—women activists and brothers at the bar alike.
Where this home should be was the question Foltz faced during the 1880s.

Her original plan when she moved to San Francisco had been to practice
while finishing her law studies and obtaining a degree from Hastings. But
soon after her move she had been involved in the *Wheeler* case for months,

while trying to keep up with law school. In describing this period in later years, Foltz said that she had "attended lectures three times a day for eighteen months" until "overstudy, lack of means, and the care of her children, prostrated her." Foltz fell seriously ill in the spring of 1881, the first of three breaks in her record of extraordinary health and energy. (The others were in 1884 and 1895.) No diagnosis was ever mentioned, but each collapse followed a period of activity and strain that was unusual even for her. Foltz moved her family back to San Jose and maintained offices there and in San Francisco. She gave up law school though she repeatedly sought a degree on the basis of her lecture attendance and her role in opening the school to women. (In 1991, at the urging of its women students, Hastings Law School finally made Clara Foltz a Doctor of Jurisprudence.)[39]

In the early vulnerable years of her practice, the one positive constant was her excellent press. "My name was on every tongue and the papers were full of flattering mention of my exploits"—as Clara Foltz remembered these days. She liked reporters and knew instinctively how to put herself in a pleasing light. A San Francisco columnist said she was "overflowing with life and humor," "quick at repartee," "a favorite of the Bar," adding: "By her womanly graces, as well as by her studious habits and patient struggles, she has won the undivided esteem of the entire profession. They have about got through laughing at her." The stories often mention her engaging personality (usually surprising to the reporter). A *St. Louis Gazette* writer found Foltz "energetic, persevering, decided, individual" and added that she "mingles daily with scores of men, brother lawyers, receiving from all respectful courtesy and preserving . . . a pure, free, unsullied womanhood."[40]

Foltz had her own ways of dealing with the all-male world in which she often moved. On a trip to Tucson to see her parents in May 1882, for instance, she was in a train car with nine men and "relieved the monotony of the railroad journey by an interesting dissertation on law." Her fellow passengers organized a Resolution of Thanks, which they signed and presented to her. Foltz's hand can be glimpsed not only in generating the story but in passing it along to the *San Francisco Post*, where papers all over the state picked it up.[41]

PRIVATE LOBBYIST: COGSWELL THE INGRATE

Around Christmas of 1882 while Foltz was living in San Jose, Dr. Henry Cogswell walked into the office she still maintained in San Francisco. Though they had not met before, each knew the other by reputation. He was one of the city's eccentrics, whose oddness people overlooked because of his wealth.

By profession a dentist, he made his money in real estate speculation. Cogswell retained Foltz to help him retract a donation he had made to the University of California some years earlier. He had given a substantial San Francisco property to be used for a College of Dentistry named after him. But the plans had faltered, and the building had fallen into disrepair. After consulting some of the university regents and other lawyers, Foltz advised Cogswell that he needed a special bill authorizing the return of the property.[42]

Though confident that such a bill would pass, Foltz told him that she could not leave her children, ranging then in age from six to sixteen, to lobby for it in Sacramento. Cogswell entreated her to move her family into the spacious San Francisco mansion he shared with his wife, Caroline. Foltz took to the doctor, who exuded a kinetic energy akin to her own, and, needing a good-paying client, agreed to his proposal.

Living with a client was a mistake that was compounded because both thought they were doing the other a favor and nothing was put in writing. Cogswell figured that the free room and board should go a long way toward paying for his lawyer's professional services; Foltz felt she was brightening his home life and making herself available to travel on his business, while enabling her to earn a much-needed fee.

The strains emerged in the letters from Foltz to Cogswell over the weeks she spent lobbying for him in Sacramento. Soon after arrival, she wrote that she had already seen a number of legislators and was promised an early hearing, but most of the letter was about her children, who had moved from San Jose into the Cogswell mansion on their own. "Please make them comfortable, and when I come home I will try to regulate everything. . . . I did not think to pay the expressman and I don't know whether Trella has enough money with her to settle with him." That same evening, Foltz dashed off another note on hotel stationery: "Passage of bill is certain. I have talked with almost every member of the Senate." She again asked urgently for word on her children and closed with "goodnight, my room is full of friends and more coming. Hope to come home flushed with victory." But it was not to be so easy.[43]

Foltz had not realized how unpopular Cogswell was, and how unwilling even her good friends at the legislature would be to return a gift freely made. She also saw that it was a far different business to be a paid lobbyist for a private client rather than an advocate for herself and all women. After weeks of "terribly annoying and tedious work" (nine by her count; four by Cogswell's), Foltz did obtain both the passage of the special bill and the governor's signature on it. Her last letter from Sacramento mingled delight in her success with irritation at Cogswell, though she tried to hide it by calling him "dear faithful friend" and signing herself "your poor tired 'girl lawyer.'" She noted that her expenses had been high, "even though I have practiced mean economy" ("in a third-rate hotel, with no money to pay my way," as she would later testify). "I have done the best I could . . . and have the proud satisfaction of knowing that no one could have done better."[44]

After Foltz's return from Sacramento in early March 1883, she and the children continued to live with the Cogswells while she lobbied the university regents to exercise their legislatively granted power to reconvey the property. She also helped Cogswell with another project. He had launched what was to be a lifelong campaign to erect water fountains dedicated to temperance in every U.S. city. Usually the fountains featured birds, flowers, and perhaps a river god or two. But the San Francisco version was a ten-foot replica of Cogswell holding a glass of water—a gift arousing no little ridicule among his fellow citizens.[45]

Arranging the donation of a site and the terms of the gift (providing for upkeep, for instance) was lawyer's work. Foltz saw to an installation in San Jose and also wrote a pamphlet about the healthful effects of water. Her role as a sort of in-house counsel reached a low point, however, some weeks after she was back in town from lobbying in Sacramento. She came home from a court appearance one afternoon to find an agitated Cogswell. He was the defendant in a case of malicious prosecution. The jury was in the box, the first witnesses had testified, and he wanted her to take over his defense. Though she thought it outlandish to dismiss his other attorneys "right in the center of the case," Foltz agreed and found herself conducting a petty battle between two grandiose personalities.[46]

It had all started when one Professor Alonzo Phelps solicited Doctor Cogswell's participation in a book called *The Great Men of the Pacific Coast* (each entry to be accompanied by a flattering steel engraving). Cogswell was pleased to pay the $250 fee to be included, and the relationship flourished for a time. But the two men quarreled—it was not clear why—and eventually Cogswell swore out a warrant for assault. The charges were dismissed when Cogswell did not appear for trial, but Phelps sued, claiming $20,000 for the humiliation and inconvenience of the arrest.

Among the witnesses that Foltz took on and presented in a full week of trial were both men and their spouses, people who heard Phelps slander Cogswell, others who saw them fight on Market Street, officials who prepared and served the warrant, and the prosecutor who failed to notify

Cogswell of the trial date. Finally, she called six men who swore to Phelps's bad reputation for peace and good order, truth, and veracity. Phelps responded with nine witnesses to his good name in the community, and Foltz cross-examined them severely.

The jury awarded Phelps $7,500, which the judge reduced to $3,500 in response to Foltz's new trial motion. But the original large jury verdict against him shook the doctor's faith in Foltz, and their relationship rapidly deteriorated. He hired another attorney to take the appeal, and within a few months, she moved out of the Cogswell mansion.[47]

Foltz continued, however, to represent Cogswell on the return of the dental school property. In early 1884, she wrote that the university regents wanted a court order directing them to return the property and promised not to defend a "friendly law suit" by Cogswell. She told him that she was "exceedingly anxious to serve you in this ancillary matter and will do all that any lawyer can do." But she also reminded him of "the ugly fact that money is a very necessary adjunct to the winning of lawsuits; for it gives leisure for preparation."[48]

Foltz claimed that Cogswell not only failed to pay her fully for her work in Sacramento, but also refused to acknowledge her advocacy efforts with the regents and preparations for suit. When he did not respond to her letter, she went to him at the house where she had recently lived. He refused to receive her, and from that point on, it was war between them for several more years. Foltz sued the doctor for her lobbying fee, and the details of their conflict came out for all to hear several years later at a jury trial. She testified that Cogswell had induced her to go to Sacramento to seek the special bill by promising: "I will see you get a home out of that property. You are energetic. You can succeed. Go there and stay and you can pass it." Three witnesses swore that they had heard Cogswell offer her the cost of a home, $5,000, at various times.[49]

A very convincing sworn deposition from her friend Charles Gunn filled in the story. He testified that Foltz objected to going to Sacramento and said, "I don't want to break up my business, I don't want to have my children all alone in this great city, and I don't like to be about a Legislature anyway." She was weeping, Gunn said, and Cogswell comforted her: "See here; you want a home, don't you? . . . You can get a home a good deal quicker this way than by remaining in your office." As librarian to the legislature during the 1883 term, Gunn also said that he saw Foltz working constantly on the dental school matter.

Cogswell denied ever agreeing to pay more than the $200 set when he first came to her office. He stressed that Foltz and her five children lived with him rent-free for many months and that he had advanced great sums for expenses, including for her library because she said "she must have books." His wife also testified to her "incessant demands for money," even at mealtimes. To counter Foltz's picture of being wrenched from her children, Cogswell conveyed a scene of her living it up in Sacramento. The newspapers reflected his insinuations, reporting, for instance, that Mrs. Foltz claimed a large fee for "lobbying around the legislature for 34 days . . . to say nothing of the nights."[50] Caroline Cogswell testified that when Foltz was in town on the weekends she ignored the children and went out to dinner and the theater with friends.

Most harmful was Mrs. Cogswell's fake-sympathetic statement about the frequent visits of Charles Gunn: "Mr. Gunn was Mrs. Foltz's lover at that time. Of course, it was very natural they should want to spend their time alone." All in all, the trial turned out to be less about the terms of the contract than it was about Clara Foltz's worth and character. On the witness stand, she defended herself with her usual wit. When asked, for instance, whether she went to her office "as any other attorney" would, she responded, "Most certainly, only a good deal more regularly and more sober than most of them."

Explaining why she had not lobbied at a public hearing, rather than approaching individuals, Foltz casually assaulted the legislature (though the comment was deserved): "Every time that was set for me to be heard they were so crowded and overwhelmed with business, gigantic schemes against the people, they didn't have time to hear it." The reported response to her performance was mixed; delight at her ready quips, applause for her courage, disapproval for her unwomanly self-promotion and display.[51]

The jury speedily returned a favorable verdict for Foltz, albeit for $1,400 rather than $5,000. Cogswell appealed, urging among other arguments that her approach to individual legislators violated the new constitutional provision against lobbying. With only slightly veiled innuendo, the brief implied that since her fee was contingent and she was desperate, Foltz might well have offered sexual favors for votes. As a final insult, Cogswell's lawyers accused her of neglecting her children while she was out lobbying.[52]

Clara Foltz won the appeal, and the court held that services rendered by an attorney at law in the interests of a client, when "no dishonest, secret, or unfair means" were used, was not lobbying in the sense prohibited by the

1879 California Constitution, nor was it generally against public policy.[53] She won, but she lost, too. The case doubtless took a toll on her personal and professional reputations. In public documents, she was shown doing unlady-like things, in places where ladies were not to be found. Suing a client for a fee was, moreover, considered unprofessional, particularly when there was no written contract and the suit would turn on one person's word against the other. Foltz knew this just as she had to know that the famously pugna-cious doctor would respond to her complaint by attacking her. She took the risk because she needed the money, but also because she wanted to prevent clients from reneging on their promises of handsome fees to women lawyers.

When she left the Cogswell mansion in late spring of 1884, Foltz moved her children to Eleventh Street in the city, rather than returning to San Jose. It was a respectable though not an affluent neighborhood, with fam-ily homes standing in wooden rows interspersed with small businesses and retail stores, boardinghouses, saloons, and churches. At about the time of the move, Foltz again collapsed, as she had in 1881, from the pace of her life. Her mother came from Tucson to nurse her back to health and stayed to help manage the San Francisco household.[54]

Social Life and Social Status

MALE PROFESSIONALS

The record in the Cogswell case reveals a great deal about Foltz's life in the early part of her career. Her witnesses, for instance, were all men, and three of them described being with her in home or office to hear Cogswell's ex-travagant promises.[55] In her own testimony, she added that David Terry, the controversial former supreme court justice, had also been present. Terry's name came up again in the trial when Cogswell's wife described him "loung-ing on the couch" in Foltz's room—an off-color picture, especially because Terry was strikingly tall and rugged, handsome by western standards.

Her brother Charles was one of the witnesses who said he heard Cogswell promise a home to his sister. He was a newspaperman, who had worked his way from office boy to editor of the *San Jose Mercury*. Throughout Foltz's career, this brother would be a major support, providing not only testimony in her lawsuit, but money, an admiring press, and employment for her sons.

Another witness who swore to hearing Cogswell discuss the large fee was James Maguire, perhaps Foltz's best and most influential ally among the lawyers of the city. Strong-looking with an outsized moustache and pleasant face, he was a popular man and a politician in the western self-made mold. The son of Irish immigrants who moved to California when he was an infant, Maguire grew up in rural Santa Cruz County and apprenticed to a blacksmith for four years. But instead of the manual labor for which he had trained, Maguire turned to school teaching and politics. At age twenty-two he was elected to the State Assembly, and after several years of reading law, he joined the bar in 1878, the same year as Clara Foltz. He was twenty-five and she was twenty-nine. They rose to prominence at the same time through charisma and hard work, without the benefit of family wealth or influence. Both were gifted orators and had large, humorous personalities. Maguire was a radical Democrat whose mentor in political economy was Henry George, advocate of the "single tax" on property and its transfer, a measure aimed directly at wealth redistribution. Fairness to workers—the right to organize and wage-hour legislation—was Maguire's other major political concern. He supported all underdogs, including women in their struggle for rights.[56]

From her first days in San Francisco, Maguire had befriended Foltz. Over the years they often had offices near each other in the Montgomery Block and elsewhere. When he was a witness for her in the Cogswell trial, Maguire was coming to the end of a six-year term on the trial court in San Francisco. He had been the rare pro-labor judge who refused to enjoin strikers or to find that union boycotts were actionable conspiracies.

The Republican press opposed Maguire's reelection, charging him with bias against property rights. Foltz defended him, writing that "the rich, as well as the poor" could obtain justice in his court because "whatever his peculiar views regarding society, they are left behind him when he ascends to the bench."[57] Ultimately, Maguire did not seek a second judicial term, but instead returned to practice for a few years and then, in 1892, ran successfully for the U.S. Congress and was twice reelected.

From the testimony in the Cogswell case and press profiles of Foltz in the first half of the 1880s, the picture emerges of her office-parlor-salon, with fresh flowers on her desk, framed pictures of her children on the wall, and a throng who "came merely to talk a few minutes on the topics of the day." Sometimes she found it necessary to close the salon, "bar out the great world," in her words, and "keep company with myself and prepare my cases."[58]

Foltz also found companionship in a Bohemian society that included not only lawyers like James Maguire, but writers, editors, actors, and artists who had rooms in or near the Montgomery Block. The men and women would repair regularly to Hjuls, the local coffee shop, to discuss politics, the latest trial or stage performance, literary shop talk, and town gossip. It was an unusual way for the sexes to mix—semiprofessionally and without the standard social conventions of proper introductions and class hierarchy. Foltz formed some lifetime friendships during these years, not only among professional men, but also with women writers.

"FEMALE SWEETHEARTS"

Two of the women Foltz saw regularly in the city were Madge Morris and Frona Wait. They had bonded at the legislative session in 1880 when they were, in Wait's description, "in the rose-garden of life . . . [e]ach bent upon beating a pathway to success in our chosen fields of endeavor." Wait wanted to be a journalist, and Morris a poet.[59]

Both women admired Clara Foltz. Morris dedicated a poem to her with lines like "Then Hail thee! Priestess of the law / Our fair-browed Portia of the West." In a similar vein, Wait published a "pen picture" of Foltz in the early 1880s—"what she is rather than what she has been through." Wait wrote that though Foltz was sometimes called "the little woman lawyer," she was actually "quite tall with a model's form and symmetry." And like many others, she noted the variability of the physical impression Foltz made: "To some she is beautiful, to others plain; to some a magnificent queen, to others a pretty student; to some a perplexed philosopher, to others a gay and brilliant society woman."[60]

Another woman writer, Ella Sterling Cummins, also published a long and much-reprinted profile of Foltz in the mid-1880s.[61] Before she interviewed Foltz, Cummins, who was not a suffragist, expected to dislike her subject, but instead she found a happy household "permeated with mother love." Lawyer Foltz apparently assured that documentary evidence supported this conclusion. Cummins quoted from a note in which Davey (a "bright boy of thirteen") secretly assured his mother that "I love you with a different love from the rest of the children." Also quoted was "a legal form drawn up to adjust domestic difficulties" addressed to "Trella Foltz, Chief Manager of the House, No 233 Eleventh St. San Francisco":

> Greeting:
> You are hereby commanded to cease interfering with the wearing apparel of the doll, known and designated by the name of "Marguerite," the property of one Virginia Foltz; and it is further ordered that the said Virginia have full

power to remove the clothes worn by the said doll "Marguerite": and this is my command. Signed and sealed with my hand and official seal: Mamma.

In addition to describing Foltz as lovingly maternal, Cummins wrote that she was "young and dashing, clever and witty," and after the interview that so charmed her, the two women became close friends.

Ella Cummins was a California character—one of Foltz's favorite types. Born in a mining camp in 1853, cradled in a rocker used for sifting gold from gravel, she married early and was widowed (actually, not fictionally like Foltz) young. She was the author of the first published novel written by a native Californian and managed to support herself and her daughter by her writing. Although she was a good storyteller, her success seems to have stemmed as much from her charm and self-confidence as from her literary talents.[62]

Cummins was one of a group that Frona Wait jokingly called Foltz's "female sweethearts"—her companions outside the women's movement. To the sweethearts, wrote Wait, a sweetheart herself, "the busy lawyer talks in an unrestrained way" not of public life, but of feminine things like "dress and society, and plans for her beautiful children."[63] Foltz's friendship with Cummins, Wait, and Morris would continue in this vein for many years.

"THE BEST PEOPLE"

Frona Wait wrote that Foltz would have shone in the highest circles, "but her home duties make society a luxury she cannot indulge in."[64] More likely, it was a luxury she could not afford and perhaps one impossible for a practicing lawyer and a women's rights activist to achieve at this time. Though Foltz's suffrage identification had lifelong benefits—enabling her career and ennobling her efforts—it also bore certain social costs.

One was the general belief that being a suffragist did not fit with being a lady. In his widely read study of the American commonwealth published at the end of the 1880s, the English writer James Bryce observed that woman suffragists were not generally among the "upper classes" in the United States. He attributed this to their call for "a general dissettlement between the sexes" and their reputation for being "too masculine in their manners and discourse."[65] Of course such things might be said especially of women lawyers who necessarily met men alone in their offices, engaged in adversary contests with them in court, and moved unescorted through the city at all hours. Great lawyers were, moreover, bold, aggressive, incisive, and zealous in the interests of justice or a client. Great ladies were not.

Favorable stories about Clara Foltz mentioned her engaging manners and excellent conversational abilities. She embraced the title of lady lawyer, "a pretty soubriquet," she said, that aided her in maintaining "a dainty manner as I browbeat my way through the marshes of prejudice and ignorance." But neither pretty sobriquets nor social skills sufficed for gaining access to the highest circles. Foltz's combination of being a suffragist, a practicing lawyer, and a single woman was too much for even the relatively relaxed rules of San Francisco society. As she wrote later, "[I] found myself and mine ostracized and ignored by the so-called 'best people' with whom my father's family had always moved."[66]

At the same time Foltz was rejected, another lady lawyer, who was also an ardent suffragist, was easily accepted in the upper reaches of society. She was Mary McHenry Keith, and her advantages were obvious. When she started law school, Mary McHenry was young, very pretty, unmarried, the daughter of a distinguished Louisiana judge, and a star graduate of the University of California. She attended Hastings without incident and was the first woman to complete the whole course and graduate—the exact achievement Clara Foltz had wanted for herself. Moreover, McHenry was chosen to give a valedictory.[67]

In her speech "The Origin and History of the Last Testament," McHenry argued for better protection for wives and children in probate while showing a scholarly command of Roman law, which she compared to English common law. Foltz wrote a warm congratulatory letter without a hint of rancor or jealousy, referring to herself as "a sort of mother of the institution." "I rejoice in your success," she said, "that at the first public graduating exercises of Hastings College of the Law, a bright and beautiful young girl comes off with the honors of the class." "You scored one for your sex," Foltz added in her note, but McHenry did it in a ladylike way—not a call to arms, but to reason.[68]

Within a year of her graduation speech, McHenry married William Keith, who was to become a renowned and financially successful landscape painter. Mrs. Keith gave up her law office and specialty in will-writing, while maintaining her open involvement with the women's movement and friendship with Susan B. Anthony. Despite her activism, Keith had the education, male protection, and ultimately wealth that allowed her to move easily on levels Foltz could not hope to attain.

Foltz was vulnerable to social slights and longed for acceptance. "I wanted to be loved by women—and men too for that matter. At least, I craved their approval," she said later. As she told the story, the social rejection receded with her growing fame, and ultimately "plates were laid at every function and I was made the toast of the most conservative."[69] But she was probably exaggerating this acceptance. What actually happened was that Foltz created her own social circle, which included suffragists and other reformers, career and working women, male lawyers and politicians. Eventually, she also found a way to include some society ladies in her sphere, even if she never quite made it into theirs. For instance, she founded the Portia Club to prepare women to vote by teaching them law. Ladies who would never consider working outside the home would come to Foltz during the 1890s to learn about exercising the privileges of citizenship (see Chapter 3).

Lawyer for the "Poor and Sick and Despairing"

Though she advertised as a family lawyer (probate and divorce), Foltz's actual specialty in the 1880s was hopeless criminal cases for those who could not afford a male attorney. She simply could not resist the pleas of people so desperate they would come to a woman lawyer. An admirer wrote that she was "patient and kind" and "served all who applied for her services, charging for them only when the party applying was able to pay."[70] Critics said she had no discretion in choosing cases.

Her "poor and sick and despairing clients" (as she called them) were a main source for an idea taking shape in Foltz's mind: that the government should pay for the defense of those charged with crime, just as it did for the prosecution. From many individual situations, she formulated the proposal for a public defender and the arguments she would use to support it. An example was the case of Charles Colby, condemned to die for murder. She came into the case after his appeals and his funds were exhausted and tried to obtain a commutation of his sentence. When she failed, Colby became, in 1880, the last person publicly hanged in Santa Cruz. On the eve of his execution, he penned an open letter thanking Clara Foltz for her "earnest and zealous efforts on my behalf." He was only sorry that she had not come into the case sooner. "They got the best lawyer in Santa Cruz to prosecute," he wrote from prison. Perhaps Foltz thought of Charles Colby years later when she urged that the unequal skills and resources of prosecution and defense made a public defender necessary.[71]

Colby was one of a number of pardon cases Foltz handled in the early 1880s—most ended more successfully, especially during the term of George Perkins, a Republican Party friend and admirer, who was the first governor under the 1879 California Constitution. He was especially responsive to pleas for juveniles and for veterans. Foltz made a good story for patriotic occasions of one such case for a client named William Johnson, who had fought in the Mexican–American War. Rather than filing formal papers, Foltz said she took the convict's friend, an aged veteran himself, to tell the governor the following tale. During the Civil War, "Johnson was herding sheep in the gold country. On July 4, 1862, he hung out the stars and stripes. About 20 desperadoes from the mines and whiskey saloons came by and shouted for him to take down 'that Yankee flag.' He heard the threats, he knew the danger, but he rushed into his cabin, brought out his six-shooters and repeating rifle and as the rebels advanced upon him cocked and cried: 'I'll shoot the first man who dares to lay his hands upon that flag.'"[72] Without a further plea from counsel, Governor Perkins took a blank pardon form from the desk and filled it out for William Johnson.

Foltz's story illustrates the informality of the pardon practice, which was entirely removed from the courts and regular procedures. Governor Perkins described his interactions with "Clara—that is, Mrs Foltz" to a commission investigating prison conditions early in his term. He said that she "came to me . . . and said she wanted me to divest my mind of all sympathy in her behalf, and then presented her case . . . for pardon of some prisoners here."[73]

As the governor indicated, Foltz did not rely on personal pleas for mercy, but put solid legal work into showing that her client's conviction was unjust or that he deserved mercy. Most of these cases for men serving long prison terms had little potential for making money, even when she won their release. In one instance, Foltz sued the witnesses whose false testimony had put her client in prison. She sought $75,000 (more than $1.5 million today) and appealed when she lost in the trial court. But the California Supreme Court held there was no cause of action against perjurers and that it was too late to sue for malicious prosecution.[74]

In her only profitable pardon case on record, Foltz took some choice property in Washington Territory as a fee for winning the release of a convicted murderer and then sold it, presumably for a good sum.[75] Her real gain from her pardon practice, however, was a firsthand look at the injustice of harsh sentencing after a trial without adequate counsel, entered without credit for rehabilitation or hope for mitigation. The experience not only inspired Foltz's public defender idea, but it also led her to campaign for a parole bill in the 1890s.

Some of her early clients found Foltz on their own, turning her "modest law office," she said, into "a rendezvous for the poor and sick and despairing, the ex-convict, the drunkard and our weak little sisters of the so-called underworld."[76] Other lawyers and friends also referred people with sad stories to the understanding woman lawyer. Often, the courts appointed her to defend the indigent accused. (In most states, courts called on lawyers to defend pro bono if the charges were serious.)

Her brother Sam, who was a schoolteacher at the time, enlisted her aid in the trial of a student's father, the aptly named William Mess. Accused of forgery, he had a court-appointed lawyer who Sam thought was inadequate. Foltz helped the attorney present an insanity defense through a parade of lay witnesses, but lost the trial and the appeal. The case gave her a close look at the difficulties of mounting a technical defense without funds for expert witnesses.[77]

Though she gathered material for her public defender proposal, won some verdicts, and received favorable press, the criminal work did not lead to a paying practice. Foltz continued to need the income from lecturing and political oratory. During the 1884 election season, while serving as a paid orator for the Republican Party, she also became involved in the campaign of Belva Lockwood for president of the United States. The experience showed Foltz how she might make money from a nationwide lecture tour.

Lecturing for Money

BELVA LOCKWOOD FOR PRESIDENT

The careers of Clara Foltz and Belva Lockwood intersected a number of times, starting in 1879 when the trial judge cited Lockwood's admission to the Supreme Court in support of his ruling for Foltz in the Hastings case. For the next few years their law practices paralleled each other, one in Washington, D.C., and the other in San Francisco. In 1884, they met when Lockwood ran for president and Clara Foltz was her elector from California.[78]

As Lockwood told the story, she received a letter from the Equal Rights Party in California nominating her; she accepted and waged a spirited campaign, with appearances across the country and much attendant publicity. She mentioned Clara Foltz only as one of her official electors. After Lockwood died in 1917, Foltz offered her own version of the nomination and campaign. It does not conflict with Lockwood's but casts events in a different light and Foltz in a larger role. In this story, the impetus for the Lockwood candidacy did not come from any organized party but from Marietta Stow, a woman "far, too far ahead of her time." (Foltz never wrote that about anybody else.)[79]

A widow whose main mission was reforming the probate laws to make them fair to women, Stow was the founder in 1880 of the Woman's Social Science Association, which published a monthly magazine, *Woman's Herald of Industry and Social Science Cooperator.* She admired Foltz, praised her extravagantly in the pages of the *Herald,* and put her name on the masthead as director of the Science of Government Section. Stow thought that running for high office was a good idea for gaining publicity for women's rights and at several points had tried to persuade others to do it. She had no luck until 1884, when Belva Lockwood wrote a sharp letter to the *Herald* about the failure of both major parties to include woman suffrage in their platforms. "It is quite time that we had our own party, our own platform, and our own nominees," Lockwood wrote. "We shall never have equal rights until we take them, nor respect until we command it."[80]

Lockwood's letter gave Stow the idea of nominating her for president, and according to Foltz, she and Stow spent a "merry half hour" composing a telegram to Lockwood from the nonexistent "equal rights party in convention assembled at San Francisco." In telling the story, Foltz made a little fun of her friend Stow, who was a serious dress reformer, a movement Foltz never joined. She was "a fine-looking, large woman [Stow was more than six feet tall] dressed in a divided skirt (the joke of everybody at that time) wearing a fedora hat adorned with the feminine touch of one funny little feather . . . her big feet shod in the commonest sense shoe ever found on the market."[81] Stow's outfit was her own design. She had her photograph made wearing her "triple S costume" at about the same time as Foltz was pictured in a tightly fitted gown of the stiff new polka-dot bombazine fabric.

The nomination letter for Lockwood included no details, and Foltz and Stowe expected no reply. To their surprise, however, "Mrs. Lockwood did not see any joke in the announcement and lost no time in notifying us of her acceptance." Even more alarming was the arrival of reporters at Foltz's door in the early morning hours, alerted by the eastern press and hungry for details of the Equal Rights Party. Showing her usual skill in dealing with the press, Foltz realized they had the goods and told the reporters how it happened. "The newspaper men, true to their cult, appreciated the situation and the laugh went round," Foltz wrote. They agreed on the spot to "treat seriously the nomination" and go along with the sport.

Meanwhile, Lockwood signed with the Slayton Lyceum Bureau to lecture across the country at the reported rate of $100 a night plus expenses, and with the expectation of campaign contributions that she would collect for herself from the audiences. She published a platform pledging "equal and exact justice without distinction of color, sex, or nationality."[82] Other planks opposed the liquor traffic, monopoly, and high tariffs and proposed uniform marriage, divorce, and inheritance laws; peace as a foreign policy; the fair allotment of the public domain; and civil service reform.

Again, according to Foltz, she and Stow took up the game, formed a slate of presidential electors, and decided that Stow should run for vice president. They designed a ballot and mailed a batch of them to the "Mayor or most popular citizen" for distribution in each of the towns where Lockwood campaigned. Though Foltz had joined in the nomination as a joke, "an impractical one" as she later called it, she did not back out of the effort. With "no end of trouble," using her best personal advocacy, she was able to secure endorsements that "would lend dignity to the 'party.'" Ellen Sargent (wife of the California senator who sponsored the Lockwood bill allowing women to practice in federal courts), Laura Gordon, Sarah Knox-Goodrich, and several other "old time and loyal suffragists" gave their names to the nomination. Foltz's friend James Maguire was also on the list.[83]

Foltz and Stow planned a "ratifying" convention, and Lockwood set out for California, stumping along the way. Concerned that she might be embarrassed by questions about the original nomination, Foltz eluded reporters and met the train a stop ahead of its official arrival at Sacramento. "I found our candidate in a tourist car, modestly lunching from a basket!" Foltz liked her looks, handsomer than her pictures, with "fine eyes, an aquiline nose and a firm mouth and rounded chin."

Lockwood's reaction to the confession about her nomination also impressed Foltz. "Like any lawyer worthy of her calling, [she] decided to go right on with her plans." Their ratifying convention went well, with the candidate "carrying herself splendidly." But Foltz's enjoyment of the scene was somewhat diluted by the "disapproval of my mother and the objections of my brothers to what they believed was a foolish waste of time." Her family feared that "serious advocacy of the impossible" would make her look like a crank.

But these fears did not materialize. Instead, Lockwood's campaign provided good publicity, on the whole, for the cause, and she won the most votes (734) in California, where Clara Foltz headed the slate of electors. The two women lawyers did not afterwards become close allies or friends, but they would meet again at an 1890 convention in Washington, D.C., and at several World's Fair events in 1893. Lockwood described Foltz in the early 1890s as "a blonde, tall and pleasant looking," who "has all the vivacity of a girl, and betrays the fondness of her sex for becoming dresses," and who managed to raise and support her several children "by her own efforts."[84]

Though the 1884 campaign began as a gag, as Foltz recalled it, and ended up requiring considerable energy, it was also an important inspiration for her. She saw the money-making potential of a tour where one could be a celebrity at each new locale while giving the same lectures many times over. Perhaps such a venture by the "Portia of the Pacific" could supply the financial base she needed for her law practice. Decisive as usual, Clara Foltz launched her career as a traveling lecturer shortly after the 1884 election.

THE "LAWYERS" LECTURE

Foltz made three nationwide lecture tours during the 1880s. Almost as much as the income, she needed what she called "a respite from a laborious practice." For seven years she had held office hours six days a week, tried cases in courts throughout northern California, and appealed her losses. She had lectured locally for money, for charity, and for the movement; lobbied the legislature for women's rights, for criminal justice reforms, and for Cogswell; stumped the state in political campaigns; and served as a suffrage leader—while maintaining her household, supporting her five children, and appearing "always genial and happy."[85]

Even long trips by steamer, rail, and overland stage to lecture four or five times a week were a relief from such intensely competing demands. Away on her own, Foltz could both indulge herself and project an image of success. Rather than staying in cheap inns "of funeral dreariness," as one woman lecturer described them,[86] or overnighting with movement allies, as most cause speakers did, she would register at the best hotel in town and then summon the press for an interview with an imposing dateline.

The profession of lecturer was in full flower in the late nineteenth century, and a number of women found acceptance on the platform that was denied them in other public vocations. In addition to Lockwood, Foltz had the examples of women's rights speakers such as Elizabeth Cady Stanton, Mary Livermore, and Lillie Devereux Blake, who made good incomes from nationwide tours. So did Frances Willard, who spoke on temperance. Anna

Sculpture of Clara Foltz lecturing. William T. Farnan, 2004, presented to the author
by Stanford Law School on the occasion of her retirement.

Dickinson had converted cause lecturing into lyceum speaking, and for money-making success Kate Field was the best model. Said at her death in 1896 to be "one of the best known women in America," her subjects ranged from Mormonism to characters in the novels of Charles Dickens.[87]

In 1873, Field described public lecturing in a book about her travels. She compared lecturers to mushrooms, appearing overnight, without time to adjust to the local atmosphere and audience tastes. Unlike musicians or actors, moreover, a lecturer "stands in his own person, on a cold barren platform, unaided by scenic effects or costume, and for an hour or more is expected to speak uninterruptedly and in such a manner as to constantly entertain."[88] Field's success in drawing large audiences under these conditions was doubtless known to Foltz as she set out on her first nationwide tour in 1885. Later in the decade, the two would meet and spend some time together in San Diego.

For her lecture subjects, Foltz drew first on her own experience. While it had yet to provide her a good living, the legal profession supplied the material for a very entertaining lecture. Titled simply "Lawyers," it mixed a number of genres—the bar speech about the nobility of the profession, the women's movement call for reform, and the personal story of adventure. She started with the last: a barbed and humorous rendering of the Hastings litigation. "I went through law school in just three days," Foltz would say, "accompanied only by a bad cold." Then she told of the other students who imitated her discreet coughs with "noises worthy of the barnyard." In a revenge passage, she declaimed: "What men these were! From that day to this I have never heard tell of one of them." The contrast was obvious. "Nor do I expect to hear much from creatures so delicate that they are disturbed by the rustling of an old dame's skirts."[89]

Growing serious about her hard-won profession, Foltz praised it as socially important—a vocation rather than a business. Acknowledging that lawyers were held in low esteem, Foltz defended the profession. Few people, she said, appreciate the "great labor" that goes into the lawyer's work. "We drop into court and watch the able advocate as he dissects an abstruse question of law; we listen to the clear exposition, the rounded periods, the faultless similes, the graceful allusions. But we do not know of the weeks and months of toil that made those sentences perfect."[90]

She believed that women lawyers would improve the profession because they would practice at a high humanitarian level, with mother-love and solicitude. Speaking of women as the first lawgivers and enforcers in everyone's life, Foltz declared, "The law *is* woman's sphere." Implicitly she was answering the argument that the practice was too dirty and rough for women—akin to the "filthy pool of politics" that was predicted to defile female voters.[91]

At the same time, Foltz brought word from the criminal courts, where most people did not go regularly, that there was a type of lawyer there who fell far below the professional standard: the degraded and ignorant "shyster," who "you can always know . . . by his soiled linen, his whiskey breath and his generally dilapidated appearance." She said there were too many of these shysters defending people and also denounced "District Attorneys who lose sight of the object for which their office was created and use it as a political tool. They often make misdemeanors a felony and an innocent man a criminal."[92] In the next decade, the shyster defense lawyers and overbearing prosecutors were to become staples of Foltz's argument for a public defender.

Foltz enjoyed the trappings of her platform career—the flowers, the flattering introductions, and the applause—much as she had her political oratory. Her rhetoric about good women and good lawyers blended with the phrases introducing her as a "loving mother, faithful daughter and wife, woman-hearted friend of humanity, wearing always the jewel of true womanhood."[93] But behind the confident lady lawyer on the platform was a scared woman who was older than she claimed, who was divorced rather than widowed, and who needed to lecture for money.

A FALLEN HERO

As she prepared for her first nationwide tour in 1885, Foltz had the "Lawyers" lecture and her women's rights speeches as a basic repertoire, but she needed something with more universal appeal to draw the crowds. She found her subject in the life of a distinguished lawyer, public servant, and Civil War hero, Edward Dickinson Baker, "the Old Gray Eagle of Mount Hood." Baker had been a great orator who had not survived to tell his own stories on the lecture circuit, which even after twenty years was still producing large audiences for Union Army veterans. Clara Foltz would, in a sense, stand in for him there.[94]

Over several hours, she traced his life from boyhood in Illinois and friendship with Lincoln to his western migration during gold rush days where, she said, Baker immediately "took first rank at the bar" in San Francisco. The centerpiece of Foltz's speech was Baker's forensic gift, which made him a genius before a jury; "his very appearance was equivalent to an acquittal," she said.[95] As illustration, Foltz told a gripping trial story, which also made a point about the high duty of defense lawyers.

In the 1850s, the gambler Charles Cora killed the only U.S. marshal in San Francisco, perhaps in self-defense, perhaps in retaliation for an insult to Cora's wife, a well-known madam. Even in the brawling, gold-rush atmosphere of San Francisco, this was seen as going too far. "A man is shot down in one of the principal streets in the chief city on the Pacific Coast, by a man who lives in a bawd-house, and who is instigated to the murderous deed by a harlot," was a typical news report.[96]

Baker took the Cora defense for a fee of $40,000 (almost $1 million today), but even this huge amount did not cover the risks of representing so despised a defendant. Lauding Baker's "personal courage" and "undaunted daring," Foltz quoted from his jury summation in Cora: "There is no wretch so steeped in all the agonies of vice and crime that I would not have a heart to listen to his cry, and a tongue to speak in his defense, though around his head all the wrath of public opinion should gather, and rage, and roar and roll, as the ocean rolls around the rock. And if I ever forget, if I ever deny, that highest duty of my profession, may God palsy this arm and hush my voice forever." There was a good deal more in this vein.[97]

Baker's summation overwhelmed the prosecution and hung the jury. But before there could be a retrial, vigilantes descended on the jail and seized, tried, and executed Cora on a single night. Rumor had it that they also were looking for Baker, who went into hiding for several months and then moved to Oregon.

In her lecture, Foltz turned from the Cora case to sketch Baker's political career as U.S. senator from Oregon and to recite from his stirring antislavery speeches, including the well-known peroration: "Long years ago I took my stand for freedom, and where the feet of my youth were planted there shall my old age march. And for one I am not ashamed of freedom. I know her power. I rejoice in her majesty. I walk beneath her banner. I glory in her strength."[98] Foltz often quoted these lines in her own speeches, applying them to women's liberation.

Finally, she brought her hero to Balls Bluff, Virginia, early in the war, where he met "nine rebel bullets, the swift-winged messengers of the death which closed the life of the glorious and well-beloved hero." Matching Baker's lush periods, she declaimed that his "speeches were poems; his words were music; his thoughts were thunderbolts. . . . When he touched upon the themes of Liberty and Union, his eyes blazed, his whole frame quivered, he looked like a god."[99]

On a September night in 1885, Foltz opened her tour by giving her Baker lecture to "one of the most fashionable and intellectual audiences ever assembled" in San Francisco, according to the *San Francisco Alta*. "[T]he city's elite"—federal and state judges; leading politicians, including several former governors; many lawyers; and "very many ladies"—were in the large audience. Most titillating to the reporters was the presence of David Terry. He created a stir partly because Edward Baker had been the chief mourner at the funeral of David Broderick, the man Terry had killed in 1859 (see Chapter 1). In his famous eulogy, Baker had assailed Terry's "intense sectional prejudice" and "weak mind with choleric passions" that led him to challenge the antislavery senator to a duel, in which there was only "the pretense of equality." Though Clara Foltz was able simultaneously to maintain Baker as hero and Terry as friend, she did not ask the same of her audience, omitting for this performance any mention of Baker's renowned "Elegy for Broderick."[100]

Terry alone in the audience would have been noteworthy, but on his arm was his client, "the lady-plaintiff" in a lawsuit against the silver king and former U.S. senator William Sharon. Calling herself Althea Sharon, the beautiful young woman claimed to be his divorced wife and sued for alimony. Sharon acknowledged her as mistress only and swore that he had already paid for her services. For months, San Francisco had been engrossed in the salacious trial testimony; the appearance of two of the principals added to the entertainment value of Foltz's lecture.[101]

"The Life of E. D. Baker," with all its purple Victorian rhetoric, became a major piece for Clara Foltz, attracting large audiences and winning uniformly favorable reviews during her lecture tours. Foltz continued giving the speech for some years, later titling it (as memories of Baker faded) "A Forgotten Hero."[102] Anyone hearing her quote Baker might well imagine Foltz in front of a jury herself. The speech also gave her a chance to talk, in the guise of biography, about the legal profession's duty to the defenseless.

SALEM, OREGON, AND MARY LEONARD

After unveiling her Baker oration in San Francisco, Foltz set out for Portland, Oregon, traveling overland and speaking wherever she could gather an audience. One Oregon paper reported that she had "won golden opinions from the press" in northern California and southern Oregon. Roseburg and Eugene turned out "intelligent audiences" who "applauded frequently" at the "surprisingly brilliant display of oratory." And in Red Bluff "many eyes in the audience were moist" as "the last words died away, softly and sweetly spoken."[103]

For Foltz personally, the most important stop was Salem, the capital, where she had lived in the early 1870s, and where she first seriously considered becoming a lawyer. "The lady who now comes to Salem, heralded by the press and hearkened to by the people," said the local paper, "in former years boarded members of the Oregon Legislature to provide her children with winter clothing and school books."[104] Foltz planned her arrival to coincide with the legislative session for old times' sake and to increase her lecture audience.

Soon after she arrived in Oregon, Foltz successfully took up the cause of women's right to practice law in the state. As she later told an interviewer for the *Mercury*, "a lady friend" visited at her hotel and explained that the courts had refused her admission, even though she was certified in Seattle. The press report continued: "Seating herself at her desk, [Mrs. Foltz] drew up the following bill: 'Hereafter women shall be admitted to practice law as attorneys, in the courts of this state, upon the same terms and conditions as men.'" "'There,' said the fair Clara, 'I think that will cover our case.'" She apparently passed the draft bill on to a legislator, perhaps an acquaintance from her boardinghouse days, and as the newspaper report continued, "Exactly forty minutes from the time she presented the bill to the lower house it had passed both houses and was in the hands of the Governor, who signed it, and it became a law." Foltz was invited inside the bar of the House, where she met with "a perfect ovation."[105]

The woman Foltz helped was Mary Leonard, who was not exactly a conventional "lady." Born to an impoverished family in Switzerland, Leonard had immigrated in her twenties to Portland. After a few years as a domestic worker and seamstress, she married the proprietor of an inn and ferry operation, who was twenty-seven years her senior. The marriage was short and stormy. While their divorce was in litigation, he died in his bed of a bullet to the brain. Leonard and a telegraph lineman who lived at the inn were indicted and tried for first-degree murder. Both were well-represented and promptly acquitted.[106]

Apparently, this experience stimulated Leonard's interest in the law. She moved to Washington Territory where she apprenticed in the office of a Seattle attorney, a friend of her defense lawyer. Admitted to practice after a creditable examination, she returned to Oregon and sought reciprocity for her Washington credentials. The Oregon Supreme Court, however, turned her away, citing the absence of a statute to overcome the "generally understood" disqualification of women to practice law.[107] That was where Clara Foltz came in, dashed off her Woman Lawyer's Bill, and saw to its passage. It was Foltz at her decisive, persuasive, sisterly best. Though the two women did not make news together again, Mary Leonard practiced in Oregon for the next twenty years, handling mostly criminal cases.

PORTLAND AND ABIGAIL DUNIWAY

The federal judge in Portland, Matthew Deady, seems to have been unusually receptive to women lawyers. He had admitted Leonard to practice though the state courts had turned her away, and he had invited Foltz to sit on the bench with him when she was in Oregon on an earlier trip. On that occasion he had written in his diary that before going into court, "she looked in my glass . . . and disposed of her curls to the best advantage." The judge commented that Clara Foltz was "bright and tries to be a man but can't forget that she is a woman always." He was in the audience for Foltz's Baker lecture in 1885 and described it in his diary as "pretty good . . . from the popular stand and quite well delivered."[108]

In addition to lecturing, Foltz also had the chance in Portland to see and consult with her friend and mentor Abigail Duniway. "The bravest of the brave, the truest of the true to the cause of women—her work precedes us all," wrote Foltz years later of the woman she called "beloved Mrs. Duniway."[109] Though Duniway was fifteen years older than Foltz, the two had very similar lives. Both were originally from the Midwest, married young and romantically, and bore many children (Duniway had a daughter and five sons). Unlike Jeremiah Foltz, Ben Duniway was a faithful and sympathetic companion and a good father, but like Jeremiah, he was a poor provider. He lost the family farm by foolishly cosigning a friend's note (against Abigail's advice) and then had an accident that rendered him a semi-invalid from 1861 until his death in 1895. Working for money became a necessity for his wife.

Duniway first opened a school and then a millinery and dressmaking shop. (Mary Leonard and Clara Foltz may have both sewed for her.) By Foltz's 1885 visit, however, Duniway's shop days were long behind her. Instead, she was making a financial success of her suffrage weekly, the *New Northwest*, and was also writing novels and lecturing for money. Speaking for suffrage and gathering subscriptions for her paper, Duniway looked for promising real estate deals as well as she went across the country. Like many other westerners, she dreamed of buying undeveloped property and selling it to future settlers for a large profit.

Clara Foltz and Abigail Duniway, so alike in biographical details, also shared some personality traits. Both were energetic, forthright and funny, physically and morally courageous, and both were quite vain and obstinate (especially in their declining years). They were, however, unlike in outward manner. A Salem paper had captured the difference in reference to Foltz's lobbying for Mary Leonard. It mentioned her "gentle ways and dignified bearing" that had accomplished "more for women in one week than a ranting, domineering, imperious woman could do in ten years."[110] The comparison was doubtless to Duniway, who was a regular lobbyist for women's rights at the legislature.

Though Foltz drew on her friend's lecture experience and even took some of her topics, their styles were distinct. Duniway was down-home and anecdotal; an admirer said she substituted "force" for "polish." She gave a lecture on Edward Baker, for instance, in which she told of knowing him personally and of her belief that his spirit had come to comfort her at the death of her only daughter.[111]

Often, Duniway spoke extemporaneously, to the alarm of Susan Anthony, who advised her, "Never attempt to speak in public without careful preparation and committing to memory everything [you] want to say."[112] Foltz followed this course, scripting her lectures along the lines taught by classic rhetoric texts, from exordium to peroration. (Because she memorized and repeated the same words and phrases, they continued to crop up in her writing and everyday speech years after she left the lecture circuit.)

Duniway disagreed with Anthony on more than speaking style. Throughout a fifty-year friendship, they clashed often on tactics and personalities. Mainly, Duniway had no patience for the endless meetings and petitioning that typified the suffrage movement. She also often disagreed with other suffragists over who was to be in charge and who deserved credit. Though Foltz was better than Duniway as both a leader and a lobbyist, she had some of the same weaknesses displayed by her mentor.

SEATTLE AND WOMAN JURORS

From Portland, Foltz traveled by steamer to Washington Territory. Soon after arriving in Seattle, she announced her plans to settle there for good once she finished her tour.[113] Although this would not be the last time Foltz became an instant convert to the charms of a place she visited, her enthusiasm for Washington Territory was well grounded. She loved the wild, beautiful scenery and at the same time was struck by the economic opportunities of the region, opening to the railroads and with statehood imminent. Best of all, women voted and served on juries in the territory, preceded in both of these advances only by Wyoming Territory. Furthermore, the male legal establishment was uncommonly receptive to women, having freely admitted two of them to practice—Mary Leonard, the vindicated murder defendant, and Lelia Robinson, a recent arrival from Massachusetts who would play an important role in the early woman's bar.[114]

In 1882 Robinson had been the first woman graduate of Boston University Law School, but the state courts had refused to admit her to practice. Citing and following Foltz's example, she drafted and lobbied a Woman Lawyers Bill through the legislature. But even when she was duly certified, no lawyer in Boston would hire her. Like Foltz and other pioneer women who did not have male relatives in the profession to help them, Robinson hung out her shingle and waited for business. She wrote of the "embarrassments and difficulties" of starting "without having had preliminary training of a practical nature in an established office." Frustrated because the little business she had was all office work, and feeling that "the public judges a woman lawyer, as it does a man, largely by his success in court," Robinson set out in the spring of 1884 for Washington Territory where people were "more liberal on the woman question."[115]

Liberal indeed; soon after her arrival, Robinson was appearing in court before juries that included members of her own sex, probably the first woman ever to do so. She wrote about the "quick-sighted and keen-scented" jury women, who were as "true as steel in their findings. If they failed in either direction, it was in sometimes being a trifle too logical, not allowing sweet pity to have its fair influence." Robinson complained particularly of one woman who "thought my Chinaman client to be guilty . . . whereas he was really quite innocent." The next week, not daring to trust the lady again, Robinson removed her peremptorily from another jury. This was probably the first time that a woman lawyer struck a member of her own sex from the jury.[116]

Clara Foltz was in Washington Territory in December 1875 and might have even witnessed the historic peremptory strike. Immediately upon arrival in Seattle, Foltz had rushed to the courthouse to see a mixed jury and wrote that such "grand evidence of progress" so moved her that she "had hard work to maintain my self control." She described one of the jurors: "a motherly-looking, intelligent woman, with hands encased in cotton gloves and bonnet strings tied snugly under her chin, listening with conscientious intent to the argument." This woman was the reality that Foltz contrasted to the stereotype—the subject of "ribald jest and unseemly denunciation" because they spent time alone with men in the jury room. She said the opponents to women jurors fell into three categories: "narrow men" who oppose progress; "mercenary men" who want the three dollars per diem; and "lawless men who fear the conscience that women bring to jury duty." Also to blame were "timid women" afraid of the "scarecrow of custom," who failed to support this important recognition of women's full citizenship.[117]

Whether she actually observed Lelia Robinson trying a case, it seems likely that Foltz met the other woman lawyer while she was in Seattle. The two may well have spoken about the difficulties of making a living. Robinson was dubious about itinerant lecturing as an income supplement. In a letter of advice to women lawyers, she emphasized that they "must prove their staying power" and pointed out that the woman who leaves her legal work, whether "for philanthropy, money or fame or all three," will be said by the world to be lecturing "because she cannot succeed in practice."[118]

Foltz was well aware of this view, but it doubtless also occurred to her that it was unfair. Male lawyers could have successful parallel careers as orators without the suspicion that they had failed in practice. At any rate, she did not have a real choice when she set forth from Seattle on her eastward swing early in 1886. For almost half a year, Foltz was on the road, speaking mainly on lawyers, E. D. Baker, and impartial suffrage. Other speech titles were "Mother and Son," "A Woman and Her Partner," "Thomas Paine" (all these were mainly concerned with women's rights), and occasionally "Ulysses Grant."

In June, she was back in Washington Territory for another round of lectures before returning home to San Francisco. Things had changed for women in the six months since her last visit. Lelia Robinson had moved back to Boston because she missed her mother and sister and could not persuade them to join her. And woman suffrage was under attack by powerful forces, with its supporters in disarray. Washington would be admitted in 1889 as a male suffrage state.

The end of woman suffrage in the territory came because the issue was enmeshed with prohibition of liquor and control of vice. In the five years that women voted, they passed local option laws creating dry counties and as grand jurors indicted saloonkeepers, gamblers, and prostitutes. Lelia Robinson described the Washington experience, writing that Chief Judge Roger Greene, a prohibitionist as well as a suffragist, had been trying for years to secure indictments against various forms of vice. But the grand juries "would quietly let the subject drop." Then, women began to serve. The "new and strange" grand jury with female members "went in person at unexpected times and seasons to inspect suspicious premises, and summoned witnesses freely." The result was a "decided emigration of gamblers and prostitutes out of the city, and a general purification of the moral atmosphere."[119] "Purification" was not universally popular, and soon the backlash started that would put an end to suffrage. In a series of criminal appeals, convicted defendants successfully objected to the composition of the grand juries that included women, partly on the grounds that the statute awarding them suffrage was invalid.[120]

By 1888, the great experiment would be over—women did not vote (or serve on juries) in Washington again until 1910. On her swing back through the territory, where she lectured for a week, Foltz may have observed a change in atmosphere. She said no more of moving her practice there. Instead, she would soon try another frontier made newly accessible by the completion of a transcontinental railroad: Southern California.

San Diego Days

SEARCHING FOR EL DORADO

Foltz went home to San Francisco in the summer of 1886, but she did not reestablish the office that her publicity described as "among the handsomest in the city," with "one of the largest and most valuable law libraries."[121] Instead, she announced that she was back for an intermission and would resume lecturing in a few months. Meanwhile, as she did on the road, Foltz created her image by dressing well and registering at a fine hotel.

Many San Franciscans conducted their social and commercial lives in hotels rather than in private homes, partly because the city's population had outstripped its housing supply, and partly because even in post–gold rush days, it still included large numbers of single people and transients. The very best hotel was the Palace, built by one of the Comstock's silver kings. Foltz probably could not afford to stay there, but she had many choices among smaller and only slightly less elegant places—the Russ, the Lick House, and the Occidental among them. Years later, Foltz wrote nostalgically about the communal life at the Occidental, that "old-time popular hostelry" where one "Major Hooper, whose memory I lovingly cherish, was the manager, and because of his gracious and manly course with all women, the majority of them who lived at the hotel were secretly, at least, just dead in love with him—myself among the number."[122] For a good part of 1886–1887 Foltz lived on her own, both in San Francisco and on her second cross-country tour.

Often in her travels, she told interviewers that she was searching for a new place to settle and practice. Like so many male westerners, she also had a constant eye out for El Dorado, the golden city where she would make her fortune. Foltz thought she had found her perfect spot in booming San Diego in the spring of 1887. She reassembled her household with her sons and younger daughters and hung out her shingle, declaring that she would "anchor me down for all the rest of my days."[123] It actually turned out to be barely three years, and they were among the most eventful and stressful of her life.

Foltz arrived in Southern California at the height of the land boom that had started two years earlier when a railroad rate war combined with a sublime climate and a burst of effective promotion to bring a sudden population surge to the previously sleepy area. All kinds of people came, many "from the adventurous classes of the world," as one observer delicately put it. There were also farmers and merchants, health and climate-seekers, bankers and brokers, and the "professional boomers who showed the natives how to make money out of wind." The atmosphere, said those who had seen both boomtowns, was much like San Francisco during the gold rush.[124]

A thousand ships berthed in San Diego in one year. Many were loaded with timber for the city that was being built, including the spectacular Hotel del Coronado with its 399 rooms, no two alike. Lots that went for $500 were sold a few months later for $2,500 per front foot. By the end of 1887, real estate was turning over at a rate of $200,000 (about $4.5 million now) in a single day. No one asked what use there was in a twenty-five-foot lot. The whole town succumbed to the charms of the boom: buggy rides behind matched pairs with silver harnesses, barbecues and brass bands, and above all real estate promoters' promises of a certain and prosperous future.[125]

The population quickly outstripped the town's infrastructure. Sewers were needed, good water was hard to come by, and unpaved streets were muddy in the winter and dusty the rest of the year. A local story told how the manager of the Florence Hotel put planking down around its grounds. One day he told the owner of a steamship company: "'This is going to be a great city. We are going to have electric street railways, motor roads to the suburbs, a ferry across the bay, a big hotel on the peninsula, and many other things.' And then, pointing with pride, he exclaimed: 'And now we have this sidewalk.'"[126]

Clara Foltz wanted to be part of the boom and one of the founders of the grand city she believed would grow from it. Her problem, as usual, was one of capital. She could make money from her profession, of course, and would be the first and only woman lawyer for miles around. But so far, being first and even being famous had not provided her with a secure financial base. So she decided to go into publishing, something that western lawyers often did on the side. Little working capital was required, and she thought the new business could meet the overhead of her law practice, introduce her to San Diego, and help promote the boom. Initially, Foltz planned a weekly on the model of Abigail Duniway's *New Northwest*, to be called the *Woman's Inquirer* and "devoted to the interests of her sex and to general literature."[127] But she ran into a better proposition and started a daily newspaper instead.

CLARA FOLTZ, EDITOR

Foltz's close friend, the poet Madge Morris, had moved to town with her new husband some months earlier, bringing with them *The Golden Era*, a monthly magazine they published. A group of San Diego businessmen had sponsored the relocation, hoping to introduce some culture to their booming town. Madge and Harr Wagner attracted a little group of "men and women of literary tastes" to go to San Diego with them."[128] Some of these were people Foltz knew from the old group of lawyers, writers, and artists who had offices around the Montgomery Block and frequented Hjuls coffee shop. Indeed, as events unfolded, Foltz was so closely connected to the *Golden Era* crowd that she may have been one of those whom the Wagners recruited to come along. At least their presence gave her another reason for the move.

Harr Wagner said he hoped to make *The Golden Era* the "pioneer literary publication of San Diego in 1887, as it was of San Francisco in 1852." Perhaps he counted on the excitement of the boom to revitalize the magazine, which had been on a long decline from its origins as the "vade-mecum of the mining camps."[129] At any rate, the *Golden Era* migrants had very high hopes for the future of San Diego.

Foltz did not say at the time why she gave up the idea of a suffrage weekly and entered the more competitive and demanding daily news business instead. Nor did she write about her San Diego days in her autobiographical columns later in life. All that can be known for sure is that on May 16, 1887, the first issue of the *San Diego Bee*, "Clara Foltz, Editor," appeared on the newsstands. At first, Foltz relied on the equipment and staff of the monthly *Golden Era*. Several of the magazine's writers were already using the free type for a daily sheet called the *Stingaree*, the local name for both sting-rays in the bay and the red-light district of town. Apparently, someone had the idea of combining Foltz's publishing plans with the going enterprise, and the raffish *Stingaree* was transmuted into the respectable *Bee*.[130]

The name was designed to emphasize the new image; bees spend their time busily gathering honey and sting only in self-defense. Her opening move was to make the paper a daily and expand its size and the number of columns to twenty-eight. Foltz was to find that it took an immense amount of labor to fill these columns every day. She purchased telegraphic services, but all of the *Bee*'s local news had to be gathered or made; everything had to be written up, then set in type, run off and proofed, printed and folded, delivered and sold day after day. On top of this, advertisements had to be solicited, bills collected, the office administered, and a payroll met. Nothing really prepared Foltz for the total absorption and relentless pace of the daily newspaper business.

With its single-column headlines and crude woodcut illustrations, her paper was similar in appearance to hundreds of others in striving settlements throughout the West. Yet Foltz aspired to more for the *Bee*. "As the faithful record of a people's existence," she wrote, the newspaper "is the history of the masses." And then, as often was the case, especially under deadline pressure, her enthusiastic rhetorical boosterism got the best of her: "Not even the gold excitement of 1849 and the succeeding ten years revealed more matchless enterprise to the world. . . . We are laying the foundations of the divinest paradise the earth has ever known."[131]

SAN DIEGO SOCIAL LIFE

Clara Foltz was "Queen Bee" to her staff—the nickname reflected her position at the paper and to a large degree her place in the town, too. As an editor and a celebrity, Foltz was in the social swing, a pleasant change from San Francisco where her isolation in a male profession and her lack of money were often issues. The *Bee* covered local society and fashion developments in greater detail than any other paper, and Foltz enjoyed the friendly San Diego scene, where, she said, "all classes are alike full of geniality and cordial feelings."[132]

On a visit back to San Francisco, Foltz held "long conferences with dressmakers and milliners," according to her friend Frona Wait, who predicted that she would soon "burst upon her new-made friends in something like her old-time glory." Apparently, Foltz had the money for a new wardrobe for the "numerous elegant parties and balls constantly taking place" in San Diego.

Many of these entertainments occurred at the Villa Montezuma, home of Jesse Shepard, whose invitations were the town's highest social prize.[133]

Shepard was a curious San Diego celebrity—though it is hard to say what exactly he did or who he was. Young and radiantly handsome, he was a performer, though not on a stage before large audiences. Rather, in his own dramatically lit parlor, Shepard played the piano and sang in different voices, displaying an impressive vocal range. He claimed that spirits from another world guided his music.[134]

Two wealthy Spiritualist brothers had brought Shepard to town and had built the Villa Montezuma to his specifications. It was almost completed when Foltz first arrived, and she reported on the decoration and finishing touches in the *Bee*.[135] A showplace in the exuberant Queen Anne style, with a jumbled profusion of purely decorative turrets, towers, and bays, its inside walls were paneled walnut, its floors were polished fir, the ceiling was covered in silver-gray faux leather, and the windows were art-glass portraits of great painters, poets, and musicians, including Jesse Shepard himself.

A younger man moved into the villa as secretary, impresario, and companion, but no rumors about the nature of their relationship appeared in the local press. Foltz was often Shepard's guest and wrote admiring reviews of his ability to "arrest the fleeting beauty of the mystic world," predicting in her understated way that the villa would become "the center of artistic and literary culture quite unlike anything of the kind on this continent."[136] Shepard was drawn to the *Golden Era* crowd and became for awhile a frequent essayist for the magazine.

Another remarkable character in Foltz's San Diego circle was the poet Joaquin Miller, called by Harr Wagner "the most picturesque figure American literature had produced." With fabulous looks and at least some writing talent, Miller defined himself as a visionary poet and untamed westerner, taking the name *Joaquin* from a Mexican revolutionary. He wore his golden hair long, tucked a red flannel shirt into leather pants, and slung a bearskin cape around his broad shoulders. When James Russell Lowell, John Greenleaf Whittier, Walt Whitman, Robert Browning, and Alfred, Lord Tennyson all died within a few months of each other, Miller saluted them as "My kingly kinsmen, kings of thought." Miller loved women in general and was especially fond of "brave, bonnie, beautiful little Madge Morris," as he once described her. Harr Wagner was his best male friend, and when the couple moved south, Miller visited often and wrote something for most issues of *The Golden Era*. On at least one occasion, he and Clara Foltz were on the same program at the Villa Montezuma, he reading his latest poem, and she reciting a dramatic passage from one of her lectures.[137]

Foltz fit well into the atmosphere of San Diego, a boomtown with a Bohemian fringe. At age thirty-six, she looked young and felt accepted and admired, enjoying the moment and expecting even more from the future. Her "beautiful children" (as she always called them) were not yet old enough to disappoint her deeply, nor so young as to need constant attention. Trella, now age twenty, was an actress with a San Francisco troupe; the two younger girls, Bertha and Virginia, twelve and ten, were in boarding school in Los Angeles and came home for holidays and summers. Her sons lived with her; Sam, age nineteen, was in charge of *Bee* circulation in the early mornings and then doubled as a courtroom clerk, also gathering legal news, for the rest of the day. David, seventeen, combined general reporting and running errands for his mother. They lived in a convenient little place near the *Bee* office on Front Street, which she named Cottage Headquarters.

For awhile, Foltz was sure that she had found her El Dorado and tried to persuade her parents to move from Tucson. But it would not be long before the San Diego boom went bust, and even before the economy collapsed, Foltz got into a an ugly battle that eventually forced her to give up the *Bee*. She took on the cause of Maria Burton, Spanish widow of an American general, who claimed to be the true owner of Mexican lands being offered for sale by prominent San Diego real estate developers.

THE *BEE* VERSUS THE INTERNATIONAL COMPANY

Opening Victory

On Friday, June 10, 1887, the *Bee* published a small paid announcement, among the many gaudy real estate advertisements that were its bread and butter:

> A Warning To the Public:
> I hereby warn those who intend to purchase lands at the "*Ensenada*" that the International Company cannot give valid titles to said lands. This property belongs to me. It is a Royal Grant, ratified, given in 1804, and confirmed by the Mexican Government in 1859 and 1868.
> Maria A. Ruiz Burton

Mrs. Burton was referring to property in Mexico, fewer than one hundred miles south of San Diego, near potentially rich mines, with a magnificent port at Ensenada. Several San Diego businessmen, organized as the International Company, had started a settlement on the land Burton said was hers.

Foltz promised an investigation of Burton's claim and rebuked the other papers for refusing to print her paid notice. The next morning's *Bee* carried a sympathetic interview with Mrs. Burton. At 7 p.m. that same night, Foltz left Sunday's paper to be typeset and went to her nearby home. As soon as she was out of the *Bee* office, six thugs stormed in, seized the type and equipment, forced the printers out of the building, and padlocked the doors.[138] Foltz's staff managed to hold on to Sunday's copy in the fray, and after being alerted, she rushed around town begging the editors of San Diego's other three papers to lend her their presses for her Sunday edition. When all of them refused, Foltz hired a carriage and set out with her men for National City, about four miles away, which had one newspaper.

Right behind her thundered the agents of the International Company. As midnight neared, the two sides met the editor of the *National City Record*. Foltz pleaded as a lady in distress. The company men said she was no lady but a blackmailer threatening to ruin a legitimate business venture by publicizing a false title unless she was compensated for her silence. They promised to prove this charge or pay the editor $1,000 by three o'clock on Sunday. He agreed to wait until that hour before aiding Foltz.

On Sunday, no *Bee* appeared, and the other papers ran stories declaring the "stingless *Bee*" deceased. The *Union* inveighed against the "irresponsible" *Bee*, pushing a title that all "who have long been residents of San Diego know to be a chestnut." Clara Foltz was called unethical, and Maria Burton, old and incompetent. By Monday, however, the *Bee* was back on the streets, with an issue printed in National City. It was only a single sheet, without the usual logo or any San Diego advertisements, but it told the whole story of the takeover, and four thousand copies sold within hours. "Only the good," Foltz observed editorially, "are raised from the dead." The resurrection lasted only two days, however, followed by a ten-day silence.[139]

During this time Foltz decided to fight and planned her campaign. At first she had said that she was interested only in giving Burton the "justice of a hearing." But when the International Company closed the *Bee* down and denounced its editor, Clara Foltz joined cause completely with Maria Burton against their mutual opponent: "the syndicate that would close the lips of free speech and pollute with their leprous hands every source of independent thought."[140] Foltz rallied all her forces for the upcoming press war.

Most important was Harr Wagner, who joined partly as a personal supporter, but also because the International Company's frontmen had duped him into selling them the *Golden Era* type and printing equipment on the condition that they continue to share it with the *Bee*. Immediately after the late-night seizure Foltz's reliable friend Charles Gunn hurried to her side from San Francisco. Both Wagner and Gunn were able writers and editors, and Foltz's regular staff was also solidly behind her initially. Somewhere, she found financial backing and purchased new type and equipment that enabled her to publish a better-looking *Bee*. In her first editorial in the new format, Foltz promised "a fearless policy" and that "the weak or unfortunate will not appeal to us in vain."[141] The press war was on.

The International Company and its chief newspaper ally, the *San Diego Union*, blasted Foltz personally through an anonymous "Scribbler." Without mentioning her name, Scribbler referred to certain "sordid . . . intellectual harlots" who are "for sale to the highest bidder." When they "are refused employment by the Republican State Committee of California, they forthwith offer themselves to the Democratic State committee." There could be no doubt this was Foltz, whose switch of political allegiance just three years before was well-known throughout the state. Scribbler went on to accuse her of first "gently hint[ing]" that she would refrain from printing damaging accusations "for a consideration" and then "[assuming] a threatening attitude and demand[ing] a specific sum as the price of silence." He suggested that she had turned to blackmail because she was "hard up financially and . . . being made desperate by the importunity of creditors." And, "Sometimes [such people] fail as lawyers, and then take to journalism where they fail the more so."[142]

For her part, Foltz's *Bee* printed legal documents purporting to show that Burton inherited the property from her grandfather, a distinguished Spanish general who received it originally from the Spanish king in gratitude for gaining military control of the Baja region. The *Bee* also published Burton's own clearly written account of her claim. Though the company men described her as a demented old woman, Burton was actually a substantial person, who had recently pseudonymously published a novel, *The Squatter and the Don* (1885), which portrayed the experience of the Spanish settlers and their descendents in the former Mexican colonies.

Every *Bee* issue had headlines warning prospective purchasers about the International Company and offering the property for sale under the Burton title instead. One story pointed out that the company had no San Diego assets, which made it judgment-proof there; another mentioned a smallpox epidemic in Ensenada. At first, the press war was exhilarating, and it was certainly good for circulation. Foltz's brother Charles reported in the *San Jose Mercury* that the *Bee* was "brighter, healthier and busier than ever. The effort of the corporation with the sounding title and sneaking methods failed entirely."[143]

Sources of the Conflict

Foltz's relationship with the International Company had begun cordially. The company men had advertised generously in the *Bee* and had entertained Foltz on a free trip to the Ensenada settlement. In return, she had written in praise of "the great syndicate" and "the enormous enterprise." She had described the organizers of the company in glowing terms: one was "tireless" and "indomitable"; another was "wealthy" and "thought-executing"; the wife of a third was a "princess of her sex"; and the chief real estate agent had a "benevolent countenance" and a "brain all afire."[144] So from their side, Foltz had accepted their hospitality and was now trying to destroy them. It was hard enough to persuade Americans to invest in land in Mexico; a clouded title could be fatal. On her side, Foltz viewed herself as a crusader for press freedom and women's rights. Simple kindness was also mixed with sacred principle: "The elastic cord of human feeling is touched" on behalf of the "defenseless widow," she said.[145]

Foltz was never one to admit, or perhaps even to experience, anything less than certainty about her own conduct or motives. Her strong sense that she was right—her opponents called it self-righteousness—would often lead her to be surprised when she faced criticism. As for the accusation of blackmail, she noted that the practice existed and condemned it, but she added that it was common for editors who "dare tell the truth, unmask fraud and expose the sham and deviltry of villains" to be "called blackmailers by those whose deeds they unveil."[146]

In fact, there were explanations short of blackmail for Foltz's dealings with the International Company. Perhaps she thought it only fair to warn them before she printed Maria Burton's claims, which they then portrayed as an illegal approach. As a lawyer, moreover, she could have been offering to settle the matter before harmful publicity. Though by modern standards Foltz's double roles here as journalist and attorney would be dubious, rules against conflicts of interest were not well-developed at the time. And neither were journalistic ethics; the line between an honest editor and a press blackmailer was surprisingly indistinct.

Foltz was certain that the other San Diego papers were on the International Company's payroll, and indeed few newspapers were totally independent in their publishing decisions. Many received regular subsidies in return for squelching unfavorable stories. In his memoir of almost fifty years of California newspapering, San Francisco journalist and publisher Fremont Older told of payments from political candidates, the Southern Pacific Railroad, and various utility companies. Without apology or excuse, Foltz herself had written in an early *Bee* editorial that she thought "newspapers should be paid for what they do not print, as well as for what they do." Maybe in context she was simply speaking about using editorial discretion, but her meaning was far from clear.[147]

Throughout July, August, and early September of 1887, the *Bee* continued to urge Burton's claim and to escalate its attacks on the International Company. The *Union* carried on its personal assaults, casting a harsh light on everything Clara Foltz did. Like an unhappily married couple, the two newspaper editors were locked in weary repetitive conflict. When Foltz told some of her stories at a patriotic celebration of the flag, for instance, the *Union* commented that her "egotism dwarfs all the rest of mankind. She delights in public occasions, but only if she is conspicuous on the program." And the *Bee* rejoined that it would be surprising news "when the envious editor of the six-day morning subsidy shall be honored with a place either conspicuous or otherwise." Public speaking was hard work, Foltz pointed out, particularly for one already "overburdened with business and home cares and responsibilities."[148]

On the Fourth of July, Foltz was again on a public platform, and this time the whole town was there. Following a huge parade, a picnic, and a speech by the local congressman, Clara Foltz abandoned the customary platitudes and placed the whole Burton matter in a feminist frame. Without preliminaries she declared: "The language of the Declaration of Independence comes to me today with a new force." Everyone knew why. "Before the echoes of the Independence bell had died away . . . while the thought of equal rights was yet burning in the brain of a new-born nation, the very builders denied to more than one half of the people the rights they were fighting to secure. The feminine half of the people were wholly discarded, and in the white robes of freemen were woven the black threads of slavery."[149]

Suffragists had been arguing in similar terms since the 1876 centennial of the Declaration of Independence, but such contentious views were not usually part of the official program. Foltz's enemies complained that the speech was another example of her irritating self-importance, putting her press war on a par with the injustices of history. The *Coronado Mercury* added: "We wish to God, you were a man, for your own sake to mind your own business and keep your tongue from wagging."[150]

By late July 1887, the International Company was on the ropes, though Burton had yet to realize a penny on her claim. And the *Bee*, which had increased its sales of advertising as a result of the press war, was losing quality because Foltz and her small staff could not fill the additional news columns. She resorted to publishing a silly serialized novel. At this point, Foltz took a break from the daily grind and traveled with her youngest, Virginia, to San Francisco for several weeks. She left the *Bee* with Charles Gunn and her staff, and her household with her teenaged children.

The Last Round

When Foltz returned to San Diego, she found that Edward Cothran, her assistant editor, had moved to a rival paper. The loss was also a personal one because Cothran was an old friend and a fellow lawyer. In fact, when they were both students, he had been one of her supporters in her struggle to join the San Jose legal club. Cothran was a facile writer, who could fill a whole column with readable reflections after a walk around town. Now, from the pages of the *San Diego Sun*, he denounced Burton's claims to own the Ensenada land: "a spent sky rocket, an exploded firecracker, a wax taper burnt to embers, a collection of rotten rags, a mist, a ghostly fire fly." "What a jumble," Foltz jeered at his mixed metaphors and under the heading "A Sudden Conversion" cast aspersions on his legal ability, his integrity, and his sanity. "Inspired by a senseless animosity," she wrote, he had sold out. Though the rest of her staff remained loyal, Cothran's departure marked the beginning of the end of Clara Foltz as crusading editor.[151]

Another major gain for the International Company forces in her absence had been Tom Fitch, a boomer extraordinaire, who had followed the western action from mining camp to metropolis for twenty-five years. People said that no boom really started till Fitch showed up. He had been in San Diego for a year, selling his handsome, entertaining self along with the "bay 'n climate."[152]

Every other day Fitch published fanciful advertisements, numbered "specials," that delighted the town and sold papers as well as property. Special number 12, for instance, described California's sudden spring when "scarlet poppies and the big yellow buttercups wave in the breeze like the plumes and banners of an elfin army."[153] While Foltz was away, Fitch had endorsed the International Company title to the Ensenada land and had withdrawn his specials from the *Bee*, which made it harder than ever to fill the daily columns.

After weeks of rumors that the end was near, Foltz announced her retirement from newspaper publishing in November. She had been editor of the *Bee* for six months. Her staff of young men, "from the associate editor up to the 'devil,'" were distraught. At a farewell banquet at the Saddle Rock restaurant, "Mrs. Foltz addressed the boys in feeling terms," and they responded with resolutions about "our kind and generous employer." A few days later, they launched a "fine little yacht" named *The Queen Bee* after Clara Foltz "in consideration of her kindness, industry and executive ability."[154]

Foltz also bid farewell in the *Bee*, writing of her "sorrow at parting with those who stood nobly by us when days were dark." She denied ever asking for or receiving payment for "the expression or suppression of any matter whatsoever" and spoke of the reforms she had wanted to promote as editor of the paper. Among these "purposes unaccomplished," she placed the building up of San Diego, establishing a manual training school, starting a home for working girls, importing the silk culture in order to provide light and profitable employment for women, and improving prison conditions. She said nothing directly of the International Company of Mexico, Maria Burton, or her press foes.[155]

Nor did Foltz publish the sale terms. These continued to be the subject of rumors circulated and denied for some months afterwards. Charles Shortridge reported in the *San Jose Mercury*, however, that she sold the *Bee* name, the printing equipment, and a one-year promise not to compete for the handsome sum of $15,000 (more than $300,000 today).[156] Moreover, most of this amount was profit for Foltz, who probably had not put any significant amount of money into the paper.

Did she win or lose? Was Clara Foltz right or wrong in the battle against the International Company? She made a lot of enemies in a small town, including some of the leading businessmen and lawyers, and, most dangerously to her good name, news reporters and publishers. Her reputation for honesty was put into question by the never fully refuted charges of press blackmail, and her reputation for good judgment by the extremes she had gone to in her championship of Maria Burton. Neither of these blows could help in her effort, thus far unsuccessful, to become not only the first woman lawyer in California, but the first woman to win a secure place among the leaders of the bar.

On the positive side, Burton's claims were heard, and though Foltz had made enemies, she had also gained friends and admirers—the warmer for being together in a battle. She made of the struggle one of her infrequent financial successes, being bought out for a good price rather than forced out. The International Company never recovered and was sold at a loss to another syndicate.[157] Ultimately, the Ensenada settlement collapsed along with the San Diego boom on which it depended. Maria Burton turned to the U.S. courts, where she recovered nothing and was left to litigate in Mexico. The *Bee* published for another half year, with Tom Fitch as editor; then it merged with the *Union*, which survived to be modern San Diego's leading paper.

LIFE AFTER THE *BEE*: BOOM AND BUST

After her retirement from the *Bee* in late 1887, Foltz relaxed from the intense pressures of daily publication and press warfare. For a few weeks, she had time for beach picnics and sunset drives in the splendid horse and buggy she bought with her *Bee* money. Charles Gunn did not return to San Francisco but joined the local bar and was Foltz's frequent escort. Together they visited her parents in Tucson for a few weeks. Laura Gordon, "lady lawyer of San Joaquin County" (as she was billed), was Foltz's guest at the Horton House, one of the town's hotels. The two did their annual planning about women's rights bills for the next legislative session.[158]

Though Foltz had announced her return to full-time law practice, she hesitated to do it, partly because the *Bee* battle's effect on potential clients was uncertain. Also, private practice may have seemed too much like publishing—demanding and detailed work, with her sex always a contentious issue. She applied to be a prosecutor, a secure lawyer's job with a regular salary, but was unable to persuade the city fathers that women were eligible—the statute required that prosecuting attorneys had to be voters.[159]

Foltz also thought of "running the circuit," as she described it, by opening branch legal offices at San Bernardino and Los Angeles. And she considered relocating completely to Los Angeles, where she had many friends and fewer enemies than in San Diego. Bertha and Virginia were in school there, and her contract not to publish another paper did not apply. On the other hand, less than a year had passed since she committed herself to San Diego for life. She genuinely loved the weather, the beauty, and the warm social scene. Most important, leaving would look like an admission of failure. In early 1888, three months after vacating the editor's chair, Foltz was still vacillating about her future, when the famous lecturer and journalist Kate Field arrived in town.[160]

Field supported herself handsomely without the drag of clients, movements, or professional responsibilities. Though she had her causes, such as cremation, anti-Mormonism, and the annexation of Alaska and Hawaii, Field's money-making lectures were more entertainment than advocacy— "An Evening with Charles Dickens" and "Musical Monologues" were typical titles. Credited with inventing the occupation of publicist, Field had persuaded Queen Victoria to try the telephone, and a grateful Alexander Graham Bell rewarded her with stock in his new company. Later, Field touted American glassware, California wines, the Paris exposition, and the Chicago World's Fair. But the product she pushed most successfully was herself. The new editors of the *Bee*, for instance, who never had a nice word for Foltz, called Field "one of the most popular of America's public women" and praised her intellect and honesty.[161]

Foltz and Field became instant friends and were often together during the winter that Field spent in San Diego. Highlighting the visit was an "exceptionally brilliant reception" at the Villa Montezuma, where the "toilettes of the ladies" were elegant and the pleasures of the evening "extended some distance into the night."[162] Foltz may have discussed with Field her most unusual idea for a new career—becoming an actress.

Kate Field had actually tried acting and enjoyed the experience even though her success had been limited. Foltz's lectures and political speeches (many dramatic and delivered in theaters) arguably prepared her for the stage. Interviewers sometimes commented that she should have been an actress; "her exquisite form, her emotional nature, her mobile features, her musical voice and grace of action" all pointed in that direction.[163]

When Foltz originally floated the idea of a stage career, Harr Wagner approved it in *The Golden Era*: "Her life has been rather dramatic, and her talent and natural fitness are peculiarly adapted for the stage."[164] He was right that she was always in a role—crusading editor the latest—and usually in costume also—whether she played the wealthy society lady, the tailored career woman, or the scholarly graduate in robe and mortarboard. Yet as much as Foltz liked to imagine a more glamorous and less litigious life, the theater was not a real alternative. She was in her late thirties, so it would have been a very late start, and with success even less certain than in law practice. Furthermore, only a few of the most celebrated actresses were able to rise above the prevailing opinion that a woman could not be entirely respectable on the stage (or even, in some places, in the audience). Foltz often compared women lawyers to women actors in the prejudice that both confronted.

In the end, she determined to stay in San Diego and try to profit directly from the boom. She did not want to be a "mud hen," the ugly name for women who speculated in the market like gamblers. Instead, Foltz set up as a real estate broker who could not only sell the property, but also do the lawyers' work of searching and clearing the titles, drafting the sales contract, and litigating if there were problems. Brokers were from economic necessity civic boosters, influential advocates for municipal improvements like electric lights and cars, sewers, fresh water, parks, public auditoriums, and the coming of *The Golden Era* to San Diego. She would be the only lady broker in town, and this would give her advantages in dealing with the wives of buyers and providing a social welcome to new settlers. Just a week before Christmas, Foltz arranged for six carriages to go to Ocean Beach and picnic on the verandah of the new hotel there. One of the people on this trip was Maria Crawford, a friend from San Francisco, who had recently moved to San Diego. Shortly afterwards, the two women announced the opening of business, bringing to 235 the number of real estate agents in town.[165]

But the turn to real estate was, like so many of Clara Foltz's business ventures, unlucky or ill-judged. Just as she started, the San Diego bubble burst and the bottom dropped out of the market. One day the Hotel del Coronado had opened with a special train of sightseers from Chicago, while land speculators were predicting a population of 150,000 for the city. The next day, people were fleeing the area, taking what was left of their capital with them. In "the gilded saloons," wrote an observer, "the generals, colonels, majors, judges, doctors and professors whom boom money had evolved from very common clay" went from French champagne to California Riesling "without tarrying at the half way house of Sauterne," and by summer, "the boys were drinking water."[166]

Clara Foltz's reaction to the sudden stillness in the real estate market was impulsive and heroic if viewed sympathetically, grandiose and grasping to her critics. She offered to go on a nationwide tour as a publicist for Southern California in the manner of Kate Field. For this she asked $10,000, which included the services of her newly arrived friend Maria Crawford as companion and aid. "Mrs. Foltz has a reputation that is world-wide and she will undoubtedly draw large crowds," said a supporter.[167]

To Foltz's enemies from the battle over the International Company, the project and its price tag were an easy target. The *National City Record*, lightly ironic, observed that while $10,000 might seem steep for an ordinary lecture, Mrs. Foltz had promised "original witticisms, well-seasoned stories, and purely original jokelets." Such "originality in this degenerate day of plagiarism and imitation," continued the writer, is worth the price. The *Bee* suggested that since her attacks on the International Company were partly responsible for the bust, she was hardly the one to be well paid by taxpayers suffering from its consequences.[168]

Foltz did go on her publicizing tour in April 1888, though probably for less than her asking price. She combined her lectures with inspections of manual training schools in the East, so the Normal School Board may have paid part of her expenses. By the time she returned several months later, the real estate collapse had taken a severe toll, and San Diego had shrunk from its peak population of almost forty thousand to sixteen thousand. Pessimists predicted that the town proper would soon look like the ghost subdivisions that now surrounded it.

In the long, anxious summer of 1888, the annual July Fourth celebration assumed added significance. It would show whether San Diego was destined to be a real city, or just a failed boomtown. The parade featured a wagon drawn by ten coal-black horses in which thirty-eight maidens in white represented the states of the Union. (Virginia Foltz wore the sash of South Carolina.) Every business and civic group marched. Clara Foltz was the sole orator of the day.[169] Unlike the previous Fourth, she did not refer to women's rights, the blot of slavery on the country's founding, or any other subject that might distress her worried fellow citizens. Rather, in less than an hour, she traced the history of liberty from its birth in the Garden of Eden to its apotheosis in America.

Foltz designed her text for delivery in short phrases (so that they could be understood when shouted without amplification), memorized and rehearsed it, and then gave it to a huge crowd in the open air. A woman in the audience wrote: "Ten years ago I heard Mrs. Clara Foltz attempt to read her first paper upon woman suffrage to a few invited guests in a small hall in San Jose. How timid her voice! How trembling her tones! Once the manuscript fell from her hands. On the Fourth of last July I saw her standing before assembled thousands in San Diego, calm, self-possessed, dignified, perfectly womanly, delivering an address, which for elegance of diction and warmth of patriotic enthusiasm I have never heard surpassed. Men listened with bared heads as she taught them beautiful truths."[170]

The brave Fourth of July civic show was reassuring. It promised that the town would survive because the people on the plaza that day had come to make a life as well as to strike it rich. Only a few years later, San Diegans would be speaking of the boom's good effects, though they much preferred the "steady growth" that followed the bust. An old resident summed up the days of the land bubble thus: "We were a lot of very ordinary toads whirled up by a cyclone until we thought we were eagles sailing with our own wings in the topmost dome of heaven."[171]

ANOTHER BATTLE OF THE SEXES:
THE WHITE DIVORCE CASE

The death of the boom made full-time law practice Foltz's only practical option in San Diego. The local bar at the time was made up of sixty-five male lawyers, a clubby group who nevertheless seemed to welcome their first woman. At this time, lawyers around the country were forming bar associations, following the lead of the New York lawyers who had organized to fight municipal and judicial corruption in the 1870s. Along with Charles Gunn, Foltz helped organize a bar association for San Diego, whose initial project was to create a library for the use of all members. Foltz's acceptance as a founder contrasted with her San Francisco experience where the bar association had remained exclusively male, with meeting rooms featuring billiards, cold meats, and hard liquor.[172]

San Diego's judiciary consisted of a magistrate, a roving commissioner, and a single judge: John Downey Works. Scholarly and sociable, Works had come from Indiana as a "health-seeker" in the early 1880s. He wrote books on pleading, practice, and ethics and was often listed as a guest at the Villa Montezuma and the town's balls and parties. Later, he would serve on the state supreme court.[173]

Judge Works's civil docket reflected the clashes typical of a western town in the midst of a boom and then a bust. The big-money cases were about the ownership and improvement of property. Contracts, debt collection, and nuisances were also frequent subjects of litigation. Far down on the list of desirable matters for lawyers were domestic disputes such as the one that provided Clara Foltz with her first jury trial in San Diego. Foltz was retained by Arvilla White, who was involved in a sad contest with Richard White, her husband of twenty-three years.

The case was procedurally confused and factually a clash of equally credible stories. It had started with the husband's suit to set aside his conveyance of the Hotel Adelphi to his wife. Judge Works found that Arvilla had made false promises and threats to induce Richard to sign away the property and that she planned to abandon him for another man. He ordered her to reconvey the hotel to her husband. Instead, Arvilla White hired Clara Foltz to try to reverse the decision.[174]

As editor of the *Bee*, Foltz had originally taken the husband's side in commenting on the case. After her retention as counsel for Arvilla, however, editor Foltz had written: "White is old and childish, he imagines that his wife is having an affair, which she has always indignantly denied and the guests at the hotel generally support her." As Arvilla's attorney, Foltz's first legal move was a fifty-page motion for a new trial on the grounds that Judge Works had been biased against the wife. At the same time, she filed an action for divorce.[175]

The Whites had married in 1864, the same year as Clara and Jeremiah Foltz. Like the Foltzes, they had started out on a midwestern farm. In the divorce complaint, Foltz detailed the sad story of the marriage from Arvilla's side. She "had borne and cared for the children, done her own housework, and at the order of Defendant has washed clothes for laboring men, cooked for hired hands in large numbers, performed the labor of men in the field and at the house." Richard, in Foltz's words, had been "lazy, indolent and idle, declaring he would not work and generally living up to his declaration." There were some allegations of physical abuse (slapping, elbowing), but the complaint focused on Arvilla's mental suffering.[176]

The story thus told was close to Clara Foltz's own experience; the lawyer knew firsthand about the frequent pregnancies, the never-ending toil, and the ineffectual and demanding husband. But the White marriage was far more tragic than hers in one respect. Arvilla had been pregnant twenty-one times in twenty-three years, but only three children survived into adulthood. She had suffered eight miscarriages, and ten of the thirteen children who had come to term had died early. One cause of the frequent miscarriages had been Richard's requirement that Arvilla "overwork and unduly exert herself at common labor" while pregnant, followed by his refusal "to provide her suitable attendance and attention although abundantly able so to have done." According to the complaint, he was also callous toward the frequent deaths. He tried to bury one stillborn baby in the stable yard and failed to attend either the deathbed or funeral of another child.

Richard's lawyers answered both the new trial motion in the hotel conveyance case and the complaint for divorce, contesting all of Foltz's factual claims. Judge Works took jurisdiction of the new trial motion even though it was based partly on charges of bias against him, and denied it. The divorce complaint went to trial late in May 1888 before an advisory jury. As usual when Clara Foltz was the lawyer, there were many spectators, including a large number of women. Richard and Arvilla gave their stories under oath as they had at the earlier trial; the two grown daughters testified for their mother, and the son-in-law was on Richard's side. Friends and neighbors disagreed about who had most injured whom. Their community property included farming implements, four hundred stands of bees, a horse and buggy, and busts of Byron and of Shakespeare.

Adultery, a crime in California (a felony if both parties were married), was the subject of conflicting testimony. Arvilla testified to Richard's constant false accusations against her, which constituted one of her grounds for divorce. Richard swore that he peeped through the keyhole and saw a man in his wife's bedroom. She responded that the meeting was innocent; the room doubled as an office, and she no longer desired sexual relations with anyone.

One problematic piece of evidence (introduced by Arvilla's lawyers at the first trial) was the claim that she had aborted a pregnancy using an umbrella wire. Richard had made the charge in a note he placed under her dinner plate, accompanied by a threat to reveal it publicly unless she stopped litigating against him. To the all-male jury in the divorce trial, the abortion allegation against the wife was probably more damaging than the revelation of the husband's blackmail. At any rate, after six days of testimony, the jury returned a verdict for Richard, denying Arvilla a divorce.

The reports of the trial in the local press, especially the *Bee*, edited by Foltz's successor and critic Thomas Fitch, were unfavorable to her. One juror interviewed by Fitch complained later that Foltz "went bobbing and flouncing around with a significant sneer" and added that it was "hard enough to be compelled to leave their business for a week and to have their ears polluted with the mass of filth . . . which Mrs. Foltz's lady friends . . . were so anxious to hear, without being subjected to contumely and insult." In the *Bee* Fitch also criticized a request Foltz had made during the trial to "pass over in silence" the "filthy and unpleasant" portions of the evidence; it was her own fault, Fitch wrote, that she failed to "select her cases and work with discretion" and so "ran the risk of having her finer feelings and sensibilities constantly trampled on."[177]

Fitch did not mention that he had previously been counsel for Arvilla White and was dismissed in favor of Foltz. But clearly he thought that a real lady should not appear in a case involving messy facts. Though Foltz did not respond on the record to his charge, she would probably have said that for women to find equal justice as litigants and witnesses, and equal access to trials as spectators and jurors, both sides should try to present the evidence in a way fit for mixed company.

The adverse comments on Foltz in the White case were just one example of Fitch's constant needling. Often, it was under the guise of a pretended compliment, as when he wrote of his hope that "our talented townswoman" would "finally drift into her proper sphere of usefulness."[178] *Sphere* was a loaded word, used against the suffragists when they wanted to vote, serve on juries, or be lawyers. Many people, perhaps most, believed that when referring to women, *sphere* should have the word *domestic* in front of it.

MARRIAGE AND THE DOMESTIC SPHERE

While she was in San Diego, Foltz passed a milestone in motherhood; Trella, her eldest child, came home to be married. "My darling first born" had been her lieutenant in the battle to keep the family together. "A beautiful daughter, looking like a porcelain picture, and but sixteen years her mother's junior, mildly exerts her sway during the mother's absence," wrote an observer about Trella in the early years of Foltz's career.[179]

Just as her mother had dreamed from girlhood of "oratory, politics and fame," so Trella had fixed on the stage. She had started by reciting at socials and opening for her mother at suffrage events. One of her earliest reviews has her at age fourteen "going through a wide range of Shakespeare's heroines with fidelity and taste." So excellent was her performance that the audience "supposed a regular course of dramatic training, but she had only had such as her mother could give her." At eighteen, Trella joined the stock company connected to the California Theater in San Francisco as an extra. But soon she took the lead for road performances of *Hazel Kirke*, a popular romance about a woman who braves all to marry for love. Though the plot was indecipherable, the play attracted attention because its characters spoke in the vernacular and it was set in a mill instead of a mansion.[180]

Trella's fiancé, Charles Gridley Toland, was a theater buff, who may have first seen her on the stage. The son of a well-known physician, he was a successful doctor himself. Old enough to be Trella's father, Charles was attractive, kind, and prosperous—a suitable husband according to any mother's reckoning. With her marriage, Trella, at age twenty, gave up her highest stage aspirations, which would have meant moving to New York City, and for a time confined herself to recitations in private parlors.

The wedding was on a Sunday afternoon at Foltz's little place in San Diego, Cottage Headquarters, with the Presbyterian minister presiding and only family present. After the ceremony, the newlyweds entrained immediately for a honeymoon in Yosemite.[181] A year later, Clara Foltz's first grandchild, William, was born.

Trella Foltz wed in the midst of a trans-Atlantic debate spurred by the women's movement about the institution of marriage and whether it oppressed women. British feminist Mona Caird started the controversy with an article in the influential *Westminster Review* claiming that for women, at least, marriage was a failure. The article "stirred the press to white heat both in England and America," as Elizabeth Cady Stanton remembered it years later. In the outpouring of commentary that followed Caird's article, Leo Tolstoy's novella *The Kreutzer Sonata* was often invoked. Tolstoy pictured married women as subjugated sexual slaves who were required to be mother, wet nurse, and mistress all at once. There were also stark passages about the death of love in daily life: "Sometimes I watched her pouring out tea, swinging her legs, lifting a spoon to her mouth, smacking her lips, and I hated her for these things." Considered extremely shocking by late Victorian standards, the story stirred so much controversy that one writer commented, "Nothing is so prolific of enmities as the subject of Tolstoi, unless it be that of the tariff."[182]

Throughout the 1880s a public woman interviewed on any topic was also asked whether she considered marriage a failure. When Kate Field stepped off the train in New York, returning from her western sojourn, it was a reporter's first question. She said she had never tried marriage and never would. But Field continued that inferior people fail at marriage, just as they fail at other things, and that bad marriages, like crimes, make news, while good unions remain private.[183]

Clara Foltz had been giving her opinion on marriage for years in her lecture "Woman and Her Partner." The title was only slightly ironic. She believed that "most of the heart-breakings of married life are due to the lack of a common center of thought between husband and wife. . . . To achieve the ideal harmony of a complete union," she said, quoting Tennyson, "liker must they grow":

The man be more of woman, she of man,
He gain in [mental] and in moral height,
Nor lose the wrestling thews that throw the world;
She mental breadth, nor fail in childward care,
Nor lose the childlike in the larger mind;
Till at the last she set herself to man,
Like perfect music unto noble words.

No one could say which is more important to the song—the music or the words. If "husband and wife would blend in the harmony of a complete union they must pursue some common theme. In marriage, as in mathematics," Foltz said, "only parallel lines keep close together."[184]

Law study, she often suggested, would make a woman a better wife and a better mother because it would enable her to be mentally parallel to her husband. Foltz did not go as far, however, as her friend Myra Bradwell, editor of the *Chicago Legal News*, who suggested that women lawyers should find mates within the profession, as Bradwell herself had done: "Married people should share the same toil and be separated in no way. If they worked side by side and thought side by side we would need no divorce courts."[185]

Foltz believed that women like men, wives like husbands, should work outside their own households to improve society. Not that she disdained the domestic arts; in fact, Foltz bragged about her cooking and sewing abilities. But unlike some female professionals (Kate Field for one) who judged it impractical to combine a public career with running a household and raising children, Foltz was an apostle for having it all.

Given Foltz's ideas about the possibility of combining marriage and career, why didn't she marry again herself? Many years later she explained: "I could only marry once. I lost my husband when we were both very young and I have never cared quite enough for any man to take the yoke again." She also admitted, "I've cracked many a heart in my time."[186]

It seems likely that one of these hearts beat in the breast of Charles Gunn, who had been at her side throughout the 1880s. At Foltz's urging, he had studied law, and they worked well together in the parallel lines she promoted. But it was always her work they did. Clara Foltz was the one with the breakthrough career, the nationwide fame, and the large ambitions, while he played the supporting actor to her leading lady. For Foltz, to marry Gunn would have been to settle—to give up on finding her equal. On balance, she was unwilling to forego the freedom that seemed near as her children left her care.

Also weighing against any formal union was Gunn's constant availability without the bonds of marriage. He made another move, apparently for Foltz's sake, in the spring of 1888, when her breach of contract lawsuit against Cogswell for her fee, filed several years earlier, finally came to trial in San Francisco. Rather suddenly, Gunn put himself beyond the jurisdiction of the California courts by departing for Tucson. This allowed his deposition taken by Foltz's lawyer to be read to the jury instead of his giving live testimony.

It also meant that Cogswell's lawyers were unable to cross-examine Gunn on his relationship with Clara Foltz, to undercut his favorable testimony by raising the suspicion that he was her lover. Though Gunn claimed that he had permanently moved to Tucson and would "grow up with the country," he returned to San Francisco shortly after the Cogswell trial ended.[187] He would continue to be in Foltz's life at many critical junctures for the next ten years. Charles Gunn never married.

Lacking Foltz's personal papers and diaries, we cannot know whether the two were in fact lovers. Mrs. Cogswell testified that they were and they looked very much like a couple, especially during their period in San Diego when they worked together in the press war and Gunn often served as Foltz's escort in society. In her last months there, however, Clara Foltz was especially far from settling into a conventional domestic scene. She found a new enthusiasm, Bellamy Nationalism, which promoted a society where men and women enjoyed complete equality free from traditional gender roles. Like many other American reformers of the time, Clara Foltz was ready for that.

UTOPIAN VISIONS IN A BUSTED TOWN: BELLAMY NATIONALISM

Despite the efforts of the faithful who remained, San Diego's promising recovery soon wilted. In the winter of 1889, the town's best asset, its wonderful climate, suddenly turned ugly, with massive floods and cold weather lasting for months. There were even a few small earthquakes along forgotten faults. Undermined by drought that preceded the floods and by the dislocations of the bust, the agricultural base deteriorated further. The railroads, whose rate war had started the boom, now colluded to raise prices so high that farmers could not ship their few surviving crops, and the men who had come to build a great city had no exit. Unemployment and crime were on the rise.

Each day seemed to bring more bad news. In mid-August 1889, the papers were full of the death of Foltz's old friend David Terry. A federal marshal guarding U.S. Supreme Court Justice Stephen Field shot and killed him at a train station near Stockton. Witnesses gave conflicting accounts, with some reporting that the marshal was protecting the justice from an assault by Terry, while others described the shooting as unprovoked.[188] All agreed that Terry was unarmed when his body was searched. On the other hand, he was known to carry a revolver and a bowie knife and had killed many men in duels and wars. Moreover, he had threatened the justice's life if he came to California for his circuit-riding duties because he had ruled against Terry's client (now his wife) in her suit to gain a share of the Sharon estate.

Though she was aware of his faults, Foltz knew Terry as a helpful friend to women's causes. She remembered him as "the gallant knight who championed" the education and employment clauses through the constitutional convention "in his incomparable manner."[189] His violent end, shot down in public, made the news shocking as well as tragic.

Things looked bleak on most fronts for Foltz as she tried to hang on in San Diego despite the bust. Political equality for women was at low ebb, locally and nationally. Foltz blamed "the vast majority of women who do not give a single fig for the privilege of voting."[190] Her law practice was failing as a result of the bad economy and of her representation of unpopular people and causes. Onto this scene, however, came a new movement that inspired Foltz and gave her a fresh intellectual framework for her lifelong commitment to women's equality and social reform more generally. It started with the publication in January 1888 of *Looking Backward: 2000–1887*, a novel by a little-known Boston lawyer, Edward Bellamy. An overnight sensation, the book sold a half million copies at a time when sales of ten thousand was considered an extraordinary success. Only *Uncle Tom's Cabin* eclipsed it during the whole century.

The book pictured a democratically socialist United States in the year 2000, in which everyone contributes to and is cared for by the state, which also owns the major industries, railroads, and means of communication. Every citizen is an equal partner in a national corporation and serves in the National Industrial Army between ages eighteen and forty-five; hence, the name *Nationalism*. In Bellamy's conception, the army would do all society's work, from housekeeping to history teaching. Presenting political philosophy packaged in a romance, the book features Julian West, who falls asleep in the nineteenth century and awakes in the twenty-first. He finds himself among the delightful, if somewhat pedantic, Leete family, including Edith, who has the same name and appearance as his real-life fiancée. New-Edith explains that she plans to marry but that no human should depend on another for basic support, nor should people be in competition for the good things of life. She tells the transfixed young man that the private umbrella is the symbol of the old culture where everyone lived for himself. In the new age, the sidewalks have rollout awnings that protect all alike.

For a few years, Bellamy Nationalism extended its own broad awning over reformers of many stripes, giving them all renewed vitality. On the eve of a major economic depression, facing an ever-widening gulf between rich and poor, many Americans embraced the vision of a new society founded on old principles of universal equality. Women, as "the greatest victims" of the previous civilization, would benefit most. They would be free actors and independent thinkers instead of "ennuied, undeveloped, and stunted at marriage, their narrow horizon bounded so often physically by the four walls of home and morally by a petty circle of personal interests," as Bellamy described the nineteenth-century woman.[191]

Suffragists along with other reformers flocked to the new movement, which spawned clubs all over the country. "California always fertile, blossomed with them," wrote an observer at the time, adding that the state born in a gold rush was "peculiarly addicted to swift enthusiasms." Another contemporary said that a Californian who was not a Nationalist was like "a Kentuckian without a corkscrew." The San Diego branch boasted six hundred members, "including the elite of the intellectuals of the city." Clara Foltz was a founding member and in 1890 the president of the club.[192]

Laura Gordon headed the Nationalists in Lodi, and Addie Ballou, another suffragist, was president of the San Francisco club. A new kind of woman reformer—more concerned with the social than with the political disabilities of gender—also joined the Bellamyite movement. Perhaps the best known of these was Charlotte Perkins Gilman. For a few years, she and Clara Foltz were California's leading Nationalists. Born into the prominent Beecher family, Gilman had left the East and her conventional marriage in the late 1880s. Upon her arrival in postboom Pasadena, she immediately joined the Bellamy Nationalists. Her particular inspiration was the movement's doctrine that every person was entitled to satisfying work regardless of sex or social station. Bellamy's proposal that housework and child-rearing should be professions supported by the state also appealed to Gilman.

Gilman made her living as a writer and lecturer, and her widely read book *Women and Economics* (1898) was an influential elaboration of Bellamy Nationalism. Even more celebrated was her thinly fictionalized account of her own nervous breakdown. *The Yellow Wallpaper* (1892), later recognized as one of the classic works of American feminism, described a young woman driven half-mad by the limitations of her life and the conventional "rest cure" for women, which counseled avoidance of mental activity as a remedy for the special ailments to which the female brain was susceptible. In both works, Gilman denied any innate variation in the abilities of the sexes, arguing that there was no such thing as a "female mind" any more than there was "a female liver."[193]

In her popular Bellamyite lectures, Gilman painted a picture of a collective society founded on sex equality and dedicated to the elimination of greed and competition. Foltz's own egalitarianism, even in this her most radical phase, was more inclined toward equality of opportunity than guaranteed equality of result. She continued to emphasize her longstanding ideal of a level playing field for both men and women and for the children of both rich and poor. There were other differences between these two Bellamy Nationalists born a decade apart. The younger Gilman was openly unconventional in her personal life, cared little for fashion, viewed domesticity and motherhood as burdens, and was contemptuous of the stunted lives of the society women Foltz envied. Foltz and Gilman agreed, however, on Nationalism's proposed method for effecting massive societal change in a civilized way. First, people should reshape the social environment through education and reform legislation. Then, over the course of time, humankind would be gradually transformed, leading peacefully and by consensus to Bellamy's egalitarian utopia. One wag called it socialism with "a silk hat."[194]

Gilman put great emphasis on internal changes in the family, with children raised free from the constraints of traditional gender roles. Foltz was more concerned with the legislative side, where Nationalists supported measures that would alter the relationship of the government to the people: public ownership of railroads and utilities, female suffrage, the referendum and recall, and most importantly for Foltz, free counsel for the criminally accused. Public defense was one of Bellamy's proposed interim reforms for reshaping the social and cultural scene. Bellamy's proposal was to eliminate private lawyers altogether and as such was quite different from Foltz's idea of a public defender. But they both agreed that justice within the criminal system should be free to all as a matter of right and that the combination of volunteers and court-appointed counsel was not working. Bellamy Nationalism brought together Foltz's two main causes: equality for women and publicly financed counsel for the criminally accused. They were to stay joined for her until both were achieved in the early twentieth century by the Progressive movement in California.[195]

Bellamy Nationalism turned out to be a short-lived movement, fading from the scene within a few years without ever developing into a full-fledged political party. But the enthusiasm it engendered helped carry many of its followers, Foltz among them, into the Populist movement and its political arm, the People's Party. The Populists adopted much of the Bellamy legislative platform. Moreover, Nationalism's emphasis on the plasticity of human nature and possibility of bringing about radical social change through alterations in education and family life deeply affected Foltz's political approach for the next decade.

Asked to comment at the opening of a reform school in 1890, for instance, she looked to "the final nationalization of capital" when there would be no chasm between rich and poor and "criminals shall cease to exist among us." She wrote that "the environment of our lives makes us what we are. . . . My spirit groans when I reflect that our great and prosperous State continues to build prisons and insane asylums and spends thousands of dollars annually for the maintenance of them but not a cent for the amelioration of the hard conditions [that drive people to crime]."[196]

LEAVING EL DORADO

Early in 1890, Foltz attended a national convention of reformers in Washington, D.C., and while there, she joined the Supreme Court bar. This time away from daily work and family cares apparently allowed her to reflect on her situation and finally to give up on San Diego. Within weeks of her return from the East, Foltz had sold her Cottage Headquarters. Eleven worthless lots and whatever remained from the $15,000 she made by selling the *Bee* were her only tangible assets from three years of hard work.[197]

As she prepared to leave San Diego, Foltz came to the end of her first decade as a public woman: lawyer, lobbyist, political orator, popular lecturer, and newspaper editor. She had been the first woman in California to serve as a legislative counsel, to prosecute a murder case, and to hold statewide office. At the same time, she had been largely disappointed by her inability to convert her growing fame into a secure financial situation, whether as a lecturer, a publisher, a real estate broker, or—what she really most wanted—a successful lawyer. If only she could make a good living at the law, Foltz felt that her other aspirations to influence political events, and to be a public thinker, would follow. In 1890, she returned to San Francisco for another try at joining the establishment bar.

THREE

Moving on a Larger Stage, 1890–1895

The 1890s

The 1890s marked the end of America's Gilded (not Golden) Age, as Mark Twain caustically named the whole postwar period. Though the decade was called "the gay nineties," the description referred to the extravagance of high society rather than to any pervasive glad spirit. Indeed, the worst depression in the nation's history ripened in 1893 and was marked by violent conflicts between capital and labor, rich and poor. Simultaneously, a great World's Fair in Chicago celebrated the technological and intellectual advances of a century in which the United States had gone from a struggling new republic to the world's most dynamic economy.

As always, Clara Foltz's life mirrored her times. At the World's Columbian Exposition in Chicago, she launched her campaign for a new legal institution, the public defender, which would ultimately become her most important legacy (see Chapter 7). But in the moment, the depression of the 1890s made it even harder for her to earn a living as a woman lawyer practicing on her own. Foltz lamented the growing gap between rich and poor, while wishing she had some wealth or at least some wealthy clients herself.

During the first half of the decade, Foltz fought for unpopular people in the San Francisco courts, promoted the public defender, ran for the office of city attorney, and started a legal organization for clubwomen, the Portia Club. She traveled to the World's Fair in Chicago and across the continent several times, attracting attention and generating positive publicity everywhere she went. It was a life unimaginable to previous generations of women.

Endings

DEATH IN THE FAMILY

The decade started on a somber note with the death of Elias Shortridge. He returned to San Jose from his long sojourn in Arizona where he had fallen ill from what may have been colon cancer. At his bedside were his wife of forty years, and three of his children, Clara, Charles, and Samuel. He was sixty-four years old. Charles Shortridge described the funeral in many columns of the *San Jose Mercury*: the "exceedingly rich and beautiful floral offerings," the pallbearers, the "vast cortege" that followed the coffin.[1]

Rather than scripture, the Unitarian minister read from the best-known nineteenth-century poem on death. "Thanatopsis" by William Cullen Bryant pictured the dying man as one who bravely approached his grave "Like one who wraps the drapery of his couch / About him, and lies down to pleasant dreams." For the rest, the minister relied on the history supplied by Elias Shortridge's children: born and raised in the "free atmosphere" of Indiana, then the western frontier; first a lawyer, then a preacher in the Christian Church, "renowned for his eloquence"; "his acquaintance with Abraham Lincoln, which had a powerful influence upon his character." The minister told of how Elias "went out to battle for existence on the frontiers of civilization. In the mining camps of Arizona, among rough white men and Apache Indians he carried no weapons, but made his way by strength of character."[2]

Foltz would make Elias's story part of her own. In one of her interviews she described him as a "well-known Christian minister" and a man of "power and eloquence" whose "sunny disposition and gifted tongue" had passed on to his daughter. She also shared her father's energy and courage—and his restless impulsivity. Elias had been the first to think she would make a good lawyer and had been her mentor and supporter as she prepared for the bar. He had modeled dedication to the public good and the duty of all citizens to take an "interest in every important question of the day." He had also prefigured her own life of sporadic and unsuccessful attempts to strike it rich.[3]

Six days before he died, Elias Shortridge wrote a will leaving all his worldly goods to "his beloved and ever faithful wife."[4] The probate records show property valued at $5,000 or $6,000 at most, plus unspecified mining claims. (No evidence indicates that any of these panned out posthumously.) Even if the value was underestimated, double the amount claimed was very little to show for a decade in the desert mines.

A few months after her father's death, Foltz set up housekeeping with her mother and children in San Francisco. Telitha Shortridge, widowed at age sixty-three, would live almost twenty more years, most of them with her daughter. "My precious mother," as she always called her, was a constant presence in Foltz's stories, treasured for counsel and support.

Grief for Elias was still fresh when Trella's doctor-husband, Charles Toland, overdosed on morphine that he had taken to ease a neuralgia attack. Trella entered the room as the office boy was trying to revive him. The *Chronicle* reported that she fainted repeatedly before reaching home, where "loving and sympathetic people endeavored to assuage the greatness of her grief."[5] Toland was survived by his son and his wife of just two years. By all accounts, their marriage had been happy and had enabled Trella to live well in one of San Francisco's best neighborhoods. She could have continued in the city as a society widow, and still young and very attractive, might easily have married again. Instead, within months of her husband's death, Trella moved to New York City, where she resumed the acting career she had given up when she married. She took William, a toddler, with her, to the apparent dismay of his Grandmother Toland, who later cut the boy from her will (see Chapter 4). Clara Foltz offered no public reaction to Trella's move, though it seems like the kind of unconventional thing she might have done herself. Later in the decade Foltz would join her daughter in New York in a quixotic attempt to make a career as a corporate lawyer.

There was one other death in the family in 1890: Jeremiah Foltz. Though Clara had claimed to be his widow for almost twenty years, it was not she, but his second wife, Kate, who filed for his Civil War pension. Perhaps his death was something of a relief for Clara Foltz, who could now tell her widowhood story without fear of his inconvenient reappearance.

LAST DAYS AS A DEMOCRAT

Returning to San Francisco in 1890 after three years in Southern California, Foltz found the city far less prosperous than when she had left. Twenty-five thousand unemployed men were on the streets, and this was only the beginning. California was in the vanguard of a nationwide depression even worse than the collapse of the late 1870s, when Foltz had first tried to make it as a lawyer in the big city. As in the earlier period, the hard times were accompanied by political unrest.

After a tour of the state at the beginning of September, Foltz wrote that though she was not by nature "an alarmist," she had found the people of all classes restless and determined that "the bounties of heaven" would no longer be "consumed by greed, and monopolized by theft."[6] She was sharpening her sentences for the coming election. Though 1890 was not a presidential election year, a U.S. Senate seat, the governorship, and the San Francisco municipal offices were up in California. For Foltz personally, the contests offered a chance for her to make some money while she tried to reestablish her law practice. Even though the Democrats had lost the last election, she assumed that her own performance, in which she had drawn huge audiences, would assure her employment as a paid campaign orator again. Moreover, things looked good for the party at the outset of the season.

The reform spirit represented by Bellamy Nationalism and the populist Farmers' Alliance would likely draw support away from the Republicans, who were associated with big business, especially with the Southern Pacific Railroad. Stephen White, the head of the Democrats' progressive wing, entered the race for the U.S. Senate against the incumbent Republican, the railroad magnate Leland Stanford. When Clara Foltz learned of White's ambition, she wrote to him: "How grand, indeed, it would be to have our great state represented for once by a young and capable man," instead of "millionaires and railroad presidents."[7] Stanford was the railroad president, and though he was also a millionaire, she was alluding to the other California senator, Democrat George Hearst. He was an old-guard Democrat, who supported the San Francisco political machine while the party reformers opposed bossism almost as much as railroads and monopolies. Edward Pond, the party's gubernatorial candidate, could not bridge the rift because of his close association with the notorious San Francisco boss Chris Buckley.

Noting the Democratic split, Stanford poured money into the Republican campaign. In the days before direct election, running meant campaigning for a majority in the State Assembly, which chose the senator. "All purchasable newspapers, all purchasable politicians are being called into camp," White wrote a friend in August. Stanford went on the stump himself and hired many of the top political orators as well, including Foltz's old nemesis from San Diego, Tom Fitch, who was paid $5,000 for the campaign.[8]

Despite the accusation of a fellow mogul that he had robbed the stockholders to finance his political objects, Stanford was a popular man in California. He had recently announced the founding of a university as a memorial to his young son, whose early death touched people's hearts. Most disappointing to White's hopes, Stanford's enemies did not help finance the campaign against him.

By mid-September, the Democrats were running aground. Urgently, Foltz wrote to White that the State Central Committee had not scheduled any appearances for her. She offered to take a month off from her practice to speak for the Democrats wherever "a large audience may be had" and assured him that she would charge a reasonable price for her services. But despite her repeated entreaties, Foltz's oratorical services went unused, and the election results were as she predicted in one of her letters. Pond lost miserably, and so did virtually every Democratic candidate. The newly elected Assembly was overwhelmingly Republican (eighty-eight to thirty-one). When asked why his party had failed, Boss Buckley quipped, "I don't know, but I think they didn't get enough votes."[9]

After the 1890 election, Clara Foltz gave up for good on the Democrats. Ultimately, she would return to the Republican Party of her father and brothers, but only after a significant fling with the radical Populists. Before making any new allegiance, however, Foltz turned to lobbying the newly elected legislature for women's rights and penal reform. It helped that she had not been on the campaign trail attacking those she was now entreating.

Beginnings

LOBBYING FOR REFORM

"The legislature of a thousand scandals" was the tag applied within months to the lawmakers who assembled in Sacramento in 1891. Originally purchased by Leland Stanford, they sold themselves many times over to other interests as well. When a hoard of empty currency wrappers was discovered in a wastebasket in the capitol library, no one was either surprised or quite sure who had been bribed for what.[10] Yet despite its sketchy reputation, morally speaking, this legislature was more responsive to Foltz's lobbying for progressive measures than any since 1878 when she had won the right to practice law.

One of her first efforts was a bill to allow parole for prisoners. Like the public defender idea, the proposal sprang mainly from Foltz's experience representing poor people accused of crime. Many clients came to her after being convicted and sentenced to long terms without the help of a good lawyer; some had no counsel at all. Often, the time for appeal had expired and their only hope was executive clemency. Foltz investigated and prepared arguments to the governor for their release.

But in 1887 this last hope for the imprisoned was blocked. The governor's secretary, one Harry Dam, was requiring a bribe to process pardon applications. Foltz told the press of a current case in which she had acquired "unimpeachable evidence" of her client's innocence and even persuaded the judge and jurors of their mistake in convicting. But, Foltz said, she could not present the case to the governor because the client had no money to "fee Dam."[11]

The fact that the pardon process was informal and hidden from public view made it peculiarly subject to corruption of this sort, and also by lawyers who took a prisoner's money and did no work and by governors who paid off supporters or received gifts in return for clemency. The applications for pardons were, moreover, numerous and time-consuming for any conscientious governor to consider. To relieve the governor and also out of concern for the difficulty of administering a prison when inmates were serving excessive and disparate sentences for the same crimes, a special commission recommended a parole system in 1887—the first such proposal in California. But the recommendation had languished for several years before Clara Foltz revived the parole idea at the 1891 legislature.[12]

Foltz's bill differed significantly from the earlier version: her parole board would be composed of citizens, plus the warden and prison doctor, rather than the politically appointed prison directors; she would make all inmates, including murderers, eligible for parole; and she provided for the prisoner's explicit right to a hearing after serving the minimum sentence, or one year if there was no minimum. The *Los Angeles Times* observed that Foltz's proposal might make things "too easy" for the criminal, yet the paper supported it in light of the recurrent scandals with the pardon system.[13]

Though it did not pass either house, Foltz's proposal laid the groundwork for the statute enacted two years later in 1893, and she was credited with "pioneer[ing] the movement for the establishment of the prison parole system in California." When Foltz conceived her statute, only a few states, notably Ohio, had tried anything like it. But the parole movement gained momentum throughout the 1890s. In the new century, the Progressives—drawn by the reliance on penological expertise (the parole board) and by the system's potential to provide more efficient and less expensive criminal justice—took up parole as one of their main prison reforms.[14]

While she was attending the legislature on the parole matter, Foltz had a few other items to promote. She and Laura Gordon continued, without any ultimate success, to petition every session for the vote. They did better on other women's causes, winning, for instance, a measure enabling married women to be executors of estates and thus to look after their own interests when widowed. No doubt, the women lawyers hoped that women executors would hire female counsel. In 1891, the legislature also passed a bill to mitigate the husband's unbounded control of property acquired during marriage. These were reforms that Foltz would list among her achievements until the end of her life.

Even more significant for Foltz herself, however, was the bill allowing women to be notaries public. She had tried to obtain the position in 1877 before she became a lawyer, but the attorney general had ruled women ineligible to serve.[15] Notary, today a minor ministerial office, was an important position in the nineteenth century, with unique statutory powers to administer oaths, authenticate acts and documents, and preserve the sworn testimony of witnesses for trial. The notary seal bore the arms of the state, and there was profit not only in the statutory fees for services, but also in the potential for a lawyer-notary to pick up an underlying legal case. A notary position was especially useful for criminal lawyers because their imprisoned clients could not otherwise sign affidavits in support of their petitions. Foltz knew the need firsthand from her pardon practice.

In California, as in most places, only voters could be notaries. Thus, for woman suffragists, the job became a symbolic step toward full citizenship. The movement press hailed each new woman notary in the same celebratory spirit as it announced women becoming lawyers, doctors, school principals, and voters in school board or municipal elections. Foltz and Gordon had lobbied steadily for a woman notary bill over the years. Opponents made their usual arguments rooted in the unbridgeable gulf between masculine and feminine spheres. Nature had not designed women to wield the notary seal! One man suggested that notaries would come from the "sappers and miners" who supported women's rights, and not from the "rank and file of her delicious, tender, modest and loveable sex."[16]

This time, however, the separate spheres argument did not hold; Foltz's notary bill passed both houses in late February, and she at once started campaigning to be the first woman in the position: "I am as anxious for women as you can possibly be for your administration," she wrote the newly elected Republican governor Henry Markham. Foltz was still officially a Democrat so she added, "You probably know of me, but if recommendation or endorsement is required I refer you to my brothers." Sam and Charles, unlike Foltz, were in good standing as Republicans. She signed herself, "Awaiting the Commission."[17]

Within a week of sending the letter, she "called upon the Governor." A news report (an obvious Foltz plant) added that the state's "leading women" had urged her to accept a notaryship, "so that the law might have a fair trial at the outset." Twice it referred to her "position at the head of the women lawyers."[18] This line of publicity looks like another round in her rivalry with Laura Gordon for "first woman" titles.

It was a hard sell for Governor Markham to give a valuable patronage appointment to a woman, especially one who had so publicly abandoned the Republican Party and stumped for the Democrats in the 1888 national election. Though he signed the notary bill, making it law, shortly after Foltz's visit, he did not appoint anybody to the job. In April, Wells Drury, the proprietor of the *Daily Evening News* in Sacramento, wrote a recommendation for Foltz. Having known her for twenty years, he assured the governor (possibly tongue in cheek) that she possessed "all the Jeffersonian requisites for the office she seeks." Then, in poignant lines for a public record, he wrote that he first met her when she "was a dressmaker in Salem, Oregon . . . working her life out to support herself and her little family. Recognizing the futility of such a struggle against the growing needs of her children, she determined to fit herself for a more remunerative calling, and so devoted herself to study of the law with that end in view. Her subsequent history you doubtless know."[19]

From desperate dressmaker to famous lawyer—this was Clara Foltz's story the way she liked it told. The governor was evidently persuaded, and he signed her commission. Foltz was to be the first woman notary public in California.

NEW POLITICS: THE POPULIST YEARS

After the 1890 state election when the Democrats refused Foltz's services and lost badly on every level, she left the party and made the easy transition to Populism. It was the route taken by many Bellamyites when Nationalism failed to become a viable political movement. The Nationalists fit well into the People's Party, which was another grand mélange of reformers and radicals pursuing disparate causes. Detractors gleefully quoted the (possibly apocryphal) peroration of a Populist orator: "I don't know exactly what we want, but we want it bad, and we want it right now." In their first platform (in

1891), the California People's Party called for government ownership of the railroads, steamship and telegraph lines, free coinage of silver, the eight-hour workday, and woman suffrage. Most of these proposals came straight from Bellamy Nationalism, which had borrowed in turn from earlier movements.

The Nationalist spin on doctrines previously seen as extreme also helped to heal the rift that had developed between organized labor and other reformers over the 1886 Haymarket bombing in Chicago. Seven policemen were killed at a Knights of Labor rally for the eight-hour workday, and though a number of anarchists were speedily arrested, tried, and convicted, the incident cast a long shadow on political association with organized labor. But the Nationalist proposals for universal employment and just compensation coupled with peaceful evolutionary change was a program that liberal reformers and their labor allies could support and take with them into the Populist coalition.

For Clara Foltz the connection with organized labor was entirely congenial. In fact, she had not blamed the Knights of Labor for Haymarket. "No organization of any consequence can exist without some villainous members who unavoidably creep into it," she editorialized in the *Bee*. She compared the Knights to organized Christianity, which had its share of "brutes, bigots and criminals."[20]

At times, Foltz proclaimed herself a working woman, though the label conflicted somewhat with her simultaneous desire for high social status. From her earliest days in California, she had sided with the Workingmen's Party of California. As editor of the *Bee*, she had hired union typographers and assailed the papers that paid below scale. In her legal practice as well, Foltz identified with working-class concerns. "My office was a sort of labor bureau," she said, adding that she often supplied poor women with clothes from her own wardrobe so that they could make a good appearance when applying for work.[21]

Not only as clients, but in her public role as a movement leader, Foltz had relationships with working women that were unusual for a middle-class suffragist. She was associated with Anna Smith, for instance, one of the most radical reformers in California. In the 1870s, Smith had roused thousands on the San Francisco sandlots. She had moved to Southern California during the boom and had become a major Nationalist organizer there. In San Diego for several years, Smith and Foltz appeared on the same platforms and signed up for the same causes.[22] From Nationalism, Smith went on to the Farmers' Alliance and then to organize for the Socialist Labor

Party—all part of the Populist coalition for a time. Though her politics were bold and her speeches were demands, Anna Smith wore a cloak of respectability. Even when she was leading a thousand unemployed men in a protest march to the strains of bagpipes and "La Marseillaise," Smith was described as "stout and shrewd," "not comely, and yet in face, in costume, in manner she seems a worthy country woman."[23]

Clara Foltz's leftist period, when she associated with Anna Smith and went from Democrat to Bellamy Nationalist to Populist, was her most personally active on the political front. In the 1892 municipal election, she ran for city attorney of San Francisco on the People's Party ticket—an ideal job that provided an office, a staff, a salary of $6,500 a year, and no restriction on outside practice or reform activities. For Foltz, it would mean an end to hustling after clients and striving to meet her overhead. Though she had little chance on a third-party ticket in an election in which her chief supporters could not vote, the magnitude of the prize made it worth the run, no matter the odds.

Moreover, the publicity might aid her practice and gain her and the People's Party name recognition for the next election. The press took Foltz's candidacy seriously, treating her on a par with her three well-respected male opponents. A story in the *Examiner* included biographies of each and woodcut pictures of the three men and Foltz, all presented as equally worthy

Newspaper artist's sketch of Clara Foltz when she ran for city attorney on the People's Party ticket. *San Francisco Examiner,* 1892.

candidates. She campaigned mainly on her "long and memorable struggle" to be admitted to the bar and on her "conspicuous efforts over thirteen years to remove the political and legal disabilities of her sex."[24]

But Foltz also ran on issues other than gender. At a large rally, for instance, she supported prizefighting, declaring that urban men had grown "puny and narrow chested" and that fists were preferable to the guns and knives commonly used to settle disputes.[25] It was the kind of stand that might well appeal to a male western electorate. However, a legal obstacle somewhat undermined the credibility of Foltz's campaign. A statute required that government officials, such as the city attorney, be electors. Previously, in San Diego, the same statute had prevented her appointment as a city prosecutor. "The code bobbed up," wrote a supporter at the time, "and said: 'No, Mrs. Foltz, you can't be a deputy because you wear a bustle instead of a cut-away coat.'"[26]

The same statute had also barred women from being notaries until Foltz and her allies won legislative relief from the exclusion in the 1891 legislative session. Foltz argued that a similar statutory amendment was not necessary to make her eligible to serve as city attorney and that she was "confident of taking the position" should she win.[27] Probably, she planned to argue that the 1879 constitutional clause enabling women to pursue any calling or vocation would allow her to serve. It was the same point she had made when Marion Todd was running for district attorney on the Greenback Labor ticket in 1881 (see Chapter 2).

Populism enlivened not only the 1892 campaign in California, but also political contests throughout the country in the presidential election year. As the nation hurtled toward economic breakdown, the major parties had little to offer in the way of platforms, candidates, or campaign excitement. Benjamin Harrison, the incumbent Republican president, had become known as "the White House iceberg." His wife's grave illness—she died two weeks before the election—only added to his personal aloofness and disinclination to campaign. Out of deference to Mrs. Harrison, Grover Cleveland also avoided much speechmaking. Neither man was popular or charismatic, even within his own ranks. One commentator joked that "each side would have been glad to defeat the other if it could do so without electing its own candidate." In terms of issues as well as candidates, the campaign between the major parties was largely a replay of 1888. Both were for the gold standard and tight currency; the Republicans backed a protectionist tariff and the Democrats free trade.[28]

By contrast, the People's Party held a rousing convention in Omaha, Nebraska. A woman activist described it as "a religious revival, a crusade, a Pentecost of politics in which . . . each spoke as the spirit gave him utterance."[29] Their platform had so many radical planks—free coinage of silver, government ownership of railroads and utilities, antiliquor proposals, a graduated income tax, the eight-hour workday, regulation of child labor, and a host of other reforms—that woman suffrage seemed a relatively modest proposal.

The presidential nominee of the People's Party, James Weaver of Iowa, campaigned extensively in California—an unusual move for a candidate of any party at this time. With him was the famous Populist orator Mary Elizabeth Lease (also known as Mary Ellen). They drew large crowds in the south and in the interior of the state, and one night in August, seven thousand people packed the Mechanics Pavilion in San Francisco. Many came to hear Lease especially, because though Californians were accustomed to women on the stump, "the Kansas Pythoness" or "Yellin' Mary," as she was known, had a unique style and persona. Plain talk, forcefully delivered, was her specialty, best shown in her signature line: "Farmers should raise less corn, and more hell." In a voice of "rare power," Lease excoriated the government "of Wall Street, by Wall Street, for Wall Street" and pleaded the case of the wageworker. As a People's Party candidate herself, Foltz may well have been at the rally, though it is far from clear what she made of Lease.[30]

Like Foltz, Lease was the first woman to be a lawyer in her state, Kansas, in 1885. Instead of practicing, however, she was a full-time oratorical agitator. Homely and unfashionable, Lease spoke in the style of a spiritualist trance preacher, hypnotic and apparently extemporaneous. Foltz contrasted with Lease in almost every way, even during her Populist period. Her clothes were beautiful, her speeches memorized, and her manner dignified. She would never have called for the audience to pelt her with silver dollars as Lease did.

The People's Party made an impressive showing in its first national campaign, polling more than one million votes and carrying four states. In California, it won a few offices, but not city attorney of San Francisco, which was taken by the Democratic candidate. Having co-opted most of the Populist issues, the Democrats held on to their reformers, while the Republicans lost a substantial bloc of their party to the Populists. The result was a sweep of state offices for the Democrats, who also delivered the state to Grover Cleveland, the winner in the presidential election. The Democratic reform leader Stephen White finally obtained the Senate seat he had long craved—with the critical aid of the Populist Assembly members, and the providential death of George Hearst, the incumbent who would have fought hard for reelection.[31]

After the 1892 election, Clara Foltz withdrew from electoral party politics for the rest of the decade. She would continue to lobby the legislature for suffrage, and for other reform causes, but not until she stumped for the Republicans in 1900 was she again a paid political orator. Perhaps her shifts of party allegiance had reduced her effectiveness. In any case, Foltz returned full time to her efforts to make a living at the law.

Practicing without Profit

CAPABLE WOMAN VERSUS HARVARD GRAD

Foltz claimed that she had made her "competency" in San Diego—that is, enough capital to allow her to live on the income derived from it. But this seems improbable, given her likely losses from the real estate bust. She returned to law practice full time, apparently hoping to establish a different sort of competency—a steady income from a reliable stream of paying clients. As always, she faced the fact that these sorts of clients were reluctant to risk hiring a woman because the prejudice against her might spill over into the merits of the case. And now there was an additional obstacle as well: one of the major economic depressions in U.S. history was under way. In its wake people had lots of legal troubles but no money to pay a lawyer. Those who could afford counsel were even less willing than usual to take a chance on a woman. The difficulty of Foltz's practice in the 1890s is encapsulated in a story she told, though it revealed more than she probably intended.

Foltz would note the "wide distinction" between a real lawyer like herself, developed by "hard study" and "years of close application," and a novice who had little more than "a brief and often desultory course of reading" resulting in "a mere sheepskin" hung on the "wall of a 2 × 4 office." She illustrated the difference with a courtroom battle between the "capable woman lawyer" (herself) and a male opponent "fresh from Harvard." At the outset of the trial, he delivered an ironic little speech about his inability, "due to his rearing, his prejudices, and his high opinion of the weaker sex," to contend with a woman at the bar. Therefore, he intended to "ignore me as a lawyer" and "treat with me as a woman only." What he meant was uncertain, but he "gallantly waved his hand toward me as if to settle the matter."[32]

Earlier in her career, Foltz had often heard such "a set speech on my sex," meant to undermine her in front of the jury. She had developed an effective response, such as she delivered in an arson case during the mid-1880s to a prosecutor who tried this tactic: "I am a woman and I am a lawyer—and what of it? I came into the practice of my profession under the laws of this state, regularly and honestly. I am not to be bullied out or worn out," and much more in this vein.[33]

In that case, the jury had returned a verdict in her favor without leaving the box. Since then, experienced local lawyers had been less ready to play explicitly on Foltz's sex. But this new man had apparently not been warned. "The young limb of the law as taught at Harvard stated his case very well and announced with a pitying glance at me, 'these facts, gentlemen of the jury, we shall prove beyond the shadow of a doubt' (he needed only to prove them by a preponderance of testimony)." He asked for $30,000 in damages.

Soon, his inexperience began to show. "He seemed unacquainted with his witnesses . . . lost or misplaced his notes . . . and proceeded through a maze of undigested questions, all of which were incompetent, irrelevant and immaterial for any purpose." The Harvard lawyer would finally founder on the law of evidence; he closed his case without introducing the written contract. For a second, Foltz said, she felt sorry for him and his "unfortunate client," and almost corrected his error. But she suppressed this motherly instinct and instead moved for dismissal of the case, which, "smiling wanly," the judge promptly granted, "to the consternation of the lawyer and his disappointed client." The jury crowded around Foltz showering approval, "in cordial recognition of my ability."

Application, experience, and her "quick insight," as she described it, "into the very bottom of a case" were the qualities on which she hoped to build a substantial law practice.[34] Yet her tale of triumph revealed, perhaps inadvertently, how far Foltz was from the kind of established client base that could bring her financial success. She was in the case only because Frank Shay, one of the chief lawyers for the Southern Pacific Railroad, had asked her to substitute for him "upon an hour's notice" while he was busy in another court.

Why did Shay give her the case? Maybe it was actually a petty matter and she exaggerated the damages to make a better story. Maybe he sent her in to hold his place until he could come and present the defense. Whatever the reason, the last-minute referral undercuts the impression that an important lawyer would employ Foltz in a big case. Referral cases, already screened and large enough to share, were the bedrock of a good practice. Foltz would never gain acceptance within the inner circle of the bar, made up of men and only men, who regularly referred cases to one another. Concern about client preference, about her inability to reciprocate, and about the untoward publicity she sometimes generated joined with simple prejudice to keep her out.

CAST ME NOT OUT:
STARKE VERSUS LADY TRUSTEES

Clara Foltz had announced a number of practice specialties in her early years at the bar: probate, divorce, real estate, and solicitor of local and foreign patents. On her return to practice in San Francisco, however, she had apparently resigned herself to being a general solo practitioner, taking what clients she could find, often including those who could not pay for her services, whether out of sympathy, on a contingent fee arrangement, or in the hope of enhancing her reputation by winning cases that attracted attention. Newspapers continued to show interest when she appeared in court, and she was reported in accidental injury cases, commercial disputes, and criminal matters.

Several of Foltz's charity cases from this period take on special importance in retrospect because they influenced her conception and promotion of the idea of a public defender—the greatest accomplishment of her law reform career. One was her challenge to the eviction of Elmira Starke from the Crocker Old People's Home. The home was a charitable institution for the indigent elderly, operated by a board of active society women, the Lady Trustees. They brought suit to evict Starke because, according to their complaint, she "entertained her son, a traveling minstrel, in her room, and brought him food from the dining room. She played quoits with the dishes and kept a light burning in her room after 9:30 p.m. She was disrespectful to the matron and used unbecoming language and was violently disobedient in her actions."[35]

Starke was another friendless woman at odds with the establishment, much like Maria Burton in San Diego. At least in representing Burton, Foltz had some hope for profit if she prevailed against the International Company. But in the Starke matter, all Foltz could win for herself in practical terms was the enmity of an important segment of San Francisco society, at the very time she was trying to reestablish her practice.

Counsel for the Lady Trustees was Charles Hanlon, who had become a lawyer in 1878, the same year as Foltz. Like her, he was a stylish dresser (Foltz called him "the Beau Brummel of the Bar"). In everything else, however, their experience was completely different. After reading law in a prestigious office, Hanlon had joined an established practice and attracted large retainers. His most celebrated cases involved breaking wills before juries, and he made an impressive income defending them as well. The fees he could command made Hanlon justly proud of his pro bono work for the Crocker Home. "Though pressed with professional cares," he was "one of the most sedulous guardians of the welfare of that excellent institution," noted one of his biographical sketches.[36]

In representing Starke against Hanlon, Foltz might have recognized his public service and offered respectful opposition. But the gentle approach to an adversary was rarely her way, and instead she ridiculed and excoriated him for what she felt was a personal attack on her client, Elmira Starke, the "sweet-faced, graceful little old woman," "the old sweetheart," the "old mother." Sarcastically, Foltz made light of the charges. All Mrs. Starke had done was bring an apple and some soda crackers to her son, a penniless minstrel. While she mended his clothes, he "sang Negro songs to his mother," which, though Hanlon charged that it disturbed the peace and dignity of the Crocker Home, "in truth delighted the old folks."

While blaming the other side for making the case "a veritable Jarndyce and Jarndyce"—a reference to the endless lawsuit imagined by Charles Dickens in *Bleak House*—Foltz filed nonstop procedural motions that delayed the court's coming to the merits of the eviction case. She challenged the court's jurisdiction, appealed the decision when she lost on that issue, and renewed her motion to dismiss at least seven times. Then she moved to disqualify the trial judge for bias, claiming that he was "disgusted" with the case because she had been "nagging after" him.[37]

With all this, it was fifteen weeks after the Crocker Home had filed for immediate ejectment of Elmira Starke before the trial started. Foltz would later describe the plaintiffs in the case, the Lady Trustees, as "wives of the ultra rich" whose "gold-mounted, harnessed thoroughbreds" stood outside the court, "a liveried hackney perched on the high seat with whip in hand." He seemed poised to strike at "the old real lady" and "her defiant counsel."

The first day of the trial saw the home administrators and inmates testify to Mrs. Starke's "anarchistic tendencies." Starke then took the stand in her own defense, denied the specifics, and claimed to be the victim of persecution. Wisely, Hanlon declined to cross-examine. He then submitted his case without argument. Any hopes that Foltz would do likewise were dashed when she promised to "make things buzz" the next day.[38]

In what the *Chronicle* called "A Brilliant Oratorical Effort by the Defendant's Fair Attorney," Foltz summed up her case.[39] Her legal position was that inmates who, like Mrs. Starke, had paid the entry fee had a life-time property interest that protected their tenancy in the home. To this she added, as if arguing to a jury rather than to a judge alone, that the Crocker Home had "no moral right" to expel this good old woman. To back up her characterization, she told Elmira Starke's story to the judge in court—and at the same time, to the whole town in the newspapers.

It was a distinctively Californian story. William Starke, from a wealthy family "of Revolutionary fame," had moved to California in 1849 to search for gold. Two years later, his fiancée, Elmira, had "crossed the plains in a prairie schooner behind an ox team" to join him in the "rough mining town of Sacramento." They were married in 1851. The couple was "happy and prosperous" and lived as "acknowledged aristocrats of the pioneers." But an accident in the mines brought an end to the idyll, mortally injuring Wil-liam. As he lay dying, the "high and mighty lords of the Comstock" took advantage of his condition and "squeezed him out" from the "rich deposits" of his mineral holdings. Elmira Starke was left alone and penniless.

"After many heart-breaking attempts to earn her way" by singing and giving piano lessons, Elmira entered the Crocker Old People's Home, with her way paid by the Mispah Club, an organization of musicians. Foltz de-scribed how she "made her room attractive by dainty etchings of her own execution" and a rag rug she sewed from "her wardrobe in the good old days." Justifying her client's "occasional digressions" on the grounds of the "peculiarities of old age" and "constitutional disturbances," Foltz repeatedly quoted the Crocker Home's motto, a verse from the sixty-first Psalm en-graved over its front door:

Cast Me Not Off in the Time of Old Age
Forsake Me Not When My Strength Faileth.[40]

The *Chronicle* reported that Foltz's "picture of the gray-haired defendant, homeless and friendless" and beset by "a host of jealous and domineering persons" had the courtroom in tears.[41] At this point, Hanlon decided that he had better argue the case for his side after all. His legal position was two-fold: Starke was a tenant at will, who could be evicted at the discretion of the trustees; and in any case, she had violated the contract of good behavior she signed upon entering the home.

His emotional appeal was to vindicate the Lady Trustees and disprove the unflattering comparison between them and their alleged victim, the real lady. Foltz remembered that the trustees sat in a row dressed in "the latest spring modes" eagerly listening to Hanlon, who extolled their "virtues, beauty and grace," "ad nauseam," as well as their "self-sacrifice" and the "long suffering patience in their heroic labor of love, etc." In response to the gestures and sneers of the Lady Trustees, Foltz moved to have them expelled from the courtroom.

The judge ruled for the Lady Trustees while complimenting Foltz. "If anyone could have won the case, you would have done so," he said.[42] Foltz was not finished with the battle, however. She brought a new suit against the Crocker Home for the money that the Mispah Club had donated for Starke's benefit. But it had already been refunded, not to Starke but to the club. So Foltz added the Mispahs to her case as defendants "and another merry war was on."

Meanwhile, she took her evicted client to her own home "where my precious mother and family tenderly administered to her every want." The "big wide awake San Francisco dailies," as Foltz called them, followed all her moves, with the happy result that an old friend and mining partner of Starke's husband, who read of her "pitiful story," came to her rescue and installed her in "his fine residence in Oakland, where she lived in comfort amid elegant surroundings." Foltz considered her representation a success because even though her lawsuits failed in court, she created the publicity that ultimately produced this rescuer for her client.

The Starke saga became a favorite in Foltz's repertoire of stories, illustrating her recurrent struggles with "wealth, entrenched behind gold bars and bank vaults" as she represented those who had "neither the courage nor the knowledge necessary to defend themselves."[43] Starke's case formed part of the background for Foltz's ideas about public defense. She saw the protection of the aged, like the defense of the criminally accused, as an important civic function that should not be left to charity administered by lady trustees or to lawyers dragooned into service. Her Bellamyite and Populist convictions increasingly favored a public duty of support and protection for the weak and unpopular.

Principles of personal liberty were involved as well in the Starke case, though perhaps less obviously than in Foltz's campaign for a public defender. She called the Crocker Home "a Bastille" and the residents who testified against Starke "terrified inmates." As she often did in criminal cases, she took upon herself the insults to her client, describing how the fashionable ladies "drew their skirts about them and smiled furtively at the bold assurance of the one woman who was not afraid, not intimidated by their uplifted brows, their pretended aristocracy."[44]

Clara Foltz's career opened her to the slights she felt from society women. Not only did she make her living in the male profession of the law, but unlike some others of the early women lawyers, who confined themselves to giving legal advice and drawing up documents, she was often in the courtroom. In a bruising adversary contest, her sharp wit and relentless pursuit of witnesses made her a great jury lawyer. These were not the qualities, however, of a gentle lady. "What! Kiss a hand which had filed charges, counter charges, demurrers and other vulgar typewritten documents in murder cases, bigamy cases, divorce cases, and other hideous litigation," read an acid little comment in the *Examiner's* society column.[45]

For years, Clara Foltz had tried to maintain a dual status as society lady and professional woman. She announced the day she would receive visitors, just as she advertised her office hours. But living in both worlds was hard and getting harder; her name splashed across the pages of the newspapers representing Elmira Starke against the Lady Trustees was not likely to result in more cards on her salver.

Respite and Reprieve: The World's Columbian Exposition

In the spring and summer of 1893, Foltz twice left her faltering San Francisco practice and went to the World's Fair in Chicago. She attended significant suffrage meetings and the first convention of women lawyers ever held anywhere. Most important, Foltz introduced her public defender proposal on a platform shared with famous male jurists at the fair's Congress of Jurisprudence and Law Reform. The World's Fair helped revive Foltz's reputation and self-confidence at a time of professional and personal struggle. With its atmosphere of optimism and progress, it allowed Foltz again, as she had on her lecture tours, to project her identity as a successful western woman lawyer. It also inspired her with an idea for joining her professional life with her social aspirations in San Francisco. Within months of her return, Foltz would found the Portia Law Club.

Half the population of the United States—twenty-six million people—passed through the fair's electric turnstiles (themselves one of its wonders) between May and September 1893. The visitors came to see the displays in two hundred buildings spread over six hundred acres, with some of the grandest outlined by electric necklaces and reflected in a lagoon plied by gondolas. It was Ancient Rome, it was Beaux Arts Paris, it was Venice, but most of all it was nineteenth-century America.

The first Ferris Wheel was the icon of the exposition, just as the Eiffel Tower had been at the 1889 World's Fair in Paris. Affording a stunning view from 264 feet above the ground, the giant wheel was powered by two engines turning a forty-five-foot axle, advertised as the largest single piece of steel ever forged. For fifty cents, riders entered a plush room about the size of a streetcar and went through three revolutions with a long pause at the top. Two thousand people could ride at once.

Though the sights were astonishing, it was the symbolism of the fair that made it important to the huge crowds in attendance. It marked the reunification of the country after the Civil War and its emergence on the world stage as a great power. The exposition's grandeur was proof of progress—more "in the last fifty years than the previous fifty centuries," said a popular orator, adding: "We live in the best age of history and the most favored portion of the globe. We stand on the summit of time."[46] Some of this was whistling in the dark— the exposition officially opened May 1, 1893, and on May 5 the stock market crashed. Throughout the summer of the fair, banks failed by the hundreds, and businesses went under by the thousands. By the end of August, farmers and factory workers were equally desperate. It was the deepest depression the country had ever experienced. Yet the harder reality pressed, the more hope people found in the gleaming White City on the banks of Lake Michigan.

Detractors criticized the treatment of racial minorities and the offhand role assigned to Native Americans in the celebration of the arrival of Columbus. Others attacked the glorified picture of urban life, the retrograde architecture, the huge amounts expended on the impermanent and extravagant when people were starving in the streets. These points, plus the ill will generated by various personal and political jealousies, dimmed the fair's radiance. Yet even the severest critics attended the fair. There was no other way to experience it—no radio, no moving pictures, no long-distance telephone (the last was a futuristic exhibit in the Electricity Building). Despite the depression, often at great sacrifice, people got themselves to Chicago in 1893. "Sell the cookstove if necessary and come," wrote the young realist author Hamlin Garland to his parents on their Nebraska farm.[47]

Every state had its own exhibition hall, and California's gigantic mission-style building was the scene of many programs and celebrations. The timing of her visits to the fair is such that Foltz may have been at the California exhibit on the opening day when the crowd spotted a celebrity they had yet to hear. "A call of 'Douglass! Douglass!' went up," and the famous black abolitionist, orator, and statesman Frederick Douglass stepped forward and praised California's free beginnings and "that spirit in her people which could invite him from the audience to the platform in recognition of the brotherhood of man."[48]

Some of Foltz's closest female friends were involved in the California exhibit. The journalist Frona Wait was on both the state and national planning commissions. Madge Morris's poem "Liberty's Bell" was widely celebrated at the fair. It told of a bell "Built of the treasures of fond human hearts" to celebrate freedom. A campaign to make such a bell for the fair gathered thousands of relics, some from historical figures, including Jefferson Davis's keys, John Brown's pike heads, Lucretia Mott's fruit knife, Abraham Lincoln's door hinges, Thomas Jefferson's kettle, and 250,000 pennies from schoolchildren.

Another ceremony that Foltz may have attended, when she was at the fair in late August, celebrated Morris's poem and honored all California writers. It was organized by Ella Cummins, an assiduous chronicler of California authors. The exhibit included Foltz's own favorite western writer, the mordant Ambrose Bierce, who characteristically wrote Cummins that he was "not convinced the best thing you can do for California literature is to call attention to it."[49]

For Foltz, the fair opened a new world where suffragists, social activists, society ladies, entrepreneurs, actresses, journalists, and literary figures mingled freely. When she saw Susan B. Anthony embrace Bertha Palmer, the Chicago socialite and national organizer of women's fair participation, Foltz must have believed that the clash between professional and society women that had frustrated her in San Francisco was not inevitable. Returning home after the fair, Foltz designed a new project to break down these barriers.

The Portia Club

FOUNDING PURPOSES

Within months of returning from her August fair visit, Foltz announced her project for bringing together the establishment ladies and the movement women: the Portia Law Club. In Chicago, Foltz probably learned about the new women's clubs that were being organized there and in eastern cities combining law study with charitable work. As Foltz described it, the aim was to attack the "poverty and distress" that resulted from women's "ignorance of the most common legal principles." Though such ignorance afflicted all classes of women, Foltz intended to start by training the upper crust, who then could presumably pass it along to others. "[A] number of society ladies, who are anxious to learn something about the management of property have submitted their names for admission," said one paper. The club held a weekly class on subjects like remedies and wills, and a bimonthly open lecture on current political issues.[50]

Among the leisured women in San Francisco, Foltz found widespread longing for learning and chafing at conventional gendered restrictions. Rich ladies could easily become virtual prisoners in their own houses, held there by hostess duties and the lack of any acceptable places for them to go in public. Although the restaurants and theaters were more open to San Francisco women of all classes than those in eastern cities, there was still little night life for upper-class women.

It was an exhilarating experience just to leave home for a few hours late in the day, unaccompanied by a male escort. Attending a law lecture had the special appeal that it challenged the widespread belief that women's minds were naturally intuitive, but not suited to logical thought. These innate differences supposedly fitted the sexes for their separate public and domestic spheres. Looking back on the 1890s, one San Francisco society woman would later observe "that the feminine intuition we heard so much of was no more than subconscious cerebration, conscious cerebration being discouraged in women."[51]

From the outset, Foltz required serious commitment from her ladies; she specified that "chatting will be restricted to the complications of promissory notes and the technicalities of Blackstone." The Portia Club was for "women's benefit and not for their amusement."[52] She also demanded prompt attendance at scheduled sessions, a change for the socialites, who specialized in dramatic late entrances.

Though the Portia Club was not explicitly a suffrage organization, the *History of Woman Suffrage* described it as an important contributor to the cause. For women to study law was in itself a political statement, partly because it was obviously good preparation for exercising the franchise and participating in government. Foltz said that the weekly classes were a first step toward a "law college" for women, which she was certain would attract students from all parts of the country. Acknowledging that many law schools were now coeducational, including Hastings by her own effort, Foltz made the case for all-female legal education. At the previously male schools, she said, a woman was "like a skeleton at a feast," who "feels that both professors and students wish she were not there."[53]

The club was a great thing for Clara Foltz, providing not only a title (dean of the Portia Law College), but also a potential source of income and clients and a way to keep her name favorably before the public. Its appeal to society women helped repair the damage she had done by portraying them as thoughtless aristocrats in the Elmira Starke case. So many of the prominent ladies in town were trustees of the Crocker Old People's Home, or had friends who were, that Foltz had found herself "ostracized and ignored by the so-called best people" after that trial.[54] She was apparently never asked to join the Century Club, for instance, even though it was prosuffrage and reformist. Of course, she was ineligible for the Pacific Association of Collegiate Alumnae, another prestigious women's organization established after the World's Fair. It was like Foltz to start her own club in these circumstances and to mold it to serve her professional and social purposes. Remembering her rejection at the start of her career by the San Jose legal club, she must have especially enjoyed having her own exclusive and much-publicized organization in the big city.

Not the least of the opportunities she found in her club was a chance to express her interest in appearance and ceremony. Foltz designed a special costume for club members: neither the split skirt of the dress reformers nor her own exquisitely tailored court suits, but "Portia gowns and caps," "striking costumes" as one headline had it.[55] They looked like academic robes and mortarboards and had the virtues of a uniform, putting all the women on an equal plane.

And what would the dean of the Portias wear? "A cardinal plush gown, trimmed with ermine and a cardinal mortarboard."[56] She had left school at age fourteen without graduating and then had faced the frustration of her efforts to obtain a law degree. Now Foltz presided over the Portia Club in full academic regalia.

The newspaper stories about the club often discussed the dress of the participants as much as the content of their programs. This was especially true on the night of a public lecture in 1894 when Foltz announced that the ladies in the audience would remove their hats, countering the custom that women must cover their heads in public. As a matter of modesty, a hat both hid the flowing hair and shadowed the face. But when women started emerging into public forums, their headwear became a constant irritation, especially during the 1890s when fashion dictated large hats to set off the immense padded shoulders and wide sleeves that were also the rage.

Though the hats blocked both sexes, Foltz promoted removal as a gift "to show the men they have some rights." She put it this way to coax women who clung to their headgear, partly because it was not easy to take off a Victorian hat—anchored with pins into hair combed to hold. Foltz assured the audience in advance that "maids will be in attendance to assist in the removal."[57] The Portia robe and the hat stories capture the drama and fresh interest Foltz stirred while seeming at the same time a little silly. Of course the real reform would be for women to go without hats, or to wear ones that did not require removal by a maid. In its programs also, Foltz's Portia Club was a mixture of society theater and high-minded purpose.

THE PORTIA SEASONS

Instead of semesters, the nascent law college was to have "seasons" of classes, lectures, and social affairs. This unorthodox academic calendar might allow the evolution of the Portia Club into the Portia College of Law by imperceptible steps. On occasion, Foltz would combine all three modes in a single evening. Thus, for the end of the first Portia season (January–June 1894), Foltz held a reception at her home. After the World's Fair she had moved to Van Ness Avenue, the newest location for the social elite. Though it did not feature the fabulous mansions of Nob Hill, or even the fading grandeur of Rincon Hill and South Park, the avenue's tree-lined streets and graceful Victorian homes made it a fine neighborhood where judges, bankers—and now one lady lawyer—had their domestic establishments.[58]

Foltz's press had previously stressed the attractions of her office—always in a fine building and featuring a great library. In the post-fair period, stories mentioned her home more often. At the Portia reception in June 1894, her "parlors were adorned with charming floral decorations," and members mingled with a "number of prominent members of the bar." The occasion mixed the musical numbers and recitations common at social gatherings with the delivery of "the Dean's report," followed by a lecture on partnership law by a distinguished male attorney.[59]

Resuming for their second season in the fall, the Portias held a public lecture and fund-raiser to furnish their clubrooms and to fit one of them out as a moot court room. "Many lawyers" and "most of the Judges in town had invested in $5 worth of the Portia pasteboards," noted one paper.[60] In their enthusiasm, however, the Portias sold three times as many tickets as the hall had seats. After some initial fluster and drawing up of chairs in the corridor, Dean Foltz introduced Rabbi Voorsanger of Temple Emmanuel, presenting him with the costly gift of the complete works of Thomas Carlyle. Though a popular speaker, he was an odd choice for the Portias because of his anti-suffrage views. Probably, Foltz was willing to put aside politics to assure a good turnout and an interesting lecture, and the rabbi provided both.

Provocatively, he attacked the club's Shakespearean namesake from *The Merchant of Venice*, arguing that Portia was neither heroine nor ideal. Her treatment of the Jew Shylock revealed her cruelty, and her false assumption of the identity of a lawyer showed her dishonesty. In response, Foltz rose in her crimson dean's regalia and "very dramatically" recited Portia's speech on the quality of mercy, which not only justified her as a model for women students of law by its eloquence, but also by its content sought to excuse the faults emphasized in the rabbi's condemnation.[61] She also said she had chosen the name because Portia was one of her favorite Shakespearean char-acters—and, of course, the press often called her the "Portia of the Pacific." So the planned Portia Law School, like the Portia Club, would in effect be named after herself.

Not everyone agreed with Foltz's program for the Portia Club, especially not with the emphasis on externals of dress, the focus on co-opting society ladies and antisuffragists, and the absence of the kind of charitable activity that characterized women's law clubs in other places. There was a schism right after the club was founded, and for awhile two groups in San Francisco called themselves the Portia Club. But Foltz's group received the press atten-tion, and for her personally, it was one of her main activities during the year and a half she spent back in San Francisco after the Chicago World's Fair.

THE PORTIAS GO TO COURT:
THE MARTIN WILL CASE

In addition to lectures and lessons at Foltz's office, the Portia Club regularly attended court trials—a movement tactic pioneered by the San Francisco suffragists. Twenty years earlier they had made headlines with a mass turn-out for the trial of Laura Fair for shooting Alexander Crittenden, a distin-guished lawyer and her adulterous lover.[62] Their point then was to protest her judgment by an all-male jury and to relieve the heavily male atmosphere of the courtroom.

Clara Foltz agreed with the need for women to attend court in order to support the woman litigant, whose situation she described to the Portia Club: "faced by a male judge, flanked by a male jury, surrounded by male lawyers . . . with a male clerk and bailiff and a mob of male bipeds in the lobby. . . . A woman, especially if she is a timid one, is at a terrible disadvantage in such a place."[63] Foltz knew firsthand what it was like being the only woman in the courthouse.

As court attendance evolved into a suffrage strategy, the justification went beyond a show of support to become an assertion of women's citizenship as well. It was also a way to prepare women for future participation in the legal system as lawyers, judges, and jurors. Along the same line, Foltz wanted her Portia Club members to share the common experience of lawyers and law students who drop in to court to observe and to learn from each other.

Women's regular court attendance stirred up a good deal of opposition. Courtrooms were places where men engaged in a thinly veiled substitute for physical conflict and where widely shared male understandings about fairness, justice, and mercy prevailed. The presence of women would change these things in subtle and unpredictable ways. Critics said that courtrooms were rough and the evidence often unfit to be heard in mixed company; no proper woman would want to attend, just as good wives and mothers did not wish to go to the polling places. But Foltz told her Portias that "the more unpleasant the revelations," the greater the duty of women to act "courageously" by offering their presence.[64]

In the summer of 1894, the Portias led a large group of women to witness a will contest trumpeted in the press as one of the greatest legal battles in the history of San Francisco. At stake was the fortune left by Henry Martin, owner of the famous Big Bear gold mine. Henry's widow offered a will in which she inherited everything. But her sister-in-law, the widow of Henry's brother, John, presented a later will in which Henry left a third of the estate to her son, Baby John. The question was why a man would leave so much to his nephew. The difficulty of Mrs. John's case was that the obvious answer cast doubt on Baby John's paternity and on her chastity.

Representing Mrs. John Martin was Grove Johnson, Foltz's old ally in the fight for the Woman Lawyer's Bill in the State Assembly. Now he was a rich and successful railroad attorney, though he continued to support political equality for women—his last progressive cause. Delphin Delmas was Mrs. Henry Martin's lawyer. Born in France, educated at Santa Clara University and Yale, Delmas was the best-known lawyer in the West. Apparently without compromising his credentials as a devout Democrat and political man of the people, he had made a fortune from law practice.[65]

The two men were in their fifties, at the top of their form, "two intellectual giants, both brilliant, both learned, both scholars, both struggling for the mastery in an almost even contest," as Foltz told the Portia Club.[66]

In appearance, Johnson was a dandy, with highly polished leather boots to the knee, a frock coat, and fresh boutonnière. His hair and beard were long and carefully tended. Delmas was balding and clean-shaven, rumpled and unprepossessing, his elegant speech a contrast to his exterior. In style, Johnson was forceful, almost fierce at times; Delmas was more polished and painstakingly prepared.

For three months, the case was tried before large crowds that the *Call* described as made up of "lawyers and women."[67] Dozens of witnesses appeared on each side and every day seemed to bring something unexpected and much that was scandalous. Documents disappeared from the clerk's office, and if found, were in altered condition; letters ruled inadmissible were splashed over the newspapers; both lawyers courted citation for contempt as they continued arguing or pursued inquiries the judge had just forbidden.

Instead of having Mrs. John shame herself by testifying to an affair between herself and Henry, Johnson relied on innuendo from witnesses who had seen the two together at late hours and inappropriate places. He also counted on the heart-winning presence of Baby John. Still in dresses, with long curls, merry blue eyes, and "cheeks like wild roses," he was in court every day.[68] Even Delmas extended a finger for Baby John to play with as the press avidly observed.

The appearance of Baby John's mother was not such a courtroom success. Members of the press all agreed that she looked overly cool and criticized her for the extravagance of her dress in contrast to the real widow, who was still in heavy mourning. Johnson did not call Mrs. John as a witness, which saved her from facing Delmas's cross-examination, while suggesting that under oath she would have revealed her affair with Henry Martin. No sooner had Johnson rested his case, however, than Delmas himself summoned Mrs. John Martin to the stand as a hostile witness. Johnson objected, and several days of legal arguments followed on the scope and shape of her proposed testimony and the relevance of Baby John's paternity to the authenticity of the will. The judge ruled that Mrs. John would have to testify, and the dramatic climax of the trial followed.

With soft insinuation rather than direct attack, Delmas set out to show that it was not clear whose baby Mrs. John had. He questioned her about other men she had targeted as the boy's father and even intimated that she had picked up the boy in a foundling home to use for this purpose. Mrs. John was a nightmare on the witness stand. She argued with the questions, refused to answer, flounced out of the courtroom and slammed the door, hectored the judge, and ended by screaming at Delmas that he had a few illegitimate children of his own.

As the testimony wound down, court watchers agreed that the case would turn on the closing arguments. Foltz anticipated the moment for the Portias: "Who would not love to listen to the great Delmas and the brilliant Johnson . . . the learning and the logic in this intellectual clash of arms. . . . They throw a subtle spell upon their auditors, who are breathless at the encounter and almost drunk with the enthusiasm."[69] The summations lived up to her advance billing.

Grove Johnson was first. He handled the central flaw of his case—the immorality and offensiveness of Mrs. John Martin—by focusing exclusively on Baby John. "The boy, the boy," he cried repeatedly, "we are fighting for the boy." Even giving Baby John his share would leave the childless Mrs. Henry Martin with more money than she could spend in her lifetime. In an astonishing finale, Johnson fell on his knees and pleaded for "the weak, helpless, innocent child." The men in the jury box reportedly wept.[70]

On the day set for Delmas to argue, the courtroom was even more crowded than usual, with women outnumbering men three to one. The *Examiner* reported that the women took advantage of the men's courtesy, as they "muscled their way to the front . . . in order to hear what Mr. Delmas would say about Mrs. John Martin [and] how Mrs. John Martin would take it." Johnson had warned the jury: "Beware of Delmas! Beware of his sarcasm, his irony, his sophistry, his vituperation, and his powers of eloquence." But Delmas displayed none of these qualities. Rather, he spoke slowly and precisely, avoiding drama and oratory. One paper reported that within a half hour, the jury "unbended a bit and appeared a trifle interested in what he had to say about wills and forgeries."[71]

In dealing with the testimony, Delmas employed a gambit that other lawyers admired, but that few dared imitate. He told the jury that his quotations from the witnesses would be "accurately, mathematically and literally correct."[72] To assure this, he asked Mrs. John's lawyers to interrupt him if he made any misstatement. Of course, if they did, it would only emphasize the adverse evidence, but if they didn't, their silence looked like acquiescence in everything that he said.

For three days Delmas proceeded to pick apart the testimony. The *Examiner* described him as answering "his adversary's brilliantly marshaled periods and tremendous force" with "cold, hard, masterful reasoning." Not until the last day of the argument did Delmas change his style, when he turned his attention from the testimony to Johnson's summation. Scornfully, he portrayed Grove Johnson as begging a verdict in the way "a maimed mendicant on the street, on bended knees, asks for alms. Shame! In an American court an American lawyer, addressing American freemen, goes upon his knees—whines and cries for a verdict. I shall treat you like men, not like grannies. I shall shed no tears. I shall deliver no address to a hired crowd of claquers who can be duplicated from any theatre. I shall appeal to your sense of justice not to your passions and emotions."[73]

Delmas's advocacy, helped along by Mrs. John's disastrous performance on the stand, carried the day. The judge's instruction favored his side, and the jury was back with a verdict for Mrs. Henry Martin in two hours. But the verdict did nothing to settle a dispute over court attendance by women between Clara Foltz and the presiding judge that had come to a head in the last weeks of the trial.

CLARA FOLTZ ROASTS JUDGE COFFEY

James V. Coffey, presiding judge of the probate court, had a reputation for being calm and judicious, but the Martin case tested his patience. Battered by the two powerful advocates, each willing to risk citation for contempt to make his case, he was also upset by the women spectators who filled virtually all the seats and made him uncomfortable in his own courtroom. The Portia Club members behaved appropriately, but other women spectators were not under Foltz's tutelage and did not understand what was expected of a courtroom audience. They applauded, gasped, and cried out. At one point, the jurors complained that the women were "constantly making comments about the evidence." Even when silent, they expressed themselves by "the most contemptuous smiles and head shakes." If the entertainment value lagged, they whispered and even dozed.[74]

While the potentially scandalous testimony of Mrs. John was pending after Delmas called her as a witness, the judge warned: "I would advise the ladies, and those of lady-like quality, not to attend court for the next few days though they can, if they insist, exercise their rights as American citizens, but I think ladies will hardly come here."[75] The women took his advice for a day or two during the legal arguments leading up to the testimony, but they were back in force when Mrs. John took the stand.

Women out of control, his courtroom out of control, Judge Coffey gave a press interview excoriating females as clients and court spectators. He did not limit his angry litany to Mrs. John; all women clients were suspicious, unreliable, unreasonable, and ungrateful. As to women spectators, they were "vulgar-minded" because they continued to attend the Martin trial even though they knew the testimony was not fit for them to hear.[76] These comments were potentially a serious blow to women's court attendance in general, and the judge seemed on the verge of throwing them out immediately.

Foltz acted at once to prevent their missing the long-awaited jury summations. Counterattacking, she organized a special Portia Club program to blast back at the judge for what he had said during his interview. In what was inevitably described as a roast of Judge Coffey, Foltz arraigned and tried him before a large public audience at the St. Nicholas Hotel. Sixty Portia Club members dressed in mortarboards and robes were in the front row; behind them were women in evening dress; and finally, there were "a few bold men who hovered around the entrance."[77] Reporters were invited, and their stories, including artists' renderings, filled many newspaper columns the following day.

The rooms were decorated with flowers, American flags, and greenery. After a musical introduction, "all eyes turned toward the central entrance. Through the door marched Mrs. Foltz preceded by a boy bearing a lamp, her face flushed with excitement, looking particularly bright in her red, red robes. Her appearance was greeted with cheers and the ex parte proceedings began." Foltz opened by observing that three types of men took the normal "badinage, wit and raillery" between the sexes too far: young ignorant men, old bitter men, or "bachelors who never had a soul big enough to capture the heart of a loving woman." The reference was obvious; Judge Coffey was forty-eight years old and had never married. She added that he was especially unqualified to talk about female clients since a search of the court records showed that he had represented only one woman in his whole career as a private lawyer.[78]

By contrast, Foltz said she herself had more than three hundred women clients, and she testified that, with the exception of two who had mental problems, they were all exemplary. Continuing the personal attack, she mocked the judge's previous career, portraying him as occupying a desk in a lawyer's office, but since no clients came to him, not actually practicing at all. Most seriously, Foltz found the judge too prejudiced to preside in cases in which women were concerned. She suggested that if he had made the same remarks about Germans that he had about women, no German person would wish to appear before him. Finally, she said that since women were involved in many cases as witnesses and litigants, Judge Coffey should probably give up presiding and "confine himself to the clerical work of the probate department, for which he seems well fitted."[79]

After intimating that the judge had customarily approved excessive fees for his bar cronies, and suggesting that the voters reject him in the coming election, Foltz turned to a defense of women's attendance as spectators at court. It served, she said, the honorable purpose of allowing them to gain "broader culture in legal matters and more practical knowledge of the machinery of justice." She concluded by calling for the "universal condemnation" of Judge Coffey. "Mrs. Clara Foltz Makes a Cutting Reply"; "The Ladies Do Him Nice and Brown; Mrs. Foltz Real Sarcastic," read the headlines in the *Call* the next day.[80]

Perhaps Foltz's reaction was disproportionate to Judge Coffey's offense. On the other hand, his statements in the interview were seriously improper and a threat to her project of educating women to be citizens. She won a victory, but as usual it was at some cost to herself. After the Portia Coffey roast the judge never again went on record against women in the courtroom. Nor did he ever give Clara Foltz any of the lucrative work of administering estates that was under his control.

Post–World's Fair Law Practice

MORE PRACTICE REALITIES

Over the years Foltz gave varying accounts of her finances, sometimes boasting "of substantial fees from those who were able to pay liberally for my forthright way of handling their business." At the same time, she said she was psychologically unable to ask for the "enormous" sums a man would demand for the same case. She also lamented that "when I received a large fee I had neither experience nor business judgment to guide me in its management."[81]

The picture seems to be one of extremes—times she was flush with a big fee and ready cash and others when she lived on credit or aid from her brothers, or headed out on a lecture tour to save face and earn the overhead. Foltz was always in search of clients and hoped that other women especially would not be prejudiced against her. She did represent a lot of women over the years, but few brought large retainers. Rich women had male protectors and advisors who selected prestigious male attorneys for them while Foltz represented the likes of Maria Burton, Arvilla White, and Elmira Starke on contingency or for no fee at all. After the World's Fair, she redoubled her efforts to attract the business of wealthy women—and no doubt part of the appeal of the Portia Club was its potential for developing new clients from among the society ladies who joined.

In a more direct approach, Foltz wrote to Jane Stanford, recently widowed by the death of her rail magnate husband, offering her services—not so much "in my own interests," so she said, as in "woman's cause." She noted that both her brothers were prominent Republicans (the late Leland Stanford's party) and added that her offices were accessible and "well appointed." At the same time Foltz wrote to one of Mrs. Stanford's male advisors: "A woman lawyer must press herself and her abilities . . . that she may rise to her proper place. . . . Recognition from Mrs. Stanford would commend me to the whole world." There is no record of an answer to either letter.[82]

"You know somewhat of my public life, and of my success," Clara Foltz could write to Jane Stanford, who undoubtedly did know because Foltz continued to generate abundant, largely favorable publicity, no matter how her finances were faring. A typical piece several months after the fair noted her appearance: "well-proportioned, graceful in pose, artistic in attire and strikingly intelligent in features." It also extolled her professional skills in the style of a paid publicist today: "her quick insight into the very bottom of a case, her ready perception of its essence, her tacit handling of disagreeable facts, her ready repartee, grace and eloquence." Concluding that she had earned "the title Portia of the Pacific," the article said she had enjoyed "phenomenal success in all her cases."[83] But even with good press like this, and the boost to her reputation from her prominent place at the fair as well as the success of the Portia Club, Foltz apparently continued to struggle through the mid-1890s in her effort to live by her law practice alone. Something close to desperation appears at work in what in better circumstances might have been a highlight of her career—the only case she brought to the U.S. Supreme Court.

This was the appeal of Alfred "Nobby" Clarke, who had been the clerk to the San Francisco police chief when Foltz first started practicing. He accumulated a fortune over several decades in that job, mainly by lending money at usurious rates to police officers. On the more respectable side, Clarke compiled several useful books of statutes on extradition and on naturalization law. Eventually, he became a lawyer himself. Like many others, Nobby Clarke fell on hard times during the financial depression of 1893, and his creditors forced him into state law insolvency proceedings. Ordered to produce a schedule of his assets, he refused, was held in contempt of court, and was imprisoned until he complied. A *Chronicle* sketch artist showed the sixty-year-old man sitting on a mattress in his underwear with his clothes hanging on nails around him, writing poetry.[84]

After unsuccessfully seeking a writ of habeas corpus from several state trial judges, Clarke appealed all the denials to the U.S. Supreme Court. The accompanying brief was a hundred or so jumbled pages assembled without any attention to the Court rules governing format, without a coherent statement of any issue of federal law that might form the substantive basis for the appeal, and without any specification of the "final" state court judgment appealed from—a prerequisite for Supreme Court jurisdiction. The Court dismissed the appeal after several irritated paragraphs attempting to sort out the "mass of confusion" created by the papers that had been filed.[85]

Clara S. Foltz was listed as the attorney on the cover of the brief. She had joined the Court bar on a trip to Washington, D.C., in 1890, the fifth woman to be a member, and was proud of the credential, which was unusual for a western lawyer. Presumably, she was simply paid for the use of her name as a member of the Court bar, and Clarke wrote the disgraceful brief himself; it bears no resemblance to her usual professional work.

She may even have been well-paid; rumor had it that Clarke fought so hard to hide his assets because he still had his fortune. That Foltz would compromise her legal reputation in this way is a mark of her hard-pressed situation. In 1895, she became involved in a case that further undermined her ability to attract paying clients. The record shows it as her last jury trial in San Francisco.

CAST ME NOT IN:

VON SCHMIDT V. THE HOME FOR INEBRIATES

Though Clara Foltz never made a consistent good living as an attorney, she did become an accomplished jury lawyer. The newspapers in the early 1890s have many examples of her prowess. None of these show her handling lucrative cases, however. Foltz is not on record as counsel in a contested will case (a California favorite) or a disputed land title (another western specialty) or a contractual dispute between wealthy people. Mostly, she went before juries on behalf of poor people either accused of crime or caught in some conflict that did not involve money.

Typical of her practice was the case of Alfred Von Schmidt, who came to her as an escapee from the Home for Inebriates. When he appeared in her office, the young man was badly beaten, "his eyes blood-shot, his front teeth gone, a raw scar upon his cheek." Years later, Foltz remembered her shock: "the Starke case had taught me the depths to which women could descend," but "the outrages committed by men upon young Alfred von Schmidt were horrible beyond belief." She determined to "expose and abolish" the Home for Inebriates.[86]

Before she filed suit, Foltz decided to get the press involved and the public on her side. She went to "the *Examiner* boys" as she called them, "as wise and kindly a bunch of good fellows as ever did service upon a great daily newspaper," and hatched a plan to place a fake inebriate in the home. It was the kind of stunt the *Examiner* had often pulled since William Randolph Hearst had become editor in the late 1880s. A poorly dressed woman reporter would pretend to faint on the street, for instance, to check out emergency services, or a male reporter would throw himself into the sea to test the ability of the lifeguards. Several of the *Examiner* staff could easily have passed as seasoned inebriates, but the editors chose Albert Munson, a prohibitionist, who according to Foltz "had never indulged in so much as a glass of beer." Munson poured a bottle of whiskey on himself, and a friend posed as a relative delivering him to the home and paying for a week in advance.

After six days, he wrote a stunning exposé of the place, claiming that the treatment would drive a perfectly sane person mad.[87] Soon after the *Examiner* story appeared, Von Schmidt, who had been recaptured, was released. A few months later, again to well-arranged publicity, Foltz filed a civil suit against the home for false imprisonment, claiming $100,000 in damages. It looked for awhile as if one of her do-gooder suits might actually generate a handsome fee on contingency.

In February 1895, with extensive publicity, the suit went to trial. E. D. Sawyer, a distinguished lawyer who served on the board of the home, represented the defendants. He was a native of New Orleans who had practiced in California since the gold rush. Known for his stories of mining camp justice, where court was held under an oak tree from which the defendant would hang if he lost, Sawyer was soft-spoken and slow moving, though eloquent in his own way.[88] The papers made much of the contrast in style with Foltz, who was quick, voluble, and full of fiery indignation.

In her attack on the absence of factual inquiry before a person was imprisoned in the home, Foltz subpoenaed a police officer to show that even the public insane asylum—not generally the model of due process—required a warrant from a judge before it would accept an inmate. Sawyer objected that there was a written statute governing the asylum. Foltz was quick to respond: "And the Home for Inebriates operates according to no law at all."[89] All observers, and presumably the jury, scored one for the woman lawyer.

The plaintiff-victim, looking very sober and entirely sane, testified to his barbarous treatment. He said his father had committed him and explained the bad blood between them in biblical terms: he was Esau to his brother's Jacob, and the old man had been unduly influenced in preferring one son over the other. Generally, Foltz's case went well, with Von Schmidt's wife and friends testifying effectively to the seriousness of his injuries and to his sobriety.[90]

Things took a turn, however, when the defense called its first witness: Colonel A. W. Von Schmidt, Sr. Sorrowfully, the handsome old man told the jury that his son had become dangerous because of a brain fever. He said that the Home for Inebriates was the only place that would take him in his condition. On cross-examination, Foltz started well enough by establishing that young Alfred was sober and temperate—which the father freely admitted. Probably, she should have stopped there.[91] But Foltz pressed him further, causing the witness to rise from his chair and declare: "Now, Mrs. Foltz, once for all let us come to the facts. I did this thing because my son was insane and I believed it for his good." Drawing himself to his full height and looking like the old warrior he was, Von Schmidt added: "And I say now that I am not ashamed of what I have done. I am glad that I had the backbone to do what was right."

Then for a few moments, as the scene was reported, lawyer and witness abandoned roles and stood facing each other, arguing heatedly—as people, as parents, about what was right in the situation. Clara Foltz finally remembered herself and resumed her professional character: "You are aware, Colonel, that I am an attorney-at-law?" The colonel responded with a straightforward statement of the prejudice that Foltz had faced so often in the courtroom: "Yes, but I am free to say that I don't believe any woman should be an attorney at law." This produced "a roar of laughter," and "Mrs. Foltz for a moment looked nonplussed," but she quickly recovered and asked whether Colonel Von Schmidt "did not think it her professional duty to champion the cause of an injured client." He replied that she should have come to him first to learn the truth and complained that she and the *Examiner* were "trying to stir up trouble in my family."

The colonel then vented his resentment over an earlier patent suit she had brought against him. Foltz had represented his brother, who was the plaintiff in the case; young Alfred had been a witness for the uncle. "That was another case I told you was a fraud," he said. "It proved a fraud and you never got a cent." Heatedly, Foltz responded that he had libeled her in the midst of the case and she had sued him for his false statements.

Again, the colonel scored, when he retorted, "Yes, you brought suit for $50,000 and afterward compromised for $150, the price of a sealskin sack," which produced "another laugh at the expense of the lady lawyer." Sealskin sacks—warm and waterproof capes—were the current women's style, so he was saying she asked for a man's damages and received a woman's token. Recovering, Foltz said pleasantly, "And now, Colonel, in the end we are good friends after all." The colonel smiled and responded, "Yes, we are friends, but you must not bring any more suits."

How the whole scene played out in the eyes of the jury is hard to say, but Foltz had better success with the next defense witness, one of the home's male nurses. Opposing counsel Sawyer had produced the actual bed and restraints used on Von Schmidt to show that they were not "fearsome instruments of torture," as Foltz called them. When the nurse took the stand, Foltz suggested that he try them on. "Enveloped in straps and buckles, the man appeared absolutely helpless," according to the *Examiner*. Foltz then questioned the bound nurse, moving about the well of the court so that he must struggle to see her. Finally, "after he had turned and twisted and gasped answers for awhile," the nurse was released.[92]

After a week of testimony, the defense rested. On rebuttal, Foltz caused a further sensation by calling the opposing lawyer, Judge Sawyer, and forcing the admission that he and his fellow board members had no idea what went on in the home. Her last witness was Albert Munson, the teetotaling *Examiner* reporter, who described the horrific mistreatment in the home.[93]

Then it was time for closing arguments, and Foltz drew a large audience, with "the fair sex . . . out in force," many of them "the lady lawyer's associates and pupils of the Portia Law Club." As a reporter portrayed the scene, "Mrs. Foltz set aside a few authorities, removed her rubbers, adjusted the comb in her hair, and began one of the opportunities of her life before a jury."[94] She started with the traditions of legal protection of liberty, Magna Carta through the Constitution, and the duties of lawyers and juries to secure and vindicate them. Preeminent among the legal restraints was the requirement of adequate procedures before restricting freedom. Yet Von Schmidt had been locked up without any due process at all "within a stone's throw of the heart of the wonderful city of San Francisco."

The Home for Inebriates faced the full blast of Foltzian rhetoric. She called it "a hideous inferno" and "a modern temple of Juggernaut," casting "its victims out upon the sands for their bones and skulls to whiten the arid plains." In closing, she gave a dramatic reading of scenes from Charles Reade's best-selling novel *Hard Cash* (1864), about a sane person locked up in a mental institution. In a nice coincidence, the hero's name was Alfred, and he was committed to the asylum by his vindictive father.

Applause was heavy when she finished, and the judge "showed his appreciation of the lady's efforts by ordering a recess of five minutes for congratulations." (Perhaps Foltz should not have held a receiving line at counsel table, which emphasized the theater of her performance rather than the wrongs done to her client.) After four hours of deliberation, the jury returned a verdict for the plaintiff, but the victory immediately turned hollow when they awarded only nominal damages of one dollar.

The jurors crowded around to congratulate Foltz, thinking that because they had found the home liable, it would have to pay her fee and the court costs. But they were wrong; by law, litigants who took less than $300 had to pay their own costs and attorneys' fees as a penalty for suing in the Superior Court instead of the lower Justice Court. The jurors even came into court the next day on their own and tried to correct the verdict, making it clear that they thought Foltz had won.[95] But of course there was nothing to be done.

Foltz grimly declared herself "not through with the case," and a few months later she testified effectively at the legislature against public funding for the home, which soon went out of business. When she retold the story of this case in print, she started it with a favorite personal maxim: "Every case furnishes a fresh adventure in pursuit of wrong." She described her two cases against custodial institutions of Victorian San Francisco as part of her crusade against oppressors who preyed on the "weak and ignorant."[96] In that, they were of a piece with her criminal cases for the indigent—and also in not producing a penny in fees.

Both the Starke and Von Schmidt cases stirred what she remembered as "much enmity" and criticism. Her style as a jury lawyer was partly behind the disapproval. Foltz was an all-out advocate, full of righteous conviction that her cause was just and her adversary wrong, if not evil. She hit hard with a passionate and personal appeal, which was particularly effective because she was a woman. Foltz lived out the prediction by one newspaper when she first started in practice that woman lawyers would be formidable opponents because they had that "mysterious . . . magnetism" more essential to forensic success than "mere eloquence . . . melodious utterance, logical force [or] imaginative capacity." The writer called it "charisma," and there can be little doubt that Foltz possessed it.[97]

But for all her trial lawyer's skills and the excellent press coverage she continued to enjoy, paying clients and large verdicts were not part of the story. Several months after the Von Schmidt case, Foltz took to the road, her usual mode for maintaining appearances when things were going badly. The *Call* announced that she was departing on an "Eastern tour," giving no further itinerary, no purpose for the trip, and no explanation for the hasty departure.[98] She may have been looking for a new place to practice—to start over where she would have fewer enemies and no history of failure. Believing that she would have a better chance as a lawyer where women were political equals, she headed first to Utah and Colorado. In both places she publicly raised the possibility that she might settle there.

At the end of an adventurous half-year of traveling, however, Foltz decided to locate in New York City. She returned to San Francisco only long enough to pack. In summing up her fifteen years of intense practice in the city of her greatest triumphs, she said that ultimately "there is little or no opportunity for a woman lawyer here."[99]

Adventures on the Road

STOPOVER IN ZION

Foltz's first destination was Salt Lake City, which was in the midst of a constitutional convention, held on the verge of Utah's admission to statehood. It had been a tough road to this point for the territory because of prejudice against the majority Mormon population. Opponents feared that Utah would become a theocratic anomaly among the states and were particularly repelled by the practice of polygamy endorsed by the founders of the religion. Though the Church of Jesus Christ of Latter-day Saints had officially disavowed plural marriage in the early 1890s, their adversaries claimed this was insincere and that it would be resumed after statehood.

The suffragists were caught in the middle of the conflict because the territory had granted women the vote in 1870; only Wyoming Territory had done it earlier. But statehood opponents urged that women's votes just doubled the church's power. Mormon men, it was said, completely controlled the women indirectly through the patriarchal culture and directly through polygamy. Already associated with free love, the suffragists feared being seen as supporting polygamy too. Yet the anti-Mormon forces were also largely antisuffrage, and the Utah women voters were responsible and impressive.[100]

Clara Foltz does not seem to have been troubled by the complicated politics. She threw herself into the convention affairs and receptions, actively supporting statehood. When a man mistook her for one of the wives of the Mormon patriarch Brigham Young, she warmly responded that she admired the late prophet and would have considered it "a great honor to have been his wife."[101]

Foltz's enthusiasm for Utah statehood may have been influenced by her hosts in Salt Lake City; she was the guest of Isaac Trumbo and his wife, friends from San Francisco. Though still a young man, Trumbo had already amassed a fortune as a miner, engineer, and businessman with interests throughout the far West. By all accounts, "Colonel" (from a short National Guard stint) Trumbo was a man of unusual charm whose lobbying and negotiation abilities were legendary. He had waged an extended lobbying campaign ("eight years of my life") to improve the image of Mormons with the U.S. Congress. Kate Field, who lectured against polygamy and Mormon culture, wrote that Utah statehood was due to "the untiring vigilance of one man. . . . Kindly, courteous, popular with all, a born diplomatist, Col. Trumbo." Trumbo expected to become one of Utah's first U.S. Senators as a reward for his statehood efforts.[102]

He had moved from his San Francisco mansion to an even grander house in Salt Lake City, slipping into town to avoid the brass band he thought would meet him. Soon he would find his expectations terribly misplaced, but in May 1895, Trumbo was still basking in his accomplishment and looking forward to his reward. Foltz's visit was full of receptions and meetings connected to the constitutional convention, sightseeing, and other social events.

The local press followed her activities, and Mrs. Trumbo was said to be a great admirer of her guest's "magnificent manner and oratorical abilities." Lauding "so lovely a society and attractive a city," Foltz declared that a brand new state would need "good constitutional lawyers" and implied that her California experience made her eminently qualified to fill the role.[103] But she wanted to look at other possibilities, too. From Salt Lake City, Foltz announced that she would go to Manitou, Colorado (where there were healing springs), and then on to Chicago and Boston. A chance meeting would drastically alter this course, however.

DIVORCE FOR "MADAME BAZETTE"

On the way to Manitou, Foltz checked into the world-famous Antlers Hotel near Pikes Peak. A Victorian heap of stone balconies and bay windows, towers and turrets, it boasted seventy-five unique rooms, many commanding views of the Rocky Mountains. On her first night in the splendid dining room where a French chef presided over service in three languages, Clara Foltz met an old friend and embarked on one of the most memorable cases of her career.

Madame Bazette, as Foltz knew her when they both lived at the Occidental Hotel in San Francisco in the mid-1880s, was seemingly a beautiful French woman, wealthy and unattached. Many years later Foltz remembered "her delightful foreign accent," her "inspiring" gowns, "her millinery, her lingerie, her jewels, her apartment." Bazette was "a born coquette," and Foltz admired her "masterful way" with "the gay gallants" at the Occidental. Foltz recalled that the admiration was mutual and Madame had even proposed taking her to Paris, until, that is, she learned that five children would be included.[104]

Despite the failed trip, the two remained friends, and when Foltz moved to San Diego, Madame visited her there. Apparently, the French lady liked the prospects in booming San Diego, and with Foltz's editorial support at the *Bee*, she tried to start a conservatory of music.[105] Investors were solicited to build an academy for performance and voice training. But the rough little town was not quite ready for Madame Bazette, and she was quick to see it and return to the Occidental. Though Foltz moved back to San Francisco in 1890, the next time she saw her friend, as she remembered it, was in the Antlers dining room.

"She came at once to my table and greeted me most cordially. 'Why, Madame Bazette!' I exclaimed. 'Hush,' she said with the tip of her dainty forefinger upon her pouting lips. 'Shhh—my name is not Bazette, but Bolles—that name was assumed for a purpose; nor am I French.'" Within the hour, Foltz heard "for the first time" the "real story" of the life of Julia Bolles and agreed to be her lawyer in a divorce suit against a millionaire miner living in Colorado Springs.

Clara Foltz, on the road looking for new opportunities, was about to hit a life-altering payday. In describing the case, she freely admitted being duped by Madame's pretense to French society; it made a better story, after all. San Franciscans, moreover, were well-known for eagerly succumbing to various pretenders. The assumption of aristocracy was only a difference in degree from the improvements that almost everyone made in their back-grounds when moving west. Though Foltz had been entirely taken in and fascinated by Madame Bazette, she was soon busy in the interest of plain Mrs. Bolles, who proved as difficult and flighty as any real coquette.

Julia Bolles had fired nineteen of her first twenty lawyers, and she now wanted Foltz to join her one remaining attorney. As Foltz later described it, that man did not accept the proposed partnership: "He began in a sort of apologetic patronizing manner by saying something about the good re-pute I sustained at the California Bar, etc. 'but I will not associate with any woman.'" Bolles dismissed him at once, and Foltz said he exited "lean and hungry-looking, with head erect."

Foltz settled down at the Antlers for the next five weeks to work on the case. Although both husband and wife wanted a divorce, they were far from agreeing on the division of property between them. And both sides had plenty of legal weaponry; Colorado law, though liberal in offering multiple grounds for divorce, was old-fashioned in providing that a suit could be defeated by showing fault in the complaining party.[106] Neither Richard nor Julia (especially in her California life as Madame Bazette) had been paragons of purity. But an all-male Colorado jury might sym-pathize more with the local wealthy man than the out-of-state coquette. On the other hand, Richard wanted to avoid publicity and to acquire his freedom.

Foltz "investigated, consulted, prepared pleadings"; listened to "a million stale, flat and unprofitable stories" about her client's "turbulent matrimo-nial career"; and developed evidence about Richard that could have "hung a dozen husbands." Her preparations were evidently effective, because the parties agreed to settle, with a rubber-stamp jury granting the divorce on grounds of desertion. The judge entered an order concluding all of Richard Bolles's financial obligations to Julia in return for an immediate cash pay-ment of $75,000 (almost $2 million today). One paper estimated that she already had stocks and other property, making the total sum she received about $200,000. Bazette-Bolles was left a rich woman.[107]

The *Rocky Mountain News* headlined the "Largest Sum Ever Granted" in the county and praised "the Celebrated Woman Lawyer of California." "It was Mrs. Foltz's first appearance in court here, and she is credited with being a shrewd, sharp lawyer." The dispatches picked up the story, which was widely reprinted with the amount of the award and the lady lawyer receiving equal billing.[108] Foltz had her due in credit—but not in cash. She had made a basic error in failing to set the fee before starting the case. As part of the settlement, moreover, she agreed to take payment from the client's award rather than having the court determine the amount and charge Richard. Now the moment of victory was marred.

"My client was very grateful—she was overjoyed in fact, her happiness was complete until I mentioned my fees for my services; and then, 'Oh how could she ever pay such a large fee as that?'" Looking back on the case many years later, Foltz was still rueful. "I am quite ashamed even now to tell the insignificant amount I named as compensation for my services." When she told her brother Sam the figure, he replied, "My dear sister, you should have a guardian."[109]

There is no record of the amount Foltz charged, but it was apparently much less than the third of the recovery, or $25,000, that she might well have asked for. Still, the sum was enough to set Foltz up to travel on to New York in style and then go with her youngest daughter on a European vacation—perhaps $10,000 (about $250,000 today). She and her client apparently remained on good terms, because Bolles entrusted Foltz with her newly won assets to invest in New York. Later in the decade Foltz would return briefly to practice in Colorado, perhaps encouraged by Julia Bolles, who stayed in the state for some years after the divorce.

"A WOMAN FIRST—THEN A LAWYER"

Foltz arrived in New York City with the mission of arranging the investment of Bolles's small fortune. Her trip east, originally a flight from failure, was beginning to look like a march of triumph. She swept into town, registered at the sumptuous new Waldorf Hotel in the heart of Manhattan, and consulted with the president of the Chemical Bank, probably the best-known banker in the country at the time.

From her imposing hotel address, as was her custom, Foltz summoned the press. Her first New York interview bears a striking resemblance to the first long piece about her in the San Francisco papers fifteen years earlier. Sent to interview a woman lawyer, a reporter expects to find a hatchet-faced dame in black broadcloth and instead discovers another kind of woman altogether. In 1879 San Francisco, Foltz was described as "rosy-featured" and "matronly," clad in a checkered apron. The New York version was "a striking society woman, who wears Paris gowns and silk petticoats, and is exceedingly womanly." "A Woman First—Then a Lawyer" was the headline in the circulation-leading *New York World*. "Now," the article continued, "though she is a remarkably young-looking woman, she is the mother of five children." Foltz stripped almost a decade from her age (from forty-six to thirty-seven) by claiming to have studied law as a teenager, instead of at age thirty. Removing desperation and defeat from her biography, she said she had been drawn to the law because as a schoolgirl she had enjoyed settling disputes among her classmates. Instead of the bitter story about the man who jeered on the day of her admission that she would fail because females were such gossips, she mildly joked that women lawyers must learn to keep secrets, as well as to maintain a "clear head" and "quiet nerves." The other qualifications for success, she said, were "a thorough education" and "a natural love of work." The interview concluded that she was on her way to Europe for her first vacation since entering the profession.[110]

Before steaming off to Southampton, however, Foltz spent several weeks in New York. She attended a house party in Newport, Rhode Island, the resort of the very rich and the place to be over the Fourth of July when she was there. Trella, "my beautiful first-born," went with her and from Newport to another resort in Catskill, New York, near where Trella's son, William Gridley Toland, now eight, attended school.[111]

Trella Foltz Toland was doing well on the New York stage, short of stardom but near to the stars in supporting roles. An autograph book she started in 1893 already featured a number of famous names from the theater. While mother and daughter were holidaying together, Clara Foltz signed the book on the page across from Nellie Melba, the Australian opera star: "To my own talented Daughter, with a love whose depth and deathlessness words cannot utter. Mama"—and under it, her full signature in her best handwriting: "Clara Shortridge Foltz, Catskill, New York, July 7th, 1895."[112]

Three days later, Foltz departed on her European voyage. She took Virginia, her youngest child, born in the last days of her marriage and raised in the turbulent early years of her career. As a young woman, she had shown an impressive contralto voice and for several years had been studying at the New England Conservatory of Music in Boston. Now Foltz proposed to have her "tried before prominent French teachers" and to investigate operatic training. It had been a long road from her first divorce case when she puzzled over a lawyer's role, sitting on her porch in San Jose "with my baby Virginia on my lap, watching the glow of the sunset through the graceful foliage of a big pepper tree."[113]

CLARA FOLTZ IN LONDON AND PARIS

The grand tour—to see the historical sites and museums of Europe—was a mark of education and success. Upper-class families traveled abroad regularly for long periods. Rich women and their daughters went to Paris for the latest fashions. Now Clara Foltz meant to do it all with the money she had made for herself. A European trip would also give her time away from daily cares to think about the next step in her professional life.

In London, mother and daughter put up at the elegant Grand Hotel near Trafalgar Square. Foltz went immediately to nearby New Bond Street and purchased "several splendid bags and trunks" to transport the finery she was planning to buy. Then it was on to Paris. Years later she remembered 44 rue de Clichy, a pleasant boardinghouse near one of the "grand magasins de nouveautés," which specialized in women's dress and trimmings. With evident pleasure, Foltz also recalled that she used her recent "fee of considerable importance" to purchase "many exquisite articles of apparel for myself" and gifts for her family and friends. But the shopping ended abruptly when Foltz became sick. A doctor advised that she was "on the verge of a very bad case of nervous break-down." Foltz blamed it on the Bolles divorce when she "toiled night and day for five weeks" with her client constantly at her side, "talking incessantly. No wonder I was ill."[114]

Clara and Virginia left Paris at once for England on their way home, but the adventures were not over yet. Crossing the English Channel on August 20, 1895, their ship, the *Seaford*, was fatally rammed by the *Lyon*, a French vessel. The story of the shipwreck became one of the epic turns in Foltz's repertoire.[115] It started when she lingered on deck to enjoy the sea air until a heavy fog came up and forced her below. Foltz described the common stateroom fitted out for ladies where "they sat in little friendly groups, chatting over the fashions" and showing off their Paris purchases. Suddenly, "a heavy stroke that seemed like the call of death roared in my ears. I instinctively knew something terrible had happened and that the steamer was doomed." She clutched Virginia and headed for the deck, shrieking at the others to follow.

The stewardess grabbed her arm and tried to quiet her. But years of public speaking in large spaces and her native decisiveness enabled Foltz to shout even louder, "and still holding to Virginia, I pushed the stewardess to the head of the stairs leading to the upper deck, while all the rest of the imperiled women were fast on our heels." Foltz was proved right when water poured through the portholes just as the last person made it up to the deck.

There, 250 passengers huddled in the heavy fog while the crew passed out life vests. Clara Foltz, who could not swim, remembered facing death "philo-sophically." Pinning her "letter of credit to Virgie's vest with my diamond brooch," she gave "full though brief instructions as to what she must do in the event we did not meet again." Luckily, the *Lyon* had survived the collision and was able to come alongside, and everybody scrambled to safety over "a stretch of sea beneath us, which foamed and hissed and surged like molten lava."

Then as the *Seaford* sank beneath the waves, there was "a mighty ex-plosion" that produced a mountain of water just as the fog lifted and the rescued passengers stood for a few minutes in rainbow light. But the ordeal was not over. The *Lyon*, also damaged and already carrying a cargo of three hundred horses, was still a good distance from shore. For five hours, the ship beat toward the coast, while the *Seaford* passengers crowded together in their life vests with the sound of the straining engines in their ears. Foltz capped her description with a Shakespearean tagline about how time and death destroy distinctions: "Verily, one touch of nature makes the whole world kin." But the initial camaraderie dissipated as a group of American lawyers on the deck engaged in a heated moot court, featuring Clara Foltz against male lawyers from the eastern states.[116]

They said the accident was an act of God and there could be no recovery for the losses. Foltz argued that the steamship company was liable: it was daylight, the water was smooth, sudden fogs were a well-known hazard of the route, and carriers had a heightened duty of care to passengers. Moreover, she had seen the captain eating a hearty lunch at the time the fog came up in-stead of taking extra precautions. No one wanted to hear criticism of the man who had just saved their lives, and the passengers turned away from Foltz.

Ten thousand people awaited their arrival, and as the travelers descended onto dry land, "a shout of joy and welcome rang from those sympathetic English cousins," as Foltz remembered it later. She also recalled the London *Chronicle's* story crediting "the presence of mind and the quick action of the American lady barrister." But the uncomfortable situation that had arisen in the debate on the deck of the *Lyon* grew worse on the special train to Lon-don, when Foltz refused to give the conductor the steamship tickets he was collecting as proof of entitlement to ride. "Poor little Virgie! She did not relish the haughty attitude of the ladies toward me, and urged me to 'give the conductor the tickets,'" Foltz wrote years later. But those tickets were Foltz's only proof of the duty she paid on five trunks, and she was not about to relinquish them.[117]

They reached London at 2 a.m., and by eight o'clock sharp, she was at the door of the American Embassy. Foltz knew what to do—she had spent a lot of time in lobbies pursuing males in authority. Handing the guard her business card, and papers that included an introduction from the mayor of San Francisco, she demanded that he present them immediately to the ambassador. Within a few minutes, she was ushered in, related her view of the accident, and asked for an introduction to "Throop and Son on Threadneedle Street," top Admiralty lawyers.

But the ambassador assured her that she could simply present her case to the steamship officers and they would certainly respond. "If there is anything an Englishman likes it is a clear and truthful statement of what one believes are his lawful rights," he told her. Foltz summed up her triumph by describing how she walked down the marble steps of the steamship company with a bag of ten-pound notes. This may be an exaggeration, however, like her claim that she was the only passenger to receive any compensation for her losses. But on the whole, her story in the press at the time and in *Struggles* later is backed by other eyewitness accounts.

Apparently, all the excitement revived Clara Foltz's health because she stayed in London for several weeks before returning to the United States. Then there followed the pleasures of the voyage home: the luxurious *City of Paris* steamer, her place at the captain's table, the eminent people onboard with a week's leisure for her to cultivate them. Many *Seaford* passengers were also on the ship, and they "treated the 'fool woman lawyer' with a great deal more respectful consideration than when standing on the deck of the freighter Lyon, all disheveled and bedraggled, we argued the question of securing damages."[118]

Shipwreck survival and steamship triumph were tales Foltz told often. The success was so entirely her own—no male ally at her side, no suffrage band at her back, and no needy, nagging client on her hands. Sometimes she would add a coda about the arrest on their arrival of the social belle of the voyage for attempting to smuggle "wondrous millinery . . . exquisite gowns, gloves by the hundreds, marvelously beautiful lingerie, and jewels."[119] For Foltz, this tacked a populist flourish onto her story, and when told together with her accounts of her own shopping spree, it illustrated her lifelong love-hate relationship with luxury and the life of leisure.

Stopping in Chicago on her way home to California, she continued the focus on shopping, telling an interviewer that in New York she had replaced many of her treasures lost at sea. Foltz showed off "a handsome dinner gown of amber chiffon and velvet trimmed with jet, another of black silk and lace, a beautiful white opera cloak and an infinite array of fine lingerie and patent leather shoes." The reporter wrote that despite her brush with death, Foltz was in jovial spirits, joking about the mermaids donning her Paris purchases.[120]

But Foltz later remembered the trip as one filled with "anxiety and discomfort."[121] Indeed, her whole five months on the road was a microcosm of Clara Foltz's life—featuring her particular brand of incredible fortune, extraordinary achievement, and wrenching bad luck. She had happened on a big case in Colorado, and then through hard work and skill managed a major payday—though not as much as she deserved. She had made some important New York connections and survived a shipwreck. She had also risked her health with an inhuman pace that drove her to a breakdown, had lost her newly won treasures, and had almost died at sea.

Leaving San Francisco

A few weeks after returning from Europe, Clara Foltz was back in San Francisco—but only to tie up loose ends and say goodbye. She had decided to move to New York City. Her last days in her home city of many years were full of farewells and tributes, especially from the Portia Club. They had held together well while she was away, and the meeting they dedicated to their founder was their fourth of the year.

In what the *Call* dramatically billed "her last appearance before a San Francisco audience," Foltz combined memoir and manifesto with commentary on current events. She predicted that someday soon women would have "the opportunity to do everything from rocking a cradle and singing a lullaby to filling the highest positions in science, medicine and law." Warmly, she spoke of the Portia Club and her hopes that "the law club movement would spread" now that "its purposes have been fully realized in San Francisco." She recalled their success in gaining equal rights to attend court, "not to gratify a desire for the sensational but to observe and learn how justice is administered." Inviting her audience to join her the next day at the courthouse, she said they could see for themselves the equality of the sexes in vying for seats.[122]

The trial that was currently absorbing the city was that of Theo Durant, "The Demon in the Belfry." He was accused of murdering two young women in the Baptist church where he was the Sunday School superintendent.[123] Only the day before Foltz's speech, there had been a near riot when two thousand people swarmed a courtroom that held two hundred. The melee started when the wives of police, politicians, and jurors were escorted into the courtroom and given the best seats.[124] This custom had never created a problem before because very few women came to court. But the Portia Club campaign had changed all that, and women were already occupying most of the places when the special guests were added, leaving no room for male spectators. In her speech, Foltz noted that the men did not object to women attending court generally but wanted them treated equally as contenders for seats. It was odd evidence of progress perhaps, but evidence (and progress) nonetheless.

She closed her talk with memories of her days lobbying the legislature in Sacramento. Because of her efforts, women could now be lawyers, notaries, and executors of estates and one day soon, she hoped, would be voters. She told of her part in the passage of a constitutional amendment granting women suffrage, which the electorate would vote on in the 1896 election (see Chapter 6). The evening ended with sentimental old songs and a zither solo.

A week later, a private farewell by invitation only was held at the Occidental Hotel, where Foltz had lived during the 1890s (and had met "Madame Bazette"). The *Call* reported how the "affectionate" Portia Law Club members clustered about Foltz. Also in attendance were Foltz's brother Sam and daughter, Bertha, recently married to Lafayette Smalley, an actor and bartender. Many lawyers and judges attended as well. No official program was planned, but Foltz's old friend James Maguire, now a U.S. congressman, spoke spontaneously, saying, "I have honored and admired her ever since she first commenced her struggle for admission to the bar against the almost universal opposition then existing." He cited her courage and praised achievements "that would be a credit to any man." Maguire said that "she has attained the greatest of skill as a lawyer," but "she has done more. With a few associates, she has made a new profession for women." Foltz was an example for all lawyers in the way she had practiced law "not with the view of achieving purely business ends," but to improve "the administration of justice." When law is conceived in such a broad way, Maguire declared, it is "the noblest of professions—worthy of noble womanhood." He concluded that she was "leaving at a time when the highest honors and emoluments await her."[125]

When she rose to reply, Foltz was choked and scarcely audible. "My ambitions have always been to challenge the admiration of men such as Judge

Maguire," she started. "I very much regret that I have found it necessary to leave my home, where I have struggled and where I have made something of a success." Referring to California as her "mother state," Foltz vowed she would also succeed in New York through "honest effort" and "noble ambition and determination."

During her final weeks in California, Foltz spoke sadly and frankly about the lack of opportunity for women lawyers in San Francisco. By contrast, in her brief time in New York, she had been "retained by two firms doing a large foreign business." Foltz could start over in the East, free of the enemies and mistakes she had made over the years, and she could shed the years as well. Her children were living on their own, and her mother could stay with Charles while she was gone. This was the moment to make her move if she was ever to do it. In Foltz's imagined New York, every opportunity was available "on demand." By the first of the year, 1896, she was "Established in Gotham," as the headlines said back home.[126]

Changing Locations, 1895–1911

New York, Denver, San Francisco, Los Angeles

A New York Lawyer

JOINING THE BAR

"Clara Foltz, for fifteen years at the San Francisco Bar," has opened a law office for general practice and for "adjusting differences without resort to the
courts," read the handsome card she sent to the press, to her acquaintances,
and to those she hoped to know in New York City. As references, Foltz
listed many of the top officeholders and judges in California. Hoping for
"a cordial welcome and a generous patronage," she took a suite in Temple
Court, near Wall Street and the press palaces of Park Row.[1]

The announcement triggered excellent press coverage: "Will Practice Law
Here: Made Her Reputation in the West" headlined the *New York Times*
on January 17, 1896, with a flattering picture. Foltz freshened up her old
stories and softened her image for the interview. She claimed that "a woman
may enter into the law and still retain all her womanly instincts." Having
been a peacemaker in her school days, she told the reporter, made her interested in settlement rather than litigation. "She has never attempted oratory,"
he wrote, "but has confined herself to those lines of speaking for which a

woman is most fitted."[2] Foltz apparently failed to mention her jury arguments or her stump speaking. The comment also contradicted a constant
theme of hers—that until women had equal opportunity, it was impossible
to know what they were fitted to do.

Generally, the new image Foltz was crafting lacked a certain consistency.
For instance, she had much to say about womanly instincts, while stressing
that she asked "no consideration for my sex, but wish my cases to be judged
on their merits. I am first of all a lawyer." In the same vein, she spoke of
dropping the "Shortridge" from her name because "I have wanted to have
my own name speak for itself." Yet plain Clara Foltz often bragged about
her brothers (one the editor of the *San Francisco Call*, and the other counsel
for the Spreckels sugar interests). Family mattered more in the East than it
did in California.

The interviewing reporter was clearly captivated, however, and did not
cross-question Foltz. He wrote that she was "striking in appearance, tall and
somewhat commanding" and remarkably "youthful." Unlike other "women
of advanced ideas," Foltz dressed fashionably and "without a trace of mannish
affection." Her offices were professional though the roses on her desk added
a "feminine touch." Among the many favorable interviews through which
Foltz presented her public persona over the years, this was one of her best.

In February, a second round of newspaper stories reported, and considerably dramatized, the routine ceremony admitting her to the practice of
law in the New York courts. An account in the *New York World* described
the interruption in "the solemn and circumstantial routine" of court business when "General Benjamin F. Tracy arose and with Chesterfieldian grace
escorted a middle-aged and prepossessing woman to the bar." It included a
large lithograph showing the general "in the act of presenting Mrs. Foltz."
The *Times* reported that while General Tracy detailed her references, and
added his personal endorsement, Foltz "stood coolly at the bar," seeming
not the "least disconcerted by the inspection of the dignitaries of the bench
or embarrassed by the crowd of male lawyers who watched her with undis-
guised interest." When the ceremony of her admission was over, "she went
out into the clerk's office, adjusted her bonnet before the glass, and went
down town alone."[3]

The picture was arresting—the sole woman in the courthouse, without
so much as a private place to fix her hat, heads out on her own to a section
of town where ladies were still rarely seen on the streets. She was a brave,
independent, and newsworthy figure, though she was not the first woman

lawyer in the city, and no one was contesting her admission. Even a famous man would not have drawn so much attention for the commonplace formality of bar admission.

That General Benjamin Franklin Tracy supported her was also significant. A prominent lawyer and political insider, Tracy was one of the founders of the Republican Party in New York. He had served as secretary of the navy under President William Henry Harrison from 1889 to 1893, earning the title "father of the fighting navy" for his part in refurbishing the fleet and encasing it in steel. Tracy also reformed the patronage excesses of the department and promoted U.S. imperialism in the Caribbean and the Pacific.[4]

Foltz called Tracy "an old friend" though it is not clear when they met. He had been a passenger on the *City of Paris* when Foltz returned from London and was a signer of a petition on behalf of Florence Maybrick, an American woman convicted of murder in England whom Foltz had supported (see Chapter 5). Tracy was also a backer of woman suffrage, though he had a mixed reputation in the movement because of his association with one of its darkest hours. In the 1870s, he had been chief counsel for Henry Ward Beecher, the charismatic preacher charged with adultery with a parishioner (see Chapter 6). The scandal absorbed the whole country, ruined many reputations, and wounded the women's movement because those involved, including Beecher, the cuckolded husband, the adulterous wife, and all the witnesses, were suffragists of one kind or another. In the course of representing Beecher, Tracy had attacked the credibility (and indeed the sanity) of a number of suffragist women. But all that was twenty years in the past when he moved the admission of Clara Foltz to the bar.

Though any bar member could have played the part, the fact that so eminent a man was Foltz's sponsor gave weight to the occasion. It would, however, be the only time their names appeared together in legal papers. Neither Tracy nor any of the other leading men at the bar would associate Clara Foltz as co-counsel in an important case. She was about to learn that it was impossible to realize her ambition: "to score a material success," to be the first woman "to make a tangible impression at the New York Bar."[5]

Nothing in her previous experience prepared Foltz for the opposition she met. By the turn of the twentieth century she was back in the West and no longer even referred to her eastern venture in press interviews. But it all started hopefully with the triumphal coverage of her bar admission. She found further encouragement in the fact that law study was flourishing among women and was connected to the movement through the Women's

Legal Education Society (WLES), an organization like Foltz's Portia Club. Indeed, the society may have been one of the attractions originally drawing her to New York.

WOMEN LAWYERS, SUFFRAGISTS, AND SOCIETY LADIES IN NEW YORK

The Women's Law Class

In most places, women were suffragists before they became lawyers. The need to be informed voters justified law study, and suffrage ideology enabled them to withstand the prejudice they met at the bar. So an active suffrage association usually produced a number of women lawyers as well as other professionals—but not in New York City in the 1880s and early 1890s. There were many suffragists, and also many women doctors, preachers, teachers, journalists, social workers, and writers, but only a handful of women lawyers. The legal profession in New York, the center of law practice in the United States, was uniquely resistant to their entry.

Kate Stoneman had been the first woman lawyer in the state in 1886—almost a decade after Foltz in California. Her experiences paralleled Foltz's in many respects; she drafted a bill allowing women to practice, lobbied it through the legislature, made an eleventh-hour plea to the governor to sign it, and then was the first to use the statute. Stoneman was also the first woman at Albany Law School, and again like Foltz, she continued to lobby for women's rights after joining the bar.[6]

But Stoneman's cases did not make headlines like Foltz's did, and few women followed her into practice. Indeed, in New York City, the first woman joined the bar in 1894—just two years before Foltz arrived. At the same time, hundreds of women, many of them among the social elite, studied law in the WLES, which then became the Women's Law Class of New York University (NYU).

The WLES started in the late 1880s when well-to-do women realized that their charity work in the city's tenements involved many legal issues. They hired a European woman lawyer to give them regular lectures at parlor meetings. Soon, the women discovered that understanding the law was a help in managing their own affairs as well as in helping poor people. Several years after the first WLES meeting, the NYU chancellor, who probably saw the wealthy people on the membership list, offered to set up a separate Women's Law Class and curriculum at the law school. From the outset, the class was an immense success. Hundreds of women graduated from the one-year program. In 1890 NYU opened its regular law school to women as well. Some people said the university did this to maintain the high tone of the separate curriculum for society ladies.

A few of the Women's Law Class graduates went on to finish the full course of law study. Stanleyetta Titus was one of these. She had joined the WLES at its inception, out of the same social-work impulses as the others, and then completed the one-year NYU program. Though Titus excelled at and loved law study, she would have concluded her exposure to law with the academic course, as most New York women did, except that her father died after suffering reverses during the economic depression. The conventional choice at that point was for Titus to live with relatives while hoping to marry, and perhaps to give lessons in piano playing or china painting. Instead, she entered the first regular law class at NYU to accept women. A prize-winning student, she graduated in 1893, apprenticed with a law firm for a year, and in the spring of 1894 joined the New York bar and became the first woman lawyer in the city.[7]

The next year, 1895, ten more women took the bar examination, most having started in the Women's Law Class. An article in the *Times* interviewed ten prominent male lawyers about the development, concluding that they mostly felt like "a magnificent mastiff towards a delightful, fluffy little scotch terrier. He doesn't mind much what she does if she does not hurt herself." One male lawyer warned that resistance to the women's legal movement was like the efforts of King Canute, "who bid the rising tide go back" and instead "it wet his royal feet."[8]

Florence Sutro

Most of the graduates of the special NYU program did not go on to complete a degree. Florence Sutro, the valedictorian of the first Women's Law Class in 1891, was typical. Already a favorite of the society reporters when she started law study, she was the young wife of a prosperous attorney. Her reputation as "an ideal clubwoman, distinguished in every branch of intellectual activity," said one story, had "spread from her own immediate salon until it had metropolitan significance."[9]

The graduation ceremonies for the Women's Law Class were important events, held in Madison Square Garden and attracting large audiences and abundant news coverage. Sutro's valedictory was titled "Why I Study Law." Reading Mansfield, Marshall, and Kent not only sharpened the intellect, she said, but also provided intrinsic satisfactions: "[L]aw is beautiful. . . . This great sense of union and order, which pervades all life," makes the study of law "one of the broadest means possible for attaining to true culture." Legal knowledge would make women better company for their men, better at managing their own property, more understanding of governmental affairs, and prepared to "enjoy the franchise." Sutro was the woman Foltz imagined when she founded her Portia Club back in San Francisco—a prosuffrage society lady who studied law. She would, in Foltz's words about the type, "come down a little to help those who are struggling to make the world better, to aid those who have the ability to do the work."[10]

The Women's Law Class, with graduates like Florence Sutro and Julia Gould (plutocrat Jay Gould's daughter), made law study, if not fashionable exactly, at least more socially acceptable, especially if done for some altruistic purpose. At the 1896 graduation of the Women's Law Class, the renowned orator and attorney Chauncey Depew raised the theme of social acceptance for practicing women lawyers. Foltz's friend the suffragist Lillie Blake reported on it in the *Woman's Journal.*[11]

Depew started by appealing to the audience's sense of noblesse oblige. Looking out over the "bright costumes of the many women who were present," he quoted from Thomas Hood's familiar poem "The Song of the Shirt," about a working woman "in unwomanly rags,"

> With eyelids heavy and red,
> In poverty, hunger, and dirt
> Sewing at once, with a double thread,
> A Shroud as well as a shirt.[12]

To his picture of women in the needle trades, who needed the help of women of privilege, Depew added the image of a girl from a respectable family whose father dies, leaving her in need of work "to support herself and possibly a widowed mother and possibly educate little brothers and sisters." But despite her aptitude for the law, she fears that going into a male profession would mean rejection by polite society. Turning to the graduates, Depew told them: "It is for you, young ladies, to preach and work against this prejudice. Most of you are pursuing this study for your own protection, but you can do missionary work for the sister who is impelled to go further."

Chauncey Depew was bold to recite "The Song of the Shirt" to a society audience, but he did not suggest that women might study law to gain wealth, political power, or fame. Not even supporters spoke in the language of Clara Foltz's ambitions. Yet Foltz would have applauded the idea that elite women could study law and be concerned with issues outside of their homes. "Eastern women seem to understand the value of a social interest in political affairs," she said after her first few months in New York.[13]

Rosalie Loew

One of the early graduates of NYU's regular law curriculum was Rosalie Loew, who joined the New York bar a few months after Foltz did. In June 1896, the two women were featured together in a big spread in *Metropolitan Magazine*. Ten photographs accompanied the article—six of Foltz and four of Loew, doing such lawyerly things as looking over a statute, arguing to a jury, and advising a client. Some of them show Foltz's office with its rolltop desk and a large portrait of herself in cap and gown. Women can be lawyers, the pictures seem to indicate, and here they are doing it.[14]

WORKING ON THE SYMPATHIES OF THE JURY.

Clara Foltz arguing to the jury, as featured in *Metropolitan Magazine*, 1896.

The text, written by Loew, was less cheerful than the engaging photos, however. Grimly, she warned that women "must take their place in the ranks by their brothers and scale the walls," even though they are handicapped because of "the energy required overcoming a probable prejudice." Nor did Loew claim any success to date for women lawyers: "they have not practiced in New York long enough to permit conclusions."

At age twenty-three, Rosalie Loew was in the second generation of American women at the bar and had faced somewhat fewer obstacles than Foltz and the other pioneers. The doors to NYU were open to women when Loew applied; her fellow students accepted her readily; the statutes of the state allowed her to practice; and the courts certified her without incident. When she wore the mortarboard, it represented degrees actually earned.[15] Yet Loew had no more choice than Clara Foltz about her first job. She could hang out her shingle alone, work as a stenographer for male lawyers (as a number of women law graduates did), or practice with a relative. In fact, Loew had even fewer opportunities because, besides being a woman, she was Jewish, at a time when anti-Semitism pervaded the New York bar. Few names like Loew, and none like Rosalie, would appear regularly on the masthead of the great corporate firms for many years. She entered her father's practice, which became Loew and Loew.

Like Foltz in her own early career, Loew drew lots of press attention—fanfare for routine cases and detailed reports about her appearance, manner, and personality. Physically, Loew was appealing: small and slender, blooming, energetic, exquisitely turned out. The phrase "no trace of mannish affectation," often said of Foltz, applied to Loew also. Her round eyeglasses, sometimes used for gestures, added to the impression of seriousness and sincerity.

Within months of writing the *Metropolitan* article, Loew left private practice and became the first woman lawyer at the Legal Aid Society, organized in the 1870s as a private charity to help poor immigrants. At her new post, she did much the same work as before, but at Legal Aid she had a regular salary. Loew's clientele resembled Foltz's own early civil practice in California—saving people from installment fraud, suing employers for the wages of workers, seeking divorce and support payments for battered wives. She also worked very hard. In the mid-1890s, Loew was the only woman lawyer in the city who went to court regularly. An article in the *Tribune* said that she "had from 18 to 23 cases on the docket a day, scattered through the eleven divisions of the Boroughs of New York. She prepares the cases, argues them in person, and is responsible for their disposal. . . . [H]er work is never ceasing."[16]

When Rosalie Loew first passed the bar, a reporter asked her father why women wanted to be lawyers anyway. William Loew responded that they desired a "distinctive identity," work and status of their own. He also believed that women would be a great "reformatory power" in the profession. His daughter Rosalie lived out his prediction. A colleague later wrote of the thousands of people Loew helped and of "her passion for justice to the wronged."[17] Yet for Foltz, it was probably disheartening to see the younger woman with all her relative advantages, unable to rise higher in the professional hierarchy. Into her old age, Foltz would complain that legal service to the poor was often the only work open to women lawyers. For herself, she sought a higher-status practice in New York.[18]

WOMEN AND THE CORPORATE BAR

Foltz hoped to join the new breed of corporate lawyers whose reputations were made in the boardroom instead of the courtroom and who were known by the prestige of their clients. One model was Joseph Choate, who had parlayed his standing as a great jury lawyer into advising Standard Oil and American Tobacco. Others were William Nelson Cromwell, whose firm represented J. P. Morgan; Elihu Root, the lawyer for big sugar; Chauncey Depew for the Erie Railroad; and George Welwood Murray, who attended to the interests of the Rockefeller family. Foltz opened an office in their midst and advertised herself as their female equivalent. No matter how well she orchestrated her presentation, however, nor how fine her setting, her manners, her references, or her reputation, she could never become one of them. The corporate bar was deeply and fundamentally prejudiced against women lawyers. Perhaps the best exemplar of intractable opposition was James Coolidge Carter, one of the most distinguished lawyers in the country.[19]

Carter was a corporate attorney, a U.S. Supreme Court advocate, a municipal reformer, a New York Bar Association founder, and an important jurisprudential theorist. Unmarried, he moved in an all-male world of practice, politics, and exclusive clubs—and he wanted to keep it that way. Interviewed on the subject, Carter said he "did not believe in women lawyers" and even suggested passage of a statute forbidding females from practicing. With "vim and animation," he attacked all women who displayed themselves in public and held that "woman" is "too full of personality" to be suited for the practice of law. "Everything is personal with her," he maintained.[20]

The exclusion of women was built right into the structure of the corporate law firms, a structure as new as the substance of the practice. Much larger than previous partnerships among lawyers, the new type of firms replaced the unpaid apprentices reading law with salaried associates, the brightest law school graduates. Even though they were bar members, these associates worked as employees of the firm for years before being considered as possible partners. Nobody left the firm unless he failed. Because the hiring involved a long-term commitment on both sides, the firms were unlikely to experiment with a woman associate—especially not a forty-six-year-old celebrity suffragist without a law degree. The other way into Wall Street practice was to bring wealthy clients into an existing partnership, which no women lawyers had the connections to do.

Only one woman had gained even a toehold in the world of big-firm New York corporate practice in the 1890s, and her situation was unique. Lavinia Lally worked in a firm as a typewriter (the same word was used for the machine and the person operating it) while attending law school. Even after passing the bar, Lally might well have continued as a secretary. Luckily for Lally, however, a number of lawyers broke off from the firm, and she was the only one with adequate knowledge of the cases they left behind. Even so, she was hired only at the associate level, though a man in the same situation might have become a partner. In press interviews, Lally spoke of hiding her female identity when cases went to court. "In the interests of my clients," she said she employed "a masculine proxy rather than appear in person and be referred to as the 'lady' instead of the 'counsel' in the case."[21]

Foltz was too old and famous to start at the bottom as an associate, so her only hope for entry into the upper reaches of the New York bar was to attract wealthy business clients. Accordingly, in her early publicity, she downplayed her jury-lawyer image, stressing instead her negotiation and lobbying abilities. She mentioned a recent matter involving $75,000 without saying it was a divorce settlement.

Portraying herself as a corporate advisor, Foltz also omitted central aspects of her life. Gone were the five children and the distracted law study "amidst the cries of my populous nursery." In fact, Foltz's preferred West Coast self-presentation as the courageous mother and crusading feminist was barely visible in most of her New York City interviews. She highlighted the Portia Club as a precursor to a "law university for women" but left out its role in the suffrage movement. Most striking was the transformation of her criminal practice and her public defender campaign into strictly "humanitarian" efforts. "She has done a great deal to ameliorate the conditions of the outcasts of society," one article concluded, as if her prior experience had been ladylike charitable work instead of spectacular and combative jury trials.[22]

A year or so into her New York practice, when she saw that entry into corporate practice would be impossible, Foltz changed tactics and tried to trade on her criminal expertise. But amidst the corruption and chaos of the local courts, she soon discovered that the netherworld of the criminal bar was as unreachable for a woman as the exalted realm of Wall Street practice. All she gained from her attempts at criminal practice was a list of telling examples establishing the pressing need for public defense.

WOMEN IN CRIMINAL PRACTICE

For Foltz, one of the main reasons a public defender was needed was the failure of prosecutors to live up to the ideals of the office. She had been lecturing about this for years. Instead of ministers of justice, she said they had become vicious adversaries, acting from motives of vanity and greed (see Chapter 7). The Manhattan district attorney exemplified every evil she had ever observed and excoriated. A newspaper exposé of the office in 1893 complained that the prosecutors "strive to convict at all hazards and by any means within their power" and "reckon their efficiency by the number and severity of sentences imposed." Favorable evidence is "not communicated to the defense and the accused is left to his own resources."[23]

Prosecutorial unfairness was more extreme in New York City because it was one element in an astonishingly corrupt scene. Tammany Hall, the infamous political machine, was in charge of both the criminal justice system and a good deal of the crime. An army of prostitutes, pimps and madams, gamblers of every stripe, regular cutthroats, and ordinary thieves paid their dues to Tammany Hall, and so did many police officers, reporters, and judges. Payoffs and bribes assured virtual immunity for everyone in the know or on the take.[24]

Except for a few brief periods of reform, the prosecutor was a Tammany man for decades, and his assistants were virtually all Tammany heelers. "Some of them were able men; others superannuated political hacks," wrote Arthur Train, the lawyer-novelist who described the office in best-selling fiction and memoirs. Train wrote that an ordinary victim of crime would have a hard time getting his case even heard by a grand jury. On the other hand, "a speedy indictment results from a short introduction" by a Tammany man. Real victims could not be heard, and there were also Tammany-instigated cases in which indictments were returned that could "never be tried because the evidence was insufficient to convict." It was a system in which "hundreds of arrests are made for no other purpose than to worry, harass, annoy, disgrace socially and bring financial disaster upon the accused."[25] Foltz had made this same point against prosecuting authorities in her World's Fair speech, though she had yet to see anything on the scale of the Tammany operation.

In other cases, prosecutors in cahoots with Tammany-linked defense lawyers would arrange for continuances until the last cent was wrung from the accused and the witnesses gave up appearing. Then the case was dismissed. When cases did go to trial, it was the custom for victorious complainants to tip the prosecutor in cash. With the prosecutor's personal financial interest added to what Foltz called "the vanity of winning cases," the trials often became "acrimonious contests of men striving for verdicts."[26] They took a different shape, however, than in San Francisco and the rural California courts where she had practiced. There, Foltz had contended with physical coarseness—men (as opponents, jurors, and witnesses) who were drunk and disorderly, abusive and bawdy. Potential for real violence, enhanced by the widespread carrying of weapons, simmered below the often-rough adversary exchange.

In New York City, on the other hand, it was not physical danger just below the surface, but pervasive corruption and mendacity. No one could tell by looking when the jurors were bribed, the judges bought, the prosecutors indentured to party bosses, or the defense lawyers members of the demimonde. And in any case, hardly anyone was looking. The criminal courts were out of sight, adjacent to the jail called the Tombs, not because so many hopes were buried there, but because it was copied from an Egyptian mausoleum. Its granite façade covered an interior of dark, airless cells that were infested with rats and often flooded because the jail was set on the marshy ground of a former cesspool. In 1895, fifty thousand people spent time in the Tombs, the length of their stay depending on whether they could raise money for bail.[27]

Far from the handsome business offices and banking establishments, the press palaces and fine shops, the Victorian mansions and pleasant apartments and hotels, the Tombs was also quite a way from Temple Court, where Clara Foltz awaited clients. She was not on hand to pick up the good cases immediately after arrest, when male lawyers and their runners streamed into the Tombs to offer their services to high-paying, or highly publicized, suspects. Even if Foltz had been located in the neighborhood, importuning at the jail was not something a woman could do and remain respectable.

Especially shocking to Foltz was the rapacity of some defense lawyers. In an 1897 law review article, she described the practices at the Tombs: "The arrested must have counsel; but few know whom to send for. Their incarceration prevents them seeking a proper attorney. Facts menace and time presses. Here is the shyster's opportunity." He or his surrogate "visits the prisoner in jail, works on his fears, secures his money and botches or neglects his cause." Sometimes, she added, the shyster employs women who "pose as angels of mercy, and advise the hiring of questionable attorneys for a share of what is in it." (These were impersonators of the real "angels"— volunteers concerned with the conditions of the urban poor in tenements and jails.) For Foltz, the harm of shysterism went to the very heart of the criminal justice system.[28]

"Innumerable" innocent people, she wrote, "boys and girls and men and women," plead guilty "because [they are] too dazed to understand their rights and legal position." Others, though they have a good defense, plead and pay a fine because "it is cheaper than counsel and they can better stand the disgrace than the money loss." Still others "are ruined by payment of counsel fees . . . robbed by shysters and . . . neglected by irresponsible court appointees."

Though Foltz had been attacking shysters for years in her lectures, she found a new level of unprofessional conduct in New York. In fact, the city was the birthplace of the term *shyster*, said to be a corruption of "Shuester," the name of a lawyer who pettifogged and judge-baited well before the Civil War. In 1889, the *Century Dictionary* defined a shyster as "one who does business trickily; a person without professional honor, used chiefly of lawyers." Most of the shysters were located near the courts and the Tombs, and the shysters supreme of the whole city, Howe and Hummel, were right across the street.[29] Out front was a forty-foot sign, garishly illuminated at night. The firm worked on regular retainer from the major criminals and gangs of the city, and its runners included newspaper reporters and police officers as well as those posing as friends or social workers. Over four decades ending in 1907, when a crusading district attorney finally closed the firm down, Howe and Hummel represented more than a thousand people accused of murder and manslaughter.

William Howe was the jury man—famous for his purple suits and display of diamonds (stickpins, studs, watch-fobs, rings, and brooches worn in the place of neckties). He was immense, on the order of William Howard Taft, with a walrus moustache and magnificent voice. Abe Hummel was as small as Howe was huge and always dressed in funereal black. Hummel was the writ writer and the appellate lawyer, though he was also quick on his feet in trial situations (and quick with his fingers too: he was an adept pickpocket, which he apparently did as a sport).

Nothing was too low for Howe and Hummel—they suborned perjury, bribed judges, and arranged for defenses in advance of the crimes. Though known for their charm and bonhomie, the pair moved through a dim and sordid world. The courthouse building where they spent their time was "one of the gloomiest structures in the world," according to Train. He described it as "a huge central rotunda, rimmed by dim mezzanines and corridors . . . crowned by a glass roof encrusted with soot through which filters a soiled and viscous light. The air is rancid." Train also described "Pontin's Restaurant . . . a stone's throw from the courts, a daily rendezvous at lunch time for the judges, the district attorney's staff and the criminal counsel. 'Pont's,' as it was called, had two rooms, an outer for the *hoi polloi*, and a smaller, containing two tables, one reserved for the General Sessions judges and the other sacred to Bill Howe and Abe Hummel." The rattle from the "well-worn dice box" on the bar went on continuously throughout the meal. No ladies dined at Pontin's.[30]

Abe Hummel happened to be in court on the day that Clara Foltz was admitted to practice. After she left, the male lawyers gathered around to chew over the novel event. "Well," said Hummel, "now we are likely to become more civilized. Which of us will have the first opportunity to show our chivalry by allowing her to win a case?"[31] The remark called for one of her cutting replies, but Foltz left the courtroom. She did attack Howe and Hummel in her writing, however, because the scale of its operations made it a good target. It was the image of this firm that Foltz was invoking when she called for replacing crooked lawyers with public defenders.

CLARA FOLTZ'S NEW YORK PRACTICE

Foltz told an interviewer in 1897 that she had been "uniformly successful" in a number of "leading cases" since her arrival in New York. But news reports of her cases showed them to be few and insignificant.[32] She handled her first criminal matter in October 1896, eight months after joining the bar.

Her client was Tom O'Connor, a fugitive from a New Jersey mental hospital, where he had been transferred after a psychotic break in prison. The state wanted him back to complete his sentence. Foltz argued that the extradition statute did not apply to the insane—"a fine point of inter-State law," which she won.[33] It was better than losing, but O'Connor's was not the kind of case that would pay the rent at Temple Court.

On the same day that Foltz went to court for O'Connor, she also "appeared" for Mrs. Sidney Beresford Pickhardt, who had been knocked over by a team of horses. The judge fined the drover five dollars for fast driving. Though Foltz had no official role because her client was only a witness, she was probably laying the groundwork for a civil suit by assuring a criminal conviction, and by helping Mrs. Pickhardt preserve her testimony. Larger litigation may also have been afoot. The lady with the high-sounding name was a former actress whose rich young husband had died within months of the wedding, leaving his fortune to her. A will contest was likely because the family had never approved of the union. Even if Mrs. Pickhardt's affairs held some promise for her attorney, however, a good fee was probably contingent and certainly far in the future.

One year from her admission to the New York bar, Foltz argued for John Greene, who sued a storage company for damaging goods worth a few thousand dollars. A story in the *Tribune* made fun of her overpreparation: "Mrs. Foltz came into court armed with a heap of law books and printed affidavits, glancing contemptuously at the youthful attorney who opposed her." He asked that the case be dismissed because the plaintiff had waited too long to sue. "Then Mrs. Foltz opened her batteries and read the contents of a pile of affidavits and nearly the contents of the law books at the rate of something like 15,000 words an hour." The judge "shuddered," the stenographer "wilted," and no decision was announced.[34]

In terms of publicity, Foltz made the most of what she had. For instance, she handled a collection matter for the writer Belle Whitney (who wrote as Dinah Sturgis). Foltz sued the *New York Herald* for withholding compensation unless Whitney could produce clippings proving they had used her stories. Apparently newspapers, which put out multiple editions every day, often delayed or avoided payment when authors could not locate their work.[35] Foltz settled for the few hundred dollars that Whitney originally billed plus costs, which did not include attorneys' fees. It was a small case even if she took some of the recovery as a fee. But Foltz said its importance lay in establishing "the right of an individual writer versus a powerful corporation," and the *Woman's Journal* noted that she had struck a blow for "every woman writer in the land who is forced to employ her pen as a means of support."[36]

All in all, Foltz's hopes of establishing a better practice for herself in New York City than she had in San Francisco were disappointed. Her plans to become a corporate lawyer were apparently frustrated rather quickly. But when she fell back to representing individuals in criminal and civil matters, only an occasional small case shows up in the reports. On the social and intellectual scene, however, Clara Foltz came closer to the New York she imagined, where everything was available "on demand."

A "New Woman" in New York

THE NEW WOMAN MOVEMENT

A magazine spread in the mid-1890s described Foltz as a "heroine of the new woman movement." The press was full of references to this new woman, whose exact identity was unclear but whose arrival was said to be near. In fact, Foltz declared to the Portia Club, the "new woman, God bless her, is here, if you only knew it." She said the new woman was "the partner of the new man," but like most who spoke on the subject, Foltz approved the concept without exactly defining it. "[I]ntelligence and a sense of freedom and equality with men" were the chief characteristics she mentioned. By this measure, many suffragists were new women, though not all new women were suffragists. In Foltz's view, however, political equality would follow naturally from the new woman's quest for the same education and opportunity that men enjoyed.[37]

One universally accepted attribute of the new woman was her physical liberation, signified by bicycle riding. Susan B. Anthony proclaimed that the bicycle "has done more to emancipate woman than any one thing in the world." Clara Foltz said it was a "tonic" and "the best relaxation from business cares." Though unlike others, Foltz did not combine bicycle riding with dress reform, she did purchase a special "bicycle suit" on her trip to Paris.[38]

In New York City, for the first time in her life, Clara Foltz found many other women like herself; in the mid-1890s the city was full of new women. As a western lawyer and character, moreover, Foltz stood out among them and generated some of the best press of her life. In addition to news stories Foltz was featured in the leading women's magazines of this period: *Godey's Lady's Book*, *Peterson's Magazine*, and *Munsey's Magazine*, among others.[39] Given the size and social complexity of the "national metropolis," as Foltz called New York, her copious publicity was an impressive accomplishment in itself.

One of the best pieces was in the *New York Times Magazine*, shortly before Foltz's forty-ninth birthday. A large portrait hid her age with dramatic half-shadows, making her look like an actress. She reiterated her standard biographical truths and fictions—married at age fifteen, widowed when very young—compressing events so that a reader would guess she was forty at most. The interviewer described her as "a tall stately blond with a fine voice" who has "been through a shipwreck and various other experiences of which she talks entertainingly." Despite her busy law practice, the story continued, Clara Foltz also enjoyed a full and satisfying social life.[40] But as with her Portia Club in San Francisco, an impressive schedule of social contacts did not translate into a stable clientage.

THE SOCIAL LIFE OF A NEW WOMAN

Trella Toland

Foltz's years in New York included more time with her eldest daughter, now approaching age thirty, than they had since Trella had been a girl. Evidence of their life together is Trella Toland's autograph book. More than two-thirds of the eighty-three entries were made when Foltz was in New York and probably reflect her connections and activities as well as Trella's.[41]

Like her mother, Trella Toland was leading the life of a new woman. Her home on 23rd Street was in the theater, restaurant, and shopping district—and near the newly electrified section of Broadway known as the "great white way." Many actors, artists, and literary types lived in the area, and the streets were alive with well-dressed, good-looking people who worked there or came to shop or dine.

Her autograph book suggests that Trella Toland was an insider in the theater world. Not only stars like Ada Rehan and Sarah Bernhardt signed it, but also Theodore Marceau, photographer of actors, and Niblo, son of one of the first impresarios in the city and founder of Niblo's Garden. In the book as well was the pastor of the "little church around the corner" in Trella's neighborhood, which had provided funeral rites for actors when other denominations refused.

Writers and journalists, such as Richard Harding Davis, who would soon be making headlines by his reporting of the Spanish–American War, also appeared in these pages. Lorimer Stoddard, a noted playwright, signed on the same page as Homer Davenport, a celebrated cartoonist whose attacks on business monopolies led to the introduction of an anticartoon bill in the

1897 New York legislature. He drew a cartoon for Trella, which someone cut from the book, perhaps to frame.

Though some of the entries were the standard sentiments of people who gave many autographs, many were personal or written on special occasions. Elizabeth Cady Stanton, for instance, signed on her birthday in 1896 ("man and woman—a simultaneous creation"). There were other figures from the women's rights movement, like George Francis Train, an early and controversial backer of Stanton and Anthony.

Clara Foltz wrote a fond inscription in July 1895, and Virginia Foltz signed a year later when she was in the city to audition for light opera: "Another California Girl Wins Laurels in New York," Trella proudly wrote about her sister's reception. But in the end, Virginia resolved to stay at the New England Conservatory of Music and then study further abroad.[42] In the summer of 1896, David, "Brother Foltzy," also signed the autograph book ("Do I love you? Yes. Have I proven it—nit"). He had moved to New York at about the same time as his mother, taking offices on Park Row to start an eastern branch of the *Call*. But nothing came of the venture, and David returned to San Francisco.

As befitted a new woman, Trella was serious about her career. She wrote a review of the London production of *Trilby* in 1896, which revealed her desire to play the lead role in this trans-Atlantic sensation. A best-selling novel and subsequent hit play, *Trilby* tells the story of an artist's model who becomes a celebrated singer when hypnotized by Svengali and of her struggles to escape his spell. It was a great role for an actress, and Trella's ambition to portray this "unique heroine" was a high aspiration.[43]

The life of an actress, including late hours and London tours, did not fit with daily mothering, so Trella boarded her son, William, from an early age at the Hudson River Military Academy in Nyack. Her decision to take him to New York with her in 1890 had repercussions five years later when his wealthy grandmother died in San Francisco and left the boy only a nominal bequest. Sam Shortridge filed a suit contesting the will on his nephew's behalf, and the papers printed large pictures of the darling boy, so mysteriously short-changed by his formerly doting grandmother. The matter was just heating up in June 1896 when Uncle Sam wrote in Trella's book "come back to us—to our home and heart; to those who love, and would serve you." Trella's return with William would certainly have helped the case, but she did not go back.[44]

After much legal maneuvering and further publicity, the will contest was settled for $20,000, a lot of money though less than half the amount claimed in the suit.[45] Several formal pictures of William and Trella from this period show a serious boy and a sad-eyed mother. They did not see much of each other, and to some it probably appeared as a case of a "new woman" abandoning the responsibilities of motherhood for her career.

Perhaps Trella had to work to support herself and William. Since she continued her career after the large settlement, however, it seems more likely that she had had enough of hands-on mothering as the oldest of five during the years after Jeremiah Foltz deserted the family. In fact, none of Foltz's children took up parenthood enthusiastically. The others were childless except for Bertha, who had a son early in her first marriage.

New Women in New Places

As new women, Clara Foltz and Trella Toland were out in public at times when most respectable ladies were at home. Foltz's office hours were from 10 a.m. to 7:30 p.m., and Trella's schedule was the irregular one of a performer. Neither had the time or place for the rounds of formal calls, parlor entertainments, and dinner parties that usually comprised social life. Yet old conventions made it hard for the new women to construct an alternative.

One night in February 1897, mother and daughter had an experience that typified the difficulties. They had attended an exhibition about x-rays, a recent invention, and were caught in a rainstorm upon leaving the hall. Ducking into a nearby restaurant, Foltz planned to ask the staff to summon a carriage but thought that she should order something before seeking this favor. When she beckoned a waiter, however, he told them "with a grin and a sneer" that unescorted women could not be served after 9:30 p.m. "You must get out," he told Foltz and pulled her chair back from the table. "The waiters and the men who were being served in the restaurant laughed aloud and chugged one another's elbows over this great joke," according to one description.[46]

Apparently, Foltz was unaware of this ban, which came about as restaurants in New York made the transition from being strictly male establishments. Indeed, by the mid-1890s many places, especially hotel restaurants, were actually seeking women's patronage. But in order to attract "nice" ladies, they had to keep the prostitutes out—thus the rule against unescorted women. (The rule was a rough fit, as successful ladies of the night might well be escorted.)

Foltz filed a lawsuit against the restaurant seeking $5,000 to compensate for her humiliation and mental distress, framing it as a civil rights case brought to "defend her sex" from unequal treatment. She encouraged publicity over the incident, making a point about women's rights and perhaps trying to force a good settlement. Though the outcome of the suit is not known, Foltz did refuse to consider settling for an apology.[47]

A few months after the restaurant incident, she again criticized inappropriate assumptions about unescorted women, this time attacking the "fly squads"—plainclothes police officers who arrested prostitutes after posing as potential customers. She claimed they were harassing respectable women and that "a half dozen law suits against officious policemen would make them respect the law they abuse."[48]

Though these suits and threatened suits show Foltz out in public at hours previously reserved for private entertaining, she also engaged in more conventional home and parlor activities. An interviewer in July 1897 reported that Foltz had "a large circle of friends" and did not neglect "her social duties."[49] One of her New York circle was Lillie Devereux Blake, who, like Foltz, was a new woman of an older generation.

Lillie Devereux Blake

Foltz first met Blake at Sarah Knox-Goodrich's house in San Jose while Blake was on a lecture tour during the 1870s. They saw each other again in San Diego in 1888 where Blake was delivering her popular title "Is It a Crime to Be a Woman?" One of her examples was a New York waitress who dressed as a man to make better wages and was sentenced to six months in jail.[50]

Unlike most of the pioneer suffragists, Blake had the background of a southern belle rather than an abolitionist reformer. She came to the women's movement in her late thirties, through the influence of Anthony and Stanton. With the passion of a convert, Blake authored a best-selling novel about marriage with the no-nuance title *Fettered for Life*, which all the suffragists were reading when Clara Foltz first started studying law. Heavily plotted and slightly risqué for the time, it featured five New York women of different classes and types but all alike in their oppression. One wanted to be a lawyer, but her father objected and she married a tyrant who ruined her life. The only character to escape a tragic female fate did it by passing as a man.[51]

Blake backed her oratorical and literary efforts with solid administrative ability and a flair for publicity. In 1886, she led a protest against the erection of the female Statue of Liberty at the "gateway of a nation in which women were not free" and hired a steamer to carry suffragists and their banners in the official opening ceremony.[52] When women were excluded from the posh Pilgrim Fathers Dinner, Lillie Blake founded a Pilgrim Mothers Dinner, which became a festive annual institution.

Her greatest contribution was her lobbying effort in Albany. Year after year, Blake arranged the introduction of bills to improve conditions for women: to provide for police matrons, for instance, and to allow suffrage, if not across the board, then for school or municipal offices. She became a familiar and efficacious figure in the capitol. One legislator credited her with "changing the whole method of the suffrage campaign, by bringing beauty and grace and charm of loveliest womanhood" to aid her arguments.[53]

Like Clara Foltz, Lillie Blake cultivated a wide circle of friends and acquaintances of different types. She proselytized for suffrage among the society women and their husbands, speaking to private gatherings as well as at conventions and rallies. Among the movement women, Blake, who was fourteen years older than Foltz, was especially attractive as a model and generous as a friend. For one thing, she loved socializing and storytelling in the tradition of her southern background, weaving entertaining tales from her own experiences, much as Foltz herself did. When she was in town, Blake held a weekly gathering where interesting people of both sexes came together for good talk over a glass of wine and a slice of cake. That kind of informal entertaining was typical of the new woman at home.

Mrs. Frank Leslie

Foltz's celebrity as a movement woman afforded access to professional and bohemian circles like those she had enjoyed in the West. For instance, one night in the fall of 1896, she was the dinner guest of "Mrs. Frank Leslie," whose entertainments were legendary. On his deathbed, Miriam Leslie's husband asked her to take over his troubled publishing empire and vindicate his reputation. She changed her own name to "Frank Leslie" and through a combination of hard work and business acumen rescued and consolidated the various Leslie publications. Throughout the 1880s, Mrs. Leslie employed hundreds of illustrators, reporters, feature writers, engravers, and printers in her Park Row offices.[54]

Mrs. Frank Leslie's age was "about thirty" for at least three decades. For many years, she held a Thursday night salon, attended by a mix of writers, visiting royalty, stage people, and politicians. Her doings were constantly in the paper: a threatened duel between two young admirers with old titles; her rumored love affair with Joaquin Miller, the poet of the Sierras; and her disastrous but brief marriage to Willie Wilde, Oscar's brother. Leslie had a series of husbands, but no children, and she spoke openly of the bad effects of pregnancy on a woman's body.

She promoted her daily regimen as ideal for the new woman. Arising around seven in the morning, Leslie took a cold plunge, worked out with barbells and pulleys, and then dressed in soft silk underneath and an outer garment so stiffened with stays that it never showed a wrinkle. Her only daytime meal was a breakfast of toast and steak. At the office by 9:00 or 9:30 a.m., she wrote columns, made the chief editorial decisions on two weekly and two monthly magazines, handled a huge correspondence, signed money orders, and made contracts. At 4:00 p.m. she drove up Park Avenue behind a fine pair of bays and started her evening activities.

Perhaps Mrs. Frank Leslie was too original and inimitable to be the ideal of a new woman. Yet she was independent, mentored other women writers, admired Susan B. Anthony, and left her fortune to the suffrage cause. Clearly, she was also taken with Clara Foltz. Several weeks after they dined together, a flattering story titled "Women Lawyers in America" appeared in *Leslie's Illustrated Weekly*, with its circulation of one million.[55] The article, which featured Foltz's profile in the center of a large photographic spread, reported that the number of women lawyers had doubtless more than doubled from the 208 counted in the 1890 census, which meant that the United States led the world in female attorneys. Prejudice and opposition were said to be fading and women to be freely admitted in all courts and most law schools—with the notable exceptions of the most elite, Columbia, Harvard, and Yale. Foltz's story—left a widow, lobbied a bill, sued Hastings—was used to illustrate the obstacles of the past. Though Mrs. Frank Leslie obviously admired Foltz, there is no indication that she referred any of the many legal matters within her purview to the woman lawyer.

The Endgame in New York

After several years, Foltz gave up the struggle to establish a lucrative practice in New York City and began looking for an exit strategy that would allow her to leave with head high and cash in hand. As usual, she was not tied down by the constraints of her established identity as a pioneer woman lawyer, suffrage leader, and emerging public intellectual. Renewing the western-style get-rich-quick bent she had shown during the San Diego land boom, she put out a handsome brochure announcing the Clara Foltz Gold

Mining Company: "A Prospect of Tenfold Profit with Return of Investment Guaranteed."[56]

The prospectus featured photographs of attractive Idaho scenery and a primitive mining operation and claimed discovery of "an enormous deposit of gold-bearing gravel." At the end were letters from mining experts opining that the gold could be easily extracted by an inexpensive technique. One of the experts was Foltz's long-time intimate Charles Gunn, at her side as usual when she was having difficulty.

Foltz had originally incorporated the gold mine in 1896 as the Idaho–Klondyke Company, probably for a client, and two years later changed the company name to her own and assembled a group of New York businessmen as investors to attract others. James T. White was president of the Foltz Company, with four of his friends and associates as officers of the corporation.

White had been a publisher in San Francisco when Foltz had burst on the public scene as the West's first woman lawyer in 1878. He had moved to New York in the mid-1880s and made a great success of an early version of *Who's Who* called *The National Cyclopaedia of American Biography*. This was the first such publication to include women as well as men, the living as well as the dead, and business and professional people in addition to statesmen, generals, and literary figures.[57]

The brochure promised that White would bring to gold mining "the same carefulness and economy" that he had shown in publishing. As a man who weighed reputations for his living, White may have decided that Foltz's name on the mining company would help sell stock, reassuring prospective buyers that a woman of her reputation would not endorse a fraudulent or wildly speculative venture. But speculative it was, and it appears that the investors lost their money. Foltz probably profited in the short run from the loan of her name, thus enabling her exit from New York, but the gold mining company was never listed in her catalog of career achievements.

It was while she was in Boise, Idaho, looking over the gold mine early in 1898 that Foltz first hinted she would soon be leaving New York, noting that her life was "cemented" to the West. By summer, she was speaking openly of her dissatisfaction with the East. Asked by a *Tribune* reporter why no woman was "a tangible success" at the New York bar, Foltz did not make her usual claim to be flourishing. Instead, she blamed the "ill-concealed, often rude opposition of the legal fraternity . . . who regard [women lawyers] as freaks rather than mental equals." Uncharacteristically revealing a weak position, and indicating that she was no longer located in the prestigious Temple Court address, she commented: "When a woman takes an office and fails to make the rent, wiseacres shake their heads and say, 'I told you so, no place for women.'" Bitterly, she added that many young men, "kindergarten lawyers," had their rent paid while they established their practices by "a mother, sister or old aunt" and in some instances by "women . . . who have forgotten more law than the kindergartener will ever know." A few months after this interview, Foltz abruptly moved her practice to Denver, Colorado.[58]

From an impressive office building in that city, she announced a specialty in mining law, particularly handling "safe" investments for her clients. She lived in the plush Brown Palace Hotel rather than in a more permanent setting. Though Foltz had no family and few friends in Denver, she apparently chose it because of her success in the Bolles divorce case. Her client Julia Bolles was still in Colorado, also living in the Brown Palace.[59]

Perhaps Foltz hoped to build a client base on that relationship, and more generally to act as an investment counselor for wealthy women in the same way she had for Bolles. Also, women had achieved suffrage in Colorado in 1893, and Foltz believed that where women voted, women lawyers could make a good living.[60] In this, she was to be disappointed more than once.

In addition to opening her practice, Foltz launched a weekly magazine named *The Mecca*, of which she would be editor and publisher. Colorado should draw "every self-respecting woman from every point of the world's compass," Foltz wrote. The magazine boosted the "bright and active young commonwealth" and featured interviews with local politicians and businessmen, society and club notes, undistinguished poetry and fiction, and editorial opinions on issues like whether the church should oppose or embrace social dancing (embrace it).[61]

After only a few issues, Foltz left Denver without any public explanation; *The Mecca* was continued by a younger couple who had helped her start it. Back in New York in January 1899, Foltz was interviewed by Theodore Dreiser, then a freelance journalist early in the career that would make him one of the major American novelists of the realist school. "The Career of a Modern Portia" was her last substantial coverage in the eastern press, which had been very attentive over two and a half years. Ironically, the article appeared in a publication titled *Success*.[62] This was one of the new low-priced magazines that started in the 1890s and catered to a wider audience than the elite periodicals like *The Century*, *Harper's*, and the *North American Review*. *Success* specialized in stories of individual achievement, usually featuring men. Thomas Edison, Andrew Carnegie, and Marshall Field were the subjects of other articles Dreiser wrote around the same time.

Portrayed on the eve of her departure from New York City, Foltz had a discouraged air. She said that "a woman with any distinctive characteristics" was apt to be "ostracized, more or less," warning that a professional woman "will find the social prejudices and inherited opinions concerning her proper sphere in life, almost insurmountable obstacles." As always, however, Foltz kept up appearances—and male writers, like the many women who interviewed Foltz, felt it important to comment on it. Dreiser described her as having "an attractive exterior" and as "a handsome blonde with a rich strong voice and an oratorical manner when aroused." He pointed out that her dress was in "the extreme of style and a Redfern gown has been no unusual costume for her." (John Redfern was an English designer who first introduced tailored suits for women.)

Although her clothes were in the latest fashion, Foltz's stories were old ones. She spoke of the Hastings case, her switch to the Democrats a decade earlier, the $75,000 settlement in the Bolles case, the shipwreck in the English Channel—not a word about law practice or other activities in New York City. By April 1899, Foltz was back in San Francisco.

In her self-presentation over the rest of her life, Foltz made no reference to the New York period, except to speak of the campaign for a public defender that she waged there. Even her homecoming interviews were vague, noting mainly that she had been "challenged at every step." While encouraging women to be lawyers, Foltz warned that they "must expect the rebuffs of the pioneer." She said she was happy to be back where she belonged— among "the patriotic, earnest and honest people of the west."[63]

The New Century in California

STARTING OVER

In San Francisco, the city Foltz always called "the cradle of my ambitions," where her early triumphs were part of the local lore, she tried for the third time to succeed at practicing law.[64] Advertising specialties in business and mining law, she set out to create a western version of the New York corporate practice she had failed to penetrate. But her reported cases were mostly the same kind of mundane matters she handled in the East.

For instance, she sued a horse-beater on behalf of the Society for the Prevention of Cruelty to Animals and tried to have a man imprisoned for defaulting on his alimony. When she lost these cases, she denounced the police court and threatened that "the women of the land would take the law into their own hands." She represented herself when a New York dentist sued for "restoring her molars" and got the bill reduced from $307 to $94. None of these matters was a good advertisement for Foltz's legal talent, nor did they portray her as a newly minted corporate lawyer after the New York model.[65]

For a time, however, soon after her return, a Southern California oil boom spurred by increased demand and improved technology brought Foltz new possibilities for practice and fresh business opportunities. "Many Quick Fortunes Made," the *New York Times* reported early in 1900, and told of the giant pool of oil being drilled in the Los Angeles area.[66] Oil was the state's third boom after gold and silver in the 1850s and land in the 1880s.

As so often in the past, with San Diego real estate, Idaho gold, and Denver as a Mecca for women, Foltz joined the booster brigade. She wrote of hope "kindled in the hearts of the people" who had been (like herself) "waiting for something to happen, knowing not what to do." Adding her own inspirational populist touch, she noted that in the past, only the rich could afford to invest, but now "the doors of the temple of fortune are wider" and people of all means "may share in the supreme opportunity which has come to us." By means of the oil boom, Foltz promised, "the poor and despairing may become opulent and happy."[67] She bought some undeveloped property near Los Angeles and set up three companies to explore and drill for oil. As usual, C. E. Gunn was with her, filing articles of incorporation for two of the businesses. Her sons and brother Charles were among the officers, and Foltz herself was the attorney for the companies.

Reprising her San Diego days, Foltz became a boom publisher. Starting in June 1901 she put out a monthly magazine, *Oil Fields and Furnaces*. On the cover, the goddess Petrolia held an oil-burning torch to guide ships laden with California crude "through the Golden Gate to our possessions . . . to bring back the treasures of the orient." The design was reminiscent of the great seal of California, on which Minerva welcomes the gold-rush ships, and at the same time it exploited the expansive imperialist sentiment generated by the Spanish–American War.

Soon after joining the boom, Foltz visited the oilfields to see with her own eyes what she was selling—"the red oil sand and oil seepages, the beds of asphalt and the formation and stratification of the rock." She wrote an account of her trip, "Through the Oil Fields A-Flying," which shows her ability to enjoy herself no matter how hard pressed. One day she stopped at a spa and took the mineral baths; on another she joined up with "a genuine young Norwegian dressed in a natty fitting summer suit" to inspect "the orange groves and their strange bedfellows the oil wells." She joked that the two of them were like "Paul and Virginia," the couple in a famous French novel who live on a paradisiacal island free of artificial social restrictions.[68]

She spent almost a week in Southern California, meeting people in the field and collecting samples (to the consternation of a man who insisted on carrying her bag later). Generally, Foltz took up the promotion of oil with great enthusiasm. Her magazine was written in the overheated language of a boom—describing the rich oilfields, praising the extraordinary engineers and businessmen in the lead, and exhorting readers to join, support, boost, and invest.

Somewhat incongruously, *Oil Fields and Furnaces* also served as an outlet for Foltz's literary writing and political commentary. Virtually one entire issue was devoted to the assassination of President William McKinley within a year of his landslide reelection. Foltz denounced his killer, a demented young man who called himself an anarchist. Although Leon Czolgosz was tried and hanged without any real defense presented for him, Foltz apparently saw no connection with the indigent accused she had so long championed.[69]

Many of the old group of lawyers and writers who used to socialize in the 1880s were together again, including Madge Morris and Harr Wagner, who were back in San Francisco from San Diego. Morris wrote a gossip column in *Oil Fields* that followed their activities. In one issue, Foltz reminisced that her friends had come to Morris's defense when Ambrose Bierce, "by far the most trenchant writer of the times," had attacked her. He made fun of Morris for using the word *howl* five straight times (referring to a coyote) in her "Ode to the Desert." Foltz reprinted the "Ode," commenting that the once solitary and silent desert it described was now filled "with the roar of machinery and the hum of industry."[70]

Instead of the Montgomery Block as in the past, the group's center was now the Parrott Building on Market and Fourth streets, where the oil companies and their attorneys were located. It was one of the most attractive new buildings in the city, with a department store on the ground level and a large central courtyard in the Parisian style. For a while Foltz reigned on the top floor as queen of the oil promoters in San Francisco.

FULL CIRCLE: RETURNING TO THE REPUBLICANS

Foltz had started the 1890s as a Bellamy Nationalist, envisioning radical change achieved in an orderly fashion by evolutionary means. Woman suffrage, public defense, and redistribution of wealth were the political aims that most interested her, and these easily translated into Populism after Nationalism failed as a full-fledged political party. When she went home to California at the end of the decade, however, Clara Foltz returned to the Republican Party, and it welcomed her back.

Foltz seems to have made the move partly from admiration for McKinley, a kindly midwestern father figure. She was an official campaigner, probably paid, in the presidential campaign of 1900. Once again, she stumped the length of California, just as she had done in the 1880s, and she also spoke in Utah and Idaho, where women could vote. And though the party made no promises, Foltz assured her Republican audiences that the new century would soon bring suffrage to the whole country.[71]

In addition to admiring McKinley, Foltz was caught up in the surge of patriotic imperialism that gripped the country as a result of the Spanish–American War, carried out during the Republican administration and in which the party's vice presidential candidate, Theodore Roosevelt, had been a hero. Many of her fellow San Franciscans supported the war and were especially keen on the battles in the Philippines, which were staged from the West. It was a point of civic pride that their city was the launching point of the new American Empire, and many thousands turned out to cheer the forces when they left and when they returned. Westerners, including Clara Foltz, believed that owning the Philippines would do wonders for their own ports and trade. "We may now dominate the world, encompass the grandest standards of commercial supremacy, and fulfill our most exalted ideals of public duty," she declared.[72]

Instead of silver or gold, the 1900 presidential campaign centered on the future of the foreign lands—Cuba, the Philippines, Guam, and Puerto Rico—acquired from Spain in the war. The Republican position was that the inhabitants of the colonies must be brought along by an indeterminate period of education before they could be considered for all the rights and benefits that Americans enjoyed. Given the nonwhite population of the islands, there was a distinct element of racism in this view.

William Jennings Bryan, running again for the Democrats, urged that Americans should free the former Spanish colonies and get out of governing faraway places altogether. Foltz did not agree with this approach, but she firmly believed as a matter of "morality, not politics," that "the constitution follows the flag," meaning that foreign people under American rule were entitled to the full rights of citizens, just as had been the case in the U.S. territories before they became states.[73]

The Republicans won the election by an overwhelming popular and Electoral College vote. Shortly afterwards, the U.S. Supreme Court held in the first of the so-called insular cases that the people of Puerto Rico enjoyed only essential rights—such as due process—rather than the full benefits of the Constitution. Mr. Dooley, a cartoon character, said that maybe the Constitution followed the flag, but the Supreme Court followed the election returns. Elihu Root, the secretary of state, joked that the Court held that "the Constitution follows the flag—but doesn't quite catch up with it." Clara Foltz, a San Francisco lawyer and oil entrepreneur, promised that "evolution will get in its work. The Supreme Court will reverse itself, as it has done many times before."[74]

On the local political level, Foltz returned to find San Francisco in the midst of a reaction to the boss rule that had flourished for most of its history. An old friend, Democrat James Phelan, had been elected mayor on a reform ticket in 1897 and had promoted the passage of a new city charter in 1898. Though the charter promised much that was never delivered—such as the public ownership of utilities—it did offer hope for relief from some of the graft, vice, and corruption that had long prevailed in the city's politics.[75]

It turned out, however, that traditions of machine politics were stronger than the reform impulses. After a crippling transportation strike ended in violence and a secret settlement in 1901, Phelan decided not to run again. A new party took over, Union–Labor, led by a new boss, Abe Ruef, a lawyer whose front man for mayor was a handsome union musician. Very soon into the new century, the city politics were as corrupt and boss-dominated as ever.[76]

All the parties, movements, leagues, and labor unions were split between reform and conservative elements. In this complex scene, one thing was still certain: there was no place for women in the power politics of the city. That had been true when Foltz left San Francisco, and if anything, the situation had grown worse for women in her absence.

Since the heartbreaking 1896 defeat of a suffrage referendum (see Chapter 6), the movement had taken a new tack. Women had shifted their public activity from direct legislative campaigns for the vote to organizing in groups dedicated to charities, education, and civic improvement. Always an ardent joiner, Clara Foltz found the new mode congenial and seemingly connected with any group that asked her. In 1902, for instance, the women's auxiliary of the Masons featured Foltz as one of the organizers of a charity ball. She was pictured looking good in the latest fashion and promising that the ball would "outdo any previous effort" and that "masks would stay on until eleven o'clock." But her other activities did not mean she gave up on suffrage; soon after her arrival she started a new club and invited prominent women like Phoebe Hearst to join her.[77]

FAMILY MATTERS

With her mother and her oldest son, Samuel, Foltz reestablished her San Francisco household. Both Samuel and David were handsome bachelors about town until 1905, when they married within months of each other. Neither had a well-defined career path, though both worked for their Uncle Charles when he was in the newspaper business and were often involved in their mother's activities, currently the oil business. Foltz's daughter Bertha was also in San Francisco, playing supporting roles in musicals and dramas. She was married to a fellow-actor, Lafayette Smalley, who doubled as the bartender at the Baldwin Hotel and Theater. They had one child, Clara's second grandson, a boy called Fay.

Both of Foltz's brothers, Sam and Charles, were in the area as well and often in the news. Samuel was in practice with the famous Delphin Delmas, but he was best known as a Republican orator, delivering fierce partisan speeches in mellifluous tones. Often on the platform dedicating a park or offering the main address on a patriotic holiday, he was an official elector for McKinley and working his way up in the party; he would eventually reach his goal of a seat in the U.S. Senate.

Charles no longer edited the *San Francisco Call*; Foltz wrote that his support of the suffragists in 1896 had resulted in his losing the post.[78] He was the more colorful and somewhat less respectable brother; his reported adventures included a bankruptcy, libel suits, and occasional brawls and contempt citations. Somewhere along the line, he read law and joined the bar. In 1908, he divorced his second wife and shortly afterward married a much younger woman, his ward, and started his third family.

On the whole, the first few years after Foltz's return from New York seem like good ones for her. Her participation in the oil boom compensated for the continued failure of her law practice to produce a large, steady income, and her social and club life appear to have been satisfying. But this happiness was interrupted in 1903 with the death of Trella at the age of only thirty-seven.[79] The cause was dropsy, a fatal swelling often associated with heart or kidney disease. Trella was appearing regularly on the New York stage and had recently married a younger man who worked for Joseph Pulitzer's *World*. In her little autograph book, she had written a note to herself just two years before she died: "I am rich in a good man's love that brings a happiness few on this earth enjoy."

Trella Evelyn, born when Foltz was a girl herself, had been comrade and collaborator as well as daughter. My "darling first born" was her tagline when she spoke of Trella, who had a role in many stories. Her death began the most tragic chapter in Foltz's life, as four of her five children would die before her: Bertha in 1915, Samuel in 1919, and David in 1932.

She seems to have dealt with Trella's loss mainly by denial. For instance, when writing to a friend soon after the death, Foltz did not speak of it. And when, after some months of absence, she was again in the press, she gave her usual lines about educating and raising five children, without mentioning that one had died.[80]

LAST DAYS IN SAN FRANCISCO

In 1904, Foltz left the Parrott Building, which may have signaled an end to oil promotion as her main activity. It is not clear what happened to the companies she incorporated, though it is likely that along with many other boom businesses, they failed to tap into the huge pool of oil that was surely there. Foltz herself stayed involved in the business for the next several decades, but the only thing that can be said with certainty is that she never struck it rich. At about the time of her move from the Parrott, her magazine merged with the *National Oil Reporter*, an organ of the Standard Oil Company, and there may have been some profit in that.

Foltz changed offices often over the years—sometimes because of a shift in her practice or associations and sometimes just ahead of the rent collector. Whatever the circumstances, she chose imposing locations among the leading lawyers, whose ranks she always aspired to join. This time, it was the Mills Building, one of the best new addresses in the city. Foltz's main activity when she made this move was as attorney for the United Bank and Trust Company. She directed a women's branch of the bank, encouraging female investors. A 1905 interview quoted her remarking on the bank's "almost phenomenal growth" in a short period. But within months of this comment, the state bank commissioners shut United down on the grounds of probable insolvency. The bank had been launched during a regulatory interregnum and was undercapitalized from the outset; some reports called it a "wildcat" bank. More than half of its assets were promissory notes from its stockholders. There were also allegations of waste and mismanagement.[81]

Foltz's name did not appear in the news stories about the bank's suspension, and it reopened after some weeks. She moved to the United Bank's offices on Bush Street, apparently to aid in its reform efforts. Whether the bank was or could have been saved is impossible to determine, however, because the 1906 San Francisco earthquake and fire devastated the business district and created a break in the record.

THE EARTHQUAKE AND FIRE OF 1906

Strangely for such a raconteur, Foltz never developed an earthquake tale for use in the many newspaper interviews in which she told her life story. Nor did she mention it in the autobiographical columns she composed from 1916 to 1918, "Struggles and Triumphs of a Woman Lawyer." Perhaps like Trella's death, the experience was too awful. Or perhaps, unlike the shipwreck in the English Channel, Foltz's part in it did not have the elements of a good story—no heroics, no unusual themes, no triumphant endings.

Foltz was living with her mother on Second Avenue when the quake struck at 5:12 a.m. on Wednesday, April 15. Always an early riser, she probably heard the sound, described as like the ocean's roar or a fast train's approach, which preceded the first short, severe shock. Then there was a pause followed by a terrifying shaking, twisting, rumbling, and wrenching that lasted forty to sixty seconds.[82]

The city suffered serious damage from the quake, but the greatest destruction was caused by ensuing fires. Within minutes, the first blazes started in the poor districts south of Market Street. Three fearful days would pass before the last one was extinguished, leaving four hundred city blocks devastated, with only a few isolated buildings still standing. Foltz's office on Bush Street was obliterated—a snapshot in a family album shows the rubble. But the fires did not reach the commercial center until the second day, and apparently Foltz was able to save her books and files. A month later she advertised her return to practice with "library and papers intact."[83]

Her diminutive rolltop desk was gone, though, and so were many of the landmarks of her life and career. Most of her office sites were damaged or demolished. The Palace Hotel where she loved to have tea, the Metropolitan Temple whose platform she had commanded, the Hall of Justice where she made headlines trying jury cases—all burned out. Only the old Montgomery Block came through, riding out the temblors and the fire because of its float construction and concrete walls.

Clara Foltz was comparatively lucky. Her home was still standing and all family members were uninjured. She was able to restart her practice out of her residence in a neighborhood where the fires had not reached and filed at least one suit across the bay in Oakland, where the courts had not been closed by the disaster.[84] But it was impossible to resume ordinary law business and social interaction, and Foltz did not join the many other San Franciscans who stayed to rebuild the city.

By December 1906, she was in Los Angeles—a move she may have contemplated earlier when she visited the oilfields and spoke of "the subtle bewitching atmosphere" of the growing town.[85] The oil boom and improved rail connections brought more residents to Southern California by the day, most of them midwesterners, a type Foltz knew well from her youth. For Clara Foltz, a perpetual seeker of fame and fortune in new places, there might still be time to get in on the ground floor of California's second metropolis.

SETTLING IN LOS ANGELES

As it turned out, Foltz spent the last thirty years of her life in Los Angeles. She achieved her highest offices there, and there she cast a legal vote, enjoying firsthand the triumph of the long suffrage struggle. There, too, she saw the establishment of the first public defender office. But these were also the years during which she lost three more of her children and experienced the passage of the California women's movement into the hands of successors who did not always appreciate her contributions.

After trying out several office buildings, she chose the Merchants Trust Building on Broadway near the Hall of Justice, with many other lawyers nearby, and announced specialties of probate and corporate law. She rented and then purchased a "big beautiful home" at 153 South Normandie, where she settled until her death in 1934.[86] Her mother and Trella's son, William, originally relocated with her, followed eventually by Samuel, David, and Bertha, excepting only Virginia who was still in the East.

From her numerous previous visits and involvement in the oil business, Foltz already had friends and connections in her new location. Woman suffrage, self-improvement, and civic clubs were flourishing—and Foltz joined many and started more (see Chapter 6). Out of all this activity would come the Progressive movement, votes for women, and a dramatic increase in the number of female attorneys.

Even though the law schools in Los Angeles, especially the University of Southern California (USC), welcomed female students, Foltz maintained her longstanding ambition, dating back to Portia Club days, to found and endow a law college devoted exclusively to training women. Soon after her arrival in the city, she started holding classes in her office every Saturday afternoon at 2 p.m. She drew about fifty students, including some well-known clubwomen. One report mentioned Foltz's handsome furnishings, "one of the finest, most up-to-date law libraries in town," and noted that her "financial status is not to be sneezed at" and that "she has earned it all by her ability as a lawyer."[87]

One of the class members was to become Foltz's chief ally in the final suffrage campaign. "Beloved Mary Foy," as Foltz referred to her, was a wealthy woman, a native daughter of Los Angeles, and a popular schoolteacher.[88] Though the women were decades apart in age, Foy, unlike some of the other younger suffragists, admired Foltz and brought out her best. Similarly, Georgia Bullock, a USC law school graduate and young enough to be one of her daughters, considered Foltz the greatest woman lawyer of all time, one whose accomplishment would never be equaled.[89]

Another woman Foltz liked was Elizabeth Kenney, whom she called, without gender limitation, "the ablest young lawyer in Los Angeles." Originally from Illinois, Kenney had graduated from Northwestern Law School and moved west in 1897. She started the Women's Pacific Coast Oil Company, in which only females could be officers but males were allowed to invest. It was apparently a great success, as was a book she published on women's and children's property rights. For many years, Foltz and Kenney signed the same petitions, joined the same clubs, appeared on the same platforms, and generally worked together for suffrage and other causes.[90]

Several years after her move, Foltz described the "heavy demands of my household" in a letter to a friend. Her mother's health had been failing, and she wrote of the hours she spent hanging "over the bed of my dear mother, lifting, bandaging, poulticing, etc. her worn body." Telitha Shortridge would linger with occasional brief revivals until early in 1910 before succumbing to heart disease at the age of eighty-five. Her children remembered her "self-sacrificing spirit" and "constant encouragement." Sons Charles and Samuel took the body back to San Jose to lie beside Elias in the Oak Hill Cemetery.[91]

Foltz had been admitted to the bar on her mother's fifty-third birthday in 1878, and for most of the next thirty-plus years they had been together. Telitha Shortridge took care of the children when Foltz went to court and on lecture tours. She was the gentle critic when her daughter exposed herself to ridicule with the presidential campaign of Belva Lockwood, and the calming helper when she brought old Mrs. Starke home to live. In the past six years, Clara had lost Trella and Telitha, the two people closest to her heart and the best witnesses to the meaning of her own life. Within months of the funeral, she received two noteworthy appointments—the first honors she celebrated without her mother. Both were indirectly tied to Foltz's suffrage activities, and both were also rewards for her pioneering efforts to reform the penal and criminal justice systems.

"SEMI-PUBLIC SERVANT"

State Board of Charities and Corrections

In February 1910, the Republican governor, James Gillett, appointed Clara Foltz to the State Board of Charities and Corrections. She would be the first woman on the board, which had been established in 1903 and empowered to investigate conditions in the charitable, correctional, and penal institutions as well as the hospitals for the insane. The naming of a woman was a result of lobbying by the California Club in San Francisco.[92]

The club had been created by suffragists shortly after the defeat of the 1896 referendum. Focusing on civic improvement rather than their own political equality, these women hoped that once the members became engaged in public affairs, they would realize that they needed the vote to achieve anything significant. It worked out as the founders had planned, and over the next decade, moderate improvement-oriented clubwomen were converted into committed suffragists in large numbers through efforts to beautify the city, rid it of rats, build playgrounds, and save Telegraph Hill. The appointment of a woman to the board overlooking prisons and charitable institutions was another of their successes.[93]

Foltz received her best publicity for a long time from this appointment. Even the antisuffrage Los Angeles Times called it "unusual and unsought." The story continued that she was "a woman of strong characteristics and marked ability," adding that "her interest in the welfare of prisoners is well known." No mention was made of the women's movement.[94]

By contrast, the Los Angeles Herald played up the feminist angle, calling Foltz an "ardent supporter of women's rights" and reporting the role of the

California Club in the appointment. For her part, Foltz "beamed happily from behind a large pile of letters and telegrams of congratulations in her handsomely furnished offices in the Merchants Trust building." She said she felt "highly honored . . . because the appointment has been given to a woman," and offered many examples of her qualifications for the post.[95]

First, she said it was "largely due to my efforts" that the board she was joining had been created by the legislature. She also told of authoring the prison parole system in California, of causing "the abolition of prisoners' cages in the police courts of San Francisco some years ago," and of promoting the hiring of prison matrons and the separation of adults and juveniles in jails and prisons. Lauding the choice, the *Law Journal of L.A.* said Foltz was "fearless, forcible, and capable" and a proven "semi-public servant." The *Tidings* called her one of the "most remarkable women of the age" and said that she possessed "all the tenderness of the true woman and the logical mind of the lawyer." It concluded that she was "peculiarly fit" for the prison board because it "requires . . . tempering of justice with mercy."[96]

Foltz's promotion of the public defender was a point in favor of the appointment, and a number of the press stories mentioned her concern for people imprisoned without adequate counsel. Immediately she turned to using her new position to revive the public defender idea and to make it a cause for women. Her first speech in her new office was on this subject. The occasion was a convention of the American Woman's League in March 1910. Originated by Edward Gardner Lewis, a wealthy Missouri publisher, the league was designed to help prepare women for political participation once suffrage was gained. Lewis funded a conglomerate of institutions, including banks, public libraries, and correspondence course universities, for this purpose.[97]

Originally, Foltz's interest in women's banking drew her to the league, but her speech to the large gathering was not about money management. Instead, she pleaded for "an even break at the bar of justice" for poor people. Foltz said she would introduce her public defender bill in the next session of the California legislature. The women of the league evidently had no doubts about the connection between public defense and female political equality; they collectively pledged their support to the proposal.[98]

Deputy District Attorney

Several months after Foltz joined the Charities and Corrections Board, she was appointed, at age sixty-one, to be a deputy district attorney, the first woman to hold the office in California. Some papers suggested she was probably the first in the country, and Foltz herself said that she was the only female prosecutor "in the world." Like the Corrections Board, this honor came to her through the efforts of organized clubwomen, this time in Los Angeles.[99]

The idea of a special prosecutor to protect the interests of women and girls originated with the Badger Club, a women's group devoted to civic improvement whose members had seen the need while doing volunteer work among the incarcerated. They urged the district attorney to create a woman's post and to select Foltz, citing her appointment to the prison board and other penal reform activities. He agreed and designated Foltz to "look into cases where women, girls, and children are affected."[100] The position was unsalaried, and she maintained her private office and her civil practice.

Foltz saw herself as better in "female" cases than men, who were "clumsy . . . when they have to deal with those weaker than themselves." She thought also that a woman prosecutor could "better find out the truth" in such cases. Though she planned to identify matters "worthy of sympathy and lenience," she rejected special treatment on account of sex. "I am a lawyer and I believe in law," she said. "If I find a woman who should pay the penalty for her acts, you will find that I will be a vigorous prosecutor."[101]

From the first, she sought to expand her role: "I look at the field from a broader standpoint than my sisters do. . . . I will do whatever is given me." On April 25, 1910, Foltz was sworn in at the side of the Lincolnesque district attorney John. D. Fredericks, and she took the occasion to speak about public defense, calling it "the one great ambition of my life." For true justice, she said, both public defenders and public prosecutors were necessary. She lauded Fredericks for his fairness and for avoiding the common attitude of district attorneys that it was their job "to furnish a culprit for every crime committed in their jurisdiction."[102]

Two months after her appointment, Foltz faced her first test as a public prosecutor. A delegation of ministers, muckrakers, and clubwomen came to her to complain because the district attorney was not pursuing the owners of property being used for organized prostitution, "the white slave traffic," as it was known at the time. The obvious response was to promise to look into the matter, thanking the interested citizens for their concern. Instead, Foltz declared, "I don't believe there is any white slave traffic in this city . . . and surely I am in a good position to know." Even if there were such a problem, she said, the male customers were the ones to punish. To hisses and heckling, Foltz added, "I who have been dignified with the beautiful soubriquet, 'sister to all men,' can't believe all men are so bad." One minister rebuked her: "A person who calls herself a public official and who says there is no white slave traffic should not be a public officer."[103]

What was Foltz thinking? First, she may have been right that organized prostitution was not a major issue. A fairly successful campaign against the trade was ongoing, and vice in Los Angeles was always tame compared with the wide-open conditions of San Francisco. Also, she probably took the group's concern as a criticism of herself and her boss, especially since the leaders were her political rivals among the new suffragists. At any rate, it was not Foltz's finest hour.[104]

Her hopes of actually trying important cases did not materialize, though she doubtless did good service for women and girls behind the scenes. Foltz was appointed for a second term in 1911, but after that, the prosecutors became full-time employees subject to civil service rules. These 1910 offices—the highest Foltz attained—both resulted from her feminist affiliations and came to her on the eve of the achievement of woman suffrage in California in 1911. In a real sense, the offices were rewards for her service to the women's movement. It is also notable that she used both appointments to promote her other great cause, the creation of a public defender. With Clara Foltz settled for good in Los Angeles, serving on the prison board and as a prosecutor, the chronological account of her life as a practicing lawyer concludes. The next three chapters cover the stories and cases, events and activities specifically related to her efforts to make her mark as a legal "thinker," to her work for women's rights, and finally to her greatest achievement, her primary role in the invention and creation of the public defender as an established feature of the American legal system.

FIVE

Clara Foltz as Public Thinker

Motivation and Style

In 1890, Matilda Gage, an organizer and historian of the women's movement, introduced Clara Foltz as a lawyer, an orator, a suffrage leader, and a "thinker."[1] Throughout the next decade, Foltz vigorously pursued her claim to that title at the same time that she continued to try for the top ranks of the practicing bar. She was often in the newspapers expressing her opinions on contested issues of the day, and she published five significant articles in prestigious law reviews—quite remarkable for a woman whose formal education had ended before the age of fifteen.

Three of Foltz's articles articulated and promoted her greatest achievement in law reform: her conception of the public defender as an institution (see Chapter 7). The other two were also impressive contributions. In "Evolution of Law," delivered at a convention of women attorneys at the 1893 World's Fair, Foltz anticipated the jurisprudence of the Progressive era. She urged that during a period of increasingly rapid technological and social transformation, legislatures representing broad public opinion must replace the courts as the main agents of change in the law. To aid legislatures in this function, Foltz proposed that the highest state court serve as an expert advisory council on needed legal reforms. Her other article, "Should Women Be Executed?," grew out of a sensational series of cases charging women with murder and criticized the tendency of other movement thinkers to advocate special rather than equal treatment for female criminal defendants. The text and context of these two pieces reveal Foltz's concerns in the 1890s when she sought to make a name as a public thinker.[2]

As she approached her fiftieth birthday, Foltz must have realized that clients with financially significant legal business were not going to choose her, or any woman, to represent them. For all her forensic skill, the jury trial route to lawyerly reputation was not open to her. Even more clearly, the new form of practice that was emerging as the most important, representation of major corporations in their business transactions, was all-male and going to stay that way for the immediate future.

If she could not become a leading jury or corporate lawyer, however, perhaps she could leave an intellectual mark on the profession, which prided itself on being studious as well as powerful and lucrative. What was the basis of ambitions extending so far beyond practicing law, making a living, and even becoming a leader of the bar? Foltz always described her father, Elias Shortridge, as her model of a thoughtful, literate, and engaged citizen, widely read and devoted to writing and speaking on public issues. Like many suffragists—Elizabeth Cady Stanton most strikingly—Foltz connected the cause of women to the general ferment of late-nineteenth-century reformism, with its mix of elements such as Socialism, free-thinking skepticism, and embrace of scientific advances. She also yearned for fame and glory, was attracted to ideas, and felt that she naturally belonged among those who shaped the thought of her time

Undoubtedly, Foltz's motivation to be a thinker had some roots also in what she termed her "imperfect education"—interrupted first by her early marriage and then by the frustration of her efforts to study law at Hastings. One way she tried to make up for both was in the maintenance of her large personal library. Many interviews over the years noted that her collection included not only law books, but fiction and poetry, history, and politics.

Foltz was an ardent reader with a powerful memory and filled her speeches with varied and apt quotations. In the midst of a closing argument, for instance, she might launch some lines from Thomas Carlyle's *Sartor Resartus*—"in immortal youth, / Unhurt amid the war of elements, / the wreck of matter, and the crash of worlds." Or she would needle the prosecutor with an eighteenth-century verse based on Matthew Prior: "Be to his virtues very kind, Be to his faults a little blind" (Foltz changed the pronoun from "her" to "his").

Quotations from the King James Bible and Shakespeare were frequent, but even when alluding to less familiar works, Foltz followed the custom of the time in assuming a fund of common knowledge in her audience. For instance, within a single article, and without identification of sources, she quoted Longfellow, "Let us, then, be up and doing, / With a heart for any fate," and Thomas Moore stanzas on the curative force of nature—"Blest power of sunshine! Genial day! / What balm, what life is in thy ray!"—and on grief—"at random driven / without one glimpse of reason or of Heaven."[3]

Long sentences with lavish quotation were characteristic of late Victorian writing and oratory. So was Foltz's tendency to hyperbole, with allies and heroes described as "grand" and "glorious," opponents and villains as "vicious" and "wicked." The style can be a little jarring today, but Foltz's acute lawyer's mind is evident in the content, and her wit and eloquence often break through across the distance of more than a century.

Clara Foltz's entry into a learned profession had given her a kind of authority available to few women. When she sought to establish herself as a "thinker," or as we would say "a public intellectual," she always spoke as a lawyer. She initiated her new identity in a speech later published as a law review article, delivered to a nationwide meeting of women lawyers at the World's Fair in 1893.

The First Women Lawyers' Meeting

WOMEN IN THE LEGAL PROFESSION

The 1893 Chicago World's Fair was a major event in the history of post–Civil War America, and also in the life of Clara Foltz. The women's movement played a large part at the fair, highlighted by Foltz's inclusion, along with leading male jurists, in the prestigious Congress of Jurisprudence and Law Reform, where she made the speech that definitively set forth her conception of the public defender. The fair also served as the occasion for the first nationwide meeting of women lawyers.

According to the 1890 census, there were 208 women lawyers in the United States, compared with 75 in 1880 and a mere 5 in 1870. It was still a minuscule number balanced against 90,000 male lawyers. An even more telling comparison was with the position of women in other professions—the almost quarter million women teachers, the 4,500 women doctors, and the 1,000-plus women members of the clergy.[4]

One reason why law was such a rare occupation for women was that it had the least plausible connection with the domestic sphere. Women doctors were nurturers, who could minister to their own sex and protect female modesty; teachers and ministers were extending the maternal role as moral instructors to the young. But the legal world was hard to reconcile with the ideal realm of purity and tender feeling that women supposedly inhabited. Like voting, practicing law involved unambiguous passage into the noisy and competitive public sphere.

Another aspect of the case against women lawyers had to do with the presumed distinction between the sexes in their mental equipment. Women were thought to be sympathetic and intuitive, but lacking in analytical and critical powers. Foltz did not oppose the idea that men and women had essential differences of this sort, but she disagreed that these legitimately dictated, either by law or social convention, mandatory limits on individual advancement. "There are two highways to the goal of truth," she said. "If we begin with facts and climb the ladder of logic, the method is inductive," and that is the one men prefer because they are emotionally "hardier, colder and under the dominion of facts." Women, on the other hand, live "under the warmer glow of ideal thought" and naturally tend toward deductive reasoning.[5]

The best results would come from "the union of these methods, the joined efforts of men and women," so Clara Foltz would often say. How do women arrive at their ideas? Directly, she claimed, doubtless describing herself. "These ideas are not reasoned . . . but simply grasped," making women quicker to understand and "to reach a result," which "in the very nature of things" would make them "reliable and efficient lawyers." She left open whether these differences were innate and thus to what extent they could be changed by education and altered social expectations.[6]

LOCATING THE LAWYERS

The women lawyers' meeting was sponsored by the Queen Isabella Association, a Chicago professional organization that, though not officially a part of the World's Fair, held many events in conjunction with it (see Chapter 6 for more on the association). Its idea was to bring together women attorneys to share practical experiences and to create an organization for mutual support. Before the Isabellas could invite the women, though, they had to locate them. One lead was the list compiled by the Equity Club, an organization formed in Michigan in the late 1880s.[7]

With the motto "All the Allies of Each," the club sponsored an annual exchange of letters among women lawyers and law students. Starting from a list of Michigan students and graduates, the group ultimately consisted of thirty-two women around the country who produced sixty letters over a four-year period. "What can be so refreshing to an aspiring soul . . . as to be simply *understood*?" one member wrote. In her letter, Clara Foltz's friend and ally Laura Gordon added, "Every woman in the legal profession must feel that want of professional companionship, that close sympathy born of mutuality of interests, which women alone can extend to a woman."[8]

Women lawyers formed local associations as well. Mary Greene from Massachusetts, an Equity Club correspondent, wrote about a Portia Club in Boston, where the women lawyers and law students met at a hotel for dinner and discussion. Another source for locating women lawyers was the movement press, which from the first trumpeted every newly made lawyer as a victory for the cause.[9] When Arabella Mansfield was admitted in 1869, for instance, Stanton and Anthony declared in martial and legalistic tones: "[T]he Bar has surrendered. Woman carried Medicine and Ministry long ago. And now the legal profession is hers. Woman is going to possess the land in common with man. The whole land and all that appertains."[10]

In 1890, Lelia Robinson produced the results of the first systematic effort to survey the entire female bar, *Women Lawyers in the United States*. She collected her information by writing to all twenty-one of the nation's law school deans, asking about women graduates, and by searching the regular as well as the movement press for every scrap of information she could find. Though women lawyers were frequently publicized curiosities, the information was unsystematic and often unreliable. Robinson complained that "the newspapers publish and republish little floating items about women lawyers along with those of the latest sea-serpent . . . one about as real as the other."[11] Of course, she could not hope to locate all those who apprenticed and practiced locally, or who married and changed their names. Yet despite the difficulties, she managed to describe the work of 120 women lawyers, more than half the number captured in the census of the same year.

A handful of women lawyers were well-known nationally, and their stories were often interconnected so that they were easily found. Membership in the bar of the U.S. Supreme Court is an example. Belva Lockwood had

been the first in 1879 after a protracted struggle and the passage of a statute admitting women to practice in the federal courts. News of her admission had been an important boost to Foltz and Gordon in their suit against
Hastings. Laura Gordon was second to apply to the Supreme Court bar,
sponsored by the same man who supported Lockwood, Albert Riddle. He
had been an abolitionist and after the war turned to the education of the
freedmen at Howard Law School. Probably through Riddle's inspiration,
Lockwood linked the two liberation movements by supporting the admission of the first southern black man, Samuel R. Lowery, the son of slaves.
Ada Bittenbender and Carrie Kilgore, the first women lawyers in Nebraska
and Pennsylvania, respectively, both joined in the 1880s, the same decade in
which they became lawyers.[12]

Early in 1890, Clara Foltz joined the Supreme Court bar while in Washington, D.C., for a suffrage convention. Later that year, Bittenbender
became the first to sponsor another woman, Emma Gillett; and Lelia
Robinson arrived on her honeymoon and was also admitted, commingling,
so she wrote in the *Woman's Tribune*, "all the poetry and romance of the
supreme event of life with the most radical and extreme departure from
the old lines." The same article proudly listed seven women, "standing high
in social and professional life," who had become members of the Supreme
Court bar in the decade since the first was admitted (a period during which
almost four thousand men joined).[13]

Using such lists as the Supreme Court bar members, the Equity Club
correspondents, and Robinson's article as well as their movement contacts
in general, the Isabellas ended up with thirty "Female Blackstones," as the
Chicago Tribune called them.[14] They ranged from Arabella Mansfield, the
first, to Charlotte Holt, who had joined the Illinois bar within the year.
A roomful of women attorneys (plus their audience and admirers) was, to
many, as astounding as any sight at the fair.

THE WOMEN LAWYERS' PROGRAM

Fourteen women lawyers were listed on the program for the meeting, which
was scheduled for two days of lectures and discussion. Many spoke about
their experiences as pioneer women. Mary Elizabeth Lease of Kansas promoted the Populist movement, Belva Lockwood talked about international
arbitration, and Mary Greene surveyed the history of women lawyers in
ancient times.[15]

On the third day, the group held a plenary session and formed the National League of Women Lawyers, with the stated purpose of allowing women lawyers "to learn from each other, to bind ourselves more closely together, to gain from growing numerical strength." Only women in actual practice for five years would be allowed to vote; others would be honorary members. The emphasis on experience made an impression on Foltz. In her first post-fair article, she stressed her "fifteen years of almost constant practice" and was described as one of "the very few women who rank high as an all round lawyer. Whether in the consulting room or at the pleaders' desk, whether arguing a knotty legal point, marshaling the facts before the court, or conducting either a civil or criminal case before a jury, she is equally at home."[16]

A sad part of the women lawyers' coming together and counting their numbers was the memorial for six of them who had died before they could attend such a meeting. Lelia Robinson Sawtelle was the most recent, dead only a few years after she had made headlines by joining the Supreme Court bar on her honeymoon. Lavinia Goodell, the first woman lawyer in Wisconsin, had been gone the longest—almost a decade—but was well-remembered at this first meeting of other first women. Goodell's death at age forty-one had roused a debate over whether women could sustain "the hard usage and severe mental application" of a legal career.[17] The issue of women's fitness came up whenever a pioneer died young. Foltz scoffed at the idea that women were physically or mentally less robust than men, though she herself had collapsed in 1881 and 1884; perhaps she thought that extreme overwork could break down a man as easily as a woman.

After the memorials came the election of officers for the new league. Chosen as first president was Florence Cronise, an early Ohio woman lawyer with twenty years at the bar. Cronise had been a small-town practitioner, doing everything from tort to probate, commercial contracts to criminal defense, and trying cases with the best of them. To the Equity Club she briskly disclaimed "any sentimental view of women's mission" other than to "honestly, earnestly and decently earn my living, doing it in the way I am most fitted for." As she assumed her new office, however, Cronise took a grander view of law practice for women. It not only "strengthened all faculties," but also deepened the "love of humanity" and broadened tolerance toward "the shortcomings of human nature." Confidently, she predicted that because the members of their new league were lawyers, they would rise above "the petty envies and jealousies that seem to creep into other associations."[18]

Thinking about the Evolution of Law

Nothing better illustrates Clara Foltz's aspiration to be recognized as a serious thinker than the words she chose for the Isabellas. She was scheduled to be the last speaker, at the end of two days of continuous lectures. This place on the program was both an honor and a challenge, and to an experienced orator like Foltz, it must also have suggested that she deliver something entertaining, inspirational, and not too demanding. Her repertoire of speeches included just the thing for such an occasion: her oft-used lecture "Lawyers." It was her personal and well-polished perspective on the profession, featuring tales of trying to break into the male preserve of the courtroom. The stories would have entertained Foltz's sister lawyers at the end of a long two days, while reminding them of her own rich experience.

Instead of this sure-fire hit, Foltz composed and delivered a lecture more abstract and intellectual than anything she had previously attempted. "Evolution of Law" was a broad jurisprudential survey, culminating in a concrete proposal for legislative reform of the law's institutional mechanisms. It was a virtuoso performance, smoothly combining familiar rhetoric from the common-law tradition with a characteristic late-nineteenth-century emphasis on historical change, while anticipating the legal thought of the twentieth-century Progressive movement.[19]

Though Foltz referred to women's rights, she did not emphasize them. This was jurisprudence, not a call to arms, and it was also the pronouncement of a confident and learned legal scholar, one perhaps already thinking of herself as a future dean of the Portia Law College. She opened by describing the profession she shared with her audience: "What a study . . . law presents! What a field it traverses!" But the field is not all sunlit; law is "an infinity of good and evil," containing "marvels of prejudice" and "a wilderness of error," yet "what amplitude of reason it unfolds!" Already, this was a departure from the usual bar speech, which would have a more purely celebratory introduction. But the women Foltz addressed knew firsthand that the law was not always a benign civilizing force.

At the same time, they were proud of becoming lawyers against the odds and had high hopes for what they could achieve though their profession. Foltz shared those hopes and expressed them in an optimistic narrative that located prejudice and error mostly in the past, increasingly retreating as "the leaves of the flower of justice have unfolded." She traced five carefully selected developments in areas of law where she and her fellow women lawyers were likely to agree there had been progress.

First was freedom of speech. She sketched the movement "by slow steps" from a "bigoted past," illustrated with vivid examples, "where no man dared to speak, even remotely, of Church or State," to a present where "the right is everywhere admitted and secured by constitutional guaranty." Next came woman's legal emancipation; she was "no longer man's slave." The husband's legal right to beat his wife, the male guardian's to compel the female ward to marry the man of his choice, had been abolished. Married women could own property and make a will, and no woman was now barred from education or the professions or from "all" of the "public places of trust and profit." The "all" was a singularly restrained reference to the suffrage crusade.

Third, workers had been freed from the more humiliating incidents of the feudal regime of master and servant. Gone were the requirements of occupational badges and distinctive clothing, meant to keep laborers or artisans in their places. Gone also was the master's right to "beat his servant into subjection" and the minute legal regulation of the wages and charges allowable for many common occupations.

Foltz then spoke of the reforms in civil procedure, the statutory replacement of the common-law writs, with their jargon, and fictions, by a "more rational" system based on "plain statement" and providing that "facts" be pleaded. These reforms were significant in the professional lives of her lawyer audience, and Foltz acknowledged their larger implications as well; the "narrow and technical path to the temple of justice" had "broadened into a highway."

Finally, she turned to the criminal justice system, whose contemporary failings she usually bitterly condemned in her public lectures. But now, Foltz the thinker, speaking from the longer perspective of history, saw great progress. The number of capital crimes had been reduced; brutal punishments like whipping, branding, mutilation, and burning at the stake had been abolished; torture of witnesses was unlawful; and trial by ordeal was gone. The defendant could testify, call witnesses, and be represented by counsel.

On the surface, Foltz's tale of law's forward steps resembled the celebratory accounts that were the usual fare for the establishment bar in the late nineteenth century. Law was progressing and was helping to make society more rational and more humane. Leading conservative lawyers would have said much the same thing. But Foltz's examples, and the forces for change she mentioned as well as the legal institutions she emphasized, departed from the standard in important ways. For one thing, her chosen areas of progress had a clear slant to the left. Freedom of speech, rights of criminal

defendants, and especially rights of women and workers were causes that
would be taken up by the Progressives of the following decades. Even on the
more arcane issue of the reform of civil procedure, she emphasized that its
main effect was to increase the access of ordinary people to the courts.

An establishment lawyer might have mentioned one or two of the reforms Foltz highlighted, but not all, and would have balanced them by emphasizing the contribution of rationalized contract and property law to the
growth of commerce, as Foltz did not. Not only did Foltz's chosen examples
of legal progress promote causes dear to reformers of her period, but they
had mostly been achieved through legislation or constitutional enactment
rather than through gradual common-law development.

Her most striking anticipation of Progressive legal thought was her promotion of democratic public opinion as the driving force behind change
in the law, and the legislature as its primary agent. The impetus for both
the progress she had described and the "wiser future jurisprudence" that
she anticipated was "the irresistible pervasive influence of numbers with a
common thought." Public opinion was the "vital spark" and "laws but the
expression of this force." If law was rooted in public opinion, it followed
that the legislature "should be the birthplace of change and reform." This
"elective body chosen by the people from its own number . . . should be
quick to feel, and prompt to respond to public demands." But as Clara Foltz
knew all too well from her extensive experience in the legislative sausage factory of Sacramento, the actual bodies fell far short of the ideal.

Most important, they lacked expertise; legislators "from the people" did
not know how to "properly draft or successfully advocate a law to crush an
evil or work a reform." Parochialism, "the petty demands of a local constituency," diverted the few legally skilled legislators into projects like "fixing a
bounty on coyote scalps." (Foltz here referred to a well-known fiasco in which
the California legislature had offered five dollars a scalp and ended with a
staggering debt and more coyotes than ever. The animals simply tripled their
litter size, and it was rumored that the supply of scalps had been augmented
by "coyote farms" in neighboring states.[20]) Finally, she said that legislators
were always tempted by the "gerrymandering measure for party benefit."

Foltz's clear-eyed catalog of the faults in the real-world legislative process echoed what conservative promoters of the common-law tradition had
long said. Their invariable response, however, was to uphold the superiority of judge-made law. Under the direction of wise jurists, the law would,
in a familiar description, "work itself pure" case by case and at the end of

the process emerge as far "superior to any Act of Parliament."[21] As Lord Edward Coke famously put it, the common law tended toward the "perfection of reason"—not the natural reason accessible to all, but rather an "artificial reason" requiring long years of specialized study of a kind that could not be expected of politicians. The best example of these arguments in Foltz's day was made by the leader of the Wall Street bar, James Coolidge Carter, against the efforts of reformers to reduce the rules of private law to a legislative code—*codification*, as it was known.[22]

Having noted the departures of actual legislatures from her democratic ideal, Foltz took a similarly balanced look at the performance of common-law courts as law reformers. She allowed that some "courageous judges" had moved the law toward the "full light of the living present" from "the darkness of a savage past." Examples included William Murray, Lord Mansfield, in his decision that the common law did not support slavery, the chancellors who had used equity to ameliorate the legal condition of widows, and the courts that had tempered the criminal code by invoking "all manner of whimsical and technical rules to prevent conviction" in capital cases.

Finally, she said, de facto law reform occurs when juries refuse to convict so that "the unjust law dies, killed without a legislative vote." But in general the courts were not a force for progress, restrained as they were by their central duty to apply existing law rather than to modify it to fit public opinion. And many of them went beyond duty in their "slavish adherence to precedent." California, for example, followed the rule developed in rain-drenched England that upstream users could use flowing water (as to turn a mill wheel) but could not remove it to irrigate crops. Ridiculous, she said, in "a State purchased from Mexico, where the common law has never prevailed and where irrigation is essential to its highest prosperity." She concluded that the judiciary was unable in itself to respond to "the demands of the hour."

This was the more true given the increasing pace of social and technological change. Foltz noted the inventions that law had been forced to assimilate in her lifetime: "the railroad, the steamship, the telegraph, the telephone, electricity, streetcar systems, patents and copyrights on all the foregoing." It was to become a commonplace among Progressive legal thinkers over the next generation that while gradual case-by-case common-law development might have suited earlier, it could not suffice in the new age.

So Foltz stayed with the conclusion she had drawn from her assumption that the law should correspond to public opinion—the legislature must take center stage in the process of evolving the law to meet society's needs. But what then to do about the defects in actual legislative performance she had experienced and described? The increasing scale and complexity of technology, demographics, and institutions were leaving parochial, inexpert, and overworked legislators less and less ready to do the assigned job.

Her response was one that Progressives would consistently champion over the next generation. Legislatures drawn from the mass of the people needed expert help. This was the "Wisconsin Idea" that underlay so much Progressive reform in the first decades of the twentieth century. Law's rational and humane evolution required knowledge of the actual, rapidly shifting conditions within increasingly complex societies, and this was to be provided by the new social sciences. The state capital and the state university, at opposite ends of the mall, must engage in constant interchange if legislation and public administration were to meet the demands of the age.[23]

Within the legal sphere, expertise meant broad knowledge of the law, ability in ascertaining inconsistencies and anachronisms within it, and skill in designing institutions and drafting legislation to correct these defects. In 1921, Benjamin Cardozo, chief judge of New York and one of the leaders of Progressive jurisprudence, would propose a Ministry of Justice whose function would be to review the laws regularly and propose corrective changes to the legislature. He drew on an idea launched a century earlier by Jeremy Bentham, which was also taken up by the other major figure in Progressive jurisprudence, Roscoe Pound, then the dean of the Harvard Law School. Cardozo's idea was eventually adopted as the New York Law Revision Commission, and similar commissions were formed in other states. Over the years, there have been many proposals, in addition to the commissions, for instituting a systematic communication between the legislature and the judiciary.[24]

Long before these developments, Clara Foltz in her speech "Evolution of Law" proposed a regular review of existing laws. But rather than establishing a ministry or commission, she would have the state supreme court act as an advisory council and suggest improvements in the statutes annually. "Better than any other body they know the evils; better than any other they know how to amend the law, for they see it in all of its phases and through the eyes of different advocates." To their expertise, she added that the supreme court justices also had a "proper pride in the perfection of their work" and a desire to build "a symmetrical system of laws that will secure substantial and equal justice to all."[25]

"Evolution of Law" was a notable performance, something well beyond the typical bar speech celebrating the glories of the profession. This was attested to by its publication as an article in the *Albany Law Journal* soon after Foltz delivered it. Widely read by lawyers around the country, the journal was one of the first and most successful of the new law reviews that sprang up during the postwar period to keep lawyers abreast of legal developments. For busy practitioners, especially those who had learned law by apprenticing, the journals were more accessible, and often more current, than the treatises on legal subjects that also marked the period. Courts began to cite them, thus marking their acceptance as important sources of legal authority.[26]

"Well-written, able and elaborate articles on new or doubtful legal subjects" was the goal of the *Albany* founder, who in 1872 coined the term *legal journalism*. His successor, the editor Foltz knew, was the genial Irving Browne, who continued the founder's policies but added an explicit purpose "to reform the laws, to render them cheap, speedy and certain," and to make the magazine "interesting." The same article that quoted Browne's aims also congratulated him on achieving them and added that under his leadership *Albany* was "undoubtedly more read and quoted by lawyers and newspapers than any of its contemporaries."[27]

Browne was interested in women's rights and found in Foltz an exponent of the cause who could write forcefully and entertainingly. He published her World's Fair public defender speech as well as "Evolution of Law." And when Foltz as thinker became involved in a series of cases featuring women accused of murder, *Albany* reported her newspaper commentary and printed "Should Women Be Executed?" This was a piece in which Foltz departed from the straight suffrage line, establishing herself as an independent thinker on equal treatment for the sexes.

Thinking about Equal Justice

MURDERESSES AND THE WOMEN'S MOVEMENT

The year from July 1896 to July 1897 was Clara Foltz's most productive period as a legal thinker. While her efforts to establish a lucrative practice in New York City languished, she wrote two articles on public defense and launched a campaign to create the office. Foltz was also a frequent commentator on the current legal scene, especially on women criminal defendants and the closely related issue of prosecutorial ethics.

Florence Maybrick, Bessie Flagler, Lizzie Borden, Maria Barbella, and Mary Alice Fleming—these were the names of women accused of homicide who fascinated the fin-de-siècle public. The cases of "the Victorian murderesses" became a common currency; novelists and preachers used them to explore the essential female nature, reformers to oppose the death penalty, the press to sell newspapers, and the women's movement to illustrate the flaws of male justice.

Clara Foltz served as counsel for Maybrick, was a mock juror trying Flagler and Fleming, and wrote an article about the Barbella case. She was widely quoted in the newspapers on all the prosecutions. Though she was called on mainly because of her connections to the women's movement, Foltz's focus was on prosecutorial misconduct and equal justice, which was different from the concerns of other female commentators on the cases.

Generally, suffragists saw the cases as examples of the fundamental unfairness involved when a woman was judged by an all-male jury. Soon after the passage of the Fourteenth Amendment, the U.S. Supreme Court had interpreted the equal protection clause to give black men the right to a jury on which their own race was eligible to serve. But the Court said nothing about a similar right for women, whether black or white.[28]

The demand for female jurors paralleled the fight for suffrage because in most places only voters could be jurors. Jury service was a mark of the full citizenship women were seeking. Moreover, the objections to women as voters—that they were incompetent, biased, and out of their sphere—were the same as those against women jurors. For the jury service arguments, Stanton and Anthony discovered early on that the individual human story was the ideal vehicle.

The first case in which the suffragists became involved was that of Hester Vaughn in 1869. She was a young Englishwoman who had married an American and immigrated, only to discover that he already had a family in Philadelphia. Left on her own, Vaughn worked as a domestic, was raped by her employer, and became pregnant. She gave birth alone, the child died almost immediately, and Vaughn was indicted for infanticide. Badly defended and swiftly convicted, she was headed for the gallows when Anthony in stirring speeches and Stanton in eloquent editorials took up her case. Stanton wrote, "If nobles cannot judge peasants or peasants nobles, how can man judge woman?" As to the canard that women should trust their fathers, husbands, and brothers to safeguard them in the justice system, Stanton said, "The Hester Vaughns,—the very class that most need protection—often have no such ties." In fact, she added, "their betrayers may *be* their judges and their jurors."[29]

Through the suffragists' efforts, the Pennsylvania governor pardoned Vaughn, and with the money they raised, she was able to return to England and make a new life. Anthony promised they would continue the individual case strategy: "As soon as we get Hester Vaughn out of prison, we will get somebody else to work for."[30]

Next, in 1870, was the case of Laura Fair, who had shot her lover, a well-known San Francisco lawyer. The jury rejected her defense of temporary insanity brought on by the victim's cruel treatment. Suffragists protested the verdict because male jurors could never understand a woman's motives or mental state. When the conviction was reversed on appeal, a second all-male jury acquitted Fair. Many people credited or blamed the movement women for the sympathetic atmosphere they created around the case.[31]

Vaughn and Fair were early cases, with publicity fairly localized, but starting in the 1890s the women accused of murder were the subject of widespread coverage fanned in New York by a press war. On one side of the battle was Joseph Pulitzer, the aging publisher of the *World*, the most successful newspaper in the city. The challenger was William Randolph Hearst, newly arrived from California where he had made the *San Francisco Examiner* into the "monarch of the dailies."[32] Hearst brought to New York his best people, hired away some of the *World*'s top staff, and set out to turn his *New York Journal*, known previously as "the chambermaid's own," into the circulation leader. Using Pulitzer's own weapons—stunts, contests, color cartoons—laid over a constant stream of sex and crime, Hearst was soon a major contender. Between them, the papers roused worldwide interest in the little band of women accused of murder in the 1890s.

FLORENCE MAYBRICK

Florence Maybrick in England was the first recipient of intense press coverage. Pulitzer's *World* led a campaign to free Florence, which featured many leading suffragists and women writers. Clara Foltz worked on the plea to re-open the case when she was in London for a few weeks in the summer of 1895.

Maybrick's case had what became the classic elements: the victim was a feckless man, the murder method was poison or other cruel means, the accused was attractive and of questionable sexual morality, and the prosecutor sought the death penalty. Her life story became familiar on both sides of the Atlantic. Born in Alabama, married to a wealthy Englishman twice her age, mother of two children, she was accused of killing her husband after he died of mysterious causes. Traces of poison were in the body, and it was revealed that Mrs. Maybrick had been soaking the arsenic off of flypaper. She said she was using it to improve her complexion—possibly a cosmetic fad at the time.

Though the evidence of murder was thin, Florence Maybrick admitted having taken a lover, and the judge instructed the jury that she had "deliberately" poisoned "a poor, helpless, sick man upon whom she has already inflicted a dreadful injury—an injury fatal to married life." The male jurors quickly convicted, and the judge imposed the death penalty. "Tried for murder, sentenced for adultery," people said, suggesting a double standard of justice and of moral conduct for men and women.[33]

Barristers and lawyers, statesmen, society ladies and suffragists, reformers and reporters protested the verdict in news stories, petitions, pamphlets, books, speeches, and mass meetings. All the efforts were aimed at winning a royal pardon because there was no court of criminal appeals in Great Britain at the time. Though Queen Victoria commuted Maybrick's sentence to life at hard labor, the movement to free her altogether only gained momentum.

On the American side, the leader was Abigail Dodge, who was a popular author and journalist writing under the pen name Gail Hamilton. She was related to James Blaine, who had run a close race for president in 1884 and was secretary of state during the Harrison administration. Twice Dodge persuaded Blaine to petition the queen through diplomatic channels; one petition was signed by notable women and the other by the top statesmen in the United States, including Benjamin Tracy, who had moved Foltz's admission to the New York bar.[34]

While working the diplomatic route, Maybrick supporters, underwritten by the *New York World*, hired distinguished British counsel to prepare an open brief on the unfair trial—a good move in the absence of an appellate court. Nothing seemed to work, however, and there was no official response. Then in 1895, the year that Clara Foltz entered the fray, some fresh evidence stirred a third wave of Maybrick protest.[35] Several witnesses came forward to say that the husband was an arsenic-eater—a little known addiction. (Some said the poison was an energizer and others that it was an aphrodisiac, though they may have been describing the same effect.) There was also new testimony about arsenic's use as a face wash—backing Mrs. Maybrick's story. At the same time, a home secretary (the cabinet officer whose recommendations influenced the exercise of the pardon power) and lord chief justice both believed to be more sympathetic to Maybrick assumed office.

In this new round, suffragists were prominent. Julia Ward Howe and Elizabeth Cady Stanton were officers of the Women's International Maybrick Association, launched in the spring of 1895. And that was the summer Clara Foltz was in London and associated with the case, though it is not clear what exactly she did. Maybe she met with counsel and discussed strategy for presenting the new evidence, or perhaps she was merely lending her "lady barrister" credentials to the cause.[36]

On her return, Foltz told a reporter that the home secretary was tired of women's "moist handkerchief" pleas. "What the case needs more than money is brains . . . hard strong arguments," she said, adding that she would like to take over but had too much other business. She "intimated that if those interested would pay her expenses, she would guarantee to go to Europe and return with Mrs. Maybrick."[37]

Nothing came of the 1895 efforts. Maybrick was released in 1904 in the regular parole process, wrote a book, lectured briefly about prison reform, and died alone in obscurity. Her most lasting memorial was the passage in James Joyce's *Ulysses* (1922) where Molly Bloom ruminated on "that Mrs. Maybrick . . . she must have been madly in love with the other fellow to run the chance of being hanged O she didnt care if that was her nature what could she do besides theyre not brutes enough to go and hang a woman surely are they."

The next case to attract widespread attention was that of Lizzie Borden in Massachusetts in 1893, accused of killing her father and stepmother. Like Maybrick, Borden was a mid-tier society lady and exceedingly well represented at trial: not poor, not defenseless, and not an appealing personality. Also, both women denied the crime rather than admitting and seeking to excuse it; their cases did not involve the arguable incapacity of males to understand a desperate female situation. Men could grasp innocence as well as women. Indeed, the all-male jury acquitted Borden in the face of strong evidence largely because she was a woman. The Borden case did not become one of the favorite stories of the women's movement.[38]

BESSIE FLAGLER

Neither Maybrick nor Borden was an ideal example of the unfairness of male justice, but the next cause célèbre was even more inappropriate for making the point. Bessie Flagler killed a black teenager who may have been stealing a pear from her father's garden in Washington, D.C. No movement formed to free Flagler, but she did not need one because her father was a man of consequence—an army general and the chief of ordnance.

Originally, the coroner ruled the boy's death accidental, but public reaction ultimately forced an indictment of Flagler for manslaughter. Her lawyers used the press to tell her side: a gang had been marauding in the neighborhood, and the police had failed to respond to complaints. Bessie Flagler had kept a gun for protection and had fired into the ground to scare the youths away. A ricochet bullet had hit Ernest Green in the heart. Flagler's skill in the use of arms was much mooted in the press, as was her character. Her temper, said the *New York World*, was "almost ungovernable when aroused, and to this her present predicament is ascribed."[39]

If ever a case called out for a jury trial, it was this one. A trial would have revealed more about the victim and provided a basis for an informed community judgment even if the jury did not include any black men or white women. In the event, however, Flagler pleaded guilty to involuntary manslaughter in closed and secret proceedings. The judge sentenced her to three hours in jail, with credit for the two she had spent when turning herself in. He also imposed a $500 fine, which her father paid immediately (making it appear he knew the sentence in advance). "Indefensible, a travesty," blasted the *World*, adding that "the poor people and the colored people are all saying there is no justice for the poor as against the rich."[40]

Actually, though the postsentence uproar was mostly about wealth and race, it was her sex that saved Bessie Flagler. No matter how rich or white, a man would not have received such a lenient sentence. Hearst saw the true nature of the story, and in his first editorial coup after taking over the *Journal*, he solicited the written opinion of twelve prominent women on the case—including Foltz. The number twelve suggested a jury, though they did not meet or deliberate.

Clara Foltz, "a prominent female lawyer of New York," censured the light sentence, concluding that "the rich and high in place may secure favours that the poor and unknown cannot reach." She was in the minority, however; seven women agreed with the result. Elizabeth Cady Stanton took the standard feminist line: "We women do not help to make the laws, why should we be condemned to suffer through them?" Stanton also mentioned "Mrs. Maybrick's pathetic case. That woman was undeniably innocent."[41]

Remarks of Stanton's sort irritated Foltz. She disapproved of the failure to distinguish different cases and of the tendency to find total excuse in the fact of sex alone. A few months after the Flagler publicity, Foltz published a sharp attack on the suffragist dogma. Her words were in the context of a far more sympathetic case, however. Maria Barbella, an illiterate seamstress, was tried twice for killing her lover.

MARIA BARBELLA

The particulars of Barbella's life and the details of her crime were mostly uncontested. A recent immigrant to New York City from Fernandina, Italy, she worked sixty hours a week in a cloak factory and lived with her parents and several siblings in the heart of Little Italy, a ghetto as poor, if not as picturesque, as her native village.[42]

On her route to work, Barbella passed the bootblack stand of Domenico Cataldo, and they struck up an acquaintance. He started walking her home and wooing her but would not come in to meet her parents. Ultimately, he induced Barbella to live with him, she said by drugging and raping her. Night and day, she begged him to marry her. After his last refusal, Barbella followed Cataldo to a local bar, where she found him playing cards. To her usual entreaties, he responded, "Only pigs marry." Swiftly, Maria Barbella pulled back his head, and using his own new razor, slit his throat from ear to ear, draining his life's blood—just the way farmers slaughtered sheep in Fernandina.

The judge appointed two unknown lawyers to defend her, practitioners without previous experience in a case of this magnitude. They visited Barbella at the prison only once during the many months between arrest and trial and never developed a theory of the defense, nor prepared their client to take the stand. Such bumblers were no match for the district attorney, reputed to have won more death verdicts than anyone in the entire United States and reportedly eager to add a woman to his record.

Facing no real opposition, the prosecutor abandoned all niceties in order to convict. He hounded and abused the young woman on the witness stand and suppressed evidence that Cataldo had reached for his stiletto when she entered the bar. In closing, the district attorney spoke man-to-man, cautioning the jurors against granting "every woman in this city who has an illicit relationship with a man the right to cut his throat with impunity."

The judge not only excluded favorable evidence, but also commanded the jury to forget mercy, to do their duty as men, to remember that "the law does not distinguish between the sexes." In July 1895, a speedy verdict of guilt was followed by a quick sentence of death. Barbella became the fifth woman scheduled for execution in New York history, the first who would die in the newly installed electric chair.[43]

At this point, in a scene more like opera than life, the Countess de Brazza, an American woman married to an Italian nobleman, steamed into town, set up at the Savoy Hotel, and launched a "Free Maria" movement. She never said why. Perhaps Barbella reminded her of the young women in the lace-making collective she ran on her husband's estate.

The countess enlisted experienced and able new lawyers, Frederick House and Emmanuel Friend. Rumor had it that these capable men were so appalled by the performance of the previous attorneys that they took the case in the name of professional duty—for expenses only. The lawyers worked on the appeal while the countess enlisted her society friends and their rich husbands—the Vanderbilts, the Iselins, the Couderts—along with journalists and politicians, to plead for clemency.

The suffragists were already on the case. Elizabeth Cady Stanton argued: "Maria [Barbella] was arrested by a male officer, locked in a prison by a male jailer, prosecuted by a male lawyer, convicted by a male jury, sentenced to death by a male judge, under a law passed by a male legislature, approved by a male Governor, and all elected male voters. She is to be electrocuted by a male warden, her body dissected by a male surgeon and finally dumped by a male undertaker in the Potters Field."[44]

With surprising rapidity, the countess and her wealthy friends, the suffragists and their media access, the lawyers and their logic, managed to turn public opinion. Originally, the press had pictured Barbella as crude and animalistic, making much of "scientific" findings like that in the *Phrenological Journal* showing that her skull demonstrated a total "lack of refinement in the social, moral and aesthetic sense." The article compared Barbella's head unfavorably to that of Susan B. Anthony, the "murderess supporter." But after the turn, Barbella was described as a delicate young woman, "helpless and ignorant of her rights," who had been denied the chance to present evidence about her mental state at the time of the murder. One of the best-known public thinkers of the day, Robert Ingersoll, wrote, "never before in the history of our country has public opinion through the press been so forcibly agitated over any one case."[45]

In April 1896 the appellate court reversed the conviction, censuring the prosecutor for withholding evidence and for inflammatory argument. It sent the case back for a new trial in which "proof may be given in the regular and orderly way, and the questions presented in [a] temperate and dispassionate manner."[46] A new jury assembled in November 1896 for a trial that little resembled the previous one. Before a new judge, Barbella's lawyers presented a defense of temporary insanity, bolstered by a history of grand mal epileptic seizures. The biggest change was Maria Barbella herself, who spoke without translation in a voice the papers called sweet and musical. Her blouse was trimmed with lace made on the estate of the Countess de Brazza.

After twenty-four days of trial, Emmanuel Friend summed up to a jury and a courtroom full of Barbella supporters. They cheered when he pointed out that "she had eliminated a man that New York would not much miss" and hissed when the prosecutor claimed that no woman could be forced to physical intimacy she did not desire. After forty minutes of deliberation, the jury acquitted Maria Barbella.

EQUAL JUSTICE AND SPECIAL TREATMENT

The Barbella saga seemed made for Clara Foltz—the personal redemption, the heroic good lawyers repairing the damage of the terrible incompetents, society ladies and suffrage women working together. Yet in November 1896, right before the Barbella retrial, Foltz published an astringent article answering a qualified yes to the question in the title: "Should Women Be Executed?" If [Maria Barbella] is guilty of murder she should receive the same punishment that would be meted out to a man for the same offense," Foltz wrote.[47]

"I know some advocates of equal rights have declared that women are not amenable to laws because they have had no voice in their making," she noted. "The position is utterly defenseless and vicious." Foreigners, criminals, and indeed most people had no voice in the making of most of the laws applicable to their conduct, yet still they must obey them. "I too believe in equality of men and women before the law" but not in claiming rights and "in the same breath" denying "equal responsibility."

The suffragists also argued that the Constitution required a jury of peers, which meant that only women could judge each other. Women jurors, it was said, would have acquitted Barbella on the grounds of "justifiable homicide." In the same vein, Mary Livermore, a preacher's wife in her seventies, declared that if a man ruined "a daughter of mine, I would strike him dead without hesitation." This was the kind of rhetoric that Foltz found insupportable and that many male thinkers used against the women's movement.[48]

"Day after day, the cause of women's suffrage receives what are, and rightly so, mortal blows at the hands of its own supporters," editorialized the

Times, expressing the common opposition view. "To anyone who believes in the rule of law, the recent public statements [on the Barbella case] demonstrate once more that women should never be granted political equality."[49] Writing just days after the 1896 election in which suffrage was defeated in California, Foltz urged her sisters in the women's movement not to cede the high ground of adherence to equal justice.

Hers was a practical as well as a principled position. Fear of antisaloon legislation had defeated the suffragists this time; fear of female jurors could be next if men believed that women would automatically acquit other women (especially ones who killed their male lovers). As a lawyer, moreover, Clara Foltz could not accept what she saw as the sentimental impulse to acquit women of homicide in the teeth of the evidence. This was "class adjudication" that was just as bad in her estimate as "class legislation"—that is, laws giving only men the right to vote or hold office. No jury, she wrote, should "acquit a woman where they would convict a man," or vice versa. "The law should acknowledge no difference between the sexes as to moral perceptions, reason, passions, volition or self control." If a person lacked these qualities, or was overwhelmed by passion, then, Foltz believed, "that was a good defense" without regard to the sex of the actor. "The victim is equally dead, whether by a man's pistol or a woman's poison." Equal justice, not special treatment, was her credo.

Foltz also attacked the argument that Barbella was entitled to the benefit of the so-called unwritten law that excused a man for killing his wife's lover (and sometimes the wife). Since that "law" was rooted in male ownership of the female body, its use to acquit women killers was illogical at best. Yet Jane Shattuck in San Francisco recently had been freed after killing her daughter's seducer in the absence of a male relative to do it.[50] Foltz did not approve of "unwritten laws" justifying homicide and objected to women grasping for their share of vigilante justice.

Furthermore, Foltz said the death penalty should be applied equally, as long as it was in force. But here was where she qualified her affirmative response to the question "should women be executed?" She made clear that she herself favored legislative abolition of what she described as "judicial murder," scoffing at the idea that official killing was "in the interest of public morals."

Her article, though lodged in a professional journal, was noticed by Foltz's sisters in the women's movement, and some chided her for weighing in on the same side as antisuffrage voices like that in the *New York Times*. "It is hardly necessary for a woman to urge that the courts shall not err on the side of mercy to her sex," editorialized the *Woman's Tribune*.[51]

But Foltz was not swayed, any more than she had been when she was mocked and attacked by men for daring to venture into the hurly-burly of the criminal courtroom. In just a thousand words, she had spoken her mind on equal justice, mistaken suffrage tactics, the jury function, and the death penalty. She had come out firmly against exempting females from the operation of the law "in these days of poisoning, throat-cutting and shooting by women." Her readers understood Foltz's references. "Throat-cutting" referred to Barbella, "shooting" to Flagler and Shattuck, and "poisoning" most famously to Maybrick, but also to another woman accused of murder in the 1890s and much in the public eye.

MARY ALICE FLEMING

In May 1896, Fleming was tried for poisoning her mother; she faced the same judge and the same prosecutor who had been reversed and rebuked a month earlier in the Barbella case. Unfazed, the district attorney again went on a rampage. In inflammatory terms, he portrayed Fleming as a promiscuous woman, a slave to sexual passion who had killed her mother for the inheritance she needed to lure back a wandering lover. Much was also made of her irregular life—never married and with three children she supported from the proceeds of an earlier successful breach-of-promise suit.[52]

Unlike Barbella at her first trial, Fleming had excellent lawyers who turned the district attorney's misconduct against him. They argued to the jury that she was "one of the People, entitled to the People's protections, entitled to the People's mercy, entitled to the People's leniency, if you please, as any other member of the community."[53] Even without the aid of good lawyers, the facts of Fleming's case did not trigger the same fears in the all-male jury as had the bloody public throat-slitting inflicted by Maria Barbella on her unfaithful lover.

Fleming's defense was that she had had nothing to do with the death of her mother, who was an arsenic eater for health and cosmetic reasons and had died from a self-administered accidental overdose. The trial featured savage cross-examinations and attacks on witnesses by both sides. Instead of "a solemn judicial inquiry involving a human life," Foltz wrote afterwards, it was "a gala tournament, in which lawyers and witnesses joined in sportive combat for the victor's laurel and to give a curious throng an American holiday."[54]

Like the twelve men in the Lizzie Borden case, the Fleming jurors could not believe a woman capable of murdering a parent. The verdict was not guilty. Not guilty was also the verdict of "The *World*'s Woman Jury," a shadow group put together by Pulitzer's paper—presumably in response to Hearst's similar "woman jury" in the Flagler case. Instead of twelve women commenting after the verdict, however, the *World* asked each woman to follow the testimony as it unfolded and then telegraph her individual decision when the actual jury retired to deliberate.[55]

Clara Foltz, whose "ability as a lawyer is nearly as well known in New York as in California, where she achieved an enviable reputation," was spokeswoman for the jury. She led nine of the women to a verdict of acquittal; three voted for guilty. The male jury was also nine to three for acquittal on the first ballot, demonstrating, said the *World*, that if the ladies could have "taken off their coats and retired to a corner," they, too, would have reached unanimity. Generally speaking, the women jurors did an excellent job of sorting the testimony, and their remarks on the evidence were perspicacious.[56]

Most promising for the future of women jurors was the fact that they were able to judge Fleming fairly despite her licentious lifestyle. Even the woman minister on the jury voted to acquit because the government had failed to connect the "weak and wicked woman" with the arsenic. Elizabeth Jordan, the woman editor who conceived the idea of the jury, scoffed at the assumption that a loose woman "would be capable of any crime that a prosecuting attorney might suggest" and added that if Mrs. Fleming had been "considered respectable, no one would ever have thought of arresting her."

Clara Foltz, defense lawyer at heart, turned Fleming's flaws in her favor, claiming that she was "shallow and volatile" and "utterly lacking in the steadfastness and intensity of purpose necessary to so shocking a crime." Foltz's focus was not the bad woman, but the vicious prosecutor. "No normal mind" could find sufficient evidence that the mother even died of arsenic poisoning, much less who administered it, or whether there was intent to kill. "[W]e do not commit judicial murder on suspicion in these days," she added. Unfortunately, the modern prosecutor has lapsed into a "very rickety and unlawful way of thinking" everyone guilty until innocence is proved, Foltz said. Instead of evaluating the evidence fairly, the prosecutor had purposefully created an "anomalous" jury by eliminating every man who had the least qualm about executing a woman. A record eleven hundred potential jurors were examined to find twelve who could pass the test.

She also accused the prosecutor of withholding exculpatory information from the defense, adding that "[s]uppressing evidence is little less than crime." Summing up her critique, Foltz said, "Such cases should not be tried, for a verdict of guilty is almost certain of reversal, a long trial is wanton waste of the people's money and an outrage on the unfortunate defendant."

Foltz's remarks on the Fleming case were published in the *World* and then picked up by the *Albany Law Journal*, where her comment on the Barbella case had earlier appeared.[57] The prosecutor's misconduct in both of these cases spurred her 1896 article in the *Criminal Law Magazine*. Titled "Duties of the District Attorney in Prosecutions," it was a definitive work that laid the groundwork for her public defender campaign (see Chapter 7).

ELIZABETH JORDAN
AND THE *WORLD*'S WOMAN JURY

The *World*'s jury was a striking assemblage of the new women so often mentioned in the press (see Chapter 4). There were two lawyers, a doctor, a preacher, writers, journalists, and clubwomen, each with an independent identity separate from that of any man. An arresting feature of the *World*'s lavish coverage was an eight-column picture: twelve women sitting in three rows of four, facing Mrs. Fleming. Patched together from individual shots of these public women, the group photo looked real and presented a startling image. Only in remote western venues had women served on juries, and no picture of an all-female jury had ever been seen.[58]

The woman who assembled the jury, and served on it herself, was Elizabeth (Kate) Jordan, the editor of the *Sunday World* and the epitome of the new woman in New York City. Single and self-supporting, her convent education and early ambitions to be a nun made her stand out among the cynical, hard-living men who dominated journalism. Nor was Jordan one of the many women reporters who created the news by writing about their own stunts or who produced such excessively sentimental pieces that they were called "sob sisters." Rather, she wrote about places women did not usually go: Chinatown back alleys, the morgue, the Tombs, the police courts. The jury box was another male location that she breached, at least symbolically, in the Fleming case.[59]

Jordan was editor of the *Sunday World* during a period when the murderess cases were much in the news, and her career, like Clara Foltz's, intersected with them at many points, in addition to the creation of the woman jury for the Fleming case. For instance, she represented her boss, Joseph

Pulitzer, in making a special plea to the White House for Florence Maybrick and was thanked in person by Maria Barbella for the favorable coverage of her second trial. Moreover, Jordan was known as the reporter "who saved Lizzie Borden" because she had written a short story about a female murderer who was acquitted after a woman reporter kept her confession a secret. Though she had covered the Borden case, Jordan denied that the tale was autobiographical.[60]

Jordan was also rumored to be the archetype for the heroine of a notorious contemporary novel by Gertrude Atherton—*Patience Sparhawk and Her Times* (1897)—about a woman reporter accused of murdering her husband. Unlike any of the real-life murder defendants, Patience was a "new woman" who, as portrayed in the novel, lived at Jordan's actual address in New York City. Convicted by an ignorant and biased all-male jury and sentenced to die in the electric chair, Sparhawk's story echoed the cases of Maybrick, Fleming, and Barbella.

Atherton was herself a new woman who, like Clara Foltz, had migrated to New York from San Francisco seeking a larger stage for her talents and who had studied newspaper culture through observing Kate Jordan at work.[61] Atherton portrayed Patience Sparhawk as completely capable of murder and her husband as fully deserving it. She combined this cold-blooded approach with an attack on New York society as crass and unfeeling. Though the book was banned in some places, it eventually became a best seller in England and the United States, and the fictional Patience Sparhawk joined the other Victorian murderesses as examples in the debates over whether women should be executed, whether they were capable of forming full murderous intent, and whether male juries were fit to fairly judge them.

Clara Foltz had weighed in on these issues in her article on the Barbella case, opining that justice had no sex and that women and men should be treated the same in all respects by the criminal justice system. In light of this piece, published only a few months before the Fleming trial, it might seem strange that she would agree to serve on the *World*'s jury. If the women differed from the men—especially if they acquitted—it could provide an example of the gendered justice she so heatedly eschewed in the article.

Composition aside, some commentators argued that mock juries would undermine public respect for the institution. Others pointed to the Lizzie Borden case where a shadow jury (eleven men and Lucy Stone) acquitted at the same time as the real jury, supposedly making the verdict more acceptable. Whatever Clara Foltz thought of shadow juries generally or of all-female shadow juries, she could hardly resist the *World*'s invitation to join this one. The publicity was too good (huge spreads in the Sunday editions: circulation three hundred thousand), especially for a lawyer trying to start a practice in New York City. Foltz knew, moreover, that she would shine in this setting because she had actually tried cases; she was almost surely the only woman in the city who knew about juries firsthand.

Her commentaries as a woman juror on the Fleming case, her Barbella article, her public defender writings, and her speech "Evolution of Law" gave Foltz stature as a significant contributor to contemporary debates about legal process and criminal justice. Attention to her ideas was the high point of her years in New York, when a lull in her practice gave her time to research and write. By the turn of the century, Foltz was well-established as a public thinker.

SIX

Working for Political Equality

Whatever else Clara Foltz was doing, she was working for women's rights, so many of her personal achievements were also evidence of the movement's progress. At major turns of her life, moreover, the suffragists showed her how to lobby in Sacramento, filled her lecture halls, paid her tuition at Hastings, and cheered her courtroom victories. Over the years, her own goals and the aims of the women's movement continued to be connected, and the history of each illuminates the other.

Much as the movement itself did, Foltz came to focus her major efforts on winning the vote, believing it the key to all other reforms. She campaigned for suffrage for more than thirty years, participating enthusiastically in launching a rump suffrage organization in 1890, working for suffrage at the 1893 World's Fair, and being involved in a post-fair suffrage campaign in California during the mid-1890s. After the presidential contest in 1896, which pitted Populist Democrat William Jennings Bryan against Republican William McKinley, Foltz concentrated for a few years on women's access to business and banking instead of to the polling place. But when suffrage became a cause for a new generation of Progressive men and women, Clara Foltz joined them to participate fully in the final victory in California. This part of the story ends in 1912 when she voted in her first presidential election.

Clara Foltz and Separate Spheres

The greatest obstacle facing Foltz and any other woman who wanted to vote (or enter a profession, hold office, or serve on a jury) was the belief that each sex had its own sphere of work and influence, inscribed in nature and ordained by nature's God. Women were destined for the exalted but limited realm of home-making and child-rearing, while men occupied the public sphere of business and government where they represented their families as well as themselves.

Clara Foltz said that whatever she tried to do, her opponents constantly "dished up . . . prattling babes, cooing doves and woman's sphere." Her lifetime strategy was to avoid, rather than to confront, the powerful, pervasive ideology. "Though very prominent in public life," starts a typical article, "Mrs. Foltz is never so happy and contented as when in the privacy of her home." Illustrating the article, which was published in a national legal magazine at the peak of Foltz's career in 1893, was a full-length photograph of her wearing an open-necked, modish gown and lightly touching a round table covered with an elegant cloth: hardly the costume or prop of a lawyer. The piece concluded that Foltz was a "standing demonstration" that a woman could be an attorney and an orator without losing "the graces, or sweetness, or beauty that crowns and glorifies woman in the home."[1]

She claimed that she loved "to wash dishes and clean and cook and sew and all the rest of it" and also said "my husband declared that I was a better cook than his dear old German mother." Foltz's motherhood was a strong point in her favor in a spheres debate, and she used it freely, even taking the children to court and on the legislative floor. Her lifelong emphasis on dress was also connected to the need to look like a true woman. She once said that "frumpish" females actually hurt the movement.[2]

As a lawyer, Foltz competed with men who feared her feminine advantage and so attacked her for being out of her sphere. She entreated them to meet her "upon the merits of law and fact without this everlasting and incessant reference to sex." On occasion, however, Foltz herself used her sex. "They called me the lady lawyer," she said, a "dainty soubriquet" that aided in "browbeating my way through the marshes of ignorance and prejudice."[3]

Clara Foltz, 1893, the year she spoke at the World's Fair. *Law Student's Helper*, 1893.

Though Foltz could not have managed the seemingly endless dialog of accusation and answer without a strong belief in women's equality, she did not develop an overall philosophy to match the separate spheres ideology. When it came to her own rights, her focus was on solving immediate problems rather than building theories. Attorney Foltz was always in search of the winning argument. Her lawyerly mindset partly explains the inconsistencies in her positions as she took up a variety of causes, styles, and commitments, some in philosophical or actual conflict with each other. Foltz could appear as both an atheistic freethinker and a Christian temperance worker; a would-be society lady and an actual working woman; a socialistic Bellamy Nationalist, a Populist, and a conservative Republican. Through changes and contradictions, however, she always remained what she once called "a woman's rights woman."[4]

The Movement for Women's Rights: 1848–1890

From the outset of the women's movement, suffrage was the greatest challenge to the separate spheres ideology. Only a few atypical women would enter the professions, speak from public platforms, or seek high office, but most adult females would be eligible to vote. As voters, their opinions might differ from those of men, causing tension in the home and strife between the sexes.

Though suffrage was one of the demands at the founding meeting of the movement in 1848 at Seneca Falls, women made little progress on that front before the Civil War and largely put aside their own cause during the conflict. Afterwards, however, the Fourteenth Amendment assuring the "privileges and immunities of citizenship" to all, and the Fifteenth Amendment enfranchising black men, made political equality for women appear less radical than it had at Seneca Falls. Moreover, women's contributions to the war effort were a further justification of their claims.

In the immediate postwar period, suffrage became the main concern of the women's movement, and it attracted many new members. But at this critical juncture, the women divided over tactics and priorities. Susan B. Anthony and Elizabeth Cady Stanton objected to the Fourteenth Amendment because it restricted the word *citizen* with the word *male* (in one section) for the first time in the Constitution. They were shocked, moreover, that the Fifteenth Amendment did not include women. Breaking with the Republican Party, they campaigned against both amendments as a betrayal.

When their former allies argued that it was "the Negro's hour," Stanton countered, "Do you believe the African race is composed entirely of males?" They had egalitarian principle on their side, but the political nation (that is, its white men) was not ready to give up patriarchy along with racial hierarchy. To some fellow reformers it was inconceivable that Stanton and Anthony could oppose the Civil War amendments in the name of their own rights.[5]

Other women leaders accepted black male enfranchisement as a first step to universal suffrage. In 1869, two competing woman suffrage societies were born out of this disagreement, one led by Anthony and Stanton, the National Woman Suffrage Association, headquartered in New York, and the other led by Lucy Stone, Julia Ward Howe, and Mary Livermore, the American Woman Suffrage Association, in Boston. Originally, the distinction between the two centered on their attitudes toward the postwar amendments and the arguments made in support of the positions. Followers of Stanton and Anthony urged that it was wrong to allow ignorant black men to vote while denying the right to educated white women. Western suffragists applied the same comparison to Chinese men, who could vote if born in the United States. Even some of those who supported citizenship for the former slaves (as Foltz did) were against the Chinese. Adding to the lack of sympathy among the western suffragists was the fact that very few of the Chinese immigrants were women.

In the cases of both the black freedmen and the Chinese immigrants, the race-based arguments led to attacks on the morality and intelligence of the "other" that are offensive today. As far as the record discloses, Clara Foltz did not rely on anti-Chinese rhetoric in her suffrage speeches or political stumping. In the hundreds of reports of her public statements, there are only two instances of such sentiments. One is in an 1875 letter to Abigail Duniway, printed in the *New Northwest*, in which Foltz complained that one Tim Wong "cast a Celestial vote" on the same day she herself had been refused at the polls. "But then Tim was born and raised in the State . . . speaks Spanish and English fluently, and crowning virtue, is the masculine persuasion. This is the first case on record, and should be the last, while woman, clothed with wisdom and armed with justice, stands knocking at the doors."[6]

The other, less mild, expression of anti-Chinese sentiment was a quotation that she attributed to Denis Kearney in her "Struggles and Triumphs of a Woman Lawyer," written in 1917: "They have no families, build no houses, live on rats, send their money back to China, and even transport their bones to the Celestial Empire for burial." Foltz added that the Chinese were "fattening upon our industries" in the 1870s.[7] The language was part of her story of California at the time when Kearney's Workingmen were the women's allies and were pitted against the Chinese (see Chapter 1). "Struggles" has many such automatic quotations in which Foltz drew on memories of speeches or texts from the period she is describing. Still, the fact that she wrote the words without disclaimer suggests that she had once endorsed such arguments and that she, like many other suffragists, failed to recognize the common humanity of other disenfranchised people.

Aside from the original causes of the schism and the related racist rhetoric, the two suffrage associations developed distinct personalities in the public mind. The Anthony-Stanton "National" stood for fundamental change in the relation of the sexes and in society generally; the Stone-Howe-Livermore "American" was more mainstream and centrist, with a focus on the vote. As if to emphasize the differences, Stanton and Anthony spoke in fiery tones through their publication *The Revolution* while Stone and Howe published the more prosaic *Woman's Journal*.

During the critical postwar period while the Republicans still felt under some obligation to women, the scandal of the century exacerbated the tension among the suffragists while distracting everyone from any common purpose. It involved Victoria Woodhull's denunciation of the famous minister Henry Ward Beecher for practicing free love while preaching against it. It was Beecher's hypocrisy that bothered Woodhull, who was a free lover herself.[8]

She revealed in her weekly newspaper that Beecher was committing adultery with the wife of his good friend and parishioner Theodore Tilton. Though there can be little doubt that Beecher indulged in the affair, he was exonerated in a church trial, and the husband's civil suit resulted in a hung jury. Every phase of the scandal was heavily publicized, and virtually all the accusers, witnesses, and commentators were suffragists.

Woodhull was associated with Stanton and Anthony in her suffrage activities, and Beecher was a friend to the American association but the scandal left suffragists on both sides of the divide with the "free lover" label. Even though Woodhull was off the scene by the end of the 1870s, she lived on in the discourse. In faraway California, for instance, when Clara Foltz wanted to be a lawyer, she was accused on the floor of the Assembly of being another Woodhull.[9]

Foltz is not on record as speaking about the scandal or being connected to either suffrage association. If asked, she would probably have aligned herself with the Anthony-Stanton National as two of her main mentors, Abigail Duniway and Laura Gordon, were on that side. On the other hand, another of her models, Sarah Knox-Goodrich, maintained relations with both associations, *The Woman's Journal* often reported on Foltz's activities, and she especially admired Lucy Stone and Mary Livermore among the American association's leaders. In short, the split does not seem to have been important to Clara Foltz. In a more general sense, historians disagree over its effect on the women's movement. Some think the schism institutionalized internecine conflict, others that it provided outlets for a wide range of views. Probably, it had both effects over the twenty years that the separation lasted.[10]

The two associations were not, moreover, always so dissimilar in either rhetoric or tactics. Suffragists from both associations joined in the "New Departure" strategy in the 1870s, for example. "Departing" from pleading for the vote, women went to the polls to demand it. They claimed that suffrage was one of the "privileges of citizenship" guaranteed under the new Fourteenth Amendment. Occasionally, the women succeeded in actually casting a ballot, but most were turned away, and some, like Susan B. Anthony, were even arrested.[11]

Still, the civil disobedience won attention and publicity, much of it positive. Sarah Knox started offering her ballot in the opening days of the New Departure and continued to do so even after the 1875 Supreme Court decision holding that the Fourteenth Amendment afforded no such right to women. In 1877, Clara Foltz also tried to vote and issued a ringing statement invoking her position as "a mother and a tax-paying citizen" against her exclusion.[12]

As the decade of the 1880s opened in California, the activists were optimistic. Led by Clara Foltz and Laura Gordon, they had won the right to practice law, opened the doors of Hastings Law School to women, and placed equal rights to employment and education in the California constitution while almost gaining the vote. Naturally, they thought that victory was close. But the women would spend the next ten years petitioning, lobbying, and rallying without another success of any kind.

The newspapers continued to be attentive, however. Suffrage meetings were widely reported, although sometimes with patronizing jokes about the women's lack of procedural knowledge. By contrast, the *Wasp* said that Foltz marched through an agenda "like a little man." Once when she had to leave a meeting early, it adjourned because, to the reporter's glee, no woman would admit that she was "older and more experienced" than the others, and thus eligible to take up the gavel.[13]

The lack of progress in California was typical of the whole suffrage scene in the 1880s. After twenty years of arduous campaigning, only Wyoming had votes for women in its constitution. North and South Dakota,

Portrait of Clara Foltz painted in 1993 by her great-grandson, Truman Toland, descendent of Foltz's oldest daughter, Trella.

Montana, and Washington joined the Union with male suffrage only. The admission of Washington in 1889 was especially painful because it had been a suffrage territory. Women had used their votes to curtail the liquor traffic and paid a heavy price in return.[14]

Many people blamed the divisiveness of the women themselves for their poor showing. It was time for the competing associations to unite, and Anthony moved decisively. In 1890, she and Lucy Stone presided over a joint convention in Washington, D.C. From the meeting emerged the National American Woman Suffrage Association, with Elizabeth Cady Stanton as president. Despite electing Stanton, the new association was more like the old American than it was like the former National. It took votes for women as practically its sole aim and moved to ally with the Woman's Christian Temperance Union, which was better financed and bigger than both the suffrage associations combined. The merger was not entirely smooth.

At about the same time that Anthony was collaborating with Stone to bring the suffragists into one national organization, her longtime lieutenant, Matilda Gage, proposed to divide them again. Gage called a convention of "liberal suffrage women" with other "liberal-thought women" to work against "their worst enemy, the Church."[15] Though she had shown no previous interest in internal movement politics or free thought, Clara Foltz was an enthusiastic participant in this convention.

A Convention of Radicals: 1890

SUFFRAGISTS AND FREETHINKERS

Matilda Gage's "Call to the Convention" to form a new suffrage organization blamed both "old" associations for failing to see the threat of organized religion. Warning of the "dangers of the hour," she decried a proposed constitutional amendment acknowledging the existence of God and requiring elected officials to be Christians. Gage also opposed mandatory Sunday rest and religious instruction in public schools and generally enjoined suffragists and freethinkers to unite in preserving the separation of church and state.[16]

Clara Foltz not only endorsed the call (along with fifty-four other reformers from twenty-three states), but wrote, "Our liberties are indeed imperiled by religious bigots who have ever stood in the broad highway of freedom and menaced free thought with an uplifted bloody cross."[17] Her words seem extreme for one raised as a preacher's daughter, but perhaps they merely reflected the zeal of a recent convert to the free thought movement.

To her role as founder of a new suffrage organization, Gage brought the classic background of a nineteenth-century reformer. Born in upstate New York, that seedbed of reform, she was the only child of a free-thinking doctor and an intellectual Scottish lady. Their home was a stop on the underground railroad for escaping slaves, and their daughter was better educated than most people's sons. Matilda Joslyn married a successful merchant and enjoyed domestic life, especially motherhood (she bore five children).[18]

Yet even as a young woman with many advantages, Gage was dissatisfied until in 1852 (just four years after Seneca Falls) she found the women's movement through Anthony and Stanton. For almost forty years, Gage wrote tracts, put out newsletters and journals, and helped to plan the annual convention in Washington, D.C. With Stanton and Anthony, she edited the first three volumes of the monumental *History of Woman Suffrage*, published in the 1880s.

"There is a word sweeter than mother, home or heaven—and that word is liberty" became her motto (taken up by others, who did not always credit Gage with the line). Gage was a strong rhetorician, writing, for instance, of the "freedom to be myself; to think my own thoughts; to act my own will; to develop in accord with my own intuitions. Freedom is necessary . . . to the growth of soul and spirit, mind and matter. No woman has ever been free."[19]

Nor would any woman be free, Gage came to think, as long as she was bound to male-centered religion. Divorcing the women's movement from the organized church became her foremost goal. At first, there was room for Gage's ideas in the liberal National association. Indeed, Stanton was fast coming to similar conclusions. But when Anthony moved to unite the rival suffrage societies, Gage objected because the Stone-Howe-Livermore American association was decidedly Christian in outlook and even had male ministers in its leadership. Worse, in her view, was the potential alliance with the Woman's Christian Temperance Union (WCTU), an organization that would openly marry religion and politics. Gage considered their revered leader, Frances Willard, "the most dangerous woman on the continent."[20]

Rather than join the merged National American association, Gage decided to form a new group combining the movements for political equality and for free thought. In launching her alternative association, she drew first on her suffrage experience. After her years of lieutenancy to Anthony, Gage knew movement workers everywhere. In the late nineteenth century, moreover, one reformer and reform led to others. Gage, like many suffragists (including Clara Foltz), was also committed to Bellamy Nationalism (see

Chapter 2). Nationalism in turn embraced additional causes, movements, and philosophies. One of these was an occult branch of Spiritualism called Theosophy. It was the Nationalism–Theosophy connection that ultimately enabled Gage to found the Woman's National Liberal Union (WNLU).

THEOSOPHISTS AND BELLAMY NATIONALISTS

Theosophy, like Spiritualism, held that life was continuous with death and that communication was possible with the deceased. The major difference was that Spiritualists believed anyone could be a medium and could summon ordinary people from the dead while Theosophists required special training in order to contact elite beings from beyond. A mysterious Russian émigré named Helena (always called "Madame") Blavatsky was Theosophy's chief apostle.[21]

People flocked to hear Madame's elevated conversation delivered through a haze of smoke from cigarettes, probably containing hashish. Madame Blavatsky claimed to communicate with the mahatmas of the occult who dictated a regime of spiritual development through training, good works, and successive reincarnations. This training period was like the series of interim reforms on the road to the final evolved state that Bellamy Nationalists promoted.

Madame Blavatsky recognized the connection in her book *The Key to Theosophy*, calling Nationalism "the first great step towards full realization of universal brotherhood." Thus, her followers took up Bellamy Nationalism's reform agenda, which included woman suffrage. Gage and her good friend Josephine Cables, editor of *The Occult World*, were among those who combined Theosophy, suffrage, and Nationalism in their thinking.[22]

Cables was recently married to William Aldrich, the scion of a wealthy New York family, who had moved to Alabama after the Civil War to make his own fortune. Some people called him a carpetbagger. Aldrich established a small mining town where, according to local legend, order, peace, and cleanliness ruled and where the black and white employees "lived in perfect harmony, with few regulations save the Golden rule."[23] In fact, Aldrich, Alabama, operated a lot like Bellamy's Nationalistic utopia.

In this Eden, William Aldrich built a palatial home for Josephine, which she named the Rajah Lodge. The couple did not withdraw into occult opulence, however, but, again according to lore, went "hand in hand to prisons" and hospitals, always heeding "the cry of the weary, the sick, and the unfortunate."[24] The Aldriches were newlyweds in 1889 when they helped Matilda

Gage organize her new liberal-thought association, combining suffragists, Theosophists, and Bellamy Nationalists—among others.

The two women published a paper called the *Liberal Thinker* to announce the founding convention, and in its pages Aldrich proposed another of Bellamy's interim reforms, a public defender. He even offered a financial reward to anyone who would help start such an office. Reading the article in a busted San Diego when she was deciding what to do next, Foltz must have seen wonderful possibilities in Gage's new organization.

Her name was listed first among the featured speakers promised at Gage's convention: "the eminent lawyer, suffragist and thinker of California." Also on the list was "Annie Besant of England." Besant was a renowned freethinker and social reformer, intimate of even more illustrious men such as Charles Bradlaugh (the first avowed atheist in Parliament) and George Bernard Shaw. Stunning in appearance, serious to the point of zealotry, Besant was called by Shaw "the greatest orator in England." On the platform she would give the Almighty five minutes to strike her dead for blasphemy and then stand in silence, with watch upheld, while the minutes passed. Besant supported woman suffrage though her main cause at the time of Gage's convention was Theosophy. To the dismay of her socialist and secularist friends, Besant had become a disciple of Madame Blavatsky.[25]

Apparently, she reconciled Theosophy and atheism because she continued to use her motto "there is no religion higher than truth" (indeed, that is what she wrote in Trella Toland's autograph book in 1890). It was a mark of Gage's departure from mainstream suffragism that she would invite Besant. Also included was the beautiful free-loving anarchist Voltaireine de Cleryre, who, clad in a Greek robe, gave a dramatic reading of an original epic poem. Neither of these presentations was the usual suffrage convention fare.[26]

In fact, everything about Gage's meeting was a challenge to her old colleagues. Following immediately on the first meeting of the newly merged National and American associations, the WNLU seemed to be piggybacking on that organization's publicity and poaching on its membership. One of the very few women to attend both meetings called one group "the standing army" and the other "the advance guard" of reform.[27] But the newspapers treated the birth of the new association as evidence that women were hopelessly divisive and fell on the latest schism with unconcealed delight.

Stanton, who had earlier supported Gage's free-thought writing, announced that she could no longer lend her name to "a secession from the suffrage ranks" and accepted the presidency of the newly merged associations.

Yet suffrage was hardly mentioned at Gage's convention, and the word did not appear in the new organization's name. The WNLU would embrace all reforms—or none, if the anarchists among them had their way. They would have no officers, dues, or "crystallized constitution." Even the word *union* was dubious among the several hundred anarchists, atheists, suffragists, socialists, spelling reformers, Theosophists, and Bellamy Nationalists representing thirty-three states who met early in 1890 in Washington, D.C. A third were men, according to Gage's report, many more than usually attended "ordinary conventions managed by women."[28]

Although the membership was unconventional, the WNLU meeting followed the ordinary course. Most of one day was devoted to resolutions, for instance. Foltz served on the committee that offered propositions about maintaining the civil character of the government and forbidding religious instruction in public schools. They passed easily.

On the afternoon of the last day, however, there occurred the first-ever national debate about public defense (see Chapter 7). Toward the end of her speech on that subject, Foltz turned without transition to woman suffrage. Seemingly out of the blue, she opened an all-out attack on the leaders of the movement. "They oppose this convention. Why? Because they have made a ridiculous failure." She said that female indifference was the main barrier to success and suggested that women would better serve their own goals by concentrating on larger societal problems. "What are the women of America doing?" she asked. "They pretend to hold meetings and clamor for the ballot when the prisons of the country are overflowing."[29]

In her peroration, Foltz proclaimed: "I have been a woman's rights woman—never in my life have I found a man who would refuse me the ballot of himself. . . . Men are only what women have made them."[30] In light of her own twenty years spent lobbying and petitioning without success, Foltz's remarks seem preposterous. She had a tendency when aroused to speak too strongly and say more than she could support. Possibly she was merely overstating the evolutionary promise of Bellamy Nationalism and saying that women must shape the environment of the young. Sometimes, too, she was intentionally provocative—to get people thinking and to gain publicity. Her remarks caused "a decided flutter" according to the *Washington Post*. Responding later to her critics, Foltz implied that she had "created a storm" on purpose because "the suffragists are asleep, or what is worse, contending against imaginary obstacles."[31] After the exciting afternoon at which Foltz presented the public defender idea and assaulted the suffrage leadership, the WNLU convention petered out in closing ceremonies. A committee that included Foltz commissioned one thousand copies of the proceedings and stationery for the new organization.

But the WNLU did not convene a second time. Foltz's interest in free thought was as short-lived as the union itself. By 1892 she was working closely with the WCTU, sworn enemy of the WNLU. Foltz's ideas about alliance with liquor-control movements varied over the years, depending largely, it seems, on her current view of what would best serve women's immediate political goals.

Clara Foltz and Liquor Control

In the early 1890s, Foltz, like many other suffragists and reformers, joined the People's Party, which was more a coalition of disparate causes than an expression of any coherent political philosophy (see Chapter 3). One group within the Populist coalition was the WCTU, which had joined with the newly united suffragists and brought fresh energy to that movement. Despite her recent free-thinking phase, Clara Foltz was quick to embrace the new workers and to become a liquor-control advocate herself.

It was not the first time. As a young woman in Salem, Oregon, in the 1870s, Foltz had worked with the WCTU, perhaps because it was the only politics for women in town. But later, lecturing in Washington Territory in 1886, Foltz rallied "an immense audience" in the Tacoma opera house against a local option bill to make the county dry. The *New Northwest* reported that "she elicited round after round of applause at frequent intervals" as she explained the inefficiencies of Prohibition "from a legal stand-point."[32]

With remarkable prescience, Foltz spoke about "the inevitable evasions of such a law" that would lead to private drinking clubs enticing youth and to black market trade attracting criminals. Recognizing "the liquor curse" and its harm to families, Foltz "advocated the high-license tax as the best and only available restricting power at present." She "urged mothers to pay less attention to Prohibition outside their homes, and more, much more, to caring for their little hoodlums that now were on the street." (*Hoodlums* was a word recently coined in San Francisco.) Instead of strict controls, Foltz proposed the elimination of "all the painted windows and screened doors that hid the inside workings of the saloons." Such a "municipal enactment could easily be enforced anywhere," she said. Once exposed to light, air, and the female gaze, the drinking places would perish.

In expressing the view that Prohibition was a mistake, Foltz was partly operating strategically rather than ideologically. As Washington Territory approached statehood (which came in 1889) there was a move to eliminate suffrage from its constitution because women had used their votes to secure Prohibition at the ballot box and indictments of liquor dealers and saloon-keepers in the grand jury room. Foltz's speech was a warning against fusing these causes.[33]

In this, she was following her mentor, Oregon suffragist Abigail Duniway, who urgently cautioned that women would lose in a fight with "the liquor power—not liquor sellers only . . . but liquor buyers and drinkers who comprise everywhere the very large majority of voters." Moreover, Duniway considered Prohibition a form of "intolerance and quackery." For a time at least, these views influenced Foltz.[34]

But by 1892, she seems to have changed her mind. For one reason, both the Prohibition Party and the WCTU were supporting suffrage. Her enthusiasm for Bellamy Nationalism, whose ideal society would eliminate addiction along with poverty and ignorance, may also have been a factor in Foltz's latest tack. Over the years, moreover, she had a lot of personal experience with alcoholism in her law practice and in her family. In 1916, having lost her daughter Bertha to its effects, Foltz would come out for "total annihilation" of the "destroyer of our home and despoiler of our children." A year later, she wrote an editorial supporting "bone-dry prohibition" and predicting that women "will lead the way to this greatest of all achievements."[35]

Finally, a decade after the passage in 1919 of the Eighteenth Amendment (establishing Prohibition), Foltz returned to her earlier views against interference "with personal liberty and thought." She said the intelligent people of the United States "should be educated to a state of temperance, not bulldozed into obeying a law."[36] Foltz's malleable and pragmatic approach to liquor regulation at different periods was typical of her political thinking generally; she was never strict about ideology—or consistency either, for that matter.

The WCTU Lobbies for Suffrage: A Legislative Victory in California

For a time in the 1890s Foltz appeared in the temperance publications and consulted frequently with their lobbyists. One WCTU member wrote that Foltz was one of the organization's strongest speakers, "ready at a moment's notice with ease and fluency." In her new alliance, personalities probably also played a role. Foltz admired Beaumelle (after the French philosopher) Sturtevant-Peet, the northern California leader of the WCTU and talented organizer who transformed the staid society into a lobbying powerhouse.[37]

Sturtevant-Peet (after her past and present husbands) pushed the vote as the essential first step to liquor control and other liberal measures. Like Foltz, she was strong, individualistic, and never publicly in doubt. During this period both women frequently tried to rouse their female followers by rebuking them. Sturtevant-Peet declared that "those who failed to ask for the ballot when they might use it for the suppression of the wrongs that affect the world" were as much to blame for "the continuance of crime and misery as those who refused to grant it."[38] In the same vein, just as she had done at the WNLU convention, Foltz berated her audiences for failing to press for the vote when men were ready to give it.

She turned out to be right about one group of men, at least—the 1892 California legislature. It passed a bill granting women school suffrage, that is, a vote for members of the school board. Most of the credit went to the WCTU workers, who gained what Foltz and Gordon, lobbying on their own and on the cheap, had been trying to achieve since 1880.

The WCTU succeeded partly because it was well-organized and well-financed, and also because its new voices spiced up the old points. One of the WCTU lobbyists, Sarah "the Sarcastic" Severance, was known for her feistiness. No one, said an observer, could picture her "clinging to the arm of a legislator and pouring into his ear sweet pleasantries." Instead, she pelted her opponents "with uncontrovertible [*sic*] facts and keen irony." For her part, Severance described the California Assembly opponents as "a set of dissipated cigar-smoking men, whom few would care to invite to the dinner table." They "range in and out, restless as polar bears, vibrating between their seats and their whisky bottles outside."[39]

The main argument against giving women the vote was the suffrage clause of the 1879 constitution, which clearly limited the franchise to men. Opponents, Severance said, "mouthed over the word 'unconstitutional'" as "children prattle a new word that strikes their fancy."[40] Despite such doubts, however, the bill passed decisively. Foltz fired off a telegram to Sturtevant-Peet in Sacramento: "Accept congratulations for yourself and Miss Severance for noble work. Woman suffrage is no joke. The State awaits its beneficent result."[41] But the governor referred the bill to a San Francisco law firm headed by a known antisuffragist for an opinion about its constitutionality, and the firm delayed its response until the ten days for signing the bill had expired. "Tricked! Tricked!" was the headline on Sarah Severance's story in the temperance paper. To have their victory snatched away by a lawyer's ploy—after they had worked for years to get the bill passed—was a bitter outcome for the suffragists. Fortunately, the opening of the World's Fair followed within months of the defeat to revive their spirits and raise morale. Generally, the effect of the fair on the women's movement and on Clara Foltz was extremely restorative even though ultimate victory remained elusive.

Women at the World's Fair: 1893

THE WORLD'S CONGRESS
OF REPRESENTATIVE WOMEN

As discussed in Chapter 3, the World's Columbian Exposition had a positive personal effect on Clara Foltz. But it also influenced her thinking about women's rights, starting with the World's Congress of Representative Women in May 1893. This was the first of seventeen great public meetings, or congresses, held in conjunction with the fair. An intellectual forum attached to the physical exposition was the brainchild of Charles Bonney, a Chicago lawyer and educator, who lined up boosters and businessmen to support it.[42]

A special building (now the Chicago Art Institute) was constructed for the world congresses with two large auditoriums and a number of smaller chambers allowing ten thousand people to attend meetings at one time. The World's Congress of Representative Women, also titled "The Woman of the Century," filled the new building to capacity from morning to night for six days. Ten thousand women in one place meeting on the subject of themselves was a sobering sight to some, and thrilling to many. Columbus may have discovered America, but "woman has discovered herself," said the Chicago Inter-Ocean.[43]

The range and variety of presentations at the congress was evidence in itself of woman's progress. Foltz had never seen anything remotely like it. One day she was speaking spontaneously at a temperance meeting, and the next she was describing the poor living conditions of Italian immigrants in San Francisco at a subcongress on labor. Jane Addams, the founder of the settlement house movement, chaired the meeting at which Mrs. A. P. Stevens, a Knights of Labor organizer and "one of the greatest female agitators," persuaded the audience to pass an antisweatshop resolution to be presented to the Illinois legislature.[44]

The huge success of the women's congress was followed by months of meetings, receptions, and rallies related to women's interests and rights. Susan Anthony, who more than any other figure had come to embody the suffrage cause, filled halls all summer long and made many converts. Even a previously hard case like the popular lecturer Kate Field yielded to Anthony's inspiration and joined the suffrage movement. The new suffragists included society women and clubwomen who were active outside the home but not in the suffrage movement. At one point, Anthony enviously compared the membership of the suffrage movement in its fourth decade (seven thousand) with that of other national organizations. The Federation of Woman's Clubs, for instance, was only three years old and boasted forty thousand members.[45] At the World's Fair at last, it seemed that all these activist women might join together in the campaign for political equality. The story of the fair's effect on the women's rights movement starts in the earliest phases of the great exposition.

SUFFRAGISTS AND SOCIETY LADIES

From the first talk of holding the fair, the suffragists, led by Susan Anthony on the federal level, sought a major role for women. Rejecting their plea for inclusion on the main planning committees, Congress instead created a separate but equal Board of Lady Managers, and Mrs. Potter Palmer, the wife of a Chicago tycoon, was chosen to head it. Stylish, bejeweled, man-pleasing, and not an avowed suffragist, she was hardly what the movement women had in mind when they fought for fair participation. However, Bertha Palmer turned out to be a superb organizer who deserves much of the credit for women's prominence at the fair so many decades before they won political equality.[46]

One of Palmer's first efforts was to gain access to all the world congresses, not just the one devoted exclusively to women in May. When the men would not agree to integrate the planning for these auxiliary meetings, Palmer set up a Woman's Branch, which carried out a congress-by-congress struggle over the particulars of participation. In the end, women spoke at fourteen congresses (all except real estate, engineering, and electricity). The high point of Clara Foltz's career was her participation in the law reform congress where she launched her idea for a public defender (see Chapter 7).[47]

Although Bertha Palmer lived in a castlelike mansion on Lake Michigan and moved in the highest social circles, she and her Chicago society lieutenants came from a local tradition of rich women involving themselves in good works. Along with other wealthy and fashionable ladies, for instance,

Palmer was active in the Chicago Club, which had fostered Jane Addams's foundation of the first settlement house in 1889. But initially their interests did not include women's rights or political equality as such. Another impressive set of Chicago women carried the banner of the movement in the fair planning. These were the women professionals, doctors, lawyers, teachers, and ministers who formed the Queen Isabella Association to prepare for women's role in the fair even before Chicago won the competition to hold it. They commissioned a large statue by a woman sculptor of the monarch holding out her jewels—presumably to Columbus, who was not portrayed. The Isabellas were the most disappointed by the naming of Bertha Palmer, rather than one of their number, to lead women's fair participation.

Even before the fair opened, there was competition between the Lady Managers and the Isabellas. As the stress of the huge enterprise began to wear on everyone, the exchange became increasingly antagonistic. The proposed Woman's Building was a particular point of contention; the Isabellas disliked its segregation of female concerns and apolitical exhibits (fine arts, handicrafts, and literary works). They predicted that the building would be an embarrassing sideshow to the fair.[48]

But the Isabellas were wrong. With its relatively human scale and comfortable places to sit, the Woman's Building was an enormous success, and Bertha Palmer's lovely face adorned many things sold there, from postcards (a fair innovation) to silver spoons. Throughout the summer of 1893, almost every day saw some program or reception at the Woman's Building, many including not only the suffragists and society ladies, but working women, black women, religious women, actresses, and reformers of every possible stripe. Only the Isabellas and their large statue were obviously excluded.

At one such meeting, Lucy Stone drew an enthusiastic crowd; from the timing, Foltz may well have been in the audience. It was the end of a long road for this grand Quaker lady, who had kept her own name in marriage, spoken for abolition, and then for women's rights, quoting from the same scripture (1 Cor. 9:16) to support both: "'Woe is unto me if I preach not the gospel of freedom for the slave." Carrie Shortridge had been a girl of fourteen when she first heard Lucy Stone; now Clara Foltz was forty-four, and Stone was making her final public address.[49]

To an audience that included clubwomen and society women as well as suffragists, she spoke proudly of women's entry into the professions and their acceptance in institutions of higher learning and on the public platform. Even as to the greatest prize of gaining the vote, there had been some progress: twenty states had adopted school suffrage, she said. Stone closed by speaking plainly: "These things have not come of themselves. They could not have occurred except as the great movement for women has brought them out and about."[50] It seems likely that Lucy Stone made some new converts that day at the Woman's Building, but they would be her last. A few months later she died.

Aftereffects of the Fair

NEW YORK AND CALIFORNIA

At the fair, Clara Foltz met with a group of "prominent women suffragists," including Anthony, Stanton, Duniway, and Stone. It must have been a high moment for her to be in this renowned company, and apparently the meeting ended any rancor over her intemperate remarks at the WNLU meeting a few years earlier. Its purpose was to plan upcoming campaigns in Colorado, Kansas, and New York.[51]

The suffragists were successful in Colorado the same year as the fair, but they failed badly in Kansas. Most of the energy and the highest hopes, however, were centered in New York, home of Anthony and Stanton and birthplace of the women's movement. Though no large eastern state had come close to granting political equality, the fair-inspired women believed that they could place suffrage in the state constitution, at a convention scheduled for 1894.

Months before the convention Anthony and other leaders were speaking six nights a week in New York City and in every city, town, and hamlet across the state. The women gathered six hundred thousand signatures on their petitions. For the first time in any suffrage campaign, reflecting the effects of the fair, the names on the petitions included those from the upper reaches of society. The socialites brought new strategies to the cause. First, they opened their parlors to suffrage meetings. Women who would never attend a public rally were willing to plot reform in well-appointed homes. Rather than going door-to-door with petitions, they invited people via a handsome card to stop by Sherry's restaurant to sign. "The famous restaurateur placed one of his handsomest rooms at the disposal of the ladies," wrote Ida Harper, a historian of the movement.[52]

The campaign was looking so good that it brought out women organized against suffrage. Despite gathering only fifteen thousand signatures on their petitions, these "remonstrants" or "antis" were treated as an important voice by the opponents of suffrage. Their style of lobbying, featuring "champagne suppers, flowers, music and low-necked dresses," contrasted with the earnest advocacy of the movement women.[53] Nor could the suffragists match the kegs of beer and jugs of whiskey provided to wavering members by the liquor interests.

In the end, after months of the most intense effort, the women lost by a vote of ninety-eight to fifty-eight—against submitting the suffrage question to the people. For Susan Anthony it was the bitterest defeat of her life. For the newly activated socialites, the losing campaign demonstrated the multifaceted nature of the opposition, which made it so hard to package the suffrage issue for political consumption. Some men feared what women would do with the ballot (for example, liquor control), some believed that voting would unsex women and wreck the social order, and others, especially the male lawyers, were simply uneasy about the uncertainties created by doubling the electorate overnight.

In many ways the New York campaign held lessons and portents for the California suffragists as well. They, too, returned from the World's Fair with renewed energy and expectations that victory was near. Clara Foltz was typical, urging "women of the coast to organize" and prophesying that "California will be one of the first States to give women the ballot."[54] Instead, like their New York sisters, the western women had in store another stunning defeat.

For several years after the fair, however, the suffrage scene was more vibrant in California than it had ever been. In all the agitation, "the Portia Law Club, Mrs. Foltz, dean, occupied a prominent place," according to the *History of Woman Suffrage*.[55] The Portias brought together suffragists and society women in the same way that the congresses and meetings of the fair had done. Foltz promised that learning law would make them better mothers and better voters when that time came.

Generally, Foltz called for "more sisterly feeling" among all classes of women. "Those in high social positions should come down a little to help those who are struggling to make the world better," she said. Like the Portia Club, other women's organizations took up the cause, though not the name of suffrage: elite women in the Pacific Association of Collegiate Alumnae; professional women and journalists in the Pacific Coast Woman's Press Association; a cross-class coalition in the Women's Educational and Industrial Union; working women in the Ladies' Assembly of the Knights of Labor— to list just a few. In addition, suffrage clubs were springing up in Southern

California, where women organized effectively for the first time. Many fresh faces emerged to lead these groups and coalitions.[56]

In San Francisco, women from various types of organizations came together for a series of meetings modeled on the World's Congress of Representative Women. Several assemblies in March 1894 were followed by "a brilliant convocation in May, a mass meeting in June," and many other "enthusiastic gatherings" throughout the next several years. The women's congress "became an intellectual force for gifted women," according to the official suffrage history.[57] The success of these congresses and the new momentum they created were at the heart of an ugly public fight in 1894 over who would lead the suffragists to the victory that seemed imminent.

Clara Foltz, who had been so keen on the fair and its effects, was largely absent from the congresses. At one on suffrage, she was a no-show on the program, and four other women spoke to fill the time allotted to her.[58] But she was right in the middle of the fight over movement leadership.

On one side was Laura Gordon, running for president of the statewide society, a job she had held for years when no one else wanted it. Now "kindergartners" in the movement were trying to oust her, according to Gordon's followers, who denounced those who would "rob her laurels."[59] On the other side was Nellie Holbrook Blinn, a political orator in several California campaigns and married to a successful businessman. She led a large group of younger women who complained that Gordon talked incessantly and wearied them with ancient history. Foltz backed Blinn and acted as her lawyer in the disputed election for president.

In an exceedingly undignified exchange of insults, Gordon called Foltz "a blue jay" who "ruffled her plumes" but did little else, and Foltz implied that Gordon was a shyster hanging about the lower corridors of the law.[60] Yet within months of their mutual attacks, the two were lobbying together in Sacramento, and their renewed partnership ended only with Gordon's death in 1907. Later, in one of life's turns, Clara Foltz faced the same kind of judgment inflicted on Gordon when college-educated suffragists assailed her old-fashioned methods and pompous style.

HEARD AT LAST: THE 1895 LEGISLATURE

The postfair renewal of the California suffrage movement bore immediate fruit in the 1894 election when the Republican Party endorsed votes for women and then won overwhelming majorities in the legislature. Several factors, in addition to the women's own efforts, contributed to this favorable result. Californians had been prepared for radical reform by the early onset of the economic depression in the state and by the strong Populist campaigns waged there for the past five years.

In the 1894 election the Republicans moved to co-opt the main Populist issues, including the free coinage of silver (to increase the money supply) and railroad regulation as well as woman suffrage. Another factor in favor of the Republicans was the unpopularity of the Democratic incumbent in the White House. Though it was not a presidential election year, Grover Cleveland's commitment to the gold standard hurt his party generally. Worse, the administration reacted with an armed response in 1894 to two bands of protestors and strikers who had widespread approval in California. One was a group of unemployed people who marched to Washington, D.C., to demand public works projects. The other was striking railway workers.[61]

At the Republican convention, Foltz's old ally, Grove Johnson of Sacramento, was largely responsible for the suffrage endorsement. Almost twenty years earlier, he had maneuvered the Woman Lawyer's Bill through the California Assembly by using his parliamentary skill—voting no at a crucial point so he would be entitled to call for reconsideration. Now in a repeat performance, he engineered an all-or-nothing vote on the whole platform—including woman suffrage—at the party convention. It was the first time in California history that a major party supported votes for women.[62]

In November, the Republicans swept the legislative offices: six out of seven U.S. congressmen and eighty-nine places in the state legislature, compared with twenty-nine for the Democrats. Though a Democrat was elected governor by a narrow margin, he was the most fiercely antirailroad candidate. Woman suffrage was one of the first items on the 1895 legislative agenda. Clara Foltz, Laura Gordon, Beaumelle Sturtevant-Peet, Nellie Holbrook Blinn, Ellen Sargent, and many other "influential women of the state" went to Sacramento for their greatest effort to date.[63]

As the movement's lawyers, Foltz and Gordon kicked off the suffrage campaign. They set out to avoid the 1893 debacle when they had succeeded in getting a suffrage bill passed, only to have the governor refuse to sign because of doubts about its constitutionality. By the time the women were done making their legal case, the chief executive said he would endorse anything the legislature submitted.

Foltz appeared initially before the Senate Committee on Elections. She did not waste time on arguments about justice but briskly called in the promise of "the party which is now in ascendancy in this commonwealth."[64]

The only issue was the form of the measure. She urged that a simple majority of the legislature could enfranchise women and presented a bill declaring that whenever the word *electors* appeared in the code, it included women as well as men.

Though the papers claimed that hers was "an entirely new view," Foltz had been urging this point for years. What was unusual this time around was that people listened. Her argument was that the state constitution did not explicitly bar women from voting, as it did some classes (for example, foreign-born Chinese, felons, and the mentally incompetent), and thus the legislature could confer the right. Suffrage by statute would require only a majority vote instead of the two-thirds needed for a constitutional amendment and would go into effect immediately. An amendment must be put to the people at the next election, meaning that even if they won, women would not actually vote until 1897.

In addition to Foltz's initial address, she and Gordon each made extended individual presentations to the Senate and Assembly judiciary committees. For almost two hours, Foltz spoke to the men like an appellate lawyer, citing cases and authorities and engaging in close legal reasoning. Laura Gordon added some history and context to Foltz's points. In particular, she called on the name of David Terry, covert ally to the women at the constitutional convention, who had brokered many of the essential compromises there without his hand being seen in the outcomes. In a "now it can be told" manner, Laura Gordon revealed that Judge Terry had personally assured her that the constitutional clause providing that no special privileges should be granted to one class that were not extended to all was meant to enable the legislature to enfranchise women.[65]

Gordon was convincing when she said that these were the unwritten understandings at the time the constitution was passed. Unlike most of the men in the legislature, she and Clara Foltz had been there in 1879 when the constitution was framed and ratified. Invoking Terry had its downsides, however, even to a group short on historical memory. Only five years had passed since his death at the hands of a U.S. marshal, and the publicity had stirred up all the old scandals. Neither the duel with the antislavery senator nor the Confederate service was likely to sit well with this current Republican legislature.

For several months, the women and their male allies lobbied and rallied for the Foltz bill. The State Assembly passed it handily, but the Senate, including many Republicans, balked and insisted on the need for a constitutional amendment. Foltz was furious, expressing her "utter contempt" for the legislators who voted against "the measure indorsed by the Republican convention and advocated by the best and brainiest men in the State."[66]

Though Foltz's statute failed, two-thirds of the legislature voted to refer the question of woman suffrage to a popular referendum in 1896—an unparalleled achievement. On this round, the women had found many new allies—"men with manly brains and men with manly hearts and courage," as Foltz described them. But the outcome left the suffragists to wage their first statewide campaign in the midst of a discordant presidential election and an economic depression.

Reflecting on the half-empty nature of the suffrage glass, Foltz "felt cast down and gloomy," according to the *Call*. The story added, improbably, that this was "the first time" for such feelings "in her successful career as journalist, lawyer and orator." But Foltz turned quickly to the half-full view, predicting "the dawn of a new era" and promising "a campaign for freedom, the like of which had not been seen or heard for many a year."

A "RED-HOT" SUFFRAGE CAMPAIGN

Foltz's prediction about the campaign came true. Susan B. Anthony arrived in California early in 1896 and with Anna Shaw and other major movement figures assumed leadership of what she called "a red-hot" campaign. Her first administrative move was to end the internecine conflict by placing Ellen Clark Sargent in charge of the statewide society instead of either Laura Gordon or Nellie Blinn. Sargent was the widow of the U.S. senator who had introduced the first federal suffrage bill and the legislation enabling women lawyers to practice in the federal courts.[67]

Sargent's appointment and the movement's headquarters in her mansion advanced the social standing of the suffragists, already improved by the World's Fair and the subsequent outburst of club activity. Women who had shown little previous interest became involved in the ratification effort. Clara Foltz missed the early months of the campaign, having moved to New York late in December 1895. But the following April, she came back to San Francisco to help. "Mrs. Foltz has just returned for a short visit, and with her characteristic energy she has already thrown herself into the thick of the fray," reported the *Call*. At a parlor meeting soon after she arrived, where Anthony was also present, Foltz helped found a new club, the Invincibles. She told the press it was "the most delightful evening" of her life: "I never appreciated the old warhorses of the movement so much."[68]

Foltz liked the parlor meeting tactic, which the local suffragists had borrowed from the New York campaign. It was a lot easier than stumping the state with its huge distances, rough terrain, one-street towns, and friendly but often indifferent people. She vowed to "carry on the fight from house to house, from Van Ness Avenue to . . ." At this point in her description, Foltz started laughing "at the incongruity into which her enthusiasm had led her"—describing guerilla warfare in upscale neighborhoods.

Her most significant contribution came in helping to win the endorsement of the *San Francisco Call*. It was the first time in any suffrage campaign that a major newspaper had given early unqualified support, and the *Call* brought in its wake most of the state press. Of course, the editor who made the bold move was Charles Shortridge, Clara Foltz's younger brother.[69] The endorsement was timed for maximum effect on the state Republican convention. Every delegate received a special edition of the paper that carried not only the prosuffrage editorial, but pages of appealing stories about the women, including an account of Anthony's reaction to hearing of the support: "For a moment the veteran suffragist . . . remained seated in her chair, the tears rolling over her wrinkled cheeks. Then, without a note of warning, she jumped from her seat and seizing her hostess, Mrs. A. A. Sargent, about the waist, executed a triumphal waltz with her through the spacious parlors, to that lady's great wonderment."[70]

When he endorsed suffrage, Shortridge had been editor of the *Call* for a year and a half, having bought it at auction for $360,000. Though he was fronting for the true purchaser, John Spreckels, the sugar king client of his brother Sam, Charles had plenty of editorial influence. In his three-year tenure, the *Call* was lively, progressive, and lavish in its coverage of the Shortridge family.[71]

The men of the big-city press, which included more than twenty daily newspapers and many magazines of political commentary, did not know what to make of Charles Shortridge at first. Some called him "the Santa Clara Simpleton," referring partly to his previous editorship of the provincial *San Jose Mercury*. But Arthur McEwen, the chief editorial writer for Hearst's *Examiner*, warned that this "ebullient rustic" meant business. "He cares nothing, this honest countryman for the artificial glitter of literary polish, but when you have read the *Call* you find yourself informed of what the world has been doing the previous day, and his local reporters have scored several scoops."[72]

McEwen captured Charles Shortridge's character as well, noting that he ran his paper "as if life were a corn-husking, San Francisco a barn, and himself the life of the party." To a cheering crowd of thousands, Shortridge declared: "I am proud of being in this fight if for no other reason than that sister of mine, who practices in the supreme court of this State—to grant her all the privileges I have. You are denying her a right to which she is entitled. . . . I pledge I will stand by you to success or defeat."[73]

Defeat was far from Foltz's mind as she headed back East. It really seemed that California, where she had started her public life speaking for suffrage, was about to give women the vote and she had played an important part in the achievement. Her feelings of efficacy were short-lived, however. In June 1896, Foltz attended the Republican National Convention in St. Louis where she saw to her dismay that despite all the positive portents, the time was not yet ripe for women's rights.

The Great Watershed Election of 1896

THE CONVENTIONS

Foltz often told her father's story of attending the first Republican convention to nominate a candidate for president where Abraham Lincoln won over better-known but less well-organized candidates. Her own Republican convention experience, by contrast, was so bleak that she never mentioned it or went to another one. It began well enough, however.

Billed in the newspapers as "the woman lawyer of New York," Clara Foltz joined her old friend Lillie Devereux Blake, an expert lobbyist from years in Albany, and a younger suffragist who was already a star organizer, Carrie Chapman Catt. The trio, three generations of woman suffragists, made an excellent team. They arrived in St. Louis several days early, set up headquarters at the labyrinthine Southern Hotel, where the power brokers were, and started lobbying individuals and state delegations.[74]

Women had been attending Republican conventions and urging a suffrage plank literally since the party's founding. But this time, they were present in vast new numbers: "several hundred well-bred, well-read, well-educated and well-to-do women," as one paper put it.[75] Even more women came from the WCTU, now completely on board for voting rights, and there were a hundred female journalists present from across the country. In addition, "hundreds of St. Louis women, with their escorts, promenaded the hotel corridors" as sightseers. "The guns of the convention," men such as the Republican boss of New York, were sighted and remarked on like monuments on a tour. But the most telling picture was in a *Harper's Weekly* article titled "Corridor of the Southern Hotel. Time 2 A.M." Not a woman, activist or tourist, appears among the milling crowd.[76]

With business being done in the dead of night when "nice" women were not out, the suffragists were at a disadvantage. Even worse, however, was the total concentration of the delegates on whether to endorse gold or silver as the monetary standard. Silver, the original cry of the farmers and other debtors and taken up initially by the Populists, stood for increasing the money supply and thus equalizing the wealth. Gold was the traditional standard and represented individual property rights and a stable currency.

"Gold bugs" and "silverites" were irreconcilable, yet both factions were prominent among the Republicans. Led by Senator Henry Cabot Lodge of Massachusetts and Thomas Platt and Chauncey Depew of New York, many powerful men were determined that the word *gold* should actually be included in the platform. The silver forces were pressing just as hard to keep the word out, and the candidate (preordained to be William McKinley of Ohio) had gained their provisional support by indicating he would run as a "straddlebug" without explicit reference to either metal.[77]

The suffragists, too, tried to be "straddlebugs" because their allies were on both sides of the divide. From western mining states where women voted and the people wanted silver came supporters like Senator Henry Moore Teller from Colorado and Isaac Trumbo from Utah. But the leaders of the goldbugs, like Depew and Lodge, were also sympathetic to woman suffrage. In short, their allies were locked in combat over an issue on which women had nothing to offer politically.

The "gold and silver wrangle," in Foltz's phrase, took all the space—psychically and even physically—in the ornate lobby of the Southern Hotel.[78] Delegates were besieged by the opposing forces on arrival and wooed steadily until they committed themselves. By the time the convention opened, it was already settled that *gold*—not *honest* or *sound* money—would be the word in the platform. With tears in his eyes, Senator Teller led the silverites, virtually all suffrage supporters, out of the convention hall and out of the party.

Unlike *gold*, the word *suffrage* did not make it into the platform, which instead had a "woman plank" referring generally to the need for "a wider sphere of usefulness" for females. The wording was the idea of Henry Blackwell (the widower of Lucy Stone), who had dashed it off on the train to the convention from Boston without consulting anyone.[79] Perhaps by coincidence (though perhaps Blackwell planned it), the leading suffrage lobbyists were absent when the platform committee passed the plank. They were

across town trying to reconcile warring factions among local women engaged in a procedural farce over who would chair a unification meeting.
By the time Foltz and the others returned, the platform committee had
accepted Blackwell's proposal.

Foltz blasted the plank in the press, calling it "twaddle" and specifically
rebutting the three propositions it contained. To the first, that "the Republican Party is mindful of the rights and interests of women," she responded
that this was not only false, but worse than previous formulations that had
at least promised "respectful consideration" of women's demands. Foltz
was even more denunciatory of Blackwell's second sentence: "Protection of
American industries includes equal opportunities, equal pay for equal work
and protection of the home." To imply that women would benefit from
high tariffs was, Foltz said, "the essence of nonsense." She had some expertise on the subject, having stumped for a whole season against protective
tariffs for the Democrats in 1888.[80]

Finally, the Blackwell plank stated: "We favor the admission of women
to wider spheres of usefulness and welcome their cooperation in rescuing
the country from Democratic and Populistic mismanagement and misrule."
As one still aligned with the Populists herself, Foltz was embarrassed by this
clause, which she said "advocates nothing, favors nothing, promises nothing" while trying to array women against the parties that might offer them
more support. Flatly, she declared that the plank was "a severe blow and
great misfortune to the woman suffragists." Though Susan Anthony was also
filled with "indignation, anger and contempt," she and other suffrage leaders decided to remain silent in light of the ongoing California campaign.[81]

By contrast, Clara Foltz was unrelenting. She had nothing but disdain
for those (notably her friend Lillie Blake) who argued that half a loaf of
bread was better than none at all, dismissing them as lacking "the courage
to acknowledge defeat; but to me there is no politics higher than truth and
no folly greater than self-delusion." A few weeks after her return from the
Republican convention, Foltz was "indignant" at reports that she would
present a suffrage plank to the Democrats, meeting in Chicago. She said
"present conditions" made an "adequate hearing" impossible and that she
would not appear before a convention that was "thinking of something else
it deemed of more importance." Indeed, she added, it was "almost irratio-
nal" for the suffragists to bother.[82]

Foltz was certainly right about the impossibility of gaining attention at
the Democratic convention. Free coinage of silver stood in for every pro-

gressive reform, and in a revival atmosphere a young ex-congressman from Nebraska, William Jennings Bryan, was nominated. His acceptance speech, which ended with the dramatic sentence "You shall not crucify mankind upon a cross of gold," became an instant classic. A few weeks later the People's Party also nominated Bryan and also omitted any reference to woman suffrage in its platform.

THE CAMPAIGN, ELECTION, AND AFTERMATH

Like the conventions, the campaign was dominated by the currency debate, which became a proxy for other oppositions in addition to sound money versus shared wealth and creditor versus debtor. The election pitted the South and West against the East and Midwest; the country against the city; youth and passion against age and wisdom. The presidential candidates were a contrast in style as well as message. McKinley was in his fifties, had served in the Civil War, and been in Congress for many years. He exuded an air of stability and calm. Refusing to compete with Bryan's exciting platform performances, McKinley ran a front-porch campaign from small-town Ohio. Instead of promising drastic change, he talked reassuringly of a "full dinner pail" and said that "good money never made times hard."[83]

Entirely absent from the political discourse was any mention of woman suffrage. Yet the women were deeply involved in the campaign as usual, doing everything but voting and attending the backroom counsels of the powerful. Though some well-financed Republican women worked for McKinley, the suffragists generally backed Bryan, and most people assumed he supported votes for women. Indeed, opponents charged that Bryan headed a dangerous mob of unbalanced men and hysterical women; others claimed that the men were weak and effeminate and the women aggressive and unsexed.

More women were on the stump than in any previous campaign, but the one most in the national spotlight was Mary Elizabeth Lease, "the Kansas Pythoness." Lease was even more denunciatory and vituperative than when she campaigned for the Populists in 1892. After she appeared in New York, the *Tribune* warned, "[B]ehind this raging virago, foaming with fury and blazing with wrath, is the wild mob of levelers eager for the general distribution of spoils; behind them the Terror, with its bloody bacchanals and merciless savagery." Foltz may have been speaking of Lease and trying to dissociate the movement from her when she derided a "great big slattern with a club in her hand and a stain on her tongue."[84]

Over the campaign season it looked like the election would be close, but McKinley won decisively and did especially well in New York, where the immigrant voters were put off by Bryan's evangelical style, teetotaling ways, and revolutionary rhetoric. The same demographics affected the vote in California, where the Republican victory in San Francisco, combined with the opposition of the liquor interests, carried defeat for the woman suffragists too. After a year of intensive campaigning, they lost with a vote of 137,000 to 110,000.[85]

Foltz felt the California defeat personally. Her brother Charles was removed as editor of the *Call* because his suffrage support hurt advertising revenues. She would later say the women's cause ruined him financially. More generally, Foltz had a large role in initiating the California campaign and had expected to savor the triumph. Instead, the election marked the end of her radical politics. She returned to the party of her father and her brothers, backed McKinley for a second term, and founded the Clara Foltz Gold Mining Company.

For a few years after the election, Foltz was largely inactive on the suffrage front. She even said in an 1899 interview that women should go slowly rather than push too fast for their rights—a sentiment so uncharacteristic that it indicates despair.[86] Returning to San Francisco after three years in New York, Foltz put her main energies into involving women in business and banking rather than in lobbying for the vote.

Victory in California
POLITICAL EQUALITY AND PROGRESSIVISM

Near the end of the World's Fair summer in 1893, Susan B. Anthony spoke of "wandering in the wilderness of disenfranchisement for forty-five years, five years longer than the children of Israel." Now, she said, the Promised Land lay just ahead.[87] Her metaphor proved all too apt; like Moses, who saw but never reached the goal, she died without casting a legal ballot.

The nineteenth century closed on fifty years of effort with only four lightly populated western states in the suffrage ranks: Wyoming, Utah, Colorado, and Idaho. Though the picture was grim on the voting front, women had made some progress during the postwar period. Notably, they won admission to higher education and gained headway in the professions. And the last decade of the century saw a fresh generation of women, partly inspired by the Chicago World's Fair, break out of their assigned sphere and start forming clubs and leagues devoted to both civic and self-improvement.

California exemplified the new shape things were taking. After the heart-breaking 1896 defeat, the suffragists did not retire to the domestic sphere but continued to organize for other purposes and sought the vote as a tool for achieving them. Women reformers met on a new plane with men who were also organizing in clubs and leagues to fight against corruption and for better and more government services to all people. From these various groups, the Progressive movement was born in California. It started in Los Angeles at about the same time Foltz moved there in 1906. A group of lawyers, journalists, and businessmen joined over dinner at a downtown café to talk about political conditions in the state. They were mostly Republicans and originally intended only to improve their own party, rather than to start a new one.[88]

Their model in this was Theodore Roosevelt, who had become president after McKinley's assassination in 1901 and moved to clean up dishonesty and unfair competition by predatory corporations. Planning to do the same thing on a state level, the California group named themselves the Lincoln–Roosevelt League. The league focused on the Southern Pacific Railroad (known as the Espee), which had been corrupting the entire government, especially the legislature, for many years.

To break the Espee's power, the progressives moved first to restore democratic control through such measures as the primary election, the referendum and recall, the direct election of senators—and woman suffrage. Many of these specific proposals and the attack on the Espee had their antecedents in Bellamy Nationalism and Populism. Yet despite her close connection with these previous movements, Clara Foltz did not become an early Progressive. Indeed, she called herself a "stand-patter Republican," the group most closely tied with the Espee.[89] Foltz's position was partly one of family loyalty. Her younger brother, Sam Shortridge, was assiduously climbing through the established party structure and would eventually serve two terms as a U.S. senator (1920–1932).

Over decades of lobbying and practicing law in California, moreover, Foltz had found many allies among the railroad's men. George Perkins, the first governor under the 1879 constitution and later U.S. senator, was an example; Grove Johnson was another. He had saved the Woman Lawyer's Bill in the California Assembly at the outset of Foltz's career and for the next thirty years as state legislator and U.S. congressman, Johnson had supported

Foltz and her cause while largely doing the Espee's bidding on matters important to it.[90]

Her old friend Johnson needed all the help he could muster in 1909 because the progressives in the legislature, still nominally Republicans, managed to pass an open primary law. It meant the end of the Espee's main forum for purchasing politicians, that is, the party conventions where candidates were bought before being elected. Almost certainly, open primaries would result in the end of Johnson's three decades as an elected official.

One of the most dramatic aspects of the situation was that Johnson's son, Hiram, long politically estranged from his father, was leading the progressive efforts. In the first open Republican primary under the new law, Hiram Johnson ran for governor against three other candidates and with the support of the Lincoln–Roosevelt League won decisively. Immediately, the well-organized reformers designed a Republican platform for the general election that included railroad regulation, direct legislation through initiative and referendum, and a host of other measures, such as a promise to submit votes for women to the people.

Of this cornucopia of reforms, Hiram Johnson campaigned on only one in the general election: busting the power of the Espee. His Democratic opponent, Theodore Bell, was also a reformer though more moderate (he said "he would not tear up the railroad with his teeth"). Foltz later complained that Johnson "never spoke one word" on behalf of woman suffrage, though "frequently importuned to do so." Generally, he did not impress her: "Every single piece of progressive legislation worthy of any consideration was already in the course of evolution long before Hiram Johnson came onto the scene," she wrote of this period.[91]

In sum, perhaps on account of her own personal and political history and loyalty, Foltz approved the Progressive principles but not the men who promoted them. As to the Progressive women, she was rivalrous in the extreme. Foltz complained bitterly that these new suffragists were trying "to take from her hands the flag which she has carried so long unsullied."[92]

LILLIAN COFFIN AND KATHERINE EDSON

Initially, Foltz's main complaint against the younger women centered on their takeover of the legislative lobbying she and Laura Gordon had done for so many years. Without financial support or recognition of any other sort, they had won bills enabling women to be lawyers, notaries, and estate executors. Year in and year out they had lobbied for suffrage. But after the

1896 defeat while Foltz was still in New York, the movement regrouped and left out Laura Gordon. In fact, Foltz wrote, the "great leaders (?) were scared half to death" that Gordon might join them and hid their departure dates for the capital. These newcomers, she added, lacked "ability or dignity of any kind" and "dished up" the "great primal principles of liberty . . . in the most inane and asinine style."[93]

Who were these women—"the nonentities" and "harpies that have been butchering and mangling a great cause"? Foltz's diatribes, even in personal correspondence, mentioned no names, but Lillian Coffin from San Francisco and Katherine Edson from Los Angeles were the two obvious targets. Both irritated Foltz, though for different reasons.[94]

Coffin was the wife of a wealthy businessman, strikingly good-looking, a former opera singer, and a clubwoman. The *Los Angeles Herald* described her as "vivacious, keen of wit, and a brilliant speaker" who wears "beautiful and becoming raiment." Publicity of this sort particularly riled Foltz, who wrote to a friend, "when it comes to beauty and good dressing, correct manners in polite life, there are others, you know." Most galling was the implicit comparison of the new and old suffragists—as when a leading male Progressive said suffrage "became a serious issue when attractive, well-dressed women took it up."[95]

Using tactics that Foltz and Gordon with their annual pilgrimages to Sacramento had not imagined, Coffin was an outstanding organizer. Before the passage of the open primary bill, one of her tactics was to lobby at the party nominating conventions, collecting commitments before the politicians were elected (like the Espee did but without bribes). In 1907, Coffin produced a great column of women dressed in white, carrying banners and waving yellow ribbons (the suffrage color) to march on the Republicans. When the convention refused to endorse suffrage, the Coffin-led ladies booed, hissed, and declined the proffered compliments.[96]

The women did, however, succeed in gaining an individual commitment from James Gillett, and when he was elected governor, they called upon him to demand that he keep his pledge and support suffrage. He rudely told them to go home where they belonged. Coffin then excoriated him so effectively in the press that the governor actually denied that he had ever given the promise. Everyone knew who was lying.[97]

Clara Foltz wrote to Gillett sympathetically, complimenting him on his "heroic treatment" of the "raw efforts of the Lillian Coffin stripe." While denigrating her rivals, Foltz flattered the governor and, without mentioning a specific post, offered her services as a true representative of women.[98] Several months later, the governor appointed her to the State Board of Charities and Corrections (see Chapter 4). Foltz said her appointment to the board showed that Gillett's female detractors were wrong about him. In an oblique reference to Coffin's methods, she added that she did not believe in "militant ways" but in "quiet and effective argument. When I meet a man who tells me that the home is woman's sphere, I do not sneer at him. I respect his ideas."[99]

Though Foltz had actually done a good deal of sneering in her own day, she had for some years, since the World's Fair, been counseling patience and understanding. "It is folly to try to argue prejudice out of anyone," she said. "It grows in the darkness of the past, and will disappear only when exposed to the light of the present."[100] Coffin and her followers made no public comment on the appointment.

Not only did the new suffragists reject Foltz's counsel on how to proceed, but as she doubtless observed, they received the kind of financial backing from wealthy women that had not been available to her and Laura Gordon. One contributor, for example, was Mary McHenry Keith, who was a non-practicing lawyer with a rich husband. Keith also started a suffrage club— the College Equal Suffrage League—that Foltz was not eligible to join.[101]

As much as Foltz inveighed against such slights from the northern California suffragists, her real nemesis was Katherine Edson in Los Angeles. Like many of the younger suffragists, Edson became interested in the vote while campaigning for other issues such as pure milk, safe food, and better working conditions for women. College-educated and a first-rate speaker and administrator, Edson typified the new breed of movement women. For instance, though she had three children, she was unsentimental about motherhood, writing at one point "how can one strong mature woman spend all her time specializing of a few children who do grow up."[102] She crossed the phrase out of her public speech but did not replace it with any Foltzian lines about home and family being a woman's highest calling. While these stylistic differences between the two women were hardly minor, they cannot fully account for the intense enmity that developed between them.

The explanation probably lies in Edson's presidency of the Political Equality League, a well-financed and prestigious suffrage organization that excluded Foltz. It had started in an unusual way as the vision of a Progressive man, who lined up one hundred other men, and then they invited a like number of women to join. Clara Foltz was not one of them. Years later she spoke resentfully of "those who came into the suffrage ranks of California in April 1910." They "little knew of the hardships of the pioneers" and labored in a field "made fallow for them and respectable withal." For these latecomers she said the suffrage campaign "was but a pleasant diversion."[103]

Instead of working in the new Political Equality League, Foltz became president of the old-fashioned Votes for Women Club. Her friend Mary Foy, a Democrat, was vice president. As the movement gained momentum, women organized against suffrage for the first time in California, just as they had done earlier in New York. Edson welcomed the opposition because she believed it would force women to take sides and inevitably develop new recruits for suffrage. Clara Foltz was scornful of the "chiffon lives" of the antisuffragists: "I prefer the working life to that of running away from duty," she said.[104]

Despite her suspicions of Hiram Johnson and the fact that her rivals were in the vanguard, Foltz threw herself into the 1910 gubernatorial campaign. Her Votes for Women Club grew to four hundred members and held weekly rallies with speeches and songs. The general election was close; Johnson won with a vote of 177,000 to 155,000, and though he barely carried San Francisco, the insurgents showed real strength in the southern counties. The Republicans, with the backing of the Progressive reformers, also won majorities in both houses of the state legislature.

Katherine Edson announced that women would be a continual presence in Sacramento until they redeemed the Republican platform promise of submitting woman suffrage to the people. But Clara Foltz had another strategy in mind, better than sending "hundreds of charming women to the Legislature" with "smiles and importuning." She had been talking for several years about her plan. "I consider the women of the state as clients who have a desperate case and yet an easy one to win if they are represented by intelligent counsel," she told the Votes for Women Club.[105] The simmering but largely submerged rivalry between Foltz and Edson was about to surface.

THE FOLTZ–EDSON FEUD ERUPTS

As the newly elected legislature started its session in 1911, Clara Foltz was there to unveil her plan. She proposed a thirty-two-word statute providing simply that woman citizens could vote. In 1895, a similar bill she drafted had passed the State Assembly but not the Senate. Instead, the legislature had adopted a constitutional amendment that had been put to a popular vote and failed the next year.[106]

No doubt Foltz had that grievous loss in mind when she insisted that the route to suffrage was through legislation. Once women had the statutory right, then they could place suffrage in the constitution at an election in which they voted. From all appearances, Foltz hoped to sweep into Sacramento, secure passage of the bill, and become once more the chief suffrage lobbyist. The *Call* described the "war flashing in her eyes for some of her sister suffragettes from Los Angeles who are expected to arrive during the week." Calling the others "dilettante suffragettes," Foltz said she came to prevent "a vast amount of unnecessary trouble and confusion" and a possible defeat.[107] Legitimate fears, yet whatever its formal legal merits, Foltz's plan was impractical. She risked splitting the affirmative votes and confusing the issue. Moreover, a legal challenge to any statute would be inevitable, and if they lost in court, the suffragists would have to start over again on the amending process.

Her insistence on a statute was an example of the divisiveness that was Foltz's besetting weakness as a movement leader. It sprang partly from the simple desire for recognition. Foltz had a tendency to stride "forward to the front of every platform," a fault she decried in others.[108] But more than ego and vanity were involved; she believed deeply that she was right and was always a little surprised when others disagreed. This supreme confidence in her own ideas, which served her well in other contexts, prevented Foltz from compromising with or conciliating perceived rivals. On the eve of women winning suffrage, she was called the "best loved and best hated" woman in Los Angeles because she felt so strongly that people were either with her or wrong.[109]

Within days of the introduction of Foltz's bill by a Democrat, Edson, Coffin, and others arrived in town to lobby a proposed constitutional amendment. It was safely through by early February. Edson claimed the "splendid victory" while Foltz, for her part, missed the quarterly meeting of the prison board because of illness, probably brought on by the news. Once recovered, she moved swiftly to take over the coming ratification campaign by asking the statewide chairman, Elizabeth Lowe Watson, to designate the Votes for Women Club as the central suffrage organization in Los Angeles. Soothingly, Watson reminded her that there was enough work for everyone and time was short. Less soothingly, she flatly stated that she would not "insult or embarrass Mrs. Edson" by appointing anyone else to be in charge in the southern counties.[110]

Watson was right about the huge job that lay ahead; the suffragists had just six months to persuade the men of the state to share political power.

"Get to work immediately and report to the committees or me just as regularly as possible," Watson's letter concluded. And Foltz did exactly that, still needling Edson whenever possible, but throwing herself into the campaign for the amendment whose necessity she had so gratuitously protested.

THE 1911 SUFFRAGE CAMPAIGN

Woman suffrage was one of twenty-three constitutional amendments submitted to the male voters of California in a special election set for October 10, 1911. No candidates, only ideas, were running—ideas about restructuring government and extending its regulatory powers, cleaning up corruption, corralling the railroad and other greedy corporations. Votes for women fit with reforms designed to strengthen democratic rule such as the referendum and recall (including of judges) and the direct election of senators.

Given their commitment to "true democracy," the Progressives had to endorse woman suffrage. Yet some of them, including Governor Johnson, were tepid in their support—while the opposition was hot. A group of well-known men (albeit mostly Espee machine politicians) designated themselves the Committee of Fifty and spoke for the "real" ladies who did not want the vote. Antisuffragists from the East came to supplement the home-grown "remonstrants."[111]

For once, Clara Foltz's increasingly outdated oratorical style suited the occasion: "Back to the husbands you have left behind in the homes you have deserted! We do not need you! We do not want you! Back! Out of our sight!" An audience six hundred strong cheered as Foltz pronounced California women too busy to sit on the "pedestals" that the antis and the Committee of Fifty were constructing for them.[112]

Opponents drew on the scare tactics that had succeeded in the past—especially the claim that woman suffrage would result in the prohibition of alcohol. Usually effective with working people and immigrant groups, the argument did not suffice this time partly because the dialog centered on civic rather than moral reform. The Progressive suffragists appealed directly to the working class on issues such as improving industrial conditions and government benefits. Moreover, liquor regulation found new support among those concerned about the effects of alcoholism on families and on the workforce.

Some WCTU members replaced their white ribbons with suffrage yellow during the campaign. Moreover, the women's groups concerned with liquor control were just one cog in the well-organized machine of more than fifty clubs, leagues, unions, and parliaments all over the state. Many of these were devoted to civic improvement and social work among the poor in addition to suffrage for themselves, making the campaign more palatable to many. Everyone worked under a loose central organization that did not try to dictate a single line on any of the issues.

For the first time, the Federation of Woman's Clubs endorsed suffrage. Despite the history of racist rhetoric by some in the movement, African American and Asian women also formed associations to seek the vote. Labor union women who had proved themselves within their organizations called in their political chits, and organized men responded. Socialists, building on the Bellamy Nationalists and the Populists, were staunch suffragists. Using new methods and strategies, women made their enfranchisement the major issue on the crowded ballot. They "automobiled" into the countryside and gathered crowds for impromptu stump speeches. In the cities, they went door-to-door and pleaded the cause to whoever answered (all unusual and brave actions). Millions of flyers, leaflets, booklets, pins, and signs were distributed.[113]

Foltz traveled "the length and breadth of the state, speaking in towns, sheep ranches, cross-roads and mining camps," raising good audiences and memories of her previous political stumping.[114] As president of the Votes for Women Club, she set a goal of five thousand members, and as they had in the gubernatorial campaign, the club held weekly rallies, this time in a hall seating eight hundred people.

Foltz and her friend Mary Foy were determined to have some fun while winning the vote. They tooled around in Foy's automobile making speeches and holding press conferences and most memorably took off in a hot air balloon, distributing suffrage flyers over the crowds below. Another fine moment was the unfurling of a gigantic "Votes for Women" banner in the golden poppy color the suffragists preferred to plain yellow.[115] It stretched across the street, directly opposite Foltz's law office. From a balcony, she pulled the cord and a brass band played while hundreds cheered and wept with joy at the imminence of victory. Foltz's office was campaign central for her club. There they held a series of noon meetings for businessmen who came for a brisk suffrage talk followed by lunch for those who had "made up their minds to place the ballot in feminine hands."[116]

With the exceptions of the *San Francisco Chronicle* and the *Los Angeles Times*, the press supported the suffragists, who proved themselves excellent media managers. They supplied reams of ready-made copy to the rural and specialized papers, held events galore, and gave interviews right and left. "Put a cross in the yes space. And put woman in her right place!" was the slogan of the hour.

Altogether, it was a remarkable effort. "The cleverest campaign ever made in the state for any cause" and "the most brilliant suffrage campaign ever waged," said the *Western Woman Voter*, noting also that it was "wholly in charge of the women of the state." Yet despite the vigorous sophisticated operation, suffrage passed by a mere 2 percent of the vote, 3,587 votes of 246,487 ballots cast.[117] More men voted on this amendment than on any other measure, and it won by the narrowest margin, with the southern counties and the countryside providing the victory. Since every vote counted, Clara Foltz was right when she said that her club's "magnificently planned campaign" was "a big factor" in the outcome. "We represented a noble division of women in the suffrage army . . . and contributed one of the brightest pages to California's history . . . one which the womanhood of the future should recall with increasing gratitude."[118]

WOMEN VOTE IN LOS ANGELES

Before the victory celebrations were over, Los Angeles women were registering to vote in a special election for mayor to be held in December 1911. Job Harriman, a union attorney and a Socialist, had won a plurality in the regular November balloting (at which women could not yet vote). His opponent in the runoff was the incumbent George Alexander, a good-government Progressive type, nominally a Republican.[119] There was little difference between the two candidates except on one issue: the Socialists supported organized labor in their efforts to unionize the city. During the previous summer, the unions had launched a major campaign with strikes, boycotts, and massive demonstrations. Mayor Alexander earned their lasting enmity by obtaining injunctions against picketing and boycotts and pushing through regulations forbidding speeches and rallies in public places.

The business community, led by Harrison Otis, conservative publisher of the *Los Angeles Times*, also strongly resisted unionization. On October 1, 1910, an explosion ripped the *Times* building, killing and injuring more than twenty people. Three leaders of the Ironworkers Union were charged; those on labor's side believed the men were falsely accused and hired Clarence Darrow, the best criminal lawyer in the country, to represent them. The trial began in October 1911, the day after the special election awarding women suffrage.[120]

It was still going on in November, and the plurality vote for Socialist Harriman for mayor was largely the result of the efforts of a fired-up labor movement. The runoff campaign that followed was full of ironies. Foremost was the conservative plea for women to register and vote—against the Socialists. Otis, in particular, pandered to the women he had been condemning only weeks before for wanting the ballot.[121]

Katherine Edson and her cohorts changed the Political Equality League into the Women's Progressive League and worked hard for the incumbent, registering women only in safe wards for Alexander. Foltz and Foy also transformed their Votes for Women Club into a civic improvement association. But they urged all eligible women to register—including Socialists.

Paradoxically, their nonpartisan stance drew the charge that Foltz had made a deal to deliver women's votes to Harriman in payment for the Socialist help in winning suffrage. While heatedly denying this, Foltz spoke proudly of her club's diversity in the earlier campaign: "In our ranks were many stanch socialists. We had many democrats and republicans as well. We had progressive republicans and standpatters. We were glad to have all of them."[122]

In the month or so that women had to register for the mayoralty runoff election, more than eighty thousand signed up to vote. One suffrage leader estimated that only ten thousand of those qualified failed to register—putting to rest for good the argument that women did not want the ballot. When Alexander won easily, people gave women the credit for saving Los Angeles from Socialism.[123] The most influential factor, however, was probably the guilty plea of the defendants in the *Times* bombing trial. Entered only days before the election, it left the coalition between Socialists and labor in disarray. Though many still believed the defendants innocent (and thought Darrow had forced the plea for reasons of his own), the formal admission of guilt stripped Harriman of the middle-class independent and Progressive voters he needed to win.

The next year brought the first statewide and national election in which California women were eligible to vote. In 1912, Clara Foltz was once again "the lady orator of the Republicans," her title in 1880 when she stumped for James Garfield. A large newspaper spread shows her with uplifted arm addressing three hundred women who supported the incumbent William Howard Taft, as against the Progressive Party ticket of Theodore Roosevelt and Hiram Johnson.[124] Even though the winner of the election was Democrat

Woodrow Wilson (probably because of the Republican split), it was surely a thrill for Foltz to cast her ballot for the first time in a presidential election.

With that vote, Clara Foltz symbolically seized the prize for which she had been working since her first public lecture in 1877. "I have written, talked and toiled" for suffrage, she said, emphasizing that in all she did, as lawyer, orator, thinker, and organizer, she had put women's rights first. Toward the end of her career, Foltz listed her achievements and concluded with the simple statement: "a leader in woman suffrage." That she surely was.[125]

In an important sense, however, Foltz gained as much from the movement as she gave to it. All her singular individual accomplishments—from winning the right to practice law to holding statewide office—were largely due to the support of the suffragists, a fact that she freely (and proudly) acknowledged. Moreover, her experience as a pioneer woman lawyer was a major source for her best and most original contribution to law reform—the public defender.

SEVEN

Inventing the Public Defender

Clara Foltz's Legacy

Clara Foltz's idea that "the law should be a shield as well as a sword" grew mainly from her experience representing poor people in the western courts. As a woman lawyer she was both newcomer and outsider in this setting and could see the injustices that the regulars missed because "deadened in feeling by constant contact." She always started her argument for a public defender by describing the criminal courts, focusing especially on the situation of the accused.[1]

Reduced to the "savage state" of self-defense, he must pay for counsel even though he is innocent according to the law, and the cost may ruin him. Of course, if he announces himself a pauper, courts in most places would appoint a lawyer for him. But Foltz said that these appointed counsels were often shysters and incompetents "wholly unequipped either in ability, skill or preparation to cope with the man hired by the State." Her solution: "For every public prosecutor there should be a public defender chosen in the same way and paid out of the same fund." She described a powerful and resourceful figure who would be the prosecutor's equal, even in some ways

his superior because the defender was representing people presumed innocent by the law. In her speeches and writings, Foltz spelled out the elements
of this representation; her defender would investigate every case for favorable evidence, would summon witnesses, would seek expert testimony, and
would prepare to cross-examine.

How did an undereducated single mother far from the centers of advanced legal thought imagine such an ideal? There were no models for the
Foltzian defender; no such office had ever existed anywhere. As a personal
achievement, her conception of the public defender ranks with opening the
legal profession to women and winning the constitutional clauses. Foltz
counted it that way: "Pioneered the establishment of the office" is how she
phrased it toward the end of her life.[2]

Her first presentation of the public defender idea on a nationwide platform was at the Woman's National Liberal Union, the rump suffrage convention she attended in 1890. Three years later, at the Chicago World's Fair,
Foltz called on the leaders of the profession to support public defense and
published the speech in a prestigious law review. Then in 1897, she put her
proposal in statutory form and saw to its simultaneous introduction in
"more than a dozen states."[3] That same year she herself presented her public
defender bill to the New York legislature.

A "new and original idea" of "great importance," declared the *Albany
Law Journal.* The *Harvard Law Review* said the public defender "certainly
merits consideration," especially amidst the "hurry and bustle" of big-city
courts, though the editors doubted the necessity in smaller places where
competent volunteer lawyers were available for appointment. The *New York
Times*, on the other hand, derided Foltz's defender as "absurd" and as the
"strange project" of "a female attorney." Likewise, the *New York Daily Tribune* held it "a ridiculous thing for the State to prosecute with one hand
and defend with the other the violation of its own statutes." By Foltz's
count, two hundred newspapers "mentioned and explained" the measure.
Of those that commented editorially, she found that 50 percent liked it and
that it met with "a favorable reception among a large class of people."[4]

Though it made a splash in the popular and professional press, the Foltz
Defender Bill did not pass anywhere in 1897. For some years afterwards,
Foltz herself seems to have largely put aside the project. But with the advent
of Progressivism in the new century, the time was right for its revival. In Los
Angeles starting around 1910, Foltz renewed her public defender campaign

while working for woman suffrage. The ultimate success of both her great causes was the crowning point of Clara Foltz's career.

Public Defender Sources

EQUAL ADVERSARIES: A CASE OF ARSON

The power of the court to assign a lawyer to the indigent accused and the duty to accept were well-established when Foltz started practicing law. A few state courts had even held that the appointed lawyers should be compensated from public funds. These liberal precedents were not followed in California, however, and their rejection was reaffirmed just a few years before Foltz joined the bar.[5]

From the beginning of her practice, she was regularly in court and often assigned to indigent cases. Soon, Foltz began advocating for a public defender. Though she said that the judges "laughed at the idea as chimerical," they "frequently appointed me to defend . . . as a sort of try-out of my own doctrine."[6] Foltz illustrated the burden on lawyers of defending for free, as well as its rewards, with one of her favorite and most emblematic trial stories.

It started in the early 1880s when Foltz was in court on some business and Judge Robert Ferral suddenly asked her to take over the defense of a man whose counsel had failed to appear for the second day of trial. "The jury is here and there is no time to lose," he said. Foltz's latest client was a young Italian immigrant, nameless in the story, described as the "sad figure in the dock." The charge was arson. Her opponent was the formidable deputy district attorney Thaddeus Stonehill. Combat veteran of two wars, he had, according to Foltz, risen to captain in the Confederacy but "by common consent everybody called him Colonel, after the manner of those gallant, loving-hearted, Southern people." His southern manners were about to fail the "Colonel," however.[7]

In his opening statement, Stonehill promised to prove that the accused set fire to his own house, a hovel on Telegraph Hill, in order to collect $500 in insurance money. Meanwhile, the jury looked at Foltz "quizzically." They had seen her vain efforts to be excused or to gain more time for preparation. What they could not see was her resolve. "Although I had not spoken a dozen words to the man whose defense had been thrust upon me, I was convinced that he was innocent of the charge of arson—that at least he was more sinned against than sinning." This was Clara Foltz's customary mental stance in criminal cases: "I believed in the defendant. This state of mind is a habit with me." In her public defender formulation, Foltz would argue that the presumption of innocence guaranteed such treatment for every defendant.

To the surprise of the courtroom audience, Foltz engaged in pointed cross-examination of the government witnesses. "I thrust the theory of the prosecutor through with the jagged shrapnels of my aroused tempestuous nature" was the way she told the story. She had overnight to prepare the defense of alibi: that her client was laying pipes in South San Francisco when the fire was set. The full defense she offered for this indigent client was a nightmare for Stonehill, the southern cavalier, as he saw himself on the verge of defeat at the hands of a woman. The word would be on the street before the jury was dismissed, and a laugh at his expense would be mandatory at the lodge and in his clubs.

As the evidence wound down, Colonel Stonehill turned to his ultimate weapon; he would make the first and the last summation to the jury: "an advantage over the defendant I have never quite believed in," said Foltz. Stonehill's scheme was to spend his first jury speech assaulting Clara Foltz, not even mentioning the evidence in the case. Instead, he would arm the jury against her slick oratory and her feminine wiles. Then in his rebuttal, when she had no chance to respond, he would discuss the evidence.

It was an old trick—defense lawyers today call it sandbagging. "Col. Stonehill was at his best. He had 'no use for a woman at the bar,' (unless she were a defendant)." While Foltz looked "calmly" on, he flayed "ambitious women who have no sense of the fitness of things, parade the streets, or enter the forum to show off'"—"women who have no child (I had five), no husband, (I was a widow), no home, (I had the dearest, cleanest little home in San Francisco)." "'SHE IS A WOMAN,' bellowed this learned limb of the law; she cannot be expected to reason: God Almighty decreed her limitations, but you can reason, and you must use your reasoning faculties against this young woman who will lead you by her sympathetic presentation of this case reeking with the vilest guilt, to violate your oaths and let a guilty man go free, etc." Finally, Stonehill sat down, "wet with perspiration."

News had gone out that there was a good show in Judge Ferral's court, and the room was crowded by the time Clara Foltz rose for her summation. Stung by the ferocity of the attack and outraged by the charge that she did not belong in the courtroom, Foltz's first words were indignant: "You well know that I am not before you by my own choice! That in obedience to a time-honored rule I am here by order of this Court trying as best I can to represent this despairing man."

Stonehill had attacked her personally, and Foltz responded in kind. "Counsel has sat here for many hours almost choked to suffocation with this mighty thought [that I am a woman]. Possibly it was the tremendous weight of this idea that sometimes made his step unsteady, his cheek more flushed and his nose a deeper crimson." At another point, she said: "Counsel intimates with a curl on his lip that I am called the lady lawyer. I am sorry I cannot return the compliment, but I cannot. I never heard anybody call him any kind of a lawyer at all."

"I am that formidable and terrifying object known as a woman," Foltz acknowledged, "while he is only a poor, helpless, defenseless man, and he wants you to take pity on him and give him a verdict in this case." In a series of cutting observations, Foltz concluded: "And now let us take it altogether. I am a woman and I am a lawyer—and what of it? It is not so new or wonderful a thing."

"I am practicing law in this city; I have offices in one of its largest buildings, and I go daily to and from those offices sober and in my right mind." This was her second dig at Stonehill's apparent propensity for drinking on the job. She told the jury that he had insulted not only her but them by assuming they would let prejudice influence their verdict. "I came into the practice of my profession under the laws of this State, regularly and honestly . . . and I have come to stay. I am neither to be bullied out nor worn out."

Expressing her individual credo, Foltz concluded the personal part of the summation. "I ask no special privileges and expect no favors, but I think it only fair that those who have had better opportunities than I, who have had fewer obstacles to surmount and fewer difficulties to contend with should meet me on even ground, upon the merits of law and fact without this everlasting and incessant reference to sex."

Turning to the facts of the case, she argued the alibi and accused Stonehill of deliberately pursuing an innocent man in his selfish desire to win and "as a sort of vicarious atonement for several other small fires on Telegraph Hill, which had aroused the resentment of a powerful insurance company." Stonehill spoke last and "roared" about "the fire bugs and arson fiends who infest our fair city" and "demanded a verdict then and there."

Sometimes a jury would be in such agreement that they would not even retire to deliberate. It happened in this case, though not as Stonehill requested. Without leaving the box, the jury acquitted the defendant "then and there." Outside the court, Clara Foltz "stood talking with the happy man and his clinging, loving young wife. . . . Hastily I took from my shoulders a soft silk scarf and tied it around her quivering little frame." Foltz watched "as hand in hand they went toward the half-burnt shack on Telegraph Hill."

The innocent man walking free into the sunset was the romantic ideal behind the public defender proposal. On the practical level, Foltz sought to free herself and other lawyers from the burden of uncompensated representation. She was frank about the weight of "pauper cases" and even said that the power to appoint was "of doubtful constitutionality" and "would only be tolerated by a profession either the most servile or the most generous." Such cases, she added, were often lost, which hurt the lawyer's reputation.[8]

Forty years after the arson case, Foltz reprinted her entire summation (considerably longer than quoted here) in "Struggles." She indicated that the personal assault drove her to deliver "a reply so tart and withal so withering." Like other prosecutors Foltz had faced, Stonehill was reacting badly to what he considered her unsporting edge with all-male juries. Irrationally (since they thought she had an unfair advantage), these same men also found it peculiarly humiliating to lose to a woman. They routinely attacked both Foltz and her client—him for his alleged crime and her for doing the dirty, unfeminine work of representing criminals. Here is the place where the public defender joined with Foltz's self-interest as a trial lawyer. A high government official, equal in pay and prestige to the prosecutor, would make defense work acceptable, even honorable, for everyone, but especially for women lawyers.

THE "SISTERHOOD OF REFORM"

The idea of public defense grew in part from Foltz's general reformist attitude toward life. Though women's rights was her main movement, she was far from a single-issue activist. Like many others, Foltz engaged what Thomas Wentworth Higginson called the "sisterhood of reform," joining together multiple causes with the assumption that loyalty to one implied support for all the others.[9]

Higginson himself, perhaps best known for leading the first black regiment in the Civil War and for championing the poems of Emily Dickinson, included in his personal "sisterhood" not only supporting abolition and suffrage, but also advocating temperance, reforming prisons, eradicating the death penalty, eliminating child labor, and establishing merit civil service. Foltz espoused Higginson's causes and more. In addition, she linked them all, including public defense, to suffrage, both in her own "sisterhood" and as an example of what women lawyers would promote in the profession, and what women voters could accomplish at the ballot box.

Prison reform, another of Foltz's concerns, also led naturally to the public defender idea. Those who worked among the imprisoned saw that many people were wrongly convicted or oversentenced. Some of the earliest proposals for a government official to protect the rights of the defendant originated with prison reformers.[10]

The experience of other pioneer women lawyers, who took criminal cases from the same combination of sympathy and necessity that drove Foltz's own practice, was another source of her formulation. The existence of a public defender would dignify and uplift their work as well as her own. Within Foltz's immediate acquaintance were Mary Leonard in Oregon, Lelia Robinson when she was in Washington Territory, Belva Lockwood in the District of Columbia, and, of course, Laura Gordon in California.

In fact, Gordon, Foltz's coadjutor and California's second woman lawyer, took criminal cases as her chosen specialty. Her view of defense work was passionate and ardent, perhaps even more so than Foltz's. Gordon thought that women with their natural understanding of human nature had a special vocation for criminal defense and described her own feelings: The defendant lays his life "in your hands and . . . tells you his every thought and motive. . . . Each life, my friend, each life has so much we cannot understand that sometimes I have looked upon the human being and I have thought, 'Oh, no one is to blame—no one.'"[11]

Perhaps the woman lawyer whose criminal defense experience was closest to Foltz's own was Marilla Ricker, in Washington, D.C. The two were both first woman notaries—one in the federal system and the other in California—and had sought the office partly in order to take sworn statements from imprisoned clients. And both Foltz and Ricker spoke of their motivation to help the poor and oppressed though their law practice.[12]

Although the reform "sisterhood" of each included such radical causes as free thought and the socialistic premises of Bellamy Nationalism, Ricker was much more unconventional in her presentation. While Foltz tried to fit her activities into the nineteenth-century ideal of true womanhood, Ricker scorned it. She claimed, for example, to enjoy "athletic games, fast horses and good living" and "did not care for children." Widowed as a young woman and left with a modest fortune, she went off alone to study abroad. In London she came under the influence of Charles Bradlaugh, the first avowed atheist elected to Parliament and famous in reform circles. Like Edward

Bellamy, he believed that when economic injustice was eradicated, crime would also wither away. In the meantime, Bradlaugh set aside time each day to counsel poor people without charge. Marilla Ricker decided to return to the United States and emulate him there, specializing in criminal cases.[13]

After apprenticing with Belva Lockwood, Ricker joined the D.C. bar in 1882 and also spent part of her time in New Hampshire, where she became the first woman lawyer in the state. Like Foltz, she charged only those who were able to pay. Ricker became widely known as "the prisoner's friend," and her practice very likely influenced Foltz's public defender idea.[14]

PRACTICING IN THE INTERESTS OF JUSTICE

As much as she liked to tell stories of poor people, like the arson defendant saved by her skills, Clara Foltz saw the attorney's role as greater than representing individuals. Long before the category of public interest lawyer existed, an admirer said that Foltz inaugurated a "new way to practice—not in the interest of business but in the interest of justice." No paying client was involved when Foltz took on such projects as working for the separation of juvenile and adult offenders, providing police matrons to care for imprisoned women, and enacting a parole system in the state.[15]

All these reforms were of a piece with the public defender idea. So was another campaign she waged to abolish the use of courtroom cages in San Francisco. That story started one day in 1892 when Foltz came to court to find her client confined in a large wire contraption next to counsel table. Immediately, she started shaking the door so vigorously that the defendant "shivering" within was afraid she would break it open and be arrested herself.[16]

Over Foltz's angry objection, the bailiff, who was the patentee of the cage, and the prosecutor persuaded the judge to keep it. Locking up the defendant had obvious security advantages, and its proponents argued that it was like the English dock, where the prisoner sits apart at trial. But to Clara Foltz, the cage was an "illegal, cowardly emblem of barbarism," "fit only for an inquisitorial age," "a libel on our civilization and an outrage upon the human heart."

On the way to court the next day, she delivered an anticages petition to City Hall and also dropped a copy by the offices of the *Chronicle*, which printed it under the headlines "Caged Like Tigers / The Care of Prisoners Made Easy / Ladies Who Declare War on the System." The supervisors passed a resolution and the mayor signed an order. Within forty-eight hours, the cages were gone forever. In her World's Fair speech, Foltz said that some states manacled prisoners in court and that California had even confined them in cages "like wild beasts until an outraged public sentiment demanded and secured their removal." She did not mention who stirred up the protest, but Foltz implied that a public defender would prevent such excesses.

BELLAMY NATIONALISM

When Clara Foltz joined the utopian Bellamyite movement in the late 1880s, it promised a society without want where crime would be largely eradicated (see Chapter 2). Meanwhile, the movement promoted a public defender to eliminate "the injustice as between the rich and poor" in the criminal courts. Bellamy's idea was to make criminal defense a public function and eradicate private lawyers altogether: "the poorest man . . . would be sure of a fair defense . . . and the richest man would not be able to get anything more." Free justice—no paid attorneys in criminal cases—was Bellamy's slogan. Elimination of the client-paid advocate was his goal.[17]

Some of "the keenest, most astute men of the professional classes" find their livelihood in "thwarting, delaying and tripping up justice at every step," he declared. Under Bellamy's plan, the "presentation of the prisoner's case would be fair, temperate and adequate, but . . . no special pleading or special devices would be employed to delay or defeat justice." His public defender would serve due process rather than the accused.

Although he recognized, as Foltz emphasized, that vindictive and unfair prosecutors were a large problem in the criminal justice system, Bellamy blamed their behavior on the provocations of private counsel. Along with the rich man's defense lawyer, Bellamy would abolish the jury he misled and the presumption of innocence he wielded. These three elements made criminal trials into a spectator sport, a competitive show, when they should be orderly and calm examinations of the evidence.[18]

Foltz liked Bellamy's "free justice" concept, and originally her defender, like his, would be available without a showing of indigence. But there the resemblance between the two ended. Far from doing away with private counsel, Foltz would make the good defense lawyer her model. Moreover, when she reduced her idea to statutory language, it provided that the affluent accused could have the option of both a paid lawyer and a public defender. Similarly, in a difficult or notorious case, the public defender representing a poor man might hire a private lawyer to help him.[19] Instead of abolishing the presumption of innocence, she argued that it created a right for each individual to receive the protection of the state when accused. Moreover, Foltz was a jury lover who had experienced winning verdicts as practically the only public power a woman could wield. Yet as different as Bellamy's conception was from hers, his promotion of the public defender helped her campaign and indirectly furnished her first national platform for discussing it.

The Public Defender Decade: 1890–1900

FOLTZ'S FIRST NATIONAL PLATFORM, 1890

The Bellamy Nationalist and successful Alabama businessman William Aldrich was interested in public defense along with his other reforms. He and his wife put it on the program when they helped Matilda Gage plan her convention for freethinkers and suffragists (see Chapter 6). "Why should not justice be free?" Aldrich wrote in the newspaper Gage published in advance of the convention. For all criminal cases he proposed public defenders, who would "be lawyers of equal ability to the District Attorney and their reputation and professional success should be based on the number of acquittals they secure for the unjustly accused." Like Bellamy, Aldrich would eliminate private counsel altogether in criminal cases. But unlike Bellamy, his main concern was the wrongful conviction (of the poor) rather than unjust acquittals (of the rich).[20]

At the WNLU convention in early 1890, Aldrich repeated his offer of seed money to experiment with the idea of a public defender in five cities: New York, Boston, Washington, D.C., Philadelphia, and Chicago. After using only a fraction of his allotted time, he introduced Clara Foltz, "who will tell you of innocent people who have been imprisoned solely because they had no one to defend them."[21]

On taking the platform, Foltz focused first on "the public persecutor," whose handsome appearance belied his actions. "Erect before the bar, in the name of law and justice, paid liberally from the treasury, he arraigns the prisoner for having committed a great crime" even though he is presumed innocent, and sometimes the prosecutor actually knows there is a good defense, and yet "he strives for the conviction." Even worse if an election is near, then indeed "in trying to make a name for himself, he harangues the judge, confuses the counsel on the other side, misleads the jury, and often convicts an innocent man." The accused needs help, but "when the poor, friendless, often innocent man appears," the court usually appoints "some pitiful pettifogger, from the kindergarten or the failures of the profession to counsel him." Finally, she brought forth the answer to overbearing prosecutors and incompetent appointees: a defender paid by the state. She said it was "astonishing" that such a system did not already exist.

At this point, the *Washington Post* reported, her speech became "a recital of her experiences in injustice to accused persons." Perhaps she told of Charles Colby, who complained from the gallows that his trial lawyers took his money and botched his case (see Chapter 2). Maybe she unfolded her tale of the arson defendant set free by her unpaid efforts. For the first time on a national program, Foltz saw how the public defender could stir a crowd. "Early in her remarks, she gained the sympathy of the audience and her strong words frequently called out bursts of applause," the *Post* continued.[22]

Another observer described her on the platform: "Grave, dignified, yet gentle and womanly her eyes kindle and sparkle till they flame, and she seems to rise in height. She is forceful, vigorous, and her sentences, every one, are clear cut and Mosaic." Foltz's speech opened an animated discussion, which pitted the male and female lawyers against each other.[23] The men thought the appointed counsel system was working well and that Foltz was exaggerating the plight of the accused. Belva Lockwood jumped into the argument, detailing her sixteen years of experience in the criminal courts of Washington, D.C. She told of innocent people who lay in jail for months, even years, because they had no attorney and also pointed out that "colored people" were especially vulnerable to this treatment.[24]

Matilda Gage called the public defender discussion "a lively episode in the proceedings."Neither she nor anyone else seemed to think that it was unrelated to the objects of the meeting. Maybe this was just good manners since Aldrich was paying for the convention. More likely, most of the people there saw a connection between public defense and the other reforms, coming as they did from Bellamy Nationalism's embrace of all causes as interim reforms on the road to utopia.[25]

Of course, there were significant unremarked differences between Foltz's conception of a public defender and Bellamy's. Most important was her belief that only an equal adversary, skilled at high-stakes jury work, could match the prosecutor and control his excesses. In a case on the eve of the World's Fair, Foltz experienced firsthand the need for her kind of defender.

UNFAIR PROSECUTORS:
PEOPLE V. WELLS, 1892

In 1892, Clara Foltz represented James Wells in the San Francisco criminal courts. Once a successful real estate man with an office near hers, he was broke and in jail when he turned to Foltz for help. Wells was the client she

CLARA FOLTZ CROSS-EXAMINES GRACIE GILBERT.

Courtroom artist's sketch of the Wells trial. *San Francisco Chronicle*, 1892.

found confined in a courtroom cage and freed through an angry publicity campaign.[26]

The incident at the outset of the trial typified the heated confrontations that would follow. Foltz thought that Wells was factually innocent and that the prosecutor was wrong even to charge him. For his part, Deputy District Attorney Walter Hinkle was irritated by her lone-woman, righteous-defender stance and her absorption of the jury and press attention. With a weak case and a strong sense that the defendant was guilty, Hinkle put aside the proprieties. Presiding was Judge James Troutt, "always urbane and with that fine bearing which characterizes the well-bred judge," as Foltz described him.[27]

In fact, the judge did display admirable calm during the adversary fireworks at the trial. Basically, the facts were undisputed—only motive and interpretation were at issue. Wells had introduced a woman named Ollie Hutchings to moneylenders; she had falsely signed the wealthy Emma Dick's name to a mortgage and received $8,000 in gold coin. Foltz's defense was that one Pilchner had actually arranged the impersonation and that Wells was hoodwinked along with the mortgage lenders. Pilchner had committed suicide hours after his arrest in the case without making any comment about it. The first prosecution witnesses were the real Miss Dick, who said she had not mortgaged the property, and the lenders, who testified that Wells had introduced them to Hutchings as Emma Dick.

On cross-examination, Foltz showed that Wells seemed shocked when told of the scam and that he had tried to help locate the woman who posed as Emma Dick. Then Ollie Hutchings took the stand for the state. The "young adventuress," as the *Chronicle* called her, was a dark-haired woman about thirty years old. Looking directly at Wells, she smiled from the witness stand—how? Observers differed: nervously, self-deprecatingly, sneeringly, triumphantly.[28]

Hutchings testified that Pilchner's only role was to introduce her to Wells and that he, not Pilchner, had set up the scheme and then paid her $1,800 for her part. Most damagingly, she swore that Wells had forced her to flee, promising to confuse the pursuit with a false description if the forgery came to light. Her tale of staking out a claim in Washington State, finding a good man to marry, and then being hunted down and arrested made her appear sympathetic.

Foltz's first move on cross was to dispel the impression of Hutchings as either distressed lady or hapless tool. Without ceremony, she attacked:

Q: You are a woman of many names, are you not? What are some of them?

A: Ollie Hutchings, Winnie Graham, Pearl Lewis, Irene Casey, and Gracie Gilbert are all I have.

To which Foltz remarked, "You have a musical ear in the choosing of them." Before the younger woman could respond, Foltz pressed her to tell how she had met Pilchner. One question later found Hutchings admitting that she had served time in the House of Corrections; for what crime remained tantalizingly open for the moment. Pleading fatigue, Foltz asked the judge to recess for the day. She wanted Ollie aka Winnie, Pearl, Irene, and Gracie to think over what was yet to come.

The next day started with a tableau that some suspected Foltz of arranging. The *Chronicle* reported: "A little boy pushed his way through the crowd and, with everybody watching him, walked quickly to where Wells was sitting and touched him on the shoulder. The man turned and kissed his son. . . . The incident distracted attention for the moment and then the examination of the witness on the stand began."[29]

Foltz concluded what all the papers called her "merciless examination" by forcing the admission that Hutchings had been a prostitute at the notorious 17 Grant Street brothel and that she had served time for soliciting young girls for the business. A news artist caught the moment—Foltz with accusing arm extended and Hutchings in shrinking attitude on the stand. But the jury could believe that the witness was lying about some things (such as the amount of her involvement) and being truthful about others (such as Wells's guilt).

Moreover, the real star of the prosecution had yet to come—the terror of the defense bar, Detective Isaiah Lees. Lees had policed San Francisco from its early days, gathering fame for always getting his man and wealth from sometimes letting him go. Foltz believed that Lees had chosen to make his case against Wells instead of the actual culprit, Hutchings, perhaps because he was "soft" on her.[30] She suggested as much in her examination of the prosecution witnesses. Naturally, Foltz did not want Lees to hear her questions and shape his testimony accordingly. Repeatedly, she entreated the court to exclude him from the courtroom—but the "plastic judge" (her words), overawed by the celebrated detective and the press coverage, refused.[31]

Authoritative and slightly menacing, Lees had more experience projecting himself as an honest witness than Clara Foltz had as a cross-examiner. Nevertheless, she controlled his answers by skillful leading questions and successfully established that Wells had described to the police the Emma Dick he knew, right down to the four different dresses he had seen her wear. The question was whether Ollie Hutchings fit this description (and secondarily whether she ever owned such clothes). A match would show that Wells was honestly trying to help the police find her, and that he, too, was duped. But if the description was off, then Hutchings was truthful in saying he was trying to confuse the pursuers.

The whole case could hang on this piece of testimony: Clara Foltz pulled out the stops. Smiling amiably, she started:

Q: Wouldn't you say, Captain Lees, that the description Wells gave of Ollie Hutchings was as good as a man could possibly give of a woman?

A: Not at all—for one thing the height was a good three inches off, which is a great deal where a woman is concerned. [Wells had said the woman was an exceptionally tall five feet, ten inches]

Q: [*mildly*] Ah, but wouldn't a woman's high heel shoe account for such a difference?

A: I don't think so—not that much difference.

Pausing for effect, Foltz seated herself, then she "suddenly stooped and took off her shoe without the slightest ceremony, holding it aloft. Undeniably the heel was very Frenchy—very high," said the *Examiner*.[32]

> Q: Do you see this shoe, Captain Lees? Would not a heel as high as this alter the height of a woman to an appreciable extent?
>
> A: Yes, [*muttering*] so would stilts.

As Foltz made this bold demonstration, "the crowd looked on admiringly, thrilled, expectant, wondering what would come next in the way of delightful sensation," according to the *Examiner*. Though "San Francisco men were accustomed," the paper said, "to a little private pirouetting when the wine is brisk," it was more than slightly risqué for a woman, especially in open court, "with unbashful fingers [to] loose the latches . . . and hold that shoe aloft for all to see."

The story then described Clara Foltz's perfect foot as revealed by the beautiful shoe—"the last on which that shoe was made was narrow, tapering, 'aristocratic.'" Continuing its lightly ironic tone, the article concluded that few would dare "call Clara Foltz handsome—such hardihood is not distributed to the many. . . . But handsome women, who would snap their jeweled fingers at Clara Foltz's learning, would fidget with envy of the feet which bear all her weight of knowledge, and like little mice, peep in and out from beneath her tailored skirts."

While the veteran police officer was momentarily stunned by her shoe display, Foltz deftly pressed him to admit that men seldom really notice the details of women's apparel. Though it was risky, she asked Lees, a trained observer, what she herself had worn the day before. He declined even to attempt a description.[33]

Then Foltz suggested that Wells had given a distinctive picture of Ollie Hutchings. He said she was tall and dark, a little heavy in the back, had full lips and an unusual gait. The only discrepancies in Wells's description were a nonexistent mole that he mentioned and a small facial scar that he missed—minor indeed for a male observer. As soon as Lees acknowledged the overall accuracy of the description, Foltz dismissed him from the stand, with a faintly disdainful "I'll have no more questions of this man."

Isaiah Lees had tasted a rare forensic defeat, sharper because delivered by a woman. From this point on, in Foltz's view, he would stop at nothing to win the verdict. The first sign of raised stakes came with the very next prosecution witness. I. C. Leavitt testified that he had often seen Wells with the deceased Pilchner, creating the inference that they acted together. On cross, Foltz brought out that Wells had actually hired Leavitt to search for the woman he knew as Emma Dick. With a flourish for each one, she introduced letter after letter from Leavitt to Wells, reporting on his mission. Then, out of the blue, came this exchange:

Q: [*by Foltz*] Did Wells tell you personally that he wanted those letters?
A: Yes, he told me further to tell the woman to skip if I found her.[34]

A trial lawyer's nightmare—the unsolicited, uncontrolled, and (Foltz thought) perjurious answer. She had no doubt about the source of this harmful outburst. "Crimson with rage," she moved to strike the answer and pointed an accusing finger at Lees. "If the Court please, I now renew and again press my motion to exclude all the witnesses from the courtroom except the one under examination." Placidly, Judge Troutt again refused to remove the famous detective, who continued to arrange countertestimony every time Foltz made a point in Wells's favor on cross-examination.

In the defense case, James Wells was her first witness and did a fine job, indicating good preparation by his lawyer. His convincing testimony probably drove the prosecutor to desperate measures in his cross-examination. Despite the evidentiary rule clearly forbidding such questions, Hinkle inquired about another alleged forgery, distant in time, not the subject of a conviction, and totally unrelated to the case. Even though Foltz's furious objections were sustained twice, the prosecutor asked three questions in the same vein, concluding with "did you not forge your father-in-law's name to a note?"[35]

In her brief, Foltz would picture Lees "with his mouth at the [prosecutor's] ear" demanding that he ask the blatantly improper questions. The *Chronicle* said that Wells "turned pale, while his counsel, Mrs. Foltz, flushed with anger. Her objections were fiery in the extreme to the 'cruel and illegal' questions." Though the trial court sustained Foltz, it was obvious that the district attorney did not care about the answers but was trying to get the inadmissible content of the questions before the jury.[36]

Foltz's anger was unabated by the time of summation. She told the jury that the district attorney had acted improperly and implied that he would not have treated an equal adversary the same way: "I deplore the fact that the law does not provide for a public defender as well as a public prosecutor." At the same time, she suggested that if Wells was a successful criminal, as the government charged, she would not be in the case. "Do you think this poor innocent man would have applied to a woman to defend him if he had money to pay some distinguished male member of the bar?" she queried.[37]

Her theory of the case was that Ollie Hutchings and several others, including Hutchings's latest husband, were the real culprits. At the mention of her husband, Hutchings screamed, "Not him. Not him. He was not in it," and made a menacing gesture toward Foltz, who "sprang aside in alarm." After the bailiff removed Hutchings, Foltz resumed: "Would you like to see your son or brother convicted on the evidence of such a woman?"[38]

Finally, Foltz pleaded with the twelve men in the box: "Remember your wives and children and think of the grief you have witnessed here. Send my client home to his family, whose devotion to this good man you have personally observed during every minute of this ordeal." When she paused, the silence was filled by the low lamentations of the entire Wells family, seated in their usual places on the front row. The jury went out at 4:20 in the afternoon; by 8 p.m. they had a verdict: guilty as charged.[39]

Foltz had her hands full trying to console the tearful and distraught client, but Charles Gunn was there to interview the jurors about the reasons for their verdict. Several told him that they had been influenced by the prosecutor's questions indicating that Wells had forged before. Foltz used Gunn's affidavit and others she gathered during the weeks after the verdict to move for a new trial on the ground of governmental misconduct and then to appeal to the California Supreme Court.

The Wells case had showcased Foltz's exceptional trial skills—both in cross-examination and in summation, and the press coverage was lavish and largely respectful. But even the "free" publicity, already compromised by losing, had its hidden costs. The shoe-removal story, for instance, made her look good on client dedication but bad on refinement and propriety. Ladies did not remove their shoes in public and wave them aloft. Her social reputation, already damaged by her recent case against the Lady Trustees of the Crocker Old People's Home (see Chapter 3), suffered further.

Not all the press was positive, moreover. The *Call*, for example, criticized her for bringing the Wells family into the courtroom and arguing emotionally for mercy on their behalf. Women lawyers try "to pervert justice, and to soften the stern conclusion of reason," a tendency that "has often been urged against the enfranchisement of their sex."[40] To lose the case and to be accused of hurting the cause were both hard to bear.

Foltz was in the middle of the Wells appellate brief, recalling the abuse and her inability to stop it, when she received an invitation to speak at the

Congress of Jurisprudence and Law Reform, scheduled for August at the World's Fair. With the trial weighing on her mind, she imagined a high-status official who could prevent unfair prosecutorial tactics. Foltz decided to use the prestigious platform to speak on behalf of public defense.

Within months of her World's Fair speech, she won the appeal in *Wells*. The opinion sounded just like Clara Foltz: "It is too much the habit of pros-ecuting officers to assume beforehand that a defendant is guilty, and then expect to have the established rules of evidence twisted, and all the features of a fair trial distorted, in order to secure a conviction. If a defendant cannot be fairly convicted he should not be convicted at all."[41]

Clara Foltz used examples from *Wells* in all her public defender speeches and writings. It also became an important legal precedent throughout the country. Forty years after Foltz won her appeal, the U.S. Supreme Court decided its first major case reversing for prosecutorial misconduct. Citing *Wells* as the most "apposite" precedent, the Court held in its now familiar language about the adversary system that the prosecutor may strike "hard blows" but not "foul ones."[42]

Wells was the case that led Foltz to make the overzealous prosecutor a principal reason for creating a public defender. Her views about this inter-connection were first fully expressed in her World's Fair speech. They were far ahead of her time.

THE CONGRESS OF JURISPRUDENCE
AND LAW REFORM, 1893

At the Chicago World's Fair in 1893, Clara Foltz appeared on a program with eminent legal thinkers from around the world. Her subject was public defenders. Drawn from her own experiences as a trial lawyer and a reformer, the speech was unlike any ever given at such a forum.

Foltz spoke at one of the seventeen international meetings held as the in-tellectual auxiliary of the fair. Except for the opening one devoted exclusively to the interests of their sex, women had to fight for inclusion in most of the world congresses. None was more contested than the Congress of Jurispru-dence and Law Reform because it seemed to many men that women had not earned a place among the top judges, professors, and lawyers. Even their supporters feared that the women were not ready for this kind of meeting.

But a committee of four women lawyers from Chicago, led by Myra Bradwell, battled for a place on the platform. The men fought them so hard on every point that they considered having their own law reform meeting, wrote Bradwell in an astringent little item in the *Chicago Legal News* about the negotiations. Finally, "at the eleventh hour," invitations went out to four women. It was too late for the two foreign women lawyers to attend, but Clara Foltz and Mary Greene (the second woman lawyer in Massachusetts) were both planning to be in town for a women lawyers' meeting. Thus, in August 1893, the two would become, in Bradwell's formulation, the first women "in the history of the world" to speak for themselves "at an international congress of lawyers."[43]

Although Foltz and Greene were participants, and a few other women were in the audience or read the papers of others, the atmosphere of the congress was unyieldingly male. Addressing the audience as "gentlemen," John Dean Caton, the oldest judge in Illinois, opened the congress. He recalled his arrival in Chicago sixty years earlier when it was a little trading post with a population of 250. There were no streets, but only Indian trails, and no law, lawyers, or courts of record. Now, the Chicago bar was eight thousand strong and hosting "legal luminaries from around the world." Those luminaries included the aristocracy of the American bar and foreign dignitaries as well: professors, judges, legislators, code makers, and text writers. It was a "select" audience—meaning small but impressive—of about two hundred people. One observer said that the turnout was low because the lawyers were involved with saving their clients and themselves from the effects of the economic depression, which was hitting bottom in August.[44]

No transcript or other complete account of the congress exists though a number of the participants, including Foltz, published their speeches in law reviews and in the *Chicago Legal News*. Belva Lockwood attended and wrote about it in the *American Journal of Politics*, but the article is little more than her notes on things that caught her interest.[45] It appears that Clara Foltz spoke on the second day, after some hours of speeches on an assortment of law reform topics. For instance, two well-known old jurisprudes were on the opening program. One was Judge Thomas Cooley of Michigan, author of *Constitutional Limitations*, the most widely used legal treatise in the United States. His speech was titled "The Administration of Civil Justice in the United States." David Dudley Field of New York, a leader of the movement to simplify law and procedure, delivered "The Codification of American Law." Lyman Trumbull of Illinois, former U.S. senator and judge, argued for reform of the laws allowing fortunes to be transmitted by descent and will.[46]

Many hours of speeches on heavy topics hardly adapted to oral presentation preceded Foltz on the program. When she took the podium, elegantly attired with a corsage of fresh flowers and with a voice that filled the room and a text that rang with provocative phrases, Clara Foltz must have been refreshing at the least. A woman speaker was a novelty in itself; a woman with a novel idea and the rolling periods of a theatrical orator was a sensation in this company.

Lasting only about half an hour, the speech was short for Foltz and devoid of personal references or patented stories. To one who knows her biography, however, she is in every line of a text taken from her jury arguments, legal briefs, lectures, and cases. For instance, the young Italian immigrant walking into the sunset, freed by her skills, materialized behind Foltz's opening paean on defending the innocent. Many of her other indigent clients would appear in the background as the speech continued.

But the case that was on her mind, as she stood at the summit of her career, was the one she had just briefed on appeal. References to *Wells*, though none explicit, are all over the text. In portraying the power of the state, Foltz first depicted the prosecutor—a composite of her opponents of the past fifteen years: "strong of physique, alert of mind, learned in the law, experienced in practice and ready of speech." Then, describing the *Wells* trial, she added: "Around and behind [the prosecutor] is an army of police officers and detectives ready to do his bidding and before him sits a plastic judge with a large discretion often affected by newspapers."[47]

Both the prosecutor and the police, she told her audience, mistakenly believe that "it is the duty of the State to convict whoever is arrested." The prosecutor "misrepresents the facts he expects to prove, attempts to get improper testimony before the jury, garbles and misstates what is allowed, slanders the prisoner and browbeats the witnesses." The police, "impelled by vanity to justify its arrests," lend highly "colored testimony and overawing presence." Again, this is straight from *Wells*.

Having pictured the force mustered to convict the guilty, Foltz compared it with the pathetic "machinery [that] is provided for the defense of the innocent." If the accused pleads his poverty, she said, the court may appoint a lawyer to defend, but these are often the "failures" or the "kindergartners" of the profession who have no resources for preparation or investigation. Foltz had used such descriptions of appointed counsel many times, starting with her "Lawyers" lecture in the 1880s.

In jury-lawyer style, Foltz described the effect on the defendant of a trial in which all the powers of his government are turned against him. Even if acquitted he "comes from the court-house a changed man. . . . Disgrace has crushed his manhood and injustice has murdered his patriotism." Having painted the scene, plainly and harshly, Foltz called forth her creation: "For every public prosecutor there should be a public defender chosen in the same way and paid out of the same fund as the public prosecutor. Police and sheriffs should be equally at his command and the public treasury should be equally open to meet the legitimate expenses."

Finally, she summoned the congress to action: "Let the criminal courts be reorganized upon a basis of exact, equal and free justice; let our country be broad and generous enough to make the law a shield as well as a sword." And a promise: "Then there will come to the State, as a natural consequence, all those blessings which flow from Constitutional obligations conscientiously kept and government duties sacredly performed."

The next morning the *Daily Inter-Ocean* wrote, "Miss [*sic*] Clara Short-ridge Foltz of the San Francisco bar, easily carried off the palm," adding that her presentation "was highly complimented by several of the most eminent jurists present." Foltz told of "the tremendous sensation caused by her plea" and claimed that her paper "Public Defenders" "called out the most comment and discussion" of any presented.[48]

It has not gone down in history that way, however. Today, the Congress of Jurisprudence and Law Reform is remembered because of Professor James Bradley Thayer of the Harvard Law School, who urged restraint in constitutional review of legislative decisions. He said courts should reverse only when there was no reasonable doubt about the error below—the same standard they applied when reviewing a jury verdict for sufficiency of the evidence.[49] Though Thayer said nothing specifically political, his analysis undermined the invalidation of progressive and protective labor laws by conservative appellate courts. His ideas stirred "deep interest" from the start, and today the speech is considered one of the greatest commentaries on constitutional law ever delivered.[50] Yet all the modern attention to Thayer's work has not previously aroused any notice of Foltz's innovative and important paper delivered from the same platform.

Perhaps the fact that the proceedings were not printed together contributed to the neglect of "Public Defenders." And Foltz's rhetorical style may have been a factor as well. Her references to a "plastic" judge, a "vicious" prosecutor, and the "sacred" performance of governmental duties, for example, were outside the usual scholarly discourse. So was her biblical phrasing—the defense was "but a shadow of the substance sought for" and the indigent accused "asks for bread and receives a stone." Moreover, Foltz gave no authority for her proposal, drew no analogies, and mentioned no other thinkers or precedents.[51]

Possibly, she was contemplating the monetary reward for starting a public defender offered by William Aldrich at the WNLU meeting a few years earlier. Her speech could have been a first step toward claiming the prize, which she would not want to share by mentioning other thinkers. Yet she also desired acceptance in this august company, and a more traditional offering would have improved her chances. In fact, her speech "Evolution of Law," which she had given a week earlier at the women lawyers' meeting (see Chapter 5), also contained an original idea but was written in academic language. Her motive in giving instead a dramatic call to action seems at least partly altruistic.

Using this precious opportunity for personal advancement, on the best platform of her life, "the very sanctuary—the holy of holies of my profession," she sought to arouse and inform these influential men about conditions in the baseline criminal courts. Most of them had no idea because by the end of the nineteenth century, as the profession grew increasingly stratified, the legal elites were far removed from this type of practice. At the same time, urbanization, industrialization, and immigration were putting tremendous pressure on the appointed counsel system.[52]

In her writing, Foltz described the scene: "Innumerable innocent boys and girls, men and women . . . robbed by shysters . . . neglected by irresponsible court appointees," pleading guilty or going to trial without an adequate defense, in jail or even if acquitted, impoverished and embittered.[53] She brought her public defender forth, whole and freestanding, as a complete solution. Despite the last-minute invitation and the lack of preparation time, Foltz was seemingly satisfied with her presentation. She repeated it throughout her statutory campaign in 1897 and in her two law review articles on prosecutors and public defenders, adding only new examples and further explication. The ideas were the same.

PUBLIC DEFENSE:
THE IDEAS AND LEGAL ARGUMENTS

Clara Foltz's legal arguments in support of public defense were almost as novel as the concept itself. First she described the fall of the prosecutor into partisan advocacy, making a defender necessary for a fair presentation of the case. Then she posited the duty of the state toward the accused and, many generations ahead of her time, spoke and wrote of a constitutional right to free counsel.[54]

Foltz opened her writings and speeches by picturing the ideal prosecutor as "a minister of public justice, aiding the court in a solemn investigation of crime . . . laying bare the truth, whatever it may be." Even in benighted times, when the "death penalty for one hundred offenses disgraced the Penal Code . . . the accused was not without a defender" because the prosecutor and the judge took special care to see that all the evidence was presented and all rights preserved.[55]

Having set the prosecutor up, Clara Foltz, a preacher's daughter, made a gripping sermon of his fall. It was a tale of power corrupting: "the vanity of winning cases" and the "lust for gold" turned him into an "indiscriminate public persecutor." She scored his patent desire "to pander to and uphold a friendly police in its frequent blunders" and commented on "the unfortunate belief, engendered by the office itself, apparently, (for they all have it after a few years' service) that the accused is always guilty." Of course, there was also the "fear of public criticism if they fail to convict."[56]

All these base motivations resulted in a trial process that little resembled "that free and impartial investigation which was the pride and boast of the English laws." Foltz's prosecutorial ideal, while not original with her, was not widely acknowledged or accepted in the late nineteenth century. Even reformers had come to believe that partisan advocacy by the government's representative was necessary and focused instead on the corruption and overbearing attitude that seemed to accompany it.[57]

Foltz proposed a skilled adversary to equalize the sides and make the presentation fair. It was an entirely new and original solution. To those who balked at the duty of the state to represent a guilty person, she responded that only the innocent would be defended. Of course, that was everybody, according to her: "Every person is presumed to be innocent . . . and the law ought to treat him as it presumes him."[58] Foltz drew no distinctions between the state's duty to the actually innocent and those who had only the presumption to sustain them.

What was true of the state was also true of the individual defense lawyer in her view. A professional lives out the law's presumption; all clients are innocent until the government meets its burden and the jury returns its verdict. Like her idea about the prosecutor's failed mission, Foltz's interpretation of the presumption as according a personal right to the defendant was novel. For authority, she cited mainly "the common conscience of men" and "the great heart of the people." Foltz added that in a high percentage of cases, the accused is actually found not guilty.[59]

Her third set of arguments had to do with the government's constitutional obligation to its people. Here, Foltz drew on John Locke's social contract theories, a staple of suffrage rhetoric, used to show that all citizens, men and women, made the same exchange with the state and should be treated equally. In the criminal context, the contention was a little different: "Each citizen surrenders his natural right to defend himself and pays his share for the support of the State, under the implied contract that . . . the government will defend his life and liberty from unlawful invasion," Foltz argued. "When therefore the rights of a person are assailed it is the duty of the government to provide him defense."[60]

Foltz's main point on the government's duty was constitutionally based. She explained that though defense counsel was denied in olden times in England (partly because most crimes were capital and the prosecutor did not charge unless the evidence of guilt was overwhelming), the opposite was true in the United States. Counsel was never forbidden and in fact was guaranteed by federal and state constitutions. But the accused must pay or go without counsel, and "thereby go without justice."[61]

The right to counsel, Foltz continued, is "subject to the same rules of interpretation" as all the other constitutional guarantees, which means that it "ought not to be impaired, nor burdens imposed to its perfect exercise." She gave many examples of burdening a right, which everyone would agree were clearly wrong—such as charging the defendant for jury expenses or for confronting the witnesses against him. Foltz claimed that counsel was the most important right, yet the defendant was forced to pay for it himself. With the increasingly complicated criminal procedure and the prosecutor's abandonment of any duty to the accused, "counsel for the defense is an absolute essential." A trial in which the accused has no lawyer is "little less than a farce" and "an invitation to the jury to convict."[62]

Seventy years after Foltz uttered these words, the U.S. Supreme Court echoed them in *Gideon v. Wainwright*, holding that "lawyers for the defense are not luxuries but necessities in criminal cases" and that the state must provide free counsel for the indigent.[63]

The Statutory Campaign, 1897

"DUTIES OF DISTRICT ATTORNEYS"

Clara Foltz went home to San Francisco after the World's Fair invigorated by her experiences there, including the reception of her public defender idea. But other than publishing her speech in a professional journal, she did nothing immediately to implement her vision. Later she said that the idea of public defense was always with her even when she was not actively pushing it—that like Banquo's ghost in *Macbeth*, "it would not down."[64]

Public defense became Foltz's main project in 1896–1897; in a single year she produced two law review articles, drafted a model statute, and campaigned for its introduction at Albany and in a number of other state legislatures. This burst of activity seems related to her struggle to get started in New York City, a period when her lack of clients gave Foltz time for research and reflection. Her situation also may have led her to seek personal profit from the public defender idea.

Right before launching her campaign, Foltz had been at the Republican Convention in St. Louis, which William Aldrich also attended. They moved in the same reform circles and could easily have met there. Newly elected to Congress, he was still interested in public defense and perhaps renewed his offer to finance the promotion of the office. Aldrich's possible offer aside, Foltz may have hoped to hold the salaried position herself if she could get it established. At the least, the publicity she stirred about upgrading criminal defense could also generate some paying cases.

Her first move was a law review article titled "Duties of District Attorneys in Prosecutions" in which she described the fall of the public prosecutor from his position as minister of public justice. It was the same point she had made at the World's Fair, in almost the same words, but now she added two hundred cases of prosecutorial misconduct from thirty-four jurisdictions. With the expertise of a trial lawyer, Foltz described the course of prosecutorial error from opening statement to inducing the court to give an improper charge. A district attorney "soothes his conscience" about bringing a weak case "by putting the responsibility on the jury." Then, she wrote, he turns around and misleads that very jury at every stage of the trial.[65]

At times the article had almost an antic spirit, as in her compilation of "justice-polluting" epithets that prosecutors used to describe the accused: "black thief—black as hell itself"; "bloody assassins"; "contemptible brute"; "grocery bully"; "midnight assassins"; "mean, wicked, low-down, dirty devil"; "pusillanimous puppy"; "sugar-loafed, squirrel-headed Dutchman"; and "terrible desperadoes." A similar run on closing arguments had twenty examples of outrageous prosecutorial remarks. In searching the digests and periodicals, Foltz discovered a shocking number of cases in a "seemingly increasing stream," lending a sense of urgency to her project.[66]

These cases were, moreover, mere "illustrations of the vices" because most "poor defendants cannot appeal, so that the wrongs done them are not recorded." Foltz concluded that appellate review was no remedy for prosecutorial misconduct because it was too slow and because of "vicious legal assumptions" like the possibility of "harmless" error. On the efficacy of instructing the jury to disregard prejudicial testimony, she was psychologically astute. "The mind is not a slate and a judge's charge a sponge. . . . One cannot forget at will; much less reject matter actually in the mind," she wrote.[67]

"Duties" appeared in *The Criminal Law Magazine*, a widely read practitioners' journal, in fall 1896. Foltz was the first woman lawyer to publish in its pages. Her next step in the public defender campaign was to draft a generic statute establishing the office. She sent her proposed bill along with excerpts from her World's Fair speech, "talking points" in today's parlance, to legislators, to the press, and to others she knew from her travels and suffrage connections. To create the sensation of a nationwide simultaneous movement, she asked that they introduce it in the first legislative session of the new year. With her usual optimism, Foltz probably expected that William Jennings Bryan would win the 1896 election, bringing into office with him progressive legislators and setting the stage for free justice. She herself planned to present the Foltz Defender Bill in the New York capital.

PUBLIC DEFENSE AND NEW YORK POLITICS

From fifteen years of lobbying for women's rights, Foltz knew how to get legislative attention: present a well-drafted bill, write up the supporting arguments, distribute press packets in advance, milk the publicity by taking the bill personally in hand, lobby individuals, and seek a public hearing. All these things—and doubtless more behind the scenes—Foltz did with skill and energy in Albany, New York, just as she had in Sacramento, California. Moreover, she was able to negotiate the arcane and divided world of New York politics with the same ease she showed on a platform with eminent scholars at the World's Fair.

On one side of the political divide was Tammany Hall, the machine that represented and manipulated the immigrant laborers of New York City, a constituency approaching half the population in the late 1890s. Aligned with the Democrats, Tammany ruled the metropolis and especially the criminal justice system. On the other side, with an equally firm grip, the Republican political boss, Thomas Platt, ran the legislature and the rest of the state.[68]

In early 1897, Platt and two of his chief deputies wrote to Foltz. Given the timing, it seems likely that they were responding to her request for support of the public defender bill.[69] The letters themselves are lost, however, and it was not one of Platt's men, but a Tammany operative, who introduced the Foltz Defender Bill in Albany. Yet the situation in New York politics was such that Platt may have counseled this move. He could have seen the public defender as a possible link in a potential alliance with Tammany, which he was seeking because the reformers in his own party were turning from a successful drive against the city boss to ridding the state of the upstate variety—that is, Platt himself.

A public defender would appeal to the Tammany constituents who would be its main consumers, and the leader of the Tammany legislative forces, Tom Grady, was an ideal person to introduce the bill. From many years of representing the immigrant poor in Albany, he understood the need. Moreover, Grady was approachable and likeable, and even in the minority, he could get a bill passed. He was also Tammany's star orator and so enjoyed perpetual press attention.

Tammany's backing did, however, have the unfortunate consequence of stirring suspicions. The *Tribune* warned that a public defender could create "an underworld trust in lawbreaking." Foltz found the charge "unworthy of a great newspaper." Yet it was not so far-fetched in a city where leading defense attorneys (often conspiring with Tammany) took fees in advance of the crime and retainers from gangs and fences. The smell of patronage boondoggle emanated from any Grady (or Platt) measure. "New offices with big salaries attached," sniffed one editorial opposing the public defender.[70]

Generally, however, the news coverage of the Foltz Defender Bill was favorable. Twice, on the day of introduction and a few weeks later, when she had a hearing on the bill, the metropolitan dailies featured it. Summing up the campaign later, Foltz said it created a "tremendous sensation." Her arrangements for a simultaneous presentation around the country also paid off in press notices. By her count, two hundred papers had stories about public defense in the winter of 1897.[71]

In interviews over the years, Foltz spoke of taking her "precious" bill "that she had spent years in preparing" to Albany on a January day. The cold of winter in upstate New York added to the drama she created around dropping a bill into the legislative hopper. Ultimately, the cold provided a sad metaphor for its reception as well, for within months, the Foltz Defender Bill was dead for the session. In fact, much of the state's business was suspended while New York City chose a mayor to replace William Strong, the reformer elected in 1884. He had lasted only one term, having displeased Boss Platt by his inattention to patronage matters, the reformers because he moved too slowly, the Tammany constituency because he enforced Sunday closing and alcohol laws on their one day off, and everyone because the economic depression persisted, making it hard for them to improve their lives.[72]

While the election was in the offing, it was impossible to rouse the public or its representatives about anything else. The new mayor would be the first to serve after the consolidation of Manhattan with Brooklyn and other outlying areas. Sixty thousand jobs would be within his patronage. Boss Platt's worst fears about the split in his own party were realized when the reformers nominated Seth Low, president of Columbia University, on a Non-Partisan ticket. Platt had "the sincerest and profoundest contempt" for nonpartisanship and was sickened by the thought of so many jobs distributed without regard to party service, so he arranged the candidacy of Benjamin Tracy on the regular Republican ticket.[73] The Republican split favored the Democrats and their nominee, an obscure Tammany-controlled judge.

Boss Richard Croker, who had fled to avoid indictment in 1894, returned from England to lead the Tammany forces with the rallying cry of "To Hell with Reform." Tom Grady called the "Tigers" to their feet cheering when he spoke of recouping their losses in recent elections: "We want revenge. We want a terrible revenge. . . . We want revenge for the lies they told, for the passions they excited. And it looks now as if we will get it!"[74] The public defender was far from the mind of its sponsor.

Seth Low campaigned against all forms of bossism, and Platt's operatives openly admitted that they would rather see a Tammany Democrat win than a Non-Partisan succeed. Indeed, many people assumed that Croker and Platt had made a deal to divide the spoils, though both denied it. The vote was close, but Tammany won. Yet most of the reformers felt as good as losers can because they had laid a solid foundation for success the next time.

For reformer Foltz, however, the election held neither immediate gain nor future promise. Back in power, the Tammany machine was absorbed with more pressing matters than the constitutional rights of the criminally accused. The male reformers who might seem her natural allies were similarly uninterested. Perhaps Foltz was misguided ever to suppose she had a chance. The motives, alliances, and shared histories of the political actors were not readily accessible to an outsider—especially to a woman. Even the

Clara Shortridge Foltz, 1919. Identified on the back of photo as "Mrs. Clara Shortridge Foltz, 7-15-19." Photo from the *Los Angeles Examiner* collection of the Regional History Center, Special Collections, University of Southern California. The apparent age of the subject indicates that this may be her actress daughter Virginia; however, Hartsock, the photographer, was well know for his heavily doctored photos. Mother and daughter looked very much alike.

familiar elements of political life were so magnified in New York as to make them different in kind. Though she used the contacts she had very well, Foltz simply did not have the lobbying power to put through a far-reaching measure like the public defender.

Recognizing after a few months that there was no hope, she gave up and took another lesson from the suffragists, who were always careful to write their own history. She published her account of the campaign, applying a triumphant gloss, treating it as a great ongoing project, and refining the arguments she had made at the World's Fair. The article, titled "Public Defenders," opened with the work of unseen hands: "Last winter . . . bills were introduced . . . in more than a dozen States." Clara Foltz herself appeared only in a footnote, receiving "hundreds of commendatory letters, from all parts of the country." She did not mention her World's Fair speech or her long one-woman effort. No Populist–Socialist, Tammany-tinged associations were visible on the surface of the text. Foltz concluded with the promise that a public defender would "promote exact and equal justice, protect the poor, save the innocent"—and last, but surely not least, "remove an unjust burden from a generous profession."[75]

She published "Public Defenders" in the nation's leading legal journal—the *American Law Review*, edited by such worthies as Oliver Wendell Holmes Jr., James Bradley Thayer, John Chipman Gray, and Jon Codman Ropes. From its first issue in 1866, the *American* was the most intellectually distinguished of the country's legal periodicals. An article published there was a sign of professional recognition previously accorded to only two other women, whose pieces were both on topics directly related to gender issues.[76]

The publication of the article concluded Clara Foltz's public defender campaign in New York. Not until she moved to Los Angeles in 1906 did she renew her efforts in a major way. There, she used her new offices of deputy district attorney and prison board director to lobby for public defense. Then she made it part of the suffrage crusade, and with women's votes, the first office of public defender was established in Los Angeles in 1913.

Enacting the Public Defender

Women won suffrage in California in a special election in 1911. The following November, Los Angeles voters passed a city charter that included the first public defender office in the country. Clara Foltz and the suffragists counted this among their major legislative achievements. "In the long fight for the franchise," said one study, women gained political skills and focus, which they used on behalf "of the ignorant and helpless and exploited everywhere."[77]

Foltz said she had been "successful in having the office created by the Los Angeles County Charter," and she must have been gratified to see the immediate effect on the atmosphere of the criminal courts.[78] Systemic evils she had described were immediately decreased: conviction of the innocent, guilty pleas by the confused, neglect by court appointees, and unfair and vindictive prosecution. From its earliest days, the Los Angeles office was a success and an inspiration to the nationwide public defender movement during the Progressive era.

Following its founding, there was a "flood of articles," committees, studies, and "a large number of bills" in state legislatures. Offices were established in jurisdictions across the country, and the idea that appointed counsel should be paid became widely accepted by courts and legislatures.[79] The Progressive-era public defender was, however, quite different from Foltz's original conception of the office. Instead of equal adversaries putting on the best case for the defense, they were officers of the court protecting the factually innocent and pleading the rest guilty. At trial, they would present the evidence in a balanced and fair way—their interest not solely that of clients, but of truth and justice. Foltz's adversarial defender had no place in the Progressive vision but was a symbol of an outworn and inefficient system for ascertaining the facts and representing the accused.[80]

Clara Foltz did not remark the difference between her model of public defense and the one enacted and practiced in the new offices. Given her tendency to view things in a positive light, she may have thought the difference unimportant, or even approved of it. In any case, there can be little doubt that in her old age, Foltz deeply enjoyed seeing the growth of the movement she started. Even if the defenders were not always as she had imagined them, the principle that defense lawyers were necessary to fair procedure was increasingly accepted.

The U.S. Supreme Court held as much in the Depression-era case *Powell v. Alabama*, decided in 1932, two years before Foltz died. Reversing convictions because the accused had no counsel, and expressing special concern for those ignorant of their rights, the opinion sounded very much like Clara Foltz in her 1893 World's Fair speech. *Powell* set the stage for *Gideon v. Wainwright* in 1963, which directly held, seventy years after she had first proposed it, that defense lawyers were necessities in criminal cases and that the government must provide a lawyer for those unable to pay for one.[81]

Today, the public defender is the main channel for defense services in the United States. The idea that the government is responsible for the fair presentation of both sides of a criminal case is a commonplace. Though the vision of *Gideon* has not been realized, mainly because many offices are chronically underfunded, there are also those public defenders that maintain the Foltzian ideal of representation. They consult, investigate, and prepare in every case, making the law, in her words, "a shield as well as a sword." Such offices enact Clara Foltz's vision—originally shaped by the situations of her "poor, sick and despairing clients" and empowered by the women's movement. They are her lasting monument.

Conclusion
Victory Roses

Though the achievements that made Clara Foltz's public life important ended in 1911 with the last suffrage campaign in California, she practiced law and sought to influence public events for two more decades. Her name cropped up in the papers repeatedly as a possible candidate for various elective offices and for judgeships. She was even mentioned for assistant attorney general of the United States in 1920, the same year her brother Sam Shortridge won the first of his two terms in the U.S. Senate. Foltz had thought of running for that office herself, but supported Sam instead.[1]

Toward the end of her life, she told a reporter that she hoped soon "to quit all this struggle . . . and to buy a new and becoming hat every week." Though she never stopped struggling, Foltz did buy a lot of new hats. High fashion continued to give her obvious pleasure, and journalists, like the one in 1931, usually commented on her appearance. "Her hair is modishly bobbed, her skirts youthfully abbreviated, and her clothes smartly up to date in style," the interviewer wrote.[2]

The comfort of Clara Foltz's old age was her wide circle of friends. She was active in Los Angeles club life, joining and founding groups right up until the end. Her most notable public activity in the years after the suffrage victory in California, was publishing a monthly magazine, *The New American Woman*, from February 1916 to July 1918. It started as a newsletter to her friends and retained a personal tone even as it went to slick paper and paid subscriptions. In her late sixties, Foltz filled thirty or so pages every month, largely by herself, with articles on national and local politics, commentary, letters, poetry, and advertisements.

The magazine also featured her autobiographical columns "Struggles and Triumphs of a Woman Lawyer," which were packed with memories of her lectures, cases, and other adventures. Foltz spoke of converting the columns into a book and at one point said she was retiring and returning to San Francisco, her "first love and the cradle of her ambitions," to do further research on it.[3] Though she also claimed to have a publisher's contract, no manuscript has survived, and the twenty-eight installments, produced on deadline over two years, omitted many salient events of her life, most notably her campaign for public defender.

She referred to *Struggles* as "hastily written," "hurried," and "thrown from the table book of memory"; many passages are repeated verbatim from lectures and oft-told stories.[4] Yet newspapers and court records confirm the actual occurrence of events she relates and the accuracy of her memory. At the same time, the disorganization and disproportionate emphasis of the chapters (for example, she has four columns on the shipwreck in the English Channel and not one word on the World's Fair) may be an indication of mental decline during her last decades. There were other signs as well that Foltz lost some of the intellectual acuity that was her chief resource during her best days.

When she reflected on her life, as compared to relating long-ago triumphs, Foltz's memories are sometimes sad. Writing in the early morning—"professional engagements in my law office begin just eight hours from now"—she remembered "no day of rest, no quiet place." She said she had spent "a life-time of self-sacrifice in a profession wholly at variance with my nature."[5] In fact, however, Foltz was well-suited to the law. She enjoyed reading and studying, writing and speaking, and using her skills to help individuals and to contribute to legal reform.

But her career had its costs. In another column, she reflected on her "unperformed duties" to her children. Quoting Wordsworth, she continued, "I think of them as they came to me bringing 'hope and forward-looking thoughts' and then of the graves of two of my little girls." She wrote this in 1918, and the next year she lost her son Samuel to tuberculosis. David died in 1932, two years before his mother. Only Virginia, her youngest, survived

APRIL 1916

The New AMERICAN WOMAN

Clara Shortridge Foltz

CLARA SHORTRIDGE FOLTZ
EDITOR AND PUBLISHER

15 CENTS A COPY
$1.50 PER YEAR

Tapestry commissioned from artist Susan Schwartzenberg by *The New American Woman* magazine, installed at the Clara Shortridge Foltz Criminal Justice Center, Los Angeles, California. Photograph by Susan Schwartzenberg, 2008.

her. Looking back sadly, Foltz regretted the hours she spent on reforms and movements while her children grew up, making "the good times I had promised them forever impossible of enjoyment." Somberly, she added, "all the pleasures of my young motherhood I sacrificed for woman's cause." Like her dark thoughts about law practice, Foltz's assessment was too harsh. She succeeded against great odds in keeping the family together, and in lighter moods, her stories reflected enjoyable moments with her children and pride in them and in herself for supporting them.[6]

In 1930, at the age of eighty-one, Clara Foltz ran for governor, appealing "to the womanhood of California." Her platform advocated a variety of reforms, ranging from equal pay for equal work to fewer jails and penitentiaries and sabbaticals for all teachers. Generally, her campaign literature was professional, if a little hyperbolic (for example, "A Knight Errantress in the Fight for Right"), and the publicity she received, respectful. According to the *New York Times*, she won eight thousand votes in the Republican primary. Four years later Foltz died of heart failure.[7]

She did not leave a will—an odd omission for someone who advertised herself as a probate lawyer. Perhaps Foltz died intestate because she did not wish to reveal how little she had accumulated in many years of practice. But her worldly goods were listed for all to see just four days after her death, when Virginia put them up for auction: Foltz's library, including her professional scrapbooks; a cookstove; two sewing machines; 113 pieces of flatware; several oil paintings; and a sterling tea set.

The major newspapers of both coasts marked the passing of California's first woman attorney.[8] Coming so long after the end of her serious public life, however, the obituaries listed her accomplishments but failed to fully capture Clara Foltz's contributions to American women and to American law. A better summing up appeared in an interview published in a Progressive magazine in 1912, on the eve of the first national election in which California women voted.[9]

The phrases in which Foltz had couched her story for fifty years flowed easily. As a girl she had heard Lucy Stone's "eloquent plea for woman's rights." Then came her "romantic marriage at fifteen" and her "widowhood" when "scarcely out of her teens." (Few were now alive who knew that this "widowhood" was in fact a divorce at age thirty.) "Facing the world with five babies," lullabies "crooned while her brain was busy with Blackstone," the long-ago rides to Sacramento "in the caboose of a cattle train, without a dollar in her pocket" to lobby for the Woman Lawyer's Bill—all were remembered, along with "the little bag of biscuits and boiled eggs" for her only refreshment.

Foltz also spoke of "the tremendous sensation created by her plea for a Public Defender" at the World's Fair and "the memorable January day when she took her precious Public Defender bill to Albany, the bill she had spent years in preparing and which will be forever known as 'the Foltz Defender bill,' which she personally introduced in thirty-two states." Interrupting the narrative, Foltz summarized for her interviewer the arguments for public defense, which were the ones she had been making since the 1880s: "The law presumes a man innocent until proved guilty; the highest function of the government is to preserve the liberty of its citizens; as a matter of common justice, the state, having provided a lawyer to prosecute should also provide a Public Defender."

Next in the story came "all the first woman things": first woman lawyer in California; first to argue a motion in the New York City courts; first to serve in a statewide office in California (the Normal School Board); first on the Charities and Corrections Board; and first to be a deputy prosecuting attorney. Then she summoned her legislative achievements, beginning with the Woman Lawyer's statute and including her early parole bill, and statutes making women eligible to be estate executors and notaries. Finally, Foltz spoke of the Portia Club and the many organizations she had headed, the last being the victorious Votes for Women Club.

Between her girlhood and the "night of triumph" when suffrage had been won in California lay decades of "scorn, ridicule and reproach"; she had "waved the flag and blown the trumpet for the laggard army." As Foltz recalled the victory night itself, she said she was weary and strained after the last hectic weeks of campaigning, "worn by the conflict of hope and despair" as the close count on woman suffrage continued for hours, followed by hours more of celebration. At the very moment of success, she had found herself weighing and balancing her past choices and asking: "Is it worth while? Have the results warranted the supreme endeavor?" Then came a knock on the door, and a messenger brought "the gift of a beloved friend—American Beauty roses, tall as the daughter of the gods, which filled the room with radiant color and a perfume that was like delicious incense. And as she clasped them to her heart she cried: 'It is worth while!'"

That was and is the end of the story, except to say that the interviewer writing it down was herself an attorney, one of a long line not yet ended—Clara Foltz's daughters in the law.

Reference Matter

Notes

Frequently cited works are identified by the following short titles:

Babcock, *First Woman*
> Barbara Allen Babcock, *Clara Shortridge Foltz: "First Woman,"* 30 ARIZ. L. REV. (1988), reprinted with a new introduction in 28 VAL. U. L. REV. 1231 (1994).

Babcock, *Inventing*
> Barbara Allen Babcock, *Inventing the Public Defender*, 43 AM. CRIM. L. REV. 1267 (2006).

Foltz, *Public Defenders*
> Clara Foltz, *Public Defenders*, 31 AM. L. REV. 393 (1897).

Foltz, Scrapbook
> Clara Foltz, Scrapbook, Huntington Library, San Marino, California.

Foltz, *Struggles*
> Clara Shortridge Foltz, *Struggles and Triumphs of a Woman Lawyer*, printed as a series in NEW AMERICAN WOMAN (1916–1918).

HWS
> HISTORY OF WOMAN SUFFRAGE, 6 vols. (1848–1920); vols. 1–3, ed. E. Stanton, S. Anthony & M. Gage; vol. 4, ed. S. Anthony & I. Harper; vols. 5 and 6, ed. I. Harper.

SHUCK, BENCH AND BAR
> OSCAR SHUCK, HISTORY OF THE BENCH AND BAR OF CALIFORNIA (1901).

WLH website
> Women's Legal History website, http://womenslegalhistory.stanford.edu; online bibliographic notes, articles on Foltz and other pioneer women lawyers.

Introduction

1. Foltz, *Struggles*, Apr. 1916.

Chapter One

1. Foltz, *Struggles*, Apr. 1916. For all twenty-eight autobiographical columns of *Struggles*, see WLH website, and *The Public Defender and the Woman's Rights Movement—1878–1913*, Women and Social Movements website, http://womhist.alexander street.com.

2. For background on Elias Shortridge, *see* SHUCK, BENCH AND BAR (Samuel Shortridge entry); and obituaries for E. W. Shortridge, *His Death at an Early Hour Yesterday Morning in This City*, SAN JOSE MERCURY, Nov. 7, 1890, and *A Good Man Laid Peacefully to Rest*, SAN JOSE MERCURY, Nov. 9, 1890, at 5. For information on Mount Pleasant, *see* Teresa Federer, *Belle A. Mansfield: Opening the Way for Others* (2002), at WLH website [hereafter Federer, *Belle Mansfield*].

3. Foltz, *Struggles*, Apr. 1916; *Mt. Pleasant Golden Age, reprinted in* SAN JOSE DAILY MERCURY, June 24, 1880, at 3 ("hard-toiling girl"). For more information on Howe's Academy, *see* Federer, *Belle Mansfield*.

4. Federer, *Belle Mansfield*. *See* Chapter 5 for more on the women lawyers' meeting at the 1893 Chicago World's Fair.

5. The two stories in which Foltz spoke of her divorce can be found in Oscar Shuck, *Clara Shortridge Foltz, A Leading Lady Lawyer*, SAN JOSE DAILY MERCURY, Aug. 20, 1882, at 5, *reprinted from* S.F. POST (writing under pen name "Scintilla Juris") [hereafter Shuck, *Leading Lady Lawyer*]; and Ella Sterling Cummins, *Clara S. Foltz, History of Her Life, Struggles and Success*, SAN JOSE DAILY MERCURY, Oct. 15, 1884, at 3, *reprinted from* SAN FRANCISCAN MAG. [hereafter Cummins, *Foltz History*].

6. Cummins, *Foltz History*.

7. The Christian Record: Pioneers of a Great Cause (unpublished manuscript, on file with the Disciples of Christ Historical Society, Nashville, Tennessee).

8. Records of military service, Jeremiah D. Foltz (on file with the National Archives, Washington, D.C.) [hereafter Foltz military records]; Cummins, *Foltz History*.

9. *The Story of a Woman*, SACRAMENTO RECORD-UNION, Feb. 25, 1879.

10. Foltz told this story to several interviewers; *see* SHUCK, BENCH AND BAR (Foltz entry); Ada M. Bittenbender, *Woman in Law, in* WOMAN'S WORK IN AMERICA 218–44 (Annie Nathan Meyer ed., 1891) (Foltz interviewed at 237–39) [hereafter Bittenbender, *Woman in Law*].

11. Shuck, *Leading Lady Lawyer*.

12. Foltz, *Struggles*, May 1916.

13. Foltz, *Struggles*, Aug. 1916. For more on Foltz's marriage and divorce, *see* Barbara Allen Babcock, *Reconstructing the Person: The Case of Clara Shortridge Foltz*, 12 BIOGRAPHY 5, 8 (1989), *reprinted in* REVEALING LIVES: AUTOBIOGRAPHY, BIOGRAPHY AND GENDER 131–40 (Susan Groag Bell & Marilyn Yalom eds., 1990) [hereafter Babcock, *Reconstructing the Person*].

14. Cummins, *Foltz History.*

15. 1851 CAL. STAT., ch. 1, § 275, at 64.

16. Clara Foltz, Letter to the Editor, N. NORTHWEST, June 15, 1877, at 2 ("times are fearful"); Foltz, *Struggles*, Mar. 1917 ("Eden of loveliness").

17. Gertrude Atherton coined the phrase "the terrible seventies" in CALIFORNIA: AN INTIMATE HISTORY (1914); Foltz, *Struggles*, Mar. 1917.

18. Foltz, *Struggles*, Mar. 1917; letter from Karl Marx to Friedrich A. Sorge (Nov. 5, 1880), *reprinted in* KARL MARX & FREDERICK ENGELS, LETTERS TO AMERICANS, 1848–1895: A SELECTION 126 (Alexander Trachtenberg ed., Leonard E. Mins trans., 1953).

19. Foltz, *Struggles*, Mar. 1917. For contemporary examples of Kearney's rhetoric, *see* 4 T. HITTELL, HISTORY OF CALIFORNIA 604, 608 (1897); 2 H. BANCROFT, POPULAR TRIBUNALS 722 (1887) ("Judge Lynch," "Hemp"); Barbara Allen Babcock, *Clara Shortridge Foltz: Constitution-Maker*, 66 IND. L.J. 849, 857–58 (1991) [hereafter Babcock, *Constitution-Maker*]; PHILIP ETHINGTON, THE PUBLIC CITY: THE POLITICAL CONSTRUCTION OF URBAN LIFE IN SAN FRANCISCO, 1850–1900 242–82 (1994) [hereafter ETHINGTON, PUBLIC CITY].

20. PHILIP S. FONER, THE WORKINGMEN'S PARTY OF THE UNITED STATES 76–77 (1984).

21. Henry George, *The Chinese on the Pacific Coast*, N.Y. TRIB., May 1, 1869; Foltz, *Struggles*, Mar. 1917.

22. Foltz, *Struggles*, Mar. 1917 ("intrepid representative"); SAN JOSE WKLY. MERCURY, Dec. 13, 1877, at 3, and S.F. CHRON., Feb. 19, 1878 (Elias Shortridge on platform with Denis Kearney).

23. S.F. CHRON., Oct. 16, 1877 ("cast their ballots aright"); JAMES BRYCE, *Kearneyism in California*, *in* 3 THE AMERICAN COMMONWEALTH 223 (1888) [hereafter 3 BRYCE, COMMONWEALTH].

24. 3 BRYCE, COMMONWEALTH 237.

25. Ibid.

26. CAREY MCWILLIAMS, AMBROSE BIERCE 136 (1967).

27. Foltz, *Struggles*, Oct. 1916.

28. For the oratorical talent of the Shortridge family and ministry of Elias Shortridge, *see* SHUCK, BENCH AND BAR 828 (Foltz entry) and 1079 (Shortridge entry).

29. Foltz, *Struggles*, May 1916.

30. *Letter from California*, WOMAN'S J., Dec. 7, 1872, at 387 ("number of the clergymen"); Clara Foltz, Letter to the Editor, N. NORTHWEST, Sept. 17, 1875, at 2 ("commanding personal appearance"); H. S. FOOTE, PEN PICTURES FROM "THE GARDEN OF THE WORLD" 226 (1888) [hereafter FOOTE, PEN PICTURES] ("fully in sympathy").

31. Foltz, *Struggles*, May 1916.

32. 3 HWS 765–66 (1876 parade).

33. WOMAN'S J., May 5, 1877, at 141 ("fire a gun" and trying to vote); J. P. MUNRO-FRASER, HISTORY OF SANTA CLARA COUNTY 768 (1881) ("pioneer mothers"); 3 HWS, at 766 ("nerved the weak").

34. Clara Foltz, Letter to the Editor, N. NORTHWEST, June 15, 1877 (Foltz

describing Owen); *In a New Field*, N. NORTHWEST, Feb. 22, 1877, at 2 (quoting the SAN JOSE MERCURY on introduction and Foltz's lecture); quotations from this lecture in subsequent paragraphs are from this latter source.

35. *Letter from California*, N. NORTHWEST, May 4, 1877, at 2.

36. Ibid., Apr. 19, 1877, at 2.

37. *Mrs. Clara M. Foltz*, N. NORTHWEST, Dec. 28, 1877, at 2 (quoting from a review in the OAKLAND TRANSCRIPT).

38. Foltz, *Struggles*, Mar. 1918; Abigail Duniway, *Editorial Comment*, N. NORTHWEST, May 4, 1877, at 2 ("a friend").

39. Foltz, *Struggles*, June 1916; the phrase about "coming events" is an old English proverb. On Spencer's illustrious career, *see* FOOTE, PEN PICTURES 86; EUGENE T. SAWYER, HISTORY OF SANTA CLARA COUNTY 84 (1922).

40. Foltz, *Struggles*, June 1916.

41. Ibid. ("preconceived notions"); *Impartial Suffrage*, SAN JOSE WKLY. MERCURY, Mar. 15, 1877, at 3–4 ("equal or his slave"); N. NORTHWEST, Feb. 22, 1878, at 2 ("strengthened and developed").

42. C. C. Stephens, *Legal Disabilities of Women in California*, WOMAN'S J., Aug. 5, 1871, at 247. For more on Stephens, *see* Babcock, *First Woman*, text at n.58.

43. Dred Scott v. Sandford, 60 U.S. 393 (1856); SAN JOSE WKLY. MERCURY, Dec. 13, 1877.

44. *A Break in the Legal Club*, SAN JOSE WKLY. MERCURY, Jan. 3, 1878 ("educated animals"); Foltz, *Struggles*, Dec. 1916.

45. *A Break in the Legal Club*, SAN JOSE WKLY. MERCURY, Jan. 3, 1878.

46. SAN JOSE WKLY. MERCURY, Jan. 10, 1878 ("call a doctor"); Foltz, *Struggles*, Dec. 1916.

47. 1851 CAL. STAT., ch. 1, § 275, at 64.

48. WOMAN'S J., Jan. 27, 1892; 3 HWS, at 757; GEORGIANA: FEMINIST REFORMER OF THE WEST: THE JOURNAL OF GEORGIANA BRUCE KIRBY (Carolyn Swift, Helen S. Giffen & Judith Steen eds., 1987) (Tator story).

49. For the story of Mansfield's acceptance in the face of a statute referring to "white male persons," *see* Bittenbender, *Woman in Law*, at 221–22; *In re* Bradwell, 55 Ill. 535 (1870); Bradwell v. Illinois, 83 U.S. 130 (1873) ("privileges or immunities"). For an explanation of the court cases involving the admission of Bradwell and Lockwood, *see* Babcock, *First Woman*, text at nn.154–69.

50. *The California Law*, WOMAN'S J., Apr. 18, 1874, at 128 ("remaining there for weeks"); 1878 CAL. STAT., ch. 1, § 275, *in* NEWMARK'S CODE OF CIVIL PROCEDURE (1880). Knox became Knox-Goodrich in 1879.

51. The Woman Lawyer's Bill thus read: "Any citizen or person resident of this state who has bona fide declared his or her intention to become a citizen in the manner required by law, of the age of twenty-one years, of good moral character, and who possesses the necessary qualifications of learning and ability, is entitled to admission as attorney and counselor in all the Courts of this state." 1878 CAL. STAT., ch. 600, §§ 1–3, at 99.

52. R. R. PARKINSON, PEN PORTRAITS: AUTOBIOGRAPHIES OF STATE OFFICERS,

LEGISLATORS, PROMINENT BUSINESS AND PROFESSIONAL MEN OF THE CAPITAL OF THE STATE OF CALIFORNIA, ALSO OF NEWSPAPER PROPRIETORS, EDITORS AND MEMBERS OF THE CORPS REPERTORIAL 105 (1878) (Murphy entry) [hereafter PARKINSON, PEN PORTRAITS]; Foltz, *Struggles*, Aug. 1916.

53. SACRAMENTO DAILY BEE, Dec. 19, 1877, at 2; SACRAMENTO RECORD-UNION, Mar. 30, 1878, at 2.

54. CAL. CONST. art. IV, § 35 (1879, repealed in 1966).

55. Foltz, *Struggles*, Aug. 1916.

56. Unnamed legislator quoted in *A Victory in California*, WOMAN'S J., Apr. 20, 1878, at 124.

57. On Laura Gordon, *see* NOTABLE AMERICAN WOMEN: A BIOGRAPHICAL DICTIONARY (Edward T. James et al. eds., 1971) (Gordon entry) [hereafter NOTABLE AMERICAN WOMEN]; for more on the relationship of Foltz and Gordon, *see* Babcock, *Constitution-Maker*, at 865–67.

58. Letter from Laura Gordon to Laura [no last name] (Feb. 16, 1877), Papers of Laura DeForce Gordon (Stein Collection, Bancroft Library, University of California at Berkeley) [hereafter Gordon Papers].

59. *See, e.g.,* SACRAMENTO UNION, Jan. 11, 1878, at 2 ("Impressionable male jurors" would "return a verdict of acquittal without leaving the box," and "the law and the facts would be simply ignored").

60. Foltz, *Struggles*, Aug. 1916.

61. *Sonnet*, PUCK, Jan. 1878, at 8–9.

62. For more on Spiritualism, *see* ANN BRAUDE, RADICAL SPIRITS, SPIRITUALISM AND WOMEN'S RIGHTS IN NINETEENTH-CENTURY AMERICA (1989); Robert J. Chandler, *In the Van: Spiritualists as Catalysts for the California Women's Suffrage Movement*, 73 CAL. HIST. 189 (1994).

63. *See* NOTABLE AMERICAN WOMEN (Woodhull entry) for a short, comprehensive account. Woodhull's involvement in the Beecher-Tilton scandal is discussed in Chapter 6.

64. BARBARA GOLDSMITH, OTHER POWERS: THE AGE OF SUFFRAGE, SPIRITUALISM AND THE SCANDALOUS VICTORIA WOODHULL 303 (1998) (speech and newspaper reaction); LOIS BEACHY UNDERHILL, THE WOMAN WHO RAN FOR PRESIDENT 143–50 (1995); MADELEINE B. STERN, THE VICTORIA WOODHULL READER 23–24 (1974) (accounts of the free-love speech).

65. SACRAMENTO DAILY BEE, Jan. 17, 1878 ("alike to head"); SAN JOSE MERCURY, Mar. 14, 1878 (reporting on Foltz's return from six weeks in Oregon); Babcock, *First Woman*, text at nn.104–6.

66. SACRAMENTO DAILY BEE, Dec. 5, 1877.

67. PEN PICTURES OF OUR REPRESENTATIVE MEN (Hugh J. Mohan, E. H. Clough & John P. Cosgrove eds.) 35 (1880) (hereafter PEN PICTURES [1880]).

68. SACRAMENTO RECORD-UNION, Feb. 26, 1878. On W. B. May, *see* PEN PICTURES (1880), at 56; *History of Woman Suffrage* gives May equal billing with Johnson for passage of the bill in the Assembly, 3 HWS, at 758. For a full description of the debate on reconsideration, *see* Babcock, *First Woman*, text at nn.97–105.

69. SACRAMENTO RECORD-UNION, Feb. 26, 1878.

70. Cummins, *Foltz History*.

71. Foltz, *Struggles*, Aug. 1916.

72. PARKINSON, PEN PORTRAITS, at 33 (about Irwin); 3 HWS, at 758 (about Gordon).

73. Foltz, *Struggles*, Aug. and Sept. 1916; for a short play based on Foltz's account, *see* Babcock, *First Woman*, text at n.111.

74. Foltz, *Struggles*, Oct. 1916; *Woman at the Bar, The First Female Lawyer of the Pacific Coast*, S.F. CHRON., Jan. 30, 1879, at 3 ("vein of fun") [hereafter *Woman at the Bar*].

75. SAN JOSE WKLY. MERCURY, Sept. 12, 1878, at 3.

76. Foltz, *Struggles*, Oct. 1916.

77. SAN JOSE TIMES MERCURY, Jan. 1, 1885 (summary of achievements); SAN JOSE WKLY. MERCURY, Oct. 3, 1878, at 1 (citing the S.F. CALL, which picked up the story from the CHICAGO INTER-OCEAN).

78. N.Y. TIMES, Sept. 27, 1878, at 4 ("attended to her family"); *Mrs. Attorney Foltz*, WOMAN'S J., Sept. 28, 1878 (quoting N.Y. WORLD).

79. *Editorial*, 30 ALB. L.J. (1885).

80. *Woman at the Bar*.

81. Foltz, *Struggles*, Feb. 1917.

82. *Woman at the Bar*.

83. The story is told in Foltz, *Struggles*, Mar.–May 1917. Foltz told the story in an abbreviated form in one of her last interviews: *West's First Portia: Then and Now*, S.F. CHRON., Mar. 21, 1931.

84. Foltz, *Struggles*, Mar. 1917.

85. Foltz, *Struggles*, Apr. 1917.

86. Ibid.

87. Foltz, *Struggles*, May 1917.

88. Ibid.

89. *Woman at the Bar*.

90. S.F. POST, Nov. 11, 1878, at 2.

91. For information on Terry, *see* A. BUCHANAN, DAVID S. TERRY OF CALIFORNIA: DUELING JUDGE 171 (1956); ALEXANDER E. WAGSTAFF, THE LIFE OF DAVID TERRY (1892); CARL BRENT SWISHER, STEPHEN J. FIELD: CRAFTSMAN OF THE LAW (1933) (chapter titled "The Terry Tragedy"); OSCAR SHUCK, BENCH AND BAR IN CALIFORNIA: HISTORY, ANECDOTES, REMINISCENCES 281 (1889).

92. D. WALDRON & T. VIVIAN, BIOGRAPHICAL SKETCHES OF THE DELEGATES TO THE CONVENTION TO FRAME A NEW CONSTITUTION FOR THE STATE OF CALIFORNIA 99 (1878) (Ayers entry) [hereafter WALDRON & VIVIAN, BIOGRAPHICAL SKETCHES].

93. For more on Roney, *see* IRA CROSS, FRANK RONEY, IRISH REBEL AND CALIFORNIA LABOR LEADER (1931).

94. Henry George, *The Kearney Agitation in California*, 17 POPULAR SCI. MONTHLY 433 (1880); 3 BRYCE, COMMONWEALTH, at 228 n.1; Doyce B. Nunis, *The*

Demagogue and the Demographer: Correspondence of Denis Kearney and Lord Bryce, 36 Pac. Hist. Rev. 269 (1967).

95. Wasp, Aug. 9, 1879, *reprinted in The Workingmen's Party of California, 1877–1882,* 55 Cal. Hist. Q. 58, 68 (1976) (collection of contemporary cartoons); 2 H. Bancroft, Popular Tribunals 742 (1887); Argonaut, Dec. 7, 1878.

96. Waldron & Vivian, Biographical Sketches, at 60–61 (Vacquerel entry).

97. Debates and Proceedings of the California Constitutional Convention 376 (1879) (Shafter) [hereafter Debates]; 3 HWS, at 752 ("Mrs. Judge Shafter" was at one of the earliest meetings to organize a suffrage society in California); Debates, at 375 (McComas).

98. *Woman Suffrage in California,* N. Northwest, July 5, 1878 ("large," "delighted," and "respectful") (letter from Clara Foltz dated June 20, 1878); 3 HWS, at 759 (description of campaign).

99. S.F. Chron., Oct. 30, 1878, at 2; *see also* Debates, at 450 (describing woman suffrage meetings in the assembly hall as an unusual and striking occurrence).

100. Wasp, Nov. 2, 1878.

101. Debates, at 408, 1007, 1009–10, 1367 (Caples's quotations), *reported in* S.F. Chron., Nov. 10, 1878, at 4.

102. Letter from Clara Foltz to Laura Gordon (Nov. 20, 1878), *in* Gordon Papers.

103. An Illustrated History of Southern California Embracing the Counties of San Diego, San Bernardino, Los Angeles and Orange 271 (1890) [hereafter Illustrated History]; Debates, at 832 (quoting Blackmer); the "low green tent" refers to the grave mound and quotes the poem "Snow-Bound" by John Greenleaf Whittier.

104. Debates, at 883, quoting William Peyton Grace, a carpenter and architectural draftsman, who was one of the stalwarts for suffrage among the Workingmen. *See* Waldron & Vivian, Biographical Sketches, at 67.

105. *See* Foltz, *Struggles,* June 1917, for quotations in this story, which Foltz also told with variations in details in Bittenbender, *Woman in Law,* at 238–39.

106. For a description of Land Office practice, *see* Gerald D. Nash, *Problems and Projects in the History of Nineteenth-Century California Land Policy,* 27 Huntington Libr. Q. 347 (1964).

107. For more on the San Francisco press, *see* Ethington, Public City, at 308–19.

108. *Woman at the Bar.*

109. Foltz, *Struggles,* June 1917.

110. Foltz, *Struggles,* Nov. 1917, for this and following paragraphs on Foltz's first days at law school. For more on Hastings, *see* Thomas Barnes, Hastings College of the Law: The First Century 120 (1978) [hereafter Barnes, The First Century].

111. *Interview with Judge Hastings,* S.F. Chron., Mar. 6, 1879, at 3.

112. *Woman at the Bar.*

113. Ibid. (Foltz quoted the letter to the *Chronicle* reporter); Barnes, The First Century, at 47 (board resolution not to admit women, Jan. 10, 1879).

114. *Woman at the Bar*; on Pomeroy's eminence, *see* BARNES, THE FIRST CENTURY, at 89.

115. Foltz, *Struggles*, Nov. 1916.

116. For a detailed account of the litigation, *see* Babcock, *First Woman*, text at nn.143–219.

117. *Woman at the Bar*.

118. SAN JOSE DAILY MERCURY, Jan. 29, 1879, at 2.

119. *Woman at the Bar* (Terry advising on strategy); Foltz, *Struggles*, Mar. 1917.

120. CAL. CONST. art. XX, § 18 (1879).

121. Letter from Charles Ringgold to Laura Gordon (Jan. 30, 1879), *in* Gordon Papers.

122. Letter from Laura Gordon to her parents (Feb. 6, 1879), *in* Gordon Papers.

123. Transcript on Appeal, Foltz v. Hoge, 54 Cal. 28 (1879); Gordon's motion, Gordon v. Hoge (on file at the California State Archives, Sacramento). Gordon asked the supreme court to take original jurisdiction because the case involved a matter of great public interest; letter from Laura Gordon to her parents (Feb. 12, 1879), *in* Gordon Papers.

124. *The Lady Lawyers*, S.F. CHRON., Feb. 15, 1878, at 2.

125. S.F. CALL, Feb. 22, 1879, at 2.

126. S.F. CALL, Feb. 25, 1879, at 1. The San Francisco and Sacramento papers all had lengthy page-one stories about the argument. The paragraphs that follow are an amalgam of the stories in the *Call*, *Chronicle*, and *Daily Alta* of Feb. 25, 1879.

127. *See In re* Goodell, 39 Wis. 232, 247 (1876).

128. *A Lady Lawyer's Retort*, FORT WAYNE INDIANA DAILY, June 8, 1881 (quoting a story in the SAN JOSE MERCURY).

129. For a chronology of the consideration of suffrage and passage of the women's clauses, *see* Babcock, *Constitution-Maker*, at 878.

130. DEBATES, at 1012.

131. Ibid., at 1368 (quoting Ayers); S.F. POST, Feb. 15, 1879 ("no blocks" and "turned the scale").

132. 3 HWS, at 759–60.

133. DEBATES, at 1422.

134. S.F. POST, Feb. 18, 1879, at 2; letter from Charles Ringgold to Laura Gordon (Feb. 29, 1879), *in* Gordon Papers.

135. DEBATES, at 1476–77.

136. S.F. CHRON., Feb. 27, 1879, at 2; DEBATES, at 1476 (querulous delegate).

137. Foltz, *Struggles*, Mar. 1917.

138. Ibid.

139. S.F. CHRON., Mar. 6, 1879, at 3 (report of the opinion).

140. Foltz, *Struggles*, Nov. 1916.

141. *A Constitution That Enlarges Their Privileges*, S.F. CHRON., Apr. 15, 1879, at 2.

142. Letter from Clara Foltz to Laura Gordon (May 6), *in* Gordon Papers (no year given, but internal evidence indicates 1879).

143. Foltz, *Struggles*, Aug. 1917; S.F. CHRON., Dec. 6, 1879, at 2.

144. SHUCK, BENCH AND BAR (Foltz entry) ("good mother"); Foltz v. Hoge, 54 Cal. 28 (1879); Bittenbender, *Woman in Law*, at 239 ("modest gold brooch").

145. For Foltz being called "Portia of the Pacific," *see, e.g.*, A WOMAN OF THE CENTURY (Frances E. Willard & Mary A. Livermore eds.) (1893) (Foltz entry) [hereafter WOMAN OF THE CENTURY]; and Chapter 3.

146. *Woman at the Bar* ("troubles"); *The Story of a Woman*, SACRAMENTO RECORD-UNION, Feb. 25, 1879, at 1.

147. Foltz military records; Foltz, *Struggles*, May 1916.

148. *Women in the Public Eye, reprinted in* INDIANAPOLIS STAR, May 5, 1910 (quoting Virginia Foltz about Jeremiah's attitude); Letter from Sarah Wallis to Laura Gordon (Mar. 7, 1879), *in* Gordon Papers.

149. Letter from Josephine Woolcott to Laura Gordon (April 19, 1879), *in* Gordon Papers ("a little worried"); divorce papers, Foltz v. Foltz (on file in San Jose Superior Court Archives) ("bitter dregs," "remove permanently"). For stories about Foltz's widowhood, *see* N.Y. TIMES MAG., July 11, 1897; *A Sketch of Clara Foltz*, 13 W. COAST MAG. 43 (1912).

150. *Woman at the Bar* ("don't believe in divorce"); *Editorial*, 54 ALB. L.J. (Mar. 7, 1896) ("sacredness of marriage").

151. Adley Cummins, *The Rights of Married Women in California*, GOLDEN ERA, Aug. 1885, at 263. For more on California's divorce laws, *see* ROBERT L. GRISWOLD, FAMILY AND DIVORCE IN CALIFORNIA, 1850–1890: VICTORIAN ILLUSIONS AND EVERYDAY REALITIES 18–20 (1982).

152. Foltz, *Struggles*, July 1916.

153. For a description of the legislature, *see* Theodore Hittell, *The Legislature of 1880*, 1 BERKELEY Q. 234 (1880).

154. WOMAN'S J., Dec. 6, 1879, at 388 ("no peace"; petition addressed to the "Honorable Senate and Assembly of the State of California" from Foltz); SKETCH-BOOK OF THE 1880 CALIFORNIA LEGISLATURE (on file at Bancroft Library, University of California at Berkeley); S.F. EXAMINER, Mar. 20, 1880, at 1; 4 T. HITTELL, HISTORY OF CALIFORNIA (1897), at 678 ("continued their storming").

155. Clara Foltz, *Brief on the Constitutionality of Woman Suffrage*, 126 PAMPHLETS 1880 (on file at the Huntington Library, San Marino, California); *see also* Chapter 6 for more on school suffrage.

156. WOMAN'S J., Dec. 6, 1879, at 388. Woman suffrage was debated on the evenings of March 11, 19, and 24, 1880; for extensive coverage of the women's arguments, *see* the *San Francisco Alta* and *San Francisco Examiner* on the day after each session.

157. S.F. EXAMINER, Mar. 20, 1880, at 2.

158. S.F. CHRON., Sept. 9, 1880, at 1.

159. *See* Laura Gordon, *Brief*, 126 PAMPHLETS 1880 (on file at the Huntington Library, San Marino, California).

160. Madge Morris, *To Clara Shortridge Foltz, reprinted in* THE LURE OF THE DESERT AND OTHER POEMS (1917) (the poem implies that she had the children with her at the legislature).

161. SAN JOSE WKLY. MERCURY, Jan. 29, 1880; a picture of Gunn is in PEN PICTURES (1880).

162. Letter from Clara Foltz to Laura Gordon (May 6, 1879), *in* Gordon Papers.

Chapter Two

1. *Woman Suffrage in California*, N. NORTHWEST, July 5, 1878, at 2 (letter from Clara Foltz). For more on the campaign, *see* Babcock, *Constitution-Maker*, at 870–72 and sources cited.

2. *Rousing Meeting*, SAN JOSE WKLY. MERCURY, Sept. 9, 1880, at 3. For more on Hardinge, *see* Robert Chandler, *Emma Hardinge: A Spiritual Voice for the Slave and the Union*, 29 DOGTOWN TERRITORIAL Q. 6 (1997).

3. *Letter from Clara Foltz*, N. NORTHWEST, *reprinted in Women to the Rescue*, SAN JOSE WKLY. MERCURY, Sept. 2, 1880; *Mrs. Clara Foltz*, S.F. CHRON., Oct. 27, 1880.

4. *Endorsing Mrs. Marian Todd*, S.F. CALL, Aug. 31, 1881, at 3. For more on Todd, *see* 1 NOTABLE AMERICAN WOMEN (Marion Todd entry); Lelia J. Robinson, *Women Lawyers in the United States*, 3 GREEN BAG (1890), at 26–27 [hereafter Robinson, *Women Lawyers*]; WOMAN OF THE CENTURY (Marion Todd entry). For more on the Greenback Labor Party, *see* WINFIELD J. DAVIS, HISTORY OF POLITICAL CONVENTIONS IN CALIFORNIA 1849–1892, at 451–52 (1893) (Greenback convention); DARCY G. RICHARDSON, OTHERS: THIRD PARTY POLITICS FROM THE NATION'S FOUNDING TO THE RISE OF THE GREENBACK-LABOR PARTY (2004).

5. Abigail Duniway, *Please Take It Down*, WOMAN'S HERALD OF INDUSTRY, Aug. 1884.

6. *Woman Suffrage in California*, N. NORTHWEST, July 5, 1878, at 2.

7. *The Career of a Modern Portia*, 2 SUCCESS, 205–6, Feb. 18, 1899 ("slurring remark"), *reprinted in* SELECTED MAGAZINE ARTICLES OF THEODORE DREISER: LIFE AND ART IN THE AMERICAN 1890S, 139–44 (Yoshinobu Hakutani ed., 1985). Regarding Foltz's price for speaking, *see* A Democrat for "Revenue Only," FRESNO REPUBLICAN, Oct. 10, 1886; SAN DIEGO BEE, June 2, 1887 (quoting story from Modesto Republican paper, which stated that when Republicans refused her price of $2,000, Foltz had a "vision like Brigham Young" and became a "new-made Democrat").

8. *Mrs. Clara Foltz Delivers a Democratic Speech*, S.F. CALL, Oct. 20, 1886, at 1 (Foltz repaying Swift); S.F. ARGONAUT, April 24, 1886 (racist rhetoric). On the American Party and the 1886 California campaign, *see* R. HAL WILLIAMS, THE DEMOCRATIC PARTY AND CALIFORNIA POLITICS, 1880–1896 104–5 (1973) [hereafter WILLIAMS, DEMOCRATIC PARTY], and WILLIAM BULLOUGH, THE BLIND BOSS AND HIS CITY: CHRISTOPHER AUGUSTINE BUCKLEY AND NINETEENTH-CENTURY SAN FRANCISCO 176–80 (1979) [hereafter BULLOUGH, BLIND BOSS].

9. S.F. CALL, Sept. 19, 1886, at 6 (quoting Swift letter); S.F. ALTA, Oct. 20, 1886, at 1 (Foltz attacking credibility of letter). For a description of Swift's letter, *see* DAVIS, HISTORY OF POLITICAL CONVENTIONS IN CALIFORNIA, 529–30.

10. S.F. CHRON., Oct. 20, 1886, at 1 ("vast audience"); S.F. CALL, Oct. 20, 1886, at 1 ("unusual number").

11. S.F. ALTA, Oct. 20, 1886.

12. For the election outcome, *see* WILLIAMS, DEMOCRATIC PARTY 104–5; on Foltz's appointment, *see* SAN DIEGO BEE, July 24, 1888.

13. Letter from Clara Foltz to Stephen White (Jan. 17, 1889) (White Papers, Department of Special Collections, Stanford University Libraries) [hereafter White Papers].

14. KEVIN STARR, INVENTING THE DREAM 69–70 (1986).

15. Letter from Morris Estee to Harrison (Sept. 22, 1888), *quoted in* WILLIAMS, DEMOCRATIC PARTY 126.

16. For sample reports of Foltz speeches, *see* S.F. EXAMINER, Sept. 7 (Tulare), Sept. 10 (Merced), Sept. 24 (Auburn), Sept. 29 (Wheatlands), and Oct. 3 (Vallejo), 1888.

17. *Eloquent Mrs. Foltz*, S.F. EXAMINER, Oct. 7, 1888. Subsequent paragraphs rely on this source.

18. S.F. EXAMINER, Oct. 5, 1888.

19. S.F. EXAMINER, Oct. 14, 1888.

20. For more on women's activities during the campaign, *see* GAYLE GULLETT, BECOMING CITIZENS: THE EMERGENCE AND DEVELOPMENT OF THE CALIFORNIA WOMEN'S MOVEMENT 1880–1911 34–42 (2000); S.F. EXAMINER, Oct. 23, Oct. 26, and Oct. 31, 1888.

21. J. MATTHEW GALLMAN, AMERICA'S JOAN OF ARC: THE LIFE OF ANNA ELIZABETH DICKINSON: THE STORY OF A REMARKABLE WOMAN (2006).

22. S.F. EXAMINER, Sept. 28, 1888 ("hangman"); SAN DIEGO BEE, Oct. 2, 1888 (Foltz's challenge).

23. *Clara Foltz, San Francisco, Cal.* 1 LAW STUDENT'S HELPER 263 (1893).

24. Foltz, *Struggles*, Oct. 1917.

25. Foltz, *Struggles*, Feb. 1917.

26. For the demographics and descriptions of San Francisco in the 1880s, *see* BULLOUGH, BLIND BOSS 100–110, and WILLIAM ISSEL & ROBERT W. CHERNEY, SAN FRANCISCO, 1865–1932, at 58–79 (1986).

27. *The Latest Horror*, S.F. CALL, Oct. 21, 1880, at 1; *A Ghastly Deed*, S.F. CHRON., Oct. 22, 1880. The *Wheeler* case was covered daily in the *San Francisco Call, Chronicle*, and *Examiner* from October 21, 1880, through February 6, 1881.

28. *A Strange Meeting, Interview with Strangler*, S.F. CHRON., Oct. 22, 1880.

29. *See* ETHINGTON, PUBLIC CITY, at 282, and sources cited for the complex story of the editor's murder. On press reaction to the insanity defense in *Wheeler*, *see, e.g.*, *A Played-Out Plea*, Jan. 8, 1881, *in* NAT'L POLICE GAZETTE (1845–1906); *"Insane Murderers,"* S.F. CHRON., Oct. 29, 1880.

30. S.F. CHRON., Dec. 23, 1880.

31. Ibid.

32. *A Forensic Female: Appearance of a Lady Lawyer in a Murder Case*, S.F. CHRON., Aug. 12, 1880.

33. *The Trial of Saldez in Judge Ferral's Court*, S.F. CHRON., Aug. 13, 1880 (sarcastic allusion); *Triumphant Woman: Victory of the Champion of Female Equality*, S.F. CHRON., Aug. 14, 1880. For more on the case, *see* Robinson, *Women Lawyers*, at 25, 26–27 (Gordon describing *Saldez*), and Babcock, *Women Defenders*, at n.33.

34. *The Wheeler Trial,* S.F. CHRON., Feb. 3, 1881 ("ruined"); EDWARD VAN EVERY, SINS OF AMERICA AS EXPOSED BY THE POLICE GAZETTE (1931).

35. *Two Females Will Be Allowed to Wag Their Tongues to Their Hearts' Content,* 38 NAT'L POLICE GAZETTE, Jan. 11, 1881, at 11 (1845–1906); *San Francisco's Female Lawyers,* 38 NAT'L POLICE GAZETTE, Mar. 5, 1881, at 8.

36. *A Strangler's Doom,* S.F. CHRON., Feb. 5, 1881 (describing summations).

37. Ibid.

38. People v. Wheeler, 60 Cal. 581 (1882); *Expiated; George A. Wheeler Pays the Death Penalty,* S.F. CALL, Jan. 24, 1884.

39. Bittenbender, *Woman in Law,* at 237–39; SAN JOSE MERCURY, May 26, 1881 (Foltz ill); Barbara Babcock, *Alma Mater: Clara Foltz and Hastings College of the Law,* 21 HASTINGS WOMEN'S LAW J. 99 (2010) (Foltz receives degree).

40. Foltz, *Struggles,* Apr. 1916 ("on every tongue"); Shuck, *Leading Lady Lawyer* (San Francisco columnist); ST. LOUIS GAZETTE, *quoted in* N. NORTHWEST, Aug. 1, 1879, at 2.

41. *A Compliment to Mrs. Foltz,* SAN JOSE DAILY MERCURY, May 30, 1882, at 3.

42. The following paragraphs rely on letters from Foltz to Cogswell (Henry D. Cogswell Papers, Bancroft Library, University of California, Berkeley) [hereafter Cogswell Papers] (including fifteen letters from Clara Foltz written between February 1883 and March 1885, as well as notes made by Cogswell about his payments to Foltz); and Transcript of Record on Appeal, Foltz v. Cogswell, 70 Cal. 201, 25 P.60 (1890) (on file with the California State Archives, Sacramento).

43. Letter from Clara Foltz to Cogswell (Feb. 14, 1883), *in* Cogswell Papers.

44. Letter from Clara Foltz to Cogswell (Mar. 7, 1883), *in* Cogswell Papers.

45. *See, e.g.,* Letter from Clara Foltz to Cogswell (Nov. 26, 1883), *in* Cogswell Papers; *A Magnificent Gift: Dr Coggswell [sic] Offers an Elegant Bronze Fountain to San Jose,* SAN JOSE DAILY MERCURY, Jan. 27, 1883, at 3.

46. Transcript of record on appeal, Phelps v. Cogswell, 70 Cal. 201, 11 P.628 (1886) (on file with the California State Archives, Sacramento).

47. Ibid. (on appeal, the sum was cut to $1,000).

48. Letter from Clara Foltz to Cogswell, Feb. 2, 1884, *in* Cogswell Papers.

49. Transcript of Record on Appeal, Foltz v. Cogswell, 86 Cal. 542, 25 P.60 (1890) (on file with California State Archives, Sacramento) (trial dates March 13–14, 1888). Subsequent paragraphs rely on this source.

50. *Don't Like Our Clara,* S.F. NEWS-LETTER, *quoted in* SAN DIEGO BEE, Mar. 22, 1888.

51. Ibid.

52. Briefs of Appellant and Respondent, Foltz v. Cogswell, 86 Cal. 542, 25 P.60 (1890) (on file in California State Archives, Sacramento).

53. Foltz v. Cogswell, 86 Cal. 542, 548, 25 P.60, 61 (1890). This was the first case decided under the antilobbying clause. CAL. CONST. art. IV, § 35 (1879, repealed in 1966).

54. Affidavit of Clara Foltz (seeking a continuance of case on grounds of illness);

transcript of Record on Appeal, Taylor v. Bidwell, 65 Cal. 489, 4 P.491 (1884) (on file with the California State Archives, Sacramento).

55. Transcript of Record on Appeal, Foltz v. Cogswell, 70 Cal. 201, 25 P.60 (1890) (on file with the California State Archives, Sacramento). Subsequent paragraphs about the testimony rely on this source.

56. Information on Maguire from SHUCK, BENCH AND BAR, at 722–23 (Maguire entry); Harold F. Taggart, *The Election of 1898 in California*, 19 PAC. HIST. REV., Nov. 1950, at 357–68 (describing Maguire's close run for governor after serving three successful terms in Congress).

57. SAN DIEGO BEE, Oct. 11, 1887.

58. *Clara S. Foltz: An Admirable Pen Picture of California's Lady Lawyer*, SAN JOSE TIMES-MERCURY, Jan. 1, 1885, at 1 [hereafter *Admirable Pen Picture*].

59. Undated notes (Wait Papers, Colburn [married name] Manuscript Collection, Box 1066, Folder 30, California State Library, Sacramento).

60. *Admirable Pen Picture*, *cited in* ELLA STERLING [CUMMINS] MIGHELS, THE STORY OF THE FILES: A REVIEW OF CALIFORNIA WRITERS AND LITERATURE 316 (1893) [hereafter MIGHELS, STORY]. (Wait authored pen pictures of Foltz.)

61. Cummins, *Foltz History*.

62. *See* ELLA STERLING [CUMMINS] MIGHELS, LIFE AND LETTERS OF A FORTY-NINERS DAUGHTER 184–89 (1934) (Cummins autobiography).

63. Frona Wait, *Column*, SAN DIEGO BEE, Oct. 10, 1887.

64. *Admirable Pen Picture*.

65. 2 BRYCE, COMMONWEALTH 424, 433.

66. Foltz, *Struggles*, Oct. 1916 ("sobriquet"); June 1917 ("best people").

67. Subsequent paragraphs rely on ETHINGTON, PUBLIC CITY *passim*; BARNES, HASTINGS COLLEGE 57–61; Noel Wise, *An Uncommon Journey: Reflections on the Life of Mary McHenry Keith* (2002), *available at* WLH website. Subsequent paragraphs rely on these sources.

68. Letter from Clara Foltz to Mary McHenry (June 1, 1882) (on file with the Keith–McHenry–Pond Collection, Bancroft Library, University of California, Berkeley).

69. Foltz, *Struggles*, Aug. 1916.

70. SHUCK, BENCH AND BAR (Foltz entry).

71. Foltz, *Struggles*, May 1918 ("poor and sick"); People v. Colby, 54 Cal. 37 (1879), 54 Cal. 184 (1880); MARGARET KOCH, SANTA CRUZ COUNTY: PARADE OF THE PAST (1973) (last public hanging); *Life for Life*, ALTA CAL., Mar. 6, 1880, at 1 (quoting open letter from Colby to the People of California that ends with thanks to Clara Foltz); *see also Charles Colby Hanged*, S.F. CHRON., Mar. 6, 1880, at 3.

72. Clara Foltz, *Speech at the Red, White and Blue Social*, SAN DIEGO BEE, July 1, 1887.

73. *Pardoning Power*, S.F. CHRON., July 23, 1881.

74. Taylor v. Bidwell, 4 P.491, 65 Cal. 489 (1884).

75. Raisback v. Carson and Dahms v. Carson [two cases], 3 WASH. TERR. 168, 13 P.618 (1887) (Supreme Court of the Territory of Washington) (cases about the

ownership of the property; Foltz mentioned in earlier transaction); on Foltz's pardon practice, *see* Chapter 3.

76. Foltz, *Struggles*, May 1918.

77. Transcript on Appeal, People v. Mess, 65 Cal. 174, 3 P.670 (1884).

78. *See* JILL NORGREN, BELVA LOCKWOOD: THE WOMAN WHO WOULD BE PRESIDENT, 124–42 (2007) [hereafter NORGREN, BELVA LOCKWOOD].

79. Belva A. Lockwood, *How I Ran for the Presidency, in* NATIONAL MAG., Mar. 1903, at 729 [hereafter Lockwood, *How I Ran*]; Clara Shortridge Foltz, *Belva A. Lockwood: First Woman Presidential Candidate*, WOMEN LAWYERS' JOURNAL 27 (1918), *reprinted from* Clara Shortridge Foltz, *Belva A. Lockwood, First Woman Presidential Candidate: Nomination in Fun by Women in Convention Assembled, in* NEW AMERICAN WOMAN (June, July, Aug. 1917) [hereafter Foltz, *Lockwood Story*].

80. Lockwood, *How I Ran*, at 729. For more on Stow, *see* REDA DAVIS, WOMAN'S REPUBLIC: THE LIFE OF MARIETTA STOW, COOPERATOR (1980); Donna Schuele, *In Her Own Way: Marietta Stow's Crusade for Probate Law Reform within the Nineteenth-Century Women's Rights Movement,* 7 YALE J. L. FEMINISM 281 (1995).

81. Foltz, *Lockwood Story*; the following story and quotations are from this source unless otherwise noted.

82. NORGREN, BELVA LOCKWOOD, at 130–32.

83. Foltz, *Lockwood Story*; WOMAN'S HERALD OF INDUSTRY, Oct. 1884 (listing a slightly different group of electors). In other parts of the country, Lockwood's most active supporters were women lawyers: Lelia Robinson in Washington Territory, Phoebe Couzins in Missouri, and Marilla Ricker in New Hampshire. NORGREN, BELVA LOCKWOOD, at 133 (discussing electors).

84. Belva Lockwood, *Women of the Supreme Court, in* GLEANINGS: A GIFT TO THE WOMEN OF THE WORLD 218 (Emily Oliver Gibbes ed., 1892).

85. WOMAN OF THE CENTURY ("a respite"); SAN JOSE DAILY MERCURY, Mar. 19, 1882, at 1.

86. RICHARD W. LEEMAN, "DO EVERYTHING" REFORM: THE ORATORY OF FRANCES E. WILLARD 14 (1992).

87. *Kate Field Dead*, N.Y. TRIB., May 31, 1896, at 7.

88. KATE FIELD, HAP-HAZARD 47–48 (1873).

89. *Lawyers*, S.F. CALL, Mar. 8, 1884; for versions of the "Lawyers" lecture, *see On Lawyers: Mrs. Clara S. Foltz's Ideas of Shyster Practitioners*, S.F. EXAMINER, Apr. 11, 1885, at 2 [hereafter *On Lawyers*], and Foltz, *Struggles*, Dec. 1917.

90. Foltz, *Struggles*, Dec. 1917.

91. Ibid.

92. *On Lawyers*.

93. SHUCK, BENCH AND BAR (Foltz entry).

94. For more on Baker, *see* OSCAR SHUCK, ELOQUENCE OF THE FAR WEST: MASTERPIECES OF E. D. BAKER 287–318 (1899) [hereafter SHUCK, MASTERPIECES]; SHUCK, BENCH AND BAR, at 13–21; ETHINGTON, PUBLIC CITY, at 181–85; HARRY C. BLAIR & REBECCA TARSHIS, THE LIFE OF COLONEL EDWARD D. BAKER: LINCOLN'S CONSTANT ALLY (1960).

95. *Mrs. Clara Foltz's Lecture*, S.F. ALTA, Sept. 17, 1885.

96. *Cited in* SHUCK, MASTERPIECES, at 306–7.

97. *Mrs. Clara Foltz's Lecture*, S.F. ALTA, Sept. 17, 1885. Unless otherwise noted, quotations in subsequent paragraphs are from this source.

98. Foltz was quoting from *The American Theater Speech, in* SHUCK, MASTER-PIECES, at 115–16 (delivered in San Francisco in 1860).

99. Clara S. Foltz, *Colonel Baker as an Orator, reprinted in* WILLIAM T. ROSS, VOICE, CULTURE AND ELOCUTION 290–91 (1886).

100. *Oration of Col. E. D. Baker over the Dead Body of Broderick*, S.F. ALTA, Sept. 19, 1859; ETHINGTON, PUBLIC CITY, at 179 n.35.

101. For accounts of the Althea Hill–William Sharon trial, see ROBERT H. KRO-NINGER, SARAH AND THE SENATOR (1964); Oscar LEWIS & CARROLL HALL, BONANZA INN 116–214 (1939); PAUL KENS, JUSTICE STEPHEN FIELD: SHAPING LIBERTY FROM THE GOLD RUSH TO THE GILDED AGE 277–90 (1997).

102. *See, e.g.*, SAN JOSE WKLY. MERCURY, Mar. 19, 1887, quoting review in Greenburg, Indiana, paper of "An American Hero"; *A Forgotten Hero*, WASH. POST, Mar. 3, 1890, at 5.

103. N. NORTHWEST, Oct. 29 and Nov. 12, 1885 ("golden opinions"); QUEEN BEE, DENVER, CO., Dec. 9, 1885 ("intelligent audiences"); SALEM DAILY STATESMAN, Oct. 25, 1885, at 3 ("many eyes," quoting the RED BLUFF SENTINEL).

104. SALEM DAILY STATESMAN, Nov. 11, 1885.

105. *The Part Played by Mrs. Foltz in the Oregon Legislature*, SAN JOSE DAILY MERCURY, Mar. 29, 1891, at 8; *Lady Lawyers Hereafter to Be Free and Unfettered*, SALEM VIDETTE, Nov. 19, 1885, *reprinted in* SAN JOSE DAILY MERCURY, Nov. 27, 1885, at 3; SALEM DAILY STATESMAN, Nov. 17, 1885 ("perfect ovation").

106. Kerry Abrams, *Folk Hero, Hell Raiser, Mad Woman, Lady Lawyer: What Is the Truth about Mary Leonard?* at WLH website.

107. *In re* Leonard, 12 Or. 93, 6 P.426 (1885).

108. PHARISEE AMONG PHILISTINES: THE DIARY OF MATTHEW P. DEADY, 1871–1892 (entries of July 1, 1882 ["looked in my glass"; "tries to be a man"] and November 21, 1885 ["pretty good"]). Foltz's time on the bench was reported in SAN JOSE MERCURY, July 7, 1882, at 2; N. NORTHWEST, July 6, 1882, at 2.

109. Letter from Clara Foltz to Clara Colby (June 6, 1904) (Clara Bewick Colby Papers, Huntington Library, San Marino, California). For more on Duniway, *see* RUTH BARNES MOYNIHAN, REBEL FOR RIGHTS: ABIGAIL SCOTT DUNIWAY (1985) [hereafter MOYNIHAN, REBEL].

110. *Lady Lawyers Hereafter to Be Free and Unfettered*, SALEM VIDETTE, Nov. 19, 1885, *reprinted in* SAN JOSE DAILY MERCURY, Nov. 27, 1885, at 3.

111. OREGONIAN, Feb. 28, 1886.

112. MOYNIHAN, REBEL, at 95.

113. N. NORTHWEST, Dec. 17, 1885, at 5.

114. Subsequent paragraphs rely on Mary Greene, *Mrs. Lelia Robinson Sawtelle: First Woman Lawyer of Massachusetts*, 7 WOMAN's L.J. 51 (1890); Sarah Killingsworth,

Lelia Robinson (1997); and Mary Nicol, *Lelia Robinson: A Second Look* (1998), at WLH website. Succeeding paragraphs rely on these sources.

115. Lelia J. Robinson, Letter to the Equity Club, 1887, *reprinted in* VIRGINIA DRACHMAN, WOMEN LAWYERS AND THE ORIGINS OF PROFESSIONAL IDENTITY IN AMERICA 66 (1993) [hereafter DRACHMAN, WOMEN LAWYERS].

116. Lelia Robinson, *Women Jurors*, 1 CHI. L. TIMES 22, 25 (1887) [hereafter Robinson, *Women Jurors*].

117. *Letter from Clara Foltz*, N. NORTHWEST, Dec. 17, 1885, at 4.

118. DRACHMAN, WOMEN LAWYERS, at 120–21.

119. Robinson, *Women Jurors*.

120. Rosencrantz v. Territory, 2 WASH. TERR. 267, 5 P.305 (1884); Harland v. Territory, 3 WASH. TERR. 131, 13 P.453 (1887); Bloomer v. Todd, 3 WASH. TERR. 599, 19 P.135 (1888); Aaron H. Caplan, *The History of Women's Jury Service in Washington*, 59 WASH. ST. BAR NEWS (2005).

121. *Admirable Pen Picture.*

122. Foltz, *Struggles*, Sept. 1917. On the Occidental and hotel life, *see* OSCAR LEWIS & CARROLL D. HALL, BONANZA INN: AMERICA'S FIRST LUXURY HOTEL (1939), and AMELIA RANSOME NEVILLE, THE FANTASTIC CITY: MEMOIRS OF THE SOCIAL AND ROMANTIC LIFE OF OLD SAN FRANCISCO 225 (1932).

123. *A New Chapter*, SAN DIEGO BEE, May 16, 1887.

124. THEODORE VAN DYKE, MILLIONAIRES OF A DAY: AN INSIDE HISTORY OF THE GREAT SOUTHERN CALIFORNIA "BOOM" 41 (1890) [hereafter, VAN DYKE, MILLIONAIRES].

125. WALTER GIFFORD SMITH, THE STORY OF SAN DIEGO 154 (1892).

126. WILLIAM E. SMYTHE, HISTORY OF SAN DIEGO, 1542–1907 431 (1907).

127. *The Women to Have an Organ in San Diego*, SAN DIEGO UNION, Apr. 13, 1887.

128. FRANKLIN WALKER, SAN FRANCISCO'S LITERARY FRONTIER 277 (1939) [hereafter WALKER, LITERARY FRONTIER]. For a history of *The Golden Era*, *see* MIGHELS, STORY, at 14–32.

129. WALKER, LITERARY FRONTIER, at 277.

130. *Editorial*, GOLDEN ERA, April 1888, describing the antecedent *Stingaree*.

131. *Editorial*, SAN DIEGO BEE, May 27, 1887.

132. *The Queen Bee*, SAN DIEGO BEE, Nov. 20, 1887; *Editorial*, SAN DIEGO BEE, June 5, 1887.

133. Frona Wait, *Fashion and Fancy*, SAN DIEGO BEE, Oct. 3, 1887; Clare Crane, *The Villa Montezuma as a Product of Its Time*, 33 J. SAN DIEGO HIST. (Spring 1987) (special edition devoted to the villa's centennial); *see also Villa Montezuma 1887–1987*, 33 SAN DIEGO HIST. 70 (1987).

134. Clare Crane, *Jesse Shepard and the Spark of Genius*, 33 SAN DIEGO HIST. 70, 107 (1987).

135. *Editorial*, SAN DIEGO BEE, May 19, 1887.

136. Ibid.

137. HARR WAGNER, JOAQUIN MILLER AND HIS OTHER SELF 8 (1929) ("most picturesque"); *Passing of Tennyson, in* THE COMPLETE POETICAL WORKS OF JOAQUIN

MILLER 225 (1902) ("kingly kinsmen"); MIGHELS, STORY 281 ("brave, bonnie"); *An Elegant Soiree*, SAN DIEGO BEE, July 27, 1887 (program at Villa Montezuma). For more on Joaquin Miller, *see* WALKER, LITERARY FRONTIER (Miller mentioned and used as an example of Western literary type throughout), and a number of respectful biographers, including MARTIN SEVERIN PETERSON, LITERARY FRONTIERSMAN (1937), and at least one debunker, M. MARION MARBERRY, SPLENDID POSEUR: JOAQUIN MILLER, AMERICAN POET (1953).

138. *"Not Quite Dead"; Futile Attempt to Crush the Bee, Russian Tactics Tried in America; A Free Press Not to Be Muzzled*, SAN DIEGO BEE, June 13, 1887. Subsequent paragraphs rely on this article, which related the events of the previous weekend.

139. *Editorial*, SAN DIEGO UNION, June 12, 1887.

140. SAN DIEGO BEE, June 26, 1887.

141. *Editorial*, SAN DIEGO BEE, June 25, 1887.

142. *Open Secrets*, SAN DIEGO UNION, June 29, 1887.

143. SAN JOSE WKLY. MERCURY, July 2, 1887.

144. *Editorial*, SAN DIEGO BEE, May 17, 28, 30, 1887.

145. *Editorial*, SAN DIEGO BEE, July 17, 1887.

146. *Editorial*, SAN DIEGO BEE, June 14, 1887 ("To falsely charge an editor with blackmail is and ought to be a criminal offense").

147. FREMONT OLDER, MY OWN STORY 28 (1919); *A Gentle Hint*, SAN DIEGO BEE, May 18, 1887.

148. SAN DIEGO UNION, July 2, 1887; SAN DIEGO BEE, July 3, 1887.

149. SAN DIEGO UNION, July 5, 1887 (text of Foltz's remarks).

150. CORONADO MERCURY, July 5, 1887, *reported in* SAN DIEGO BEE, July 15, 1887.

151. SAN DIEGO SUN, Aug. 23, 1887, *quoted in* SAN DIEGO BEE, Aug. 26, 1887.

152. WESTERN CARPETBAGGER: THE EXTRAORDINARY MEMOIRS OF "SENATOR" THOMAS FITCH 175 (Eric N. Moody ed., 1978).

153. SAN DIEGO BEE, Aug. 26, 1887.

154. *No Sale of the Bee*, SAN DIEGO BEE, Oct. 28, 1887; *The Bee Banquet*, SAN DIEGO BEE, Nov. 17, 1887; *The Queen Bee*, SAN DIEGO BEE, Nov. 20, 1887.

155. *Good Bye*, SAN DIEGO BEE, Nov. 17, 1887.

156. SAN DIEGO BEE, Dec. 31, 1887, *reprinted from* SAN JOSE MERCURY (Foltz no longer editor).

157. *See* AN ILLUSTRATED HISTORY OF SOUTHERN CALIFORNIA 406 (1890), describing the Ensenada situation in terms favorable to Burton.

158. SAN DIEGO BEE, Oct. 11, 1887 ("lady lawyer"). Throughout December of 1887, the *San Diego Bee* reported Foltz's social activities: Dec. 6 (Trella in town); Dec. 14 (Gunn and Foltz to Tucson); and Dec. 22 (Laura Gordon visit).

159. *See Editorial*, SAN DIEGO BEE, Sept. 18, 1887 (cannot be a deputy prosecutor because she "wears a bustle instead of a cutaway coat").

160. *Miss Kate Field, The Distinguished Litterateur, Arrives in the City*, SAN DIEGO BEE, Feb. 8, 1888.

161. SAN DIEGO BEE, Feb. 11, 1888.

162. SAN DIEGO BEE, Feb. 19, 1888.

163. Cummins, *Foltz History.*

164. GOLDEN ERA, Dec. 1888, at 754.

165. *See A Brilliant Party of Pleasure-Seekers Picnic at Ocean Beach and Visit Point Loma and Roseville,* SAN DIEGO BEE, Dec. 19, 1897; SAN DIEGO BEE, Jan. 10, 1888 (announcement of real estate practice).

166. VAN DYKE, MILLIONAIRES 145.

167. SAN DIEGO BEE, Apr. 4 and 12, 1888. Also, *see Clara Foltz to Boom San Diego,* L.A. TIMES, Apr. 13, 1888.

168. SAN DIEGO BEE, Apr. 3, 1888 (quoting the NATIONAL CITY RECORD).

169. *Boom! Bang! San Diego Celebrates Independence Day,* SAN DIEGO BEE, July 6, 1888; *Speech of Clara S. Foltz,* SAN DIEGO UNION, July 6, 1888.

170. *Letter,* WOMAN'S TRIB., Nov. 10, 1888, at 6.

171. VAN DYKE, MILLIONAIRES 150, quoting an "old timer."

172. Formation of the bar reported in SAN DIEGO BEE, Oct. 23 and 26, 1887; KENNETH M. JOHNSON, BAR ASSOCIATION OF SAN FRANCISCO: THE FIRST ONE HUNDRED YEARS 4, 12 (1972); SMYTHE, HISTORY OF SAN DIEGO, at 432 (number of lawyers as of September 1888).

173. For more on Works, *see* SHUCK, BENCH AND BAR (Works entry).

174. Opinion, Aug. 22, 1887, *in* Record of the White Divorce, Arvilla White v. Richard White (1888) (San Diego District Court, 18th Judicial District of California, 1887–1888, appendix to the new trial motion filed by Clara Foltz, found in Research Archives, San Diego Historical Society) [hereafter White v. White Archives].

175. SAN DIEGO BEE, Aug. 11, 1887 (supporting husband); SAN DIEGO BEE, Sept. 21, 1887 (supporting wife); *The Bee Again Called to the Unpleasant Task of Airing Dirty Family Linen,* SAN DIEGO BEE, Oct. 26, 1887 (describing complaint).

176. Complaint for Divorce, filed Oct. 24, 1887, White v. White Archives. Subsequent paragraphs refer to this complaint.

177. SAN DIEGO BEE, May 28 and June 7, 1888.

178. SAN DIEGO BEE, Nov. 12, 1888.

179. Cummins, *Foltz History.*

180. SAN JOSE MERCURY, May 17, 1882 (quoting ST. HELENA STAR). For more on nineteenth-century theater in San Francisco, *see* EDMOND M. GAGEY, THE SAN FRANCISCO STAGE 128–64 (1950), and FREDERICK G. ROSS, THE ACTOR FROM POINT ARENA (1977).

181. *Marriage of Dr. C. T. Tolland [sic] and Miss Trella Foltz,* S.F. CALL, Oct. 29, 1888.

182. Mona Caird, *Marriage,* WESTMINSTER REVIEW 186–201 (1888), reprinted in MONA CAIRD, THE MORALITY OF MARRIAGE AND OTHER ESSAYS ON THE STATUS AND DESTINY OF WOMEN (1983); ELIZABETH CADY STANTON, EIGHTY YEARS AND MORE: REMINISCENCES 1815–1897, 381 (1898) ("stirred the press"); WILLIAM SHIRER, LOVE AND HATRED: THE STORMY MARRIAGE OF LEO AND SONYA TOLSTOY 131 (1994) ("sometimes I watched"; suggesting that the story pictured the Tolstoys' marriage); THOMAS FITCH, ANNA MARISKA FITCH, BETTER DAYS; OR, A MILLIONAIRE OF TOMORROW 191 (1891) ("nothing is so prolific").

183. *See Is Marriage a Failure?* San Diego Bee, Oct. 15, 1888.

184. Foltz, *Struggles*, July 1916 (quoting Tennyson, *The Princess*, Canto 7). Foltz was evidently writing from memory because she substituted the word *mental* for *sweetness* in the second quoted line.

185. Myra Bradwell, *All Dabble in the Law*, Chi. Trib., May 12, 1889, at 2.

186. Foltz, Scrapbook, Interview (New York paper, Feb. 1928).

187. San Diego Bee, Mar. 31, 1888.

188. *See, e.g., David S. Terry Killed*, N.Y. Times, Aug. 15, 1899.

189. Foltz, *Struggles*, Mar. 1917.

190. S.F. Call, Nov. 22, 1890.

191. Edward Bellamy, Looking Backward (Daniel H. Borus ed., 1995) 156 (1888).

192. Charlotte Perkins Stetson Gilman, The Living of Charlotte Perkins Gilman, 1860–1935 122 (1972) (originally published in 1935) ("swift enthusiasms"); Arthur E. Morgan, Edward Bellamy 266–67 (1944) (other quotes).

193. Charlotte Perkins [Gilman] Stetson, Women and Economics: A Study of the Economic Relation between Men and Women as a Factor in Social Evolution 149 (1900).

194. F. I. Vassault, *Nationalism in California*, 15 Overland Monthly 660 (1890).

195. On the relationship of Bellamy Nationalism and the public defender, *see* Babcock, *Inventing*, at 1298–1301, and Chapter 7.

196. *Letter from Clara Foltz*, San Diego Bee, Jan. 31, 1890.

197. Letter from Foltz to Robert Waterman (Apr. 23, 1890) (Waterman Papers, California State Archives, Sacramento) (explaining her financial situation and seeking a loan).

Chapter Three

1. San Jose Daily Mercury, Nov. 7, 1890 (death); Nov. 9, 1890 (funeral).

2. Ibid.

3. *Foltz, Mrs. Clara Shortridge, in* Woman of the Century 293–94 (description of Elias); Foltz, *Struggles*, Apr. 1916 ("interest in every").

4. San Jose Daily Mercury, Jan. 4, 1891.

5. *Dr. Toland's Death, He Expires Suddenly at His Office, His Wife Prostrated by Finding the Dead Body of Her Husband*, S.F. Chron., Apr. 7, 1891; *see* similar stories in Daily Alta, Apr. 9, 1891; S.F. Examiner, Apr. 7, 1891; *Obituary*, S.F. Call, Apr. 7, 1891.

6. Letter from Clara Foltz to Stephen White (Sept. 21, 1890), *in* White Papers.

7. Ibid.

8. Williams, Democratic Party, at 44 (1973) (White quotation); Western Carpetbagger: The Extraordinary Memoirs of "Senator" Thomas Fitch 179 (Eric N. Moody ed., 1978) (Stanford payment).

9. Letter from Clara Foltz to Stephen White (Sept. 21, 1890), *in* White Papers ("a large audience"); Bullough, Blind Boss 221 ("I don't know").

10. BULLOUGH, BLIND BOSS, at 224–25 and 314–15 n.54. *See also* Alexander Callow Jr., *The Legislature of a Thousand Scandals*, 39 HIST. SOC. S. CAL. Q. 340 (1957).

11. *The Pardon-Broking Iniquity*, L.A. TIMES, Nov. 26, 1887.

12. For the background of parole reform, *see* Sheldon L. Messinger, John E. Berecochea, David Rauma & Richard A. Berk, *The Foundations of Parole in California*, 19 L. & SOC. REV. 1, 69–106 (1985).

13. *Mrs. Foltz's Penological Bill*, L.A. TIMES, Feb. 23, 1891.

14. Clara Shortridge Foltz, in BENCH AND BAR OF SAN FRANCISCO AND CALIFORNIA 109 (1926) ("pioneer[ing] the movement"); DAVID J. ROTHMAN, CONSCIENCE AND CONVENIENCE: THE ASYLUM AND ITS ALTERNATIVES IN PROGRESSIVE AMERICA (1980) (parole movement as Progressive measure).

15. SAN JOSE WKLY. MERCURY, Nov. 1, 1877, at 3.

16. *The Female Notary*, 31 CHI. LEGAL NEWS, Jan. 10, 1898, at 21 (quoting the *West Virginia Bar*).

17. CAL. POL. CODE at 792, 794 (as amended) (1891); Letter from Clara Foltz to H. H. Markham (Feb. 28, 1891) (H. H. Markham Papers, California State Archives, Sacramento) [hereafter Markham Papers].

18. SAN JOSE DAILY MERCURY, Mar. 7, 1891, at 3 (quoting S.F. REPORTER).

19. Wells Drury to H. H. Markham (Apr. 10, 1891), *in* Markham Papers.

20. *Editorial*, SAN DIEGO BEE, May 17, 1887.

21. *True Dignity* (editorial), SAN DIEGO BEE, May 20, 1887 (assailed the papers); Foltz, *Struggles*, May 1918 (office a labor bureau).

22. EVERETT W. MACNAIR, EDWARD BELLAMY AND THE NATIONALIST MOVEMENT, 1889 TO 1894, at 203–4, 245 (1957) (Foltz and Smith on the same platforms); Letter from Anna Smith, LIBERAL THINKER (Jan. 1890) (Smith introducing Foltz to the free-thought movement).

23. S.F. EXAMINER, Apr. 28, 1894. For more on Smith's career, *see* MARI JO BUHLE, WOMEN AND AMERICAN SOCIALISM, 1870–1920 74, 120 (1981).

24. *Attorney and Counselor, An Office for the Protection of the City's Millions*, S.F. EXAMINER, Oct. 22, 1892.

25. *Could the Suppression of Prize Fights Be Beneficial? A Woman Speaks Out*, S.F. CALL, Oct. 23, 1892.

26. SAN DIEGO BEE, Oct. 17, 1887.

27. *Attorney and Counselor, An Office for the Protection of the City's Millions*, S.F. EXAMINER, Oct. 22, 1892.

28. PAUL F. BOLLER JR., PRESIDENTIAL CAMPAIGNS: FROM GEORGE WASHINGTON TO GEORGE W. BUSH 165 (1984) [hereafter BOLLER, CAMPAIGNS] ("White House iceberg") and at 145 ("each side").

29. ANNIE L. DIGGS, THE STORY OF JERRY SIMPSON 105–6 (1908).

30. *Wild Cheering for Weaver, The People's Party Candidate Addresses a Vast Gathering, Mrs. Lease Pelted with Dollars*, S.F. EXAMINER, Aug. 10, 1892.

31. For more on the election and aftermath, *see* WILLIAMS, DEMOCRATIC PARTY, at 160–67; Harold Taggart, *The Senatorial Election of 1893 in California*, 19 CAL. HIST. SOC. Q. 59 (1940).

32. Foltz, *Struggles*, July 1918, for this and subsequent paragraphs unless otherwise noted.

33. For the arson case, *see* Chapter 7 and Foltz, *Struggles*, Jan.–Mar. 1918.

34. CLARA FOLTZ, 3 THE TRAVELER (1893), at 24 [hereafter FOLTZ, TRAVELER].

35. *Mrs. Starke Resists*, S.F. CALL, June 17, 1892 [hereafter *Mrs. Starke Resists*]. Elmira Starke's story is also reported in the *Chronicle* and the *Examiner*, June 17–19, 1892, and told in Foltz, *Struggles*, Mar.–Apr. 1918. In the story that follows, quotations are from Foltz, *Struggles*, Apr. 1918, unless otherwise noted.

36. Foltz, *Struggles*, Mar. 1918 ("Beau Brummel"); SHUCK, BENCH AND BAR, at 854 ("Though pressed"). For Hanlon's impressive income, *see Charles F. Hanlon, in* BENCH AND BAR OF SAN FRANCISCO AND CALIFORNIA 109 (1926) ($90,000 in fees for one suit).

37. *Mrs. Starke Resists.*

38. *Elmira's Eviction*, S.F. CHRON., June 18, 1892 [hereafter *Elmira's Eviction*].

39. *Elmira to Be Fired*, S.F. CHRON., June 19, 1892.

40. Foltz, *Struggles*, Mar. 1918.

41. *Elmira's Eviction.*

42. Ibid.

43. Foltz, *Struggles*, May 1918.

44. *Is It a Bastille?* S.F. CALL, Mar. 16, 1894; Foltz, *Struggles*, Apr. 1918.

45. William Chambliss, S.F. EXAMINER, *quoted in* DORIS MUSCATINE, OLD SAN FRANCISCO: THE BIOGRAPHY OF A CITY 374–75 (1975).

46. John J. Ingalls, *quoted in* DONALD L. MILLER, CITY OF THE CENTURY: THE EPIC OF CHICAGO AND THE MAKING OF AMERICA 494 (1996).

47. Garland *quoted in* RAY GINGER, AGE OF EXCESS 161 (1964).

48. FINAL REPORT OF THE CALIFORNIA WORLD'S FAIR COMMISSION 93 (1894).

49. Ambrose Bierce *quoted in* EMILY WORTIS LEIDER, CALIFORNIA'S DAUGHTER 131–32 (1991).

50. *For Needy Women: The Movement Started in Their Behalf*, S.F. CALL, Jan. 9, 1894 ("poverty and distress"); *Now the Portia Law Club*, S.F. EXAMINER, Jan. 20, 1894 ("number of society ladies") [hereafter *Now the Portia*].

51. AMELIA RANSOME NEVILLE, THE FANTASTIC CITY: MEMOIRS OF THE SOCIAL AND ROMANTIC LIFE OF OLD SAN FRANCISCO 249 (1932).

52. S.F. CALL, Mar. 3, 1895, at 4–5.

53. 4 HWS, at 479; *Now the Portia.*

54. Foltz, *Struggles*, June 1917.

55. *Portia Law Club, Ambitious Organization of Ladies: Its Object the Establishment of a Law College for Women, Striking Costumes*, S.F. CALL, Jan. 4, 1894, at 7.

56. Ibid.

57. *No Bonnets on Tuesday Night*, S.F. CALL, Mar. 3, 1895 ("to show the men"); *Ladies Removed Their Headgear*, S.F. CALL, Mar. 6, 1895 ("maids will be in attendance").

58. DORIS MUSCATINE, OLD SAN FRANCISCO 362–63 (1975).

59. S.F. CHRON., June 12, 1894, *quoted in* CHI. LEGAL NEWS, Jun. 23, 1894, at 345.

60. *Modern Portias: The St. Nicholas Parlors Too Small for the Club's Admirers,*

S.F. CALL, Nov. 4, 1894, at 2. Unless otherwise noted, subsequent paragraphs rely on this source.

61. *See* WILLIAM SHAKESPEARE, THE MERCHANT OF VENICE, act. 4, sc. 1 ("The quality of mercy is not strained . . .").

62. KENNETH LAMOTT, WHO KILLED MR. CRITTENDEN? 284–85 (1963) (suffragists attending the trial); *see also* Chapter 5 for more on *Fair* case.

63. *A Judge Condemned*, S.F. CHRON., Sept. 2, 1894, at 22 (speaking of a woman litigant, although the quotation was equally applicable to herself as the lone woman lawyer).

64. Ibid.

65. For more on Delmas, *see* SHUCK, BENCH AND BAR, at 625.

66. *Kissed by Henry*, S.F. CALL, July 27, 1894.

67. *Was It His Son?* S.F. CALL, July 31, 1894. For daily newspaper articles on the trial, *see* the *Call, Chronicle, Examiner,* and *Evening Bulletin* for July 10, 1894–Sept. 26, 1894. Newspapers in San Jose and Sacramento also followed the case extensively.

68. *The Kissing in the Case*, S.F. EXAMINER, July 25, 1894.

69. *Portia Club Meeting*, S.F. EXAMINER, Sept. 2, 1894.

70. *For the Boy*, S.F. CALL, Sept. 20, 1894.

71. *Appealed to Their Reason*, S.F. EXAMINER, Sept. 21, 1894.

72. Ibid.

73. Ibid. ("brilliantly marshaled"); *Talking against Baby John*, S.F. EXAMINER, Sept. 25, 1894 ("maimed mendicant").

74. *Watched through the Blinds*, S.F. EXAMINER, Aug. 3, 1894 (women spectators made him uncomfortable); *The Martin Will*, S.F. BULLETIN, Aug. 6, 1894 ("constantly making comments"); *Light Will Fail*, S.F. BULLETIN, Aug. 7, 1894 (whispered and dozed).

75. *As Her Enemy's Witness*, S.F. EXAMINER, Aug. 11, 1894.

76. *Coffey Rebuked*, S.F. CALL, Sept. 2, 1894.

77. *A Judge Condemned*, S.F. CHRON., Sept. 2, 1894.

78. *Fair Women and the Law: Mrs. Clara Foltz Makes a Cutting Reply to the Cold Criticisms of Judge Coffey*, S.F. EXAMINER, Sept. 2, 1894.

79. Ibid.

80. S.F. CALL, Sept. 2, 1884.

81. Foltz, *Struggles*, Sept. 1917.

82. Letter from Clara Foltz to Jane Stanford and Letter from Clara Foltz to H. C. Nash (Aug. 28, 1893) (Box 2, Folder 33, Jane Stanford Papers, Department of Special Collections, Stanford University Libraries).

83. TRAVELER, at 24.

84. *Judges Cannot Bluff Him: "Nobby" Clarke in Jail Talks about the Superior Judges*, S.F. EXAMINER, Oct. 24, 1893 (sketch). For more on Clarke, *see* 3 THE BAY OF SAN FRANCISCO: THE METROPOLIS OF THE PACIFIC COAST AND ITS SUBURBAN CITIES 343–45 (1892) (Clarke entry) [hereafter BAY OF SAN FRANCISCO].

85. Clarke v. McDade, 165 U.S. 168 (1897).

86. Unless noted otherwise, direct quotations that follow are from Foltz, *Struggles*, May 1918.

87. *Cruelties in a Madhouse: Six Days for a Reporter*, S.F. EXAMINER, May 29, 1894.

88. SHUCK, BENCH AND BAR, at 522 (Sawyer entry).

89. *How Von Schmidt Was Used at the Home*, S.F. CALL, Feb. 7, 1895.

90. *Said He'd Send Her Too*, S.F. BULLETIN, Feb. 7, 1895 (wife and friends testifying).

91. *See Defends the Home: The Story of Colonel Von Schmidt*, S.F. CHRON., Feb. 7, 1895, for subsequent references to father's testimony.

92. Quotations in this paragraph from *Strapped to the Same Bed: Scenes in the Trial of the Suit against the Managers of the Home for Inebriates*, S.F. EXAMINER, Feb. 12, 1895.

93. *A Verdict for Von Schmidt*, S.F. EXAMINER, Feb. 14, 1895 (describing last day of testimony).

94. *See Against Dr. Potter Von Schmidt Was Maltreated at the Home: Attorney Clara Foltz's Powerful Plea for Her Client: The Blundering Work of the Jury*, S.F. CHRON., Feb. 13, 1895, for this and subsequent paragraphs.

95. *Jurors Regret a Blunder*, S.F. CALL, Feb. 14, 1895.

96. Foltz, *Struggles*, May 1918.

97. *Editorial*, SACRAMENTO RECORD-UNION, Feb. 26, 1879.

98. S.F. CALL, Apr. 28, 1895.

99. *Interview with Clara Foltz*, S.F. CALL, Oct. 15, 1895.

100. *See* NORGREN, BELVA LOCKWOOD 110–23, on suffragists and Utah statehood.

101. *Political and Personal*, SALT LAKE TRIB., May 11, 1895.

102. Edward Leo Lyman, *Isaac Trumbo and the Politics of Utah Statehood*, 41 UTAH HIST. Q., 128 (1973), quoting Field at 130 and letter from Trumbo to Mormon Church leaders, Jan. 6, 1896, about his lobbying services at 144. For more on Trumbo, *see* 2 BAY OF SAN FRANCISCO, at 486–87 (Trumbo entry); *Obituary*, S.F. CHRON., Nov. 9, 1912.

103. *A Noted Visitor, Mrs. Clara S. Foltz of San Francisco, May Locate Here*, NEW STAR, May 7, 1895.

104. *See* Foltz, *Struggles*, Sept. 1917, for her telling of the story in this and subsequent paragraphs.

105. SAN DIEGO BEE, Aug. 10 and 12, 1887.

106. 3 MILLS ANN. STAT., Colorado, Ch. 43, 1562, 1566 (1904).

107. Richard Johnson Bolles v. Julia Sherman Bolles (June 11–12, 1895) (complaint, answer and cross-claim, order and decree) (District Court, El Paso Cty., Colo.) (on file in court archives and with the author); *Mrs. Bolles Gets a Divorce*, DENVER REPUBLICAN, June 13, 1895.

108. *Big Alimony Allowed*, ROCKY MOUNTAIN NEWS, June 13, 1895, at 1; *Given a Divorce*, FORT WAYNE SENTINEL, June 12, 1895 (reprint).

109. Foltz, *Struggles*, Sept. 1917.

110. *Woman at the Bar* (description of Foltz in San Francisco); *Clara Foltz in New York*, S.F. CALL, July 18, 1895 (*reprinted from* N.Y. WORLD).

111. *Number Guests for the Fourth at Newport: The Clambake Club to Have an Outing—Mrs. Kernochan's Lawn Party*, N.Y. TIMES, July 4, 1895.

112. Trella Toland's Autograph Book, at WLH website.

113. Foltz, *Struggles*, Apr. 1917.

114. Foltz, *Struggles*, Sept. 1917; for more on Paris at the time, *see* KARL BAEDE-KER, BAEDEKER'S PARIS AND ITS ENVIRONS (1888).

115. *See* Foltz, *Struggles*, Sept.–Dec. 1917 and Jan. 1918, for her telling of the story quoted throughout this section. For coverage in the U.S. press, *see Paid for Lost Property*, S.F. CALL, Oct. 6, 1895; *Mrs. Foltz Home Again*, Oct. 15, 1895; *Incidents of Seaford's Wreck*, N.Y. TIMES, Aug. 21, 1895. For coverage in the British press, *see The Sinking of the Seaford*, DAILY GRAPHIC, Aug. 22, 1895; *Alarming Collision in the Channel, Foundering of the Seaford, Escape of 300 Passengers and Crew*, DAILY TELEGRAPH, Aug. 21, 1895; *The Wreck of the S.S. "Seaford" by a Passenger*, PALL MALL GAZETTE, Aug. 23, 1895.

116. *See* Foltz, *Struggles*, Oct. 1917, for this and subsequent paragraphs.

117. Foltz, *Struggles*, Nov. 1917, for this and subsequent paragraphs.

118. Foltz, *Struggles*, Dec. 1917.

119. Foltz, *Struggles*, Jan. 1918.

120. *Mrs. Foltz in a Collision at Sea*, CHI. DAILY TRIB., Oct. 1, 1895, at 3.

121. Foltz, *Struggles*, Nov. 1917.

122. *A Representative Lady Advocate Says a Last Public Word*, S.F. CALL, Oct. 31, 1895.

123. *See* Hildegarde Tellhut & Anthony Boucher, *"The Demon in the Belfry"—The Case of Theodore Durrant* (1895), *in* SAN FRANCISCO MURDERS 51–121 (Marie F. Rodell ed., 1947).

124. *See The Corridors Rang with Strife, It Was a Day of Wild Riot around Judge Murphy's Court*, S.F. EXAMINER, Oct. 30, 1895; S.F. CHRON., Oct. 30, 1895 ("A Parisian mob in conduct rattled boisterously at the door").

125. *All Bade Her Godspeed*, S.F. CALL, Nov. 5, 1895, for this and the next paragraph.

126. *Mrs. Foltz Home Again*, S.F. CALL, Oct. 15, 1895 ("retained by two firms"); *Established in Gotham: Mrs. Clara Foltz Opens an Office at the Metropolis of the Nation*, S.F. CALL, Jan. 18, 1896.

Chapter Four

1. S.F. CALL, Jan. 18, 1895. A copy of the card, with jottings on the back by Elizabeth Cady Stanton, is in THE PAPERS OF ELIZABETH CADY STANTON AND SUSAN B. ANTHONY (Patricia Holland & Ann Gordon eds., 1991).

2. *Will Practice Law Here: Made Her Reputation in the West*, N.Y. TIMES, Jan. 17, 1896; subsequent quotations are from this source.

3. *Mrs. Foltz to the Bar*, N.Y. WORLD, Feb. 21, 1896; N.Y. TIMES, Feb. 21, 1896.

4. For more information on Tracy, *see* BENJAMIN FRANKLIN COOLING, BENJAMIN FRANKLIN TRACY: FATHER OF THE MODERN AMERICAN FIGHTING NAVY (1973).

5. *Women Who Practice Law; But Little Encouragement Is Offered to New Aspi-*

rants; Those Who Are Succeeding Find That It Is Wiser to Employ a Masculine Proxy to Argue Cases, N.Y. DAILY TRIB., July 2, 1898, at 7 [hereafter *Women Who Practice*].

6. For more on Stoneman, *see* Judge Judith S. Kaye, *How to Accomplish Success: The Example of Kate Stoneman*, 57 ALB. L. REV., 961 (1994).

7. For more on Titus, *see Women's Power to Invent: What She Has Accomplished in Business and the Professions*, N.Y. TIMES, Mar. 11, 1894; *To Practice Law Her Desire*, N.Y. TIMES, Apr. 10, 1894; *Melle Stanleyetta Titus*, 3 L. STUDENT'S HELPER, 75 (1896).

8. *Our Learned Brother: Interviewed as to His Attitude toward His Sister-in-Law*, N.Y. TIMES, June 16, 1895.

9. *These Women Know Law, but They Don't Look at All Like Typical Lawyers*, N.Y. TIMES, Apr. 11, 1891; on Sutro, *see A High Priestess of the Temple of Music*, CLUB-WOMAN MAG., June 1899.

10. Mrs. Theodore Sutro, *Why I Study Law*, SUCCESS MAG., Oct. 1912 (reprinted from graduation speech); *A Representative Lady Advocate Says a Last Public Word*, S.F. CALL, Oct. 31, 1895 ("come down a little").

11. Lillie Devereux Blake, *Our New York Letter*, WOMAN'S J., May 9, 1896, at 149 (description of the speech and huge turnout, one thousand people, for the ceremony).

12. *Our Women Graduates in Law*, N.Y. DAILY TRIB., Apr. 30, 1896, for this and subsequent paragraphs.

13. *Mrs. Foltz on Suffrage: The Well-Known Lady Lawyer Compares the East with the West*, S.F. CALL, Apr. 1, 1896.

14. Rosalie Loew, *Women Lawyers of the New York Bar*, METROPOLITAN MAG., June 1896, at 279–84; subsequent paragraphs rely on this source.

15. For more on Loew and her later career, *see* Rada Blumkin, *Rosalie Loew Whitney: The Early Years as Advocate for the Poor* (2001), and DANIELLE HAAS-LAURSEN, ROSALIE LOEW WHITNEY: LAWYER, CRIME FIGHTER, JUDGE, POLITICAL ACTIVIST, SUFFRAGIST (2001), both at WLH website.

16. N.Y. DAILY TRIB., July 2, 1898.

17. *Our Learned Brother: Interviewed as to His Attitude toward His Sister-in-Law*, N.Y. TIMES, June 16, 1895; Dudley Sicher, *Memorial of Rosalie Loew Whitney*, YEAR-BOOK OF THE ASSOCIATION OF THE BAR OF THE CITY OF NEW YORK (1940).

18. In her written answers to a questionnaire included in the first in-depth study of women lawyers, Foltz said it was a mistake for women to devote themselves to legal aid and charity work exclusively. *See* Beatrice Doerschuk, *Women in the Law: An Analysis of Training, Practice and Salaried Positions* (Dec. 1920), *available at* http://nrs.harvard.edu/urn-3:RAD.SCHL:717741, Bureau of Vocational Information (New York).

19. For more on Carter, *see* Lewis Grossman, *James Coolidge Carter and Mugwump Jurisprudence*, 20 L. HIST. REV. 3 (2002); 2 HISTORY OF THE BENCH AND BAR OF NEW YORK (1897) (Carter entry).

20. *Modern Portias in Practice; What Prominent Attorneys Think of Women Attorneys*, N.Y. TIMES, Mar. 11, 1894.

21. *Women Who Practice*.

22. Foltz, *Struggles*, Oct. 1916 ("amidst the cries"); Alice Severance, *Talks with Successful Women*, GODEY'S MAG., May 1, 1896.

23. *Why Not a Public Defender?* DAILY MERCURY, May 10, 1893.

24. On Tammany Hall, *see* Carolyn B. Ramsey, *The Discretionary Power of "Public" Prosecutors in Historical Perspective*, 39 AM. CRIM. L. REV. 1339 (2002); ARTHUR TRAIN, MY DAY IN COURT 8–11 (1939) [hereafter TRAIN, MY DAY].

25. TRAIN, MY DAY, at 13.

26. Clara Foltz, *World's Fair Speech*, 48 ALB. L.J. 248 (1893).

27. For the Tombs, *see* BURROWS, GOTHAM, at 636.

28. *See* Foltz, *Public Defenders*, for this and the next paragraph.

29. *See Mrs. Clara S. Foltz's Idea of Shyster Practices*, DAILY EXAMINER, Apr. 11, 1885; RICHARD H. ROVERE, HOWE AND HUMMEL: THEIR TRUE AND SCANDALOUS HISTORY 6, 10 (1947) (origin of the word *shyster*).

30. ARTHUR TRAIN, THE PRISONER AT THE BAR 97 (1906).

31. *Mrs. Foltz to the Bar*, N.Y. TIMES, Feb. 21, 1896.

32. *Foltz Interview*, N.Y. TIMES MAG., July 11, 1897 [hereafter *Foltz Interview*].

33. *Her First Criminal Case*, N.Y. TIMES, Oct. 29, 1896.

34. *Wilted under Feminine Verbosity*, N.Y. DAILY TRIB., Feb. 19, 1897.

35. *See A Precedent; A Case of Importance to Newspaper Writers*, N.Y. TIMES, July 19, 1897.

36. *Mrs. Whitney Wins Her Lawsuit*, WOMAN'S J., June 26, 1897, at 202.

37. *In the Public Eye*, MUNCEY'S MAG., Sept. 1895 ("heroine"); *For the New Woman: Clara S. Foltz, A Brilliant Lawyer, Defends Her*, CHI. DAILY TRIB., June 24, 1895 ("new woman" and following quotations).

38. 2 IDA HUSTED HARPER, LIFE AND WORK OF SUSAN B. ANTHONY 859 (1898) (Anthony quotation); *Mrs. Foltz in a Collision at Sea*, CHI. TRIB., Oct. 1, 1895 (Foltz quotation).

39. *See* Alice Severance, *Talks with Successful Women*, GODEY'S MAG., May 1, 1896; *Women Lawyers*, L'ILLUSTRATION, Nov. 6, 1897; *People Talked About*, 7 PETERSON'S MAG., May 1897.

40. *Foltz Interview*.

41. *Trella Toland and Her Autograph Book*, at WLH website. Subsequent references rely on this source.

42. *See Another California Girl Wins Laurels in New York*, S.F. CALL, July 19, 1896.

43. Trella Foltz Toland, *England's Trilby Boom; The Craze Started in America, Reaches the British Capital*, S.F. CALL, Jan. 19, 1896 (London dateline). On the Trilby effect, *see* THOMAS BEER, MAUVE DECADE: AMERICAN LIFE AT THE END OF THE NINETEENTH CENTURY 48–50 (1926); THEODORE DREISER, NEWSPAPER DAYS: AN AUTOBIOGRAPHY 545–46 (T. D. Nostwich ed., 1991) (describing the "strange psychologic effect" of the novel on him and on "most of the intelligentsia of America").

44. *Will of Mrs. Toland*, S.F. CALL, Nov. 30, 1895; *The Child Is Reaching Out for His Own, a Contest Made of the Will of Mrs. Mary B. Toland*, S.F. CALL, Dec. 28, 1895; Signature in Autograph Book, June 22, 1896 (Uncle Sam).

45. The story was heavily covered in the *Call* (Charles Shortridge was the editor). *See, e.g., Baby Toland Will Have a Big Nest Egg, Grandmother's Estate Settled, He Gains Nearly $20,000, Compromise Effected after Many Days,* S.F. CALL, Sept. 9, 1898.

46. *Mrs. Foltz, New York's Leading Woman Lawyer, Refused Food in a Restaurant Because She Was Unattended by a Man,* CHI. LEGAL NEWS, Feb. 28, 1897, at 243 (quotations); *see also Clara Foltz It [sic] Mad; A Gotham Restaurant Enforces a Rule against Her,* L.A. TIMES, Feb. 28, 1897.

47. *A Pained Restaurant Keeper,* NEWARK DAILY ADVOCATE, Apr. 3, 1897.

48. N.Y. WORLD, June 27, 1897, at 26.

49. *Foltz Interview.*

50. KATHERINE BLAKE & MARGARET LOUISE WALLACE, CHAMPION OF WOMEN 168 (1943) [hereafter CHAMPION OF WOMEN] (quoting a clipping from the SAN JOSE DAILY MERCURY, July 27, 1888).

51. The book was first published in 1874 and reprinted several years later. A definitive modern biography of Blake is GRACE FARRELL, LILLIE DEVEREUX BLAKE: RETRACING A LIFE ERASED (2002).

52. Ibid., at 155.

53. CHAMPION OF WOMEN, at 85.

54. The dinner is reported in Trella Toland, *A Budget of Interesting News and Gossip about the California Colony in the Eastern Metropolis,* S.F. CALL, Nov. 1, 1896. For more on Leslie, *see* MADELEINE B. STERN, PURPLE PASSAGE: THE LIFE OF MRS. FRANK LESLIE (1953); NOTABLE AMERICAN WOMEN (Leslie entry).

55. *Women Lawyers of America,* LESLIE'S ILLUSTRATED WKLY., Dec. 3, 1896, at 363, *reprinted* (with pictures) *in* S.F. CALL, Dec. 13, 1896. The other women lawyers pictured were Kate Pier of Wisconsin; Blanche Fearing, Ada Kepley and Ellen Martin of Chicago; and Emma Humphrey Haddock of Iowa.

56. *A Promising Enterprise,* Brochure, New York Public Library (no date, but internal evidence shows 1898 for issuance); subsequent paragraphs rely on this source.

57. James T. White, *Introduction,* THE NATIONAL CYCLOPAEDIA OF AMERICAN BIOGRAPHY vii–x (1891); for more on White, *see* 27 THE NATIONAL CYCLOPAEDIA OF AMERICAN BIOGRAPHY 44 (1939) (James T. White entry); *White Obituary,* N.Y. TIMES, Apr. 5, 1920.

58. *Eminent New York Attorney Now in Boise,* IDAHO DAILY STATESMAN, Feb. 21, 1898 ("cemented"); *Women Who Practice.*

59. Brown Palace registration records show Foltz's arrival there on October 18, 1898, and departure on the last day of December 1898. Report of her circular is found in CHI. LEGAL NEWS, Oct. 29, 1898; MECCA, Mar. 11, 1899, at 6 (Mrs. J. Sherman Bolles moved to Brown Palace after the Antlers in Colorado Springs was destroyed by fire).

60. *See* CHI. LEGAL NEWS, Nov. 26, 1898, at 116 (raising the likelihood that Foltz chose Denver because of woman suffrage).

61. *What the Mecca Is and Is Not,* 2 MECCA, Nov. 19, 1898, at 1.

62. *The Career of a Modern Portia,* 2 SUCCESS, Feb. 18, 1899, at 205–6, *reprinted in* SELECTED MAGAZINE ARTICLES OF THEODORE DREISER, LIFE AND ART IN THE

AMERICAN 1890s, 139–44 (Yoshinobu Hakutani ed., 1985); subsequent paragraphs rely on this article.

63. WOMAN'S TRIB., May 20, 1899.

64. *Mrs. Foltz Drops Legal Profession*, S. F. CHRON., Mar. 18, 1931 ("cradle of my ambitions").

65. *Clara Foltz Raps the Police Judges, Denounces Them as Youngsters Unfit to Hold Office*, S.F. CALL, July 14, 1899; *Let Women Take Law in Their Hands, Attorney Clara Foltz Very Angry at Judge Hall, Refused to Send Man to Prison at Her Request*, OAKLAND TRIB., Feb. 6, 1900, at 2; *Dr. Payne Gets Judgment*, S.F. CALL, Sept. 3, 1902 (dentist).

66. *Oil Boom in California, Los Angeles County the Centre of a Growing Industry, Many Quick Fortunes Made*, N.Y. TIMES, Mar. 2, 1900.

67. *Discovery*, OIL FIELDS AND FURNACES 1, June 1901 [hereafter *Discovery*]; subsequent paragraphs rely on this source.

68. Clara Foltz, *Through the Oil Fields A-Flying, In the Upper Ojai Valley*, OIL FIELDS AND FURNACES 74, Aug. 1901 [hereafter Foltz, *Through the Oil Fields*].

69. Clara Foltz, *McKinley the Beloved*, OIL FIELDS AND FURNACES, Sept. 1901.

70. OIL FIELDS AND FURNACES 51, Sept. 1901.

71. WOMAN'S J., Nov. 3, 1900, at 345.

72. *Discovery*.

73. *The Constitution and the Flag* (editorial), OIL FIELDS AND FURNACES 14, July 1901.

74. DeLima v. Bidwell, 182 U.S. 1 (1901) (first significant insular case); STUART CREIGHTON MILLER, BENEVOLENT ASSIMILATION: THE AMERICAN CONQUEST OF THE PHILIPPINES 157 (1982) (quotations from Dooley and Root); Clara Foltz, *Comment*, OIL FIELDS AND FURNACES 1, Nov. 1901. For more on the legal doctrine involved in the insular cases, *see* BARTHOLOMEW H. SPARROW, THE INSULAR CASES AND THE EMERGENCE OF AMERICAN EMPIRE (2006).

75. ETHINGTON, PUBLIC CITY, at 387–98 (the politics of municipal charter reform).

76. For more on the Union–Labor Party, *see* WALTON BEAN, BOSS RUEF'S SAN FRANCISCO: THE STORY OF THE UNION LABOR PARTY, BIG BUSINESS AND THE GRAFT PROSECUTION (1952).

77. *"Folly" Will Be the Queen at Eastern Star Masquerade, Golden Gate Chapter of the Order Is Preparing to Give a Fancy Dress Ball*, S.F. CALL, Mar. 22, 1902; *New Club: The Cause of the Fair Sex to Occupy the Members*, S.F. CALL, Jan. 17, 1900; Clara Shortridge Foltz to Phoebe Hearst, Jan. 18, 1900 (Hearst Papers, Bancroft Library, Berkeley, California; on letterhead of Victory Mining Company, showing Foltz as counsel).

78. Foltz, *Struggles*, July 1918.

79. *Obituary*, N.Y. TIMES, Jan. 4, 1903.

80. Letter from Clara Foltz to Clara Colby (June 6, 1904) (Colby Papers, Huntington Library, San Marino, California); *To Organize Business Women; New Undertaking of First of State's Women Lawyers*, L.A. TIMES, June 21, 1905 [hereafter *To Organize*].

81. *To Organize.* For more on the bank, *see A Frisco Bank Closed, United Bank and Trust Co.'s Business Suspended by Commissioners,* N.Y. TIMES, Oct. 22, 1905; *Money Ready for Any Run, United Bank and Trust Company's Allegation, Commissioners May Prevent Opening of Doors,* L.A. TIMES, Oct. 23, 1905; *Violations of Law Charged, Serious Allegations against Bank's Officials, District Attorney May Take a Hand in the Case,* L.A. TIMES, Nov. 3, 1905.

82. Books and websites abound on the 1906 San Francisco earthquake, and all quote extensively from eyewitness accounts. On this score I found particularly useful MALCOLM E. BARKER, THREE FEARFUL DAYS: SAN FRANCISCO MEMOIRS OF THE 1906 EARTHQUAKE AND FIRE (2006); DAN KURZMAN, DISASTER! THE GREAT SAN FRANCISCO EARTHQUAKE AND FIRE OF 1906 (2001); GLADYS HANSEN & EMMET CONDON, DENIAL OF DISASTER: THE UNTOLD STORY AND PHOTOGRAPHS OF THE SAN FRANCISCO EARTHQUAKE AND FIRE OF 1906 (1989); and GORDON THOMAS & MAX MORGAN WITTS, THE SAN FRANCISCO EARTHQUAKE (1971).

83. *Classified Ad under Attorneys at Law,* OAKLAND TRIB., May 24, 1906, at 17.

84. *Legal Announcements,* OAKLAND TRIB., Apr. 21, 1906, at 12.

85. Foltz, *Through the Oil Fields,* at 74.

86. Letter from Clara Foltz to Ida Harper (Mar. 2, 1918) (on file in the Harbert Collection, Huntington Library, San Marino, California).

87. Foltz, Scrapbook, clipping from unknown Los Angeles paper, Oct. 19, 1910 (mentions that school has been in existence for several years).

88. Foltz, *Struggles,* Apr. 1916. On Foy, *see* Jane Apostal, *Mary Emily Foy: "Miss Los Angeles Herself,"* 78 S. CAL. Q. 2 (1996), and Chapter 6 (Foy in the suffrage campaign).

89. Letter from Georgia Bullock to Clara Shortridge Foltz (Mar. 28, 1928) (Bullock Papers, Box 25, UCLA Special Collections, Los Angeles).

90. OIL FIELDS AND FURNACES 63, Sept. 1901 ("ablest young lawyer"). On the success of the women's company, *see* LIONEL V. REDPATH, PETROLEUM IN CALIFORNIA: A CONCISE AND RELIABLE HISTORY OF THE OIL INDUSTRY OF THE STATE 82 (1900).

91. Letter from Clara Foltz to Clara Colby (Apr. 8, 1909), *in* Colby Papers; *Death Comes Quickly: Mrs. Shortridge Passes Away at Daughter's Home in This City, at Age of Eighty-Five Years,* L.A. TIMES, Jan. 11, 1910; *Mrs. F. C. [sic] Shortridge Called to Final Rest, Highly Esteemed Woman Who Resided in San Jose for Many Years,* SAN JOSE MERCURY, Jan. 12, 1910.

92. *Los Angeles Woman Put on Prison Board,* L.A. HERALD, Feb. 11, 1910.

93. For more on the California Club's campaigns, see GAYLE GULLETT, BECOMING CITIZENS: THE EMERGENCE AND DEVELOPMENT OF THE CALIFORNIA WOMEN'S MOVEMENT, 1880–1911 133–37 (2000).

94. L.A. TIMES, Feb. 11, 1910, *in* Foltz, Scrapbook.

95. *Los Angeles Woman Put on Prison Board,* L.A. HERALD, Feb. 11, 1910.

96. *Mrs. Foltz, Lawyer, Is Given State Office,* L.A. EXAMINER, Feb. 11, 1910 ("largely due" and "abolition"); *Honor for Mrs. Foltz,* L.J. OF L.A., Feb. 11, 1910; *Unsolicited Honors Worthily Bestowed,* TIDINGS, Feb. 18, 1910.

97. On the American Woman's League, *see* NORGREN, BELVA LOCKWOOD, at 219–20.

98. *Women's League to Have $50,000 House*, L.A. HERALD, Mar. 6, 1910, *in* Foltz, Scrapbook.

99. *A Woman District Attorney*, N.Y. TIMES, Apr. 25, 1910, *in* Foltz, Scrapbook (first in the country); *Honors for Mrs. Foltz*, L.A. CAL. J., Apr. 20, 1910 (Foltz quotation).

100. *Badger Club Wants Woman Prosecutor*, L.A. EXAMINER, Mar. 11, 1910.

101. *Innovation: First Woman Prosecutor!* L.A. TIMES, Apr. 24, 1910.

102. *Oath of Prosecutor Taken by Mrs. Foltz*, L.A. CAL. EXPRESS, Apr. 25, 1910.

103. *Reform Meeting Ends in Wild Disorder*, L.A. EXAMINER, June 28, 1910.

104. On the anti-vice campaign in Los Angeles, *see* Gerald Woods, *A Penchant for Probity: California Progressives and the Disreputable Pleasures, in California Progressivism Revisited* 99, 106 (William Deverell & Tom Sitton eds., 1994).

Chapter Five

1. THE LIBERAL THINKER (Matilda Gage & Josephine Cables Aldrich eds., 1890) [hereafter LIBERAL THINKER].

2. Clara Foltz, *Evolution of Law*, 48 ALB. L.J. 206 (1893); Foltz, *Should Women Be Executed?* 54 ALB. L.J. 309 (1896).

3. *See* Foltz, *Through the Oil Fields A-Flying*, OIL FIELDS AND FURNACES 58–59, Sept. 1901, quoting Henry Wadsworth Longfellow's *A Psalm of Life* (1848) and Thomas Moore's *Lalla Rookh* (1817).

4. Dept. of the Interior, Census Office, 1 REPORT ON POPULATION OF THE UNITED STATES AT THE ELEVENTH CENSUS: 1890, Part 2, at ci (1897); *see also* VIRGINIA G. DRACHMAN, SISTERS IN LAW: WOMEN LAWYERS IN MODERN AMERICAN HISTORY 253 (1998) (Table 2 charting the "decennial growth of women and men lawyers" from 1870 to 1960).

5. Clara Foltz, *Editorials on Women Lawyers*, SAN DIEGO BEE, Aug. 7, 21, and 28, 1887 (lecture text).

6. Foltz, *Struggles*, July 1916 (lecture text).

7. For more on the Equity Club, *see* DRACHMAN, WOMEN LAWYERS.

8. Ibid., at 50–51.

9. Ibid., at 186–87. On Mary Ann Greene, *see* Kathryn Johnson, *"A Pioneer Woman": The Scholar and Lawyer* (2006), at WLH website.

10. *Woman as Lawyer*, 1 REVOLUTION 4, 10 (July 8, 1869).

11. Robinson, *Women Lawyers*, at 10 (1890). For an analysis of Robinson's findings and a reprint of her 1890 article, *see* Barbara A. Babcock, *Making History: Lelia Robinson's Index to American Women Lawyers*, 2 GREEN BAG 65 (1998).

12. NORGREN, BELVA LOCKWOOD, at 73, 83 (Lockwood supporting Lowery); for Bittenbender and Kilgore, *see* Mary L. Clark, *The First Women Members of the Supreme Court Bar, 1879–1900*, 36 SAN DIEGO L. REV. 87, 93 (1999).

13. WOMAN'S TRIB., Apr. 12, 1890, at 1.

14. *Female Blackstones Meet Today, Three Days Convention of Women Lawyers at Isabella Club House*, CHI. TRIB., Aug. 3, 1893.

15. For descriptions of the meeting and speakers, *see "Queen Isabella Association":*

Women Lawyers at the Isabella Club House, 25 CHI. LEGAL NEWS, Aug. 5, 1893, at 421, 451; *Women Lawyers Meet, Women as Attorneys*, DAILY INTER-OCEAN, Aug. 3, Aug. 5, 1893. *See also* the Chicago History Society for Ellen Martin's papers and the Archives of the Isabella Association (including the call to the meeting and the meeting minutes).

16. *The Modern Portias*, 32 WOMAN's J., Aug. 12, 1893 ("learn from each other"); *Interview*, LAW STUDENT's HELPER, Oct. 1893.

17. Robinson, *Women Lawyers*, at 24, quoting Goodell's obituary in the *Chicago Journal*.

18. DRACHMAN, WOMEN LAWYERS, at 148 ("any sentimental view"); *Women Lawyers at the Isabella Club House*, 25 CHI. LEGAL NEWS, Aug. 5, 1893, at 451.

19. Clara Foltz, *Evolution of Law*, 48 ALB. L.J. 345 (1893); subsequent paragraphs rely on this source for all Foltz quotations.

20. *See* Alexander Callow Jr., *The Legislature of a Thousand Scandals*, 39 HIST. SOC'Y S. CAL. Q. 340, 347 (1957) (reporting that in 1893, $200,000 was appropriated to reclaim forty thousand coyote scalps).

21. Omychund v. Barker, 1 Ark. 21, 26 E.R. 15 (1744) (argument of Solicitor General William Murray, later Lord Mansfield).

22. EDWARD COKE, 1 COMMENTARIES ON THE LAWS OF ENGLAND 97b ("Reason is the life of the law; nay the common law is nothing else but reason, which is to be understood of an artificial perfection of reason, gotten by long study, observation, and experience, and not of every man's natural reason"); on Carter, *see* Lewis Grossman, *James Coolidge Carter and Mugwump Jurisprudence*, 20 L. & HIST. REV. 577 (2002).

23. *See* CHARLES MACCARTHY, THE WISCONSIN IDEA (1912).

24. *See* Benjamin Cardozo, *A Ministry of Justice*, 35 HARV. L. REV. 357, 461 (1921); MICHAEL ZANDER, THE LAW-MAKING PROCESS (6th ed. 2004); Kristen David Adams, *The American Law Institute: Justice Cardozo's Ministry of Justice?* 32 S. ILL. L.J. 173 (2007).

25. Presumably, Foltz did not know that one state had already adopted the exact arrangement she had advocated, and it had not been a success. In its 1870 constitution, Illinois had charged the state supreme court to report annually to the legislature on changes in the law that it thought desirable. The provision had turned into a dead letter, as the court, busy with its judicial duties, never took seriously its role as legislative advisor. But the idea of an advisory council of respected lawyers serving the role she spelled out would in the next century be widely adopted, in the form of state law revision commissions. Ben Heineman, *A Law Revision Commission for Illinois*, 42 ILL. L. REV. 697, 702 (1948) (describing the establishment of a commission by Ill. Laws 1869, 49).

26. On the founding of law reviews, *see* R. STEVENS, LAW SCHOOL: LEGAL EDUCATION IN AMERICA FROM THE 1850S TO THE 1980S (1983); and Michael I. Swygert & Jon W. Bruce, *The Historical Origins, Founding, and Early Developments of Student-Edited Law Reviews*, 36 HASTINGS L.J. 739 (1985).

27. *Editorial*, 6 ALB. L.J. 201 (1872) (founder quote); *Editorial, Irving Browne*, 1 GREEN BAG 509 (1889) ("undoubtedly more read").

28. Strauder v. West Virginia, 100 U.S. 303 (1879).

29. KATHLEEN BARRY, SUSAN B. ANTHONY: A BIOGRAPHY OF A SINGULAR FEMI-
NIST 216–17 (1988) (Anthony's stirring speeches); ALMA LUTZ, A BIOGRAPHY OF
ELIZABETH CADY STANTON, 1815–1902, at 162–63 (1940).

30. LYNN SHERR, FAILURE IS IMPOSSIBLE: SUSAN B. ANTHONY IN HER OWN
WORDS 218 (1995).

31. *See* Fair v. State, 43 Cal. 137 (1872); KENNETH LAMOTT, WHO KILLED MR.
CRITTENDEN? 284–85 (1963).

32. DAVID NASAW, THE CHIEF: THE LIFE OF WILLIAM RANDOLPH HEARST 98
(2000).

33. J. H. LEVY, THE NECESSITY OF CRIMINAL APPEAL AND THE MAYBRICK CASE
370–78 (1899).

34. Gail Hamilton, *An Open Letter to the Queen*, 155 N. AM. REV. 257, 260–61
(1892).

35. *See Hope for Mrs. Maybrick,* N.Y. WORLD, Aug. 23, 1895.

36. *Mrs. Foltz's Mission*, S.F. CALL, Sept. 1, 1895 (Foltz in London to "assist" in
Maybrick case), and same item in N.Y. WORLD, Aug. 31, 1895; *see also The Maybrick
Case*, WOMAN'S TRIB., Oct. 26, 1895, at 138; *Women's International Maybrick Associa-
tion*, TO-DAY'S WOMAN, July 30, 1895.

37. *Mrs. Foltz in a Collision at Sea*, CHI. DAILY TRIB., Oct. 1, 1895, at 3.

38. *See* Cara W. Robertson, *Representing "Miss Lizzie": Cultural Convictions in the
Trial of Lizzie Borden*, 8 YALE J. L. & HUMAN. 351 (1996).

39. *Miss Flagler Indicted*, N.Y. WORLD, Nov. 1, 1895.

40. *A Travesty on Justice*, N.Y. WORLD, Feb. 28, 1896.

41. *Aristocracy in America*, SPECTATOR, Mar. 21, 1896, at 408–9, *reprinted in* N.Y.
TIMES as *America's Privileged Classes*, Apr. 3, 1896.

42. IDANNA PUCCI, THE TRIALS OF MARIA BARBELLA: THE TRUE STORY OF A
NINETEENTH-CENTURY CRIME OF PASSION (1997) [hereafter PUCCI, THE TRIALS].
Unless otherwise noted, subsequent quotations are from and paragraphs rely on
this source, which is based on newspaper accounts.

43. On women and the New York electric chair, *see* STUART BANNER, THE DEATH
PENALTY 188 (2002).

44. N.Y. WORLD, July 19, 1895, *quoted in* PUCCI, THE TRIALS, at 120–21.

45. *Phrenological Journal quoted in* PUCCI, THE TRIALS, at 154–55; WOMAN'S TRIB.,
Nov. 28, 1896 ("helpless and ignorant"); Ingersoll *quoted in* PUCCI, THE TRIALS, 149.

46. People v. Barberi [*sic*], 31 CRIM. L. MAG. 449, 462 (Apr. 1896).

47. Clara Shortridge Foltz, *Should Women Be Executed?* 54 ALB. L.J. 309 (1896);
subsequent paragraphs rely on and quote from this source.

48. *Editorial,* WOMAN'S TRIB., Nov. 28, 1896, at 1; Livermore *quoted in* PUCCI,
THE TRIALS, at 120.

49. *New York Times quoted in* PUCCI, THE TRIALS, at 155–56.

50. *See* People v. Jane Shattuck, 49 P.315, 109 Cal. 673 (1895) (reversing conviction in first trial); *Mrs. Jane Shattuck's Case*, N.Y. DAILY TRIB., Feb. 16, 1896 (criticizing verdict of acquittal in retrial).

51. *Editorial*, WOMAN'S TRIB., Jan. 28, 1896.

52. JAMES LIVINGSTON, ARSENIC AND CLAM CHOWDER: MURDER IN GILDED AGE NEW YORK (2010), has a detailed account of the trial and its setting. Jury selection started on May 11 and the verdict was returned on June 24, 1896.

53. *Quick Verdict Expected*, N.Y. TIMES, June 23, 1896, at 8.

54. *Editor's Note*, 54 ALB. L.J. 38–39 (1896).

55. *Mrs. Fleming and the Sunday World's Woman Jury, These Twelve Clever Women Who Think for Themselves Are Considering the Evidence and Will Render a Verdict from the Woman's Standpoint When the Case Is Closed*, SUNDAY WORLD (New York), June 21, 1896, at 21 [hereafter *Mrs. Fleming and the World's Woman Jury*].

56. *Women in Celebrated Legal Cases*, 18 CRIM. L. MAG. & REP. 479, 480–81 (1896) ("enviable reputation" and describing the shadow jury); *Woman Jury in the Fleming Case*, SUNDAY WORLD (New York), June 28, 1896, at 23 ("taken off their coats" and reporting verdict) (quotations in subsequent paragraphs are from this source unless otherwise noted).

57. *Editorial Note*, 54 ALB. L.J. 38 (1896).

58. *Mrs. Fleming and the World's Woman Jury*.

59. For more on Jordan, *see* NOTABLE AMERICAN WOMEN (Jordan entry).

60. ELIZABETH JORDAN, THREE ROUSING CHEERS 78–82 (Maybrick), 135 (Barbella), 120–23 (Lizzie Borden) (1938).

61. ELIZABETH JORDAN, THREE ROUSING CHEERS 86–88; EMILY WORTIS LEIDER, CALIFORNIA'S DAUGHTER: GERTRUDE ATHERTON 145–49 (1991) (Atherton and Jordan).

Chapter Six

1. Foltz, *Struggles*, Aug. 1916; *Clara Foltz, San Francisco, Cal.*, 1 L. STUDENT'S HELPER 263, 264 (1893).

2. Foltz, *Struggles*, May 1916; *Clara Foltz Sure Frumpish Women Injure Suffrage*, DENV. POST, June 1, 1910.

3. Foltz, *Struggles*, Jan. 1918, Oct. 1916.

4. MATILDA GAGE, WOMAN'S NATIONAL LIBERAL UNION: REPORT OF THE CONVENTION FOR ORGANIZATION, Feb. 24–25, 1890, at 77 [hereafter GAGE REPORT].

5. THEODORE STANTON & HARRIET S. BLATCH, ELIZABETH CADY STANTON AS REVEALED IN HER LETTERS, DIARY AND REMINISCENCES 104–6 (1920).

6. *Letter from Clara Foltz*, N. NORTHWEST, Sept. 17, 1875, at 2.

7. Foltz, *Struggles*, Mar. 1917.

8. For more on Beecher and Woodhull, *see* BARBARA GOLDSMITH, OTHER POWERS: THE AGE OF SUFFRAGE, SPIRITUALISM AND THE SCANDALOUS VICTORIA WOODHULL (1998), and DEBBY APPLEGATE, THE MOST FAMOUS MAN IN AMERICA: THE BIOGRAPHY OF HENRY WARD BEECHER (2006).

9. Foltz, *Struggles*, Aug. 1916.

10. For analysis of the positive effects of the schism, *see* Ellen Carol DuBois, *The Radicalism of the Woman Suffrage Movement: Notes toward the Reconstruction of*

Nineteenth-Century Feminism, in WOMEN, LAW AND THE CONSTITUTION (Kermit Hall ed., 1987).

11. Adam Winkler, in *A Revolution Too Soon: Woman Suffragists and the Living Constitution*, 76 N.Y.U. L. REV. 1456 (2001), examines the use of the "New Departure" tactic.

12. Minor v. Happersett, 88 U.S. 162 (1875); WOMAN'S J., May 5, 1877, at 141.

13. S.F. WASP, Sept. 16, 1881, at 183 (noting also that Foltz had "a fine baritone voice and a pleasant pug nose"); S.F. MORNING CALL, Sept. 7, 1881, at 4.

14. *See* T. A. Larson, *The Woman Suffrage Movement in Washington*, 67 PAC. NW. Q. 49 (1976).

15. LIBERAL THINKER, at 1.

16. GAGE REPORT, at 3–6 (reprinting the *Call*).

17. LIBERAL THINKER, at 5.

18. For more on Gage, *see* SALLY ROESCH WAGNER, SHE WHO HOLDS UP THE SKY (1998); LEILA R. BRAMMER, EXCLUDED FROM SUFFRAGE HISTORY: MATILDA JOSLYN GAGE, NINETEENTH-CENTURY AMERICAN FEMINIST (2000).

19. CHAMPION OF WOMEN 115.

20. KATHY KERN, MRS. STANTON'S BIBLE 124 (2001) (quoting letter from Gage to Stanton, July 13, 1888, *reprinted in* WOMAN'S TRIB., Aug. 18, 1888). Kern explores the development of Stanton's anticlerical beliefs.

21. For more on Theosophy and Madame Blavatsky, *see* SYLVIA CRANSTON, H. P. B.: THE EXTRAORDINARY LIFE AND INFLUENCE OF HELENA BLAVATSKY (1993); WARREN SYLVESTER SMITH, THE LONDON HERETICS 1870–1914 (1967).

22. Blavatsky quoted in ARTHUR MORGAN, EDWARD BELLAMY 264 (1944). For the connection of Theosophy and Nationalism, *see* SYLVIA BOWMAN, EDWARD BELLAMY ABROAD 385–99 (1962); for more on Cables, see WOMAN OF THE CENTURY (Josephine Cables Aldrich entry).

23. HENRY EMFINGER, MY HOME TOWN: ALDRICH ALABAMA 2 (1959) (privately printed pamphlet).

24. Ibid., at 6. For more on Aldrich, *see* BIOGRAPHICAL DIRECTORY OF THE UNITED STATES CONGRESS 519 (1989) (William Aldrich).

25. LIBERAL THINKER, at 1 ("eminent lawyer"); WOMEN WITHOUT SUPERSTITION: "NO GODS—NO MASTERS" (Annie Laurie Gaylor ed., 1997), at 272 (Annie Besant entry) ("greatest orator"). For more on Besant, *see* ROGER MANVELL, THE TRIAL OF ANNIE BESANT AND CHARLES BRADLAUGH (1976); ARTHUR NETHERCOT, THE FIRST FIVE LIVES OF ANNIE BESANT (1960).

26. For more on Voltaireine, *see* PAUL AVRICH, AN AMERICAN ANARCHIST: THE LIFE OF VOLTAIRINE DE CLEYRE (1978).

27. Olympia Brown, *The Two Conventions*, WIS. CITIZEN, Mar. 1890.

28. WASH. POST, Feb. 9, 1890 (Stanton interview); GAGE REPORT, at 91.

29. GAGE REPORT, at 76–77.

30. Ibid., at 76.

31. WASH. POST, Feb. 25, 1890; *Mrs. Foltz Replies to Critics*, WOMAN'S TRIB., May 10, 1890, at 146.

32. GAGE REPORT, at 77 (Foltz related that she had worked for the WCTU); N. NORTHWEST, July 1, 1886, at 1; subsequent paragraphs rely on this article.

33. *See* NORMAN H. CLARK, THE DRY YEARS, PROHIBITION AND SOCIAL CHANGE IN WASHINGTON 57 (1965); *see also* Chapter 2.

34. RUTH BARNES MOYNIHAN, REBEL FOR RIGHTS: ABIGAIL SCOTT DUNIWAY 143–46 (1985); *see also* ABIGAIL SCOTT DUNIWAY, PATH BREAKING: AN AUTOBIOGRAPHICAL HISTORY OF THE EQUAL SUFFRAGE MOVEMENT IN PACIFIC COAST STATES 100 (1914).

35. NEW AMERICAN WOMAN, June 1916, at 8, and May 1917, at 17.

36. *U.S. Can Learn*, unknown newspaper, Jan. 25, 1929, *in* Foltz, Scrapbook.

37. PAC. ENSIGN, June 8, 1893, at 4; for more on the emergence of the WCTU into suffrage work and Sturtevant-Peet's leadership, *see* GAYLE GULLETT, BECOMING CITIZENS: THE EMERGENCE AND DEVELOPMENT OF THE CALIFORNIA WOMEN'S MOVEMENT, 1880–1911, at 77–83 and n.44 (2000) [hereafter GULLETT, BECOMING CITIZENS].

38. Letter from Mrs. Tracy Cutler, WOMAN'S J., May 7, 1892, at 23 (quoting Sturtevant-Peet).

39. *Notes Taken in Sacramento*, 3 PAC. ENSIGN, Mar. 9, 1893, at 2 (describing Severance); *Tricked! Tricked!* 3 PAC. ENSIGN, March 30, 1893, at 3–4 (Severance report on passage of the bill).

40. *Tricked! Tricked! supra.*

41. Reprinted in 3 PAC. ENSIGN, Mar. 15, 1893.

42. *See* DICTIONARY OF AMERICAN BIOGRAPHY (1957) (Bonney entry); *The World's Congress Auxiliary of the World's Columbian Exposition*, 23 CHI. LEG. NEWS 250 (1891) (featuring Bonney with a picture); DAVID F. C. BURG, CHICAGO'S WHITE CITY OF 1893, at 235–85 (1976) (chapter on the World's Congress Auxiliary).

43. CHI. INTER-OCEAN, May 16, 1893, at 1.

44. PAC. ENSIGN, June 8, 1893 (reporting on temperance meeting); CHI. INTER-OCEAN May 22, 1893, at 3 (labor meeting).

45. For more on Field's "conversion" to suffrage, *see* GARY SCHARNHORST, KATE FIELD: THE MANY LIVES OF A NINETEENTH-CENTURY AMERICAN JOURNALIST 218 (2008); on Anthony's talk, *see* Susan B. Anthony, *Organization among Women as an Instrument in Promoting the Interests of Political Liberty*, *in* THE CONGRESS OF WOMEN: HELD IN THE WOMAN'S BUILDING, WORLD'S COLUMBIAN EXPOSITION, CHICAGO, U.S.A., 1893 (Mary Kavanaugh Oldham Eagle ed., 1894) [hereafter CONGRESS OF WOMEN].

46. On Mrs. Potter Palmer, *see* ISHBEL ROSS, SILHOUETTE IN DIAMONDS: THE LIFE OF MRS. POTTER PALMER (1960); on women's participation at the fair, *see* Gayle Gullett, *Our Great Opportunity: Organized Women Advance Women's Work at the World Columbian Exposition of 1893*, 87 ILL. HIST. J. 259 (1994).

47. For more on women's participation, *see* Ellen M. Henrotin, *The Great Congresses of the World's Fair*, COSMOPOLITAN MAG., Mar. 1893, at 626; Henrotin, *The Coming Congresses at Chicago*, 23 WOMAN'S J. 406 (1892).

48. On the rivalry between the Palmer forces and the Isabellas, *see* JEANNE MADELINE WEIMANN, THE FAIR WOMEN: THE STORY OF THE WOMAN'S BUILDING AT THE WORLD'S COLUMBIAN EXPOSITION OF 1893 (1981); Matthew J. Sanders, *An Introduction to Phoebe Wilson Couzins* (2000), *available at* WLH website.

49. Lucy Stone, *The Progress of Fifty Years, in* CONGRESS OF WOMEN, at 58.

50. Ibid.

51. *Meeting of Equal Suffragists,* DAILY INTER-OCEAN, May 21, 1893, at 5.

52. IDA HUSTED HARPER, 2 LIFE AND WORK OF SUSAN B. ANTHONY 764 (1898).

53. Ibid., at 770.

54. PAC. ENSIGN, June 8, 1893, at 4.

55. 4 HWS, at 479.

56. *A Representative Lady Advocate Says a Last Public Word,* S.F. CALL, Oct. 31, 1895. For more on postfair California clubs and activities, *see* GULLETT, BECOMING CITIZENS, at 65–106; REDA DAVIS, CALIFORNIA WOMEN: A GUIDE TO THEIR POLITICS, 1885–1911, at 78 (1967).

57. 4 HWS, at 479–80.

58. *Men and Women; Both Should Have Equal Rights to Vote,* MORNING CALL, June 3, 1894 (Foltz absent; others speak during her time).

59. *Two Bodies Lay Claim to the Same Charter and Title—Both to Elect Officers,* S.F. CALL, July 1, 1894. For more on the fight between the suffragists, *see* GULLETT, BECOMING CITIZENS, at 88–89.

60. *What Mrs. Gordon Says of Her Rival,* S.F. CALL, Sept. 13, 1894; *Tiger Orbs,* S.F. CALL, Sept. 14, 1894 (Foltz's reply).

61. *See* CARLOS A. SCHWANTES, COXEY'S ARMY: AN AMERICAN ODYSSEY 130–32 (1985); on California sympathy for railroad strikes, including among farmers, *see* WILLIAMS, DEMOCRATIC PARTY, at 195–96.

62. For Johnson's maneuver, *see* S.F. CALL, Feb. 7, 1895; for more on the convention, *see* WINFIELD J. DAVIS, POLITICAL CONVENTIONS IN CALIFORNIA 1849–1892 (1893).

63. GULLETT, BECOMING CITIZENS, at 82–83.

64. *For Equal Suffrage, Clara Foltz Talks to the Senators, An Entirely New View of a Question That Has Vexed Many Great Minds,* S.F. CALL, Jan. 25, 1895.

65. *Voice of the Woman,* S.F. CALL, Feb. 9, 1895, at 3. For more on Foltz and Gordon lobbying, *see* GULLETT, BECOMING CITIZENS, at 83–84

66. *Just a Glimmer of Light Ahead,* S.F. CALL, Mar. 21, 1895; subsequent paragraphs rely on this source.

67. *See* Susan Schreiber Edelman, *"A Red Hot Suffrage Campaign": The Woman Suffrage Cause in California, 1896,* 2 CALIF. SUP. CT. HIST. SOC'Y YEARBOOK (1995) [hereafter Edelman, *Red Hot Suffrage Campaign*].

68. *Mrs. Foltz on Suffrage, Many Clubs Being Formed,* S.F. CALL, Apr. 1, 1896; subsequent paragraphs rely on this source.

69. *Good News from California,* 8 WOMAN'S TRIB., at 13, May 16, 1896 (quoting Anthony: "In 29 years of campaigning, this is [the] first time that a paper has given timely support").

70. *The Call Declares for Woman Suffrage, Miss Susan B. Anthony Dances in her Delight,* S.F. CALL, May 3, 1896.

71. *See New Era Dawns, The Morning Call Sold by Auction,* S.F. CALL, Jan. 5, 1895.

72. JOHN BRUCE, GAUDY CENTURY 247 (1948).

73. S.F. CALL, June 27, 1896.

74. *See Woman Suffragists Hopeful, Expect to Secure a Favorable Plank in the Platform,* N.Y. TIMES, June 14, 1896; Lillie Devereux Blake, *Our New York Letter,* WOMAN'S J., June 27, 1896 [hereafter Blake, *Our New York Letter*].

75. *Women at St. Louis,* WOMAN'S J., June 27, 1896 (quoting the Dover, N.H., *Enquirer*).

76. HARPER'S WKLY., Special Convention Issue, June 27, 1896, at 609, 629, and 632.

77. For the story on the backstage lobbying for gold, *see* Henry B. Blackwell, *The Battle of the Standards,* WOMAN'S J., June 27, 1896.

78. *Interesting Women,* N.Y. L.J., July 20, 1896.

79. For the wording of the plank and an account of Missouri suffragists, *see* Blake, *Our New York Letter,* and Blackwell, *A Missouri Tangle,* WOMAN'S J., June 27, 1896, at 204 and 205.

80. Originally made in the *Syracuse Sunday Herald,* June 28, 1896, Foltz's attack was widely reprinted; *see, e.g.,* WOMAN'S TRIB., July 11, 1896, at 66.

81. Ibid.; HARPER, ANTHONY, at 880.

82. *Mrs. Foltz Indignant,* S.F. CALL, July 8, 1896.

83. MELANIE SUSAN GUSTAFSON, WOMEN AND THE REPUBLICAN PARTY, 1854–1924, at 80–81 (2001).

84. N.Y. TRIB., Aug. 13, 1896; *Mrs. Foltz on Suffrage,* S.F. CALL, Apr. 1, 1896.

85. For the outcome of the campaign, *see* GULLETT, BECOMING CITIZENS, at 94–99; ETHINGTON, PUBLIC CITY, at 398–401; Edelman, *Red Hot Suffrage Campaign,* at 181–82.

86. *The Career of a Modern Portia,* 2 SUCCESS, Feb. 18, 1899, at 205–6, *reprinted in* SELECTED MAGAZINE ARTICLES OF THEODORE DREISER: LIFE AND ART IN THE AMERICAN 1890S, at 140 (Yoshinobu Hakutani ed., 1985).

87. *Susan B. Anthony Speaks on the Suffrage Question; Sees the Promised Land,* DAILY INTER-OCEAN, Aug. 9, 1893, at 8.

88. On the formation of the Progressive movement, *see* KEVIN STARR, INVENTING THE DREAM: CALIFORNIA THROUGH THE PROGRESSIVE ERA 235–36 (1985); GEORGE E. MOWRY, THE CALIFORNIA PROGRESSIVES (1951) (providing the classic account of the California movement) [hereafter MOWRY, PROGRESSIVES]; *cf.* CALIFORNIA PROGRESSIVISM REVISITED (William Deverell & Tom Sitton eds., 1994) (essays taking issue with Mowry on various accounts).

89. *How Women Will Vote,* S.F. CALL, Nov. 5, 1911 (Foltz claiming to be a lifelong Republican and a "stand-patter" at that).

90. On Grove Johnson's politics, *see* SPENCER C. OLIN JR., CALIFORNIA'S PRODIGAL SONS: HIRAM JOHNSON AND THE PROGRESSIVES, 1911–1917 (1968); RICHARD COKE LOWER, A BLOC OF ONE: THE POLITICAL CAREER OF HIRAM W. JOHNSON (1993).

91. Mowry, Progressives, at 33 (1963) (quoting Bell); Clara Foltz, *Open Letter to the Governor*, S.F. Chron., Aug. 23, 1916.

92. *Women at War in Suffrage Campaign; Foltz Statute Plan Starts the Fight*, L.A. Examiner, Jan. 4, 1911.

93. Letter from Clara Foltz to Clara Colby (June 26, 1908), *in* Colby Papers.

94. Ibid. (Apr. 8, 1909).

95. L.A. Herald, Apr. 3, 1909; Letter from Clara Foltz to Clara Colby (June 26, 1908), *in* Colby Papers; Fresno Morning Republican, Apr. 25, 1911 (quoting Progressive Chester Rowell).

96. *See* Gullett, Becoming Citizens, at 170–71.

97. Ibid., at 164, 166–67, 172, 177–78, and 181. For further descriptions of Gillett's broken promise, *see* 6 HWS, at 40–42; Rebecca Mead, How the Vote Was Won: Woman Suffrage in the Western United States, 1868–1914, at 124, 126–32, 134, 142 (2004).

98. Letter from Clara Foltz to Governor James N. Gillett (Nov. 22, 1909) (Gillett Papers, California State Archives, Sacramento).

99. *Los Angeles Woman Put on Prison Board*, L.A. Herald, Feb. 11, 1910.

100. *To Be a Good Mother Should Study Law, Says This Portia*, N.Y. Evening Telegram, May 28, 1910.

101. On Keith and the collegiate club, *see* Gullett, Becoming Citizens, 184–85.

102. Gullett, Becoming Citizens, at 189. For more on Edson, *see* Jacqueline R. Braitman, *A California Stateswoman: The Public Career of Katherine Phillips Edson*, 65 Cal. Hist. 82 (1986); Judith Raftery, *Los Angeles Clubwomen and Progressive Reform*, *in* California Progressivism Revisited 144, 158–64 (William Deverell & Tom Sitton eds., 1994).

103. Foltz, *Editorial*, New American Woman, June 1916. For the formation of the Political Equality League, *see* Gullett, Becoming Citizens, at 182–84.

104. *Let Antis Stick to Chiffon Life; Helps Cause*, unknown L.A. newspaper, *in* Foltz, Scrapbook.

105. *Mrs. Clara S. Foltz Resigns as President of Suffrage Club*, L.A. Examiner, Nov. 11, 1910.

106. *See Women at War in Suffrage Campaign; Foltz Statute Plan Starts the Fight*, L.A. Examiner, Jan. 4, 1911.

107. *Suffragette Camp Riled*, S.F. Call, Jan. 3, 1911.

108. Letter from Clara Foltz to Clara Colby (June 2, 1907), *in* Colby Papers (comparing lesser women striding to the front of Laura Gordon).

109. *Badger Club Wants Woman Prosecutor*, L.A. Examiner, Mar. 11, 1910.

110. *Hurrah for the California Men, They Passed the Suffrage Amendment in the Senate 33 to 7 in the House 65–6*, Woman's Standard, Mar. 1911, at 2 ("splendid victory"); Letter from Elizabeth Lowe Watson to Clara Foltz (Feb. 12, 1911) (Harbert Collection, Huntington Library, San Marino, California).

111. *See* Davis, California Women, at 125 ("The San Francisco Call said [the Committee of Fifty] was composed of a bevy of corrupt legislators once entrenched

in Sacramento"); Foltz, *Struggles*, Apr. 1916, at 10 (describing the Committee of Fifty on the fifth anniversary of suffrage).

112. Jane Apostol, *Why Women Should Not Have the Vote: Anti-Suffrage Views in the Southland in 1911*, 70 S. CAL. HIST. Q. 29–42 (Spring 1988); *Granting of Suffrage Sacred Duty People Must Rule, Says Sen. Works*, L.A. HERALD, *in* Foltz, Scrapbook.

113. On the campaign, *see* GULLETT, BECOMING CITIZENS; REBECCA MEAD, HOW THE VOTE WAS WON: WOMAN SUFFRAGE IN THE WESTERN UNITED STATES, 1868–1914 (2004); Susan Englander, *Class Conflict and Class Coalition in the California Woman Suffrage Movement, 1907–1912* (1992) (unpublished Ph.D. dissertation).

114. SELINA SOLOMONS, HOW WE WON THE VOTE IN CALIFORNIA: A TRUE STORY OF THE CAMPAIGN OF 1911, at 31 (1912) (and generally for more on Foltz's activities and a lively contemporary account).

115. *Hundreds Cheer Suffrage Banner; Band Plays as Streamer Unfurls*, L.A. HERALD, Aug. 12, 1911.

116. *Suffragists to Hang Banner Today; Yellow Flag to Span Thoroughfare*, L.A. HERALD, Aug. 11, 1911.

117. W. WOMAN VOTER, Nov. 1911, at 3; GULLETT, BECOMING CITIZENS, at 191–92.

118. Jennie Allen, *The Fight for a Public Defender*, 13 W. COAST MAG. 41 (Oct. 1912) (interviewing Foltz).

119. For a description of the 1911 mayoral campaign, *see* Judson A. Grenier, *Hiram Johnson and the Progressive Years*, *in* THE RUMBLE OF CALIFORNIA POLITICS 1848–1970, at 165, 181–82 (Royce D. Delmatier, Clarence F. McIntosh & Earl G. Waters eds., 1970).

120. For the case and its background, *see* GEOFFREY COWAN, THE PEOPLE V. CLARENCE DARROW: THE BRIBERY TRIAL OF AMERICA'S GREATEST LAWYER (1993).

121. On women's involvement in the runoff campaign, *see* Sherry J. Katz, *Redefining 'The Political': Socialist Women and Party Politics in California, 1900–1920*, *in* WE HAVE COME TO STAY: AMERICAN WOMEN AND POLITICAL PARTIES, 1886–1960 (Melanie Gustafson, Kristie Miller & Elisabeth I. Perry eds., 1999); *see also* Katz, *Frances Nacke Noel and Sister Movements: Socialism, Feminism, and Trade Unionism in Los Angeles, 1909–1916*, 67 CAL. HIST. 180, 181–89 (1988).

122. *How the Women Will Vote*, S.F. CALL, Nov. 5, 1911, at 45.

123. Mabel Craft Deering, *The Woman's Demonstration, How They Won and Used the Vote in California*, COLLIER'S, Jan. 6, 1912, at 17.

124. *Taft Followers, Confident of Victory*, S.F. CALL, Mar. 5, 1912.

125. Letter from Clara Foltz to Clara Colby (June 28, 1908), *in* Colby Papers; WHO'S WHO IN LOS ANGELES COUNTY (1928–29).

Chapter Seven

1. Clara Foltz, *The Rights of Persons Accused*, Address to the Congress on Jurisprudence and Law Reform during the Chicago World's Fair, 48 ALB. L.J. 248 (1893) [hereafter Foltz, World's Fair Speech] for quotes in this and the next paragraph; *see also* Foltz, *Public Defenders*.

2. HISTORICAL AND CONTEMPORARY REVIEW OF BENCH AND BAR IN CALIFORNIA 109 (1926) (Foltz entry) [hereafter BENCH AND BAR IN CALIFORNIA].

3. Foltz, *Public Defenders*, at 393 and n.2.

4. ALB. L.J., Jan. 21, 1897, at 8; Editorial, *Public Defenders*, 10 HARV. L. REV. 514 (1896–97); *Editorial*, N.Y. TIMES, Jan. 23, 1897, at 6; *Public Defenders*, N.Y. DAILY TRIB., Jan. 25, 1897, at 6; Foltz, *Public Defenders*, at 393 and n.2.

5. Lamont v. Solano County, 49 Cal. 158, 159 (1874) (holding that California lawyers have a professional duty to serve when appointed).

6. Foltz, *Struggles*, Jan. 1918.

7. The arson case is told in Foltz, *Struggles,* Jan–Mar. 1918; quotations that follow are from these sources unless otherwise noted. The early 1880s is the date because it is the only time Ferral and Stonehill served concurrently.

8. Foltz, World's Fair Speech, at 250.

9. Higginson quoted in Howard N. Meyer, *Introduction*, THE MAGNIFICENT ACTIVIST: THE WRITINGS OF THOMAS WENTWORTH HIGGINSON 1823–1911, at 8 (2000). For more on Higginson, *see* BRENDA WHITEAPPLE, WHITE HEAT: THE FRIENDSHIP OF EMILY DICKINSON AND THOMAS WENTWORTH HIGGINSON (2008); TILDEN EDELSTEIN, STRANGE ENTHUSIASM (1968). For more on the linkages among various nineteenth-century reforms, see *Preface*, RONALD G. WALTERS, AMERICAN REFORMERS, 1815–1860, ix (1978); BONNIE S. ANDERSON, JOYOUS GREETINGS: THE FIRST INTERNATIONAL WOMEN'S MOVEMENT, 1830–1860 (2000).

10. *See, e.g.*, *A County Attorney for the Defense of Criminals*, 8 PRISONERS' FRIEND, Oct. 1855, at 58 (1845–1861), for such a proposal.

11. Gordon Interview, *The Women Who Are Helping to Make This a Great City*, S.F. CALL, July 18, 1897, at 27. For a description of Gordon's criminal practice, *see* Babcock, *Women Defenders in the West*, 1 NEV. L.J. 1, 10–12 (2001).

12. *See* WOMAN OF THE CENTURY (Ricker entry); for more on Foltz and the notaryship, *see* Chapter 3.

13. Ibid. On Bradlaugh, *see* WARREN SYLVESTER SMITH, THE LONDON HERETICS, 1870–1914 (1967).

14. Robinson, *Women Lawyers*, at 12.

15. *All Bade Her Godspeed*, S.F. CALL, Nov. 5, 1895. For a listing of Foltz's reform projects, *see* THE NATIONAL CYCLOPEDIA OF AMERICAN BIOGRAPHY (1930) (Foltz entry).

16. Foltz, *Struggles*, June 1918, for this and subsequent paragraphs.

17. *How to Secure Free and Speedy Justice and Stop Lynching*, 2 NEW NATION 419–20, July 2, 1892, for this and the next paragraph; *see also Let Us Have Free Justice*, 3 NEW NATION 214, Apr. 29, 1893; Babcock, *Inventing*, at 1298–1301.

18. ARTHUR LIPOW, AUTHORITARIAN SOCIALISM IN THE UNITED STATES: EDWARD BELLAMY AND THE NATIONALIST MOVEMENT 75 n.53 (1982).

19. Foltz, Defender Bill, *in* Babcock, *Inventing*, at 1272–73.

20. William Aldrich, *Public Defenders*, LIBERAL THINKER, Jan. 1890, at 3–4.

21. GAGE REPORT, at 72–79, for this and subsequent paragraphs; *see also* WOMAN'S TRIB., Mar. 15, 1890, at 85.

22. *A "Liberal" Platform*, WASH. POST, Feb. 26, 1890.

23. *What a Boston Paper Has to Say of a Former San Jose Lady*, SAN JOSE DAILY MERCURY, May 8, 1890, at 3 (quoting Susan Wixon in the *Boston Investigator*); Matilda Gage, FREETHINKER, May 1890, at 263 ("It was remarkable to note in what different spirit the proposition was received by the lawyers taking part in the discussion; the men opposing, the women sustaining it").

24. NORGREN, BELVA LOCKWOOD 179–81.

25. GAGE REPORT, at 79–80.

26. For the Wells trial, *see* Babcock, *Inventing*, at 1285–87, and Foltz, *Struggles*, June 1918.

27. Foltz, *Struggles*, June 1918.

28. *Wells on Trial: Gracie Gilbert Repeats Her Charges: An Uncomfortable Fire of Questions: The Life History of a Young Adventuress—Scenes in the Courtroom*, S.F. CHRON., Oct. 11, 1892. Subsequent paragraphs rely on this source.

29. *The Dick Forgery*, S.F. CHRON., Oct. 12, 1892; subsequent paragraphs rely on this source.

30. On Lees, *see* THOMAS S. DUKE, CELEBRATED CRIMINAL CASES OF AMERICA *passim* and picture at 63 (1910).

31. Clara Foltz, Defendant's Brief, People v. Wells, 34 P.1078 (Cal. 1893) (No. 21027) [hereafter Foltz, Defendant's Brief]. Foltz also used the term "plastic judge" in her World's Fair Speech.

32. *She Kicked Off Her Shoe: Clara Foltz Puts Her Dainty Bottine in Unblushing Evidence*, S.F. EXAMINER, Oct. 13, 1892, for this and subsequent paragraphs unless otherwise noted.

33. *Waved Her Shoe in Court*, S.F. CALL, Oct. 13, 1892.

34. *Too Much Evidence, a Private Detective's Bad Admission*, S.F. CALL, Oct. 13, 1892, for this and subsequent paragraphs.

35. *Wells Testifies in His Own Behalf*, S.F. CHRON., Oct. 14, 1892, for this and subsequent paragraph.

36. Foltz, Defendant's Brief.

37. *The Case Argued*, S.F. EXAMINER, Oct. 15, 1892, at 3.

38. *An Angry Wife's Protest*, S.F. CHRON., Oct. 15, 1892.

39. *See Wells Convicted . . . He Weeps When He Hears the Verdict: His Attorney Tries to Console Him but Her Efforts Are in Vain*, S.F. CHRON., Oct. 15, 1892.

40. *Women as Lawyers*, S.F. CALL, Oct. 17, 1892.

41. People v. Wells, 34 P.1078, 1079–80 (Cal. 1893).

42. Berger v. United States, 295 U.S. 78, 89 (1935).

43. *Women in the Law Reform Congress*, 25 CHI. LEGAL NEWS 435 (1893), *reprinted in* 48 ALB. L. REV. 147 (1893).

44. *Judge Caton's Remarks*, 25 CHI. LEGAL NEWS 431 (1893) ("legal luminaries"); Belva Lockwood, *The Congress of Law Reform*, 3 AM. J. POL. 321, 323 (1893) (one observer).

45. For Lockwood's piece, see Lockwood, ibid.

46. On the attendance of Cooley, *see Politics and Law*, DAILY INTER-OCEAN,

Aug. 8, 1893, at 1; on Field's attendance, *see How to Rule a City*, CHI. DAILY TRIB., Aug. 10, 1893.

47. Foltz, World's Fair Speech, for this and subsequent paragraphs. Comparisons to the Wells case are based on Defendant's Brief, People v. Wells, 34 P.1078 (Cal. 1893) (No. 21027); Foltz, *Public Defenders*, at 415–16.

48. DAILY INTER-OCEAN, Aug. 9, 1893, at 8; 13 W. COAST MAG. 43, 44 (1912); Clara Foltz, 1 LAW STUDENT'S HELPER 304 (1893).

49. James B. Thayer, *The Origin and Scope of the American Doctrine of Constitutional Law*, 7 HARV. L. REV. 129, n.1 (1893).

50. DAILY INTER-OCEAN, Aug. 10, 1893, at 8 ("very profound, logical and exhaustive treatise and called forth deep interest"). For modern interest in Thayer's work, see Thomas C. Grey, *Thayer's Doctrine: Notes on Its Origin, Scope and Present Implication*, 88 NW. U. L. REV. 28–41 (1993).

51. Foltz, World's Fair Speech, at 249; *see* Heb. 11:1 ("faith is the substance of things hoped for") and Matt. 7:9 ("if his son ask for bread, will he give him a stone?").

52. S.F. CALL, Sept. 14, 1894 ("very sanctuary"). For changes in the legal profession, *see* Michael McConville & Chester L. Mirsky, *Understanding Defense of the Poor in State Courts: The Socio Legal Context of Non-Adversarial Advocacy*, 10 STUDIES L. POLITICS & SOC'Y 217 (1990); RICHARD HOFSTADER, AGE OF REFORM 156–58 (1955); and Robert Gordon, *The Ideal and the Actual in the Law: Fantasies and Practices of New York City Lawyers 1870–1910*, *in* THE NEW HIGH PRIESTS (1984).

53. Foltz, *Public Defenders*, at 393.

54. Babcock, *Inventing*, at 1280–1313, covers in detail the legal arguments and sources for Foltz's conception of the public defender. Subsequent paragraphs refer to her World's Fair Speech, *Public Defenders*, and *Duties of District Attorneys in Criminal Prosecutions*, 18 CRIM. L. MAG. & REPORTER 415 (1896) [hereafter Foltz, *Duties*].

55. Foltz, World's Fair Speech, at 248; *Duties*, at 415; *Public Defenders*, at 393.

56. Foltz, *Duties*, at 416–17.

57. Foltz, *Public Defenders*, at 395 ("free and impartial"). For the originality of the "minister of public justice," *see* Babcock, *Inventing*, at 1283–85.

58. Foltz, *Public Defenders*, at 402.

59. Foltz, World's Fair Speech, at 248; *Public Defenders*, at 42 n.1 (statistics on innocence).

60. Foltz, World's Fair Speech, at 250. For use of the Lockean contract argument, *see* DORIS WEATHERFORD, A HISTORY OF THE AMERICAN SUFFRAGE MOVEMENT 40 (1998).

61. Foltz, *Public Defenders*, at 394 and n.4 (citing 4 WILLIAM BLACKSTONE, COMMENTARIES 355 [1765–1769]).

62. Foltz, World's Fair Speech, at 248.

63. 372 U.S. 335, 341–45 (1963).

64. *Editor's Note*, 55 ALB. L.J. 66 (1897).

65. Foltz, *Duties*, at 417.

66. Ibid., at 421–22.

67. Ibid., at 424.

68. For more on New York politics at the time, *see* DAVID C. HAMMACK, POWER AND SOCIETY: GREATER NEW YORK AT THE TURN OF THE CENTURY (1982); RICHARD L. MCCORMICK, FROM REALIGNMENT TO REFORM: POLITICAL CHANGE IN NEW YORK STATE, 1893–1910 (1981); HAROLD F. GOSNELL, BOSS PLATT AND HIS NEW YORK MACHINE: A STUDY OF THE POLITICAL LEADERSHIP OF THOMAS C. PLATT, THEODORE ROOSEVELT, AND OTHERS (1924).

69. The signatures of Thomas Platt and two of his chief lieutenants, Lemuel Quigg and Edward Lauterback, torn off from letters, appear in Trella Toland's autograph book, dated 1897.

70. N.Y. TRIBUNE, Jan. 25, 1897; Foltz, *Public Defenders,* at 393 n.1; *Public Defenders,* WASH. POST, Feb. 12, 1897.

71. Foltz, *Public Defenders,* at 393 n.1; for news coverage, *see Mrs. Clara Foltz Urges the Appointment of a Public Defender: Hearings on Bills before the New York Judiciary Committee,* N.Y. DAILY TRIB., Jan. 25, 1897, at 6; *A Bill for a Public Defender,* ALB. EVENING J., Jan. 21, 1897; N.Y. TIMES, Jan. 22, 1897, at 4; *How Mrs. Clara Foltz Would Provide Counsel for Those Who Are Too Poor to Employ a Lawyer,* BROOKLYN EAGLE, Jan. 23, 1897, at 7; EVENING TIMES, Jan. 25, 1890.

72. Jennie Allen, *The Fight for a Public Defender,* 13 W. COAST MAG., Oct. 1912 ("precious" bill); *New York Legislature: Indications That It Will Not Be Possible to Close the Session before the First of May, Important Matters Pending, Programme in the Two Houses for This Week—Hearings by Committees—Measures That Are Regarded as Dead,* N.Y. TIMES, Apr. 5, 1897.

73. HAROLD F. GOSNELL, BOSS PLATT AND HIS NEW YORK MACHINE: A STUDY OF THE POLITICAL LEADERSHIP OF THOMAS C. PLATT, THEODORE ROOSEVELT, AND OTHERS 233 (1924).

74. David C. Hammack, POWER AND SOCIETY—GREATER NEW YORK AT THE TURN OF THE CENTURY 118 (1982) (quoting N. Y. WORLD, Oct. 14 and 15, 1897).

75. Foltz, *Public Defenders,* at 393 n.1, n.2, 403.

76. On the *American, see* Roger C. Cramton, *"The Most Remarkable Institution": The American Law Review,* 36 J. LEGAL EDUC. 1 (1986). The two articles authored by women are Martha Strickland, *The Common Law and Statutory Right of Woman to Office,* 17 AM. U. L. REV. 670 (1883), and Mary A. Greene, *Privileged Communications between Husband and Wife,* 24 AM. U. L. REV. 779 (1890).

77. ELIZABETH KEMPER ADAMS, WOMEN PROFESSIONAL WORKERS 73 (1921). On the public defender provision of the charter, see LOS ANGELES COUNTY CHARTER, § 23, at 20 (2006); R. S. Gray, *The Public Defender,* 4 J. AM. INST. CRIM. L. & CRIMINOLOGY 650 (1913–14).

78. BENCH AND BAR IN CALIFORNIA (recording that Foltz "pioneered the movement for the establishment of the office of Public Defender," authored bills introduced in the "legislature of thirty-two states," and had the public defender included in the Los Angeles charter and in statewide legislation in 1921). For the effect of the bill, *see* Walton J. Wood, *Unexpected Results from the Establishment of the Office of Public Defender,* 7 J. AM. INST. CRIM. L. & CRIMINOLOGY 592–97 (1917).

79. REGINALD HEBER SMITH, JUSTICE AND THE POOR 116 (1919) ("flood of articles"); A. Mabel Barrow, *Public Defender: A Bibliography*, 14 J. AM. INST. CRIM. L. & CRIMINOLOGY 556 (1924) (collects outpouring of articles and studies). For the influence of the Los Angeles office on later developments, *see* Babcock, *Inventing*, 1270–74.

80. For a detailed comparison of the Foltzian and Progressive defenders, *see* Babcock, *Inventing*, at 1274–77.

81. Powell v. Alabama, 287 U.S. 45, 71 (1932); Gideon v. Wainwright, 372 U.S. 335 (1963).

Conclusion

1. *See, e.g.*, Foltz, Scrapbook; S.F. EXAMINER, Feb. 19, 1912 (Foltz announces for state Senate); L.A. HERALD, March 8, 1916 (Foltz contemplates run for U.S. Senate). The assistant attorney general post went to a younger woman from Los Angeles, Mabel Walker Willebrandt. Though Foltz claimed that she had been offered the job and turned it down (S.F. CHRON., June 29, 1921), there is good evidence that Sam Shortridge could not get the appointment through because of opposition from Los Angeles women, including the younger Progressive women. *See* DOROTHY M. BROWN, MABEL WALKER WILLEBRANDT, A STUDY OF POWER, LOYALTY, AND LAW, at 46–47 (quoting letters from Katherine Edson and others to Hiram Johnson and Meyer Lissner).

2. Zilfa Estcourt, *Mrs. Foltz Here to Write Memoirs of Life in Law*, S. F. CHRON., Mar. 21, 1931, at 15.

3. *Mrs. Foltz Drops Legal Profession*, S.F. CHRON., Mar. 18, 1931.

4. Foltz, *Struggles*, Sept. 1917 (hasty, hurried); Apr. 1916 ("table book of memory").

5. Foltz, *Struggles*, Dec. 1917.

6. Foltz, *Struggles*, Mar. 1918.

7. *Shortridge's Sister Out for Governorship; She Whacks Her Male Rivals in California*, N.Y. TIMES, Feb. 15, 1930, at 3; campaign leaflets (Alice Park Papers, Huntington Library, San Marino, California); *Obituary: Mrs. Clara Foltz, Lawyer, Is Dead: Suffrage Champion and First Woman to Practice Law on Pacific Coast; Tried to Be Governor*, N.Y. TIMES, Sept. 3, 1934, at 13 (eight thousand votes). But, *see* Mortimer D. Schwartz, Susan L. Brandt & Patience Milrod, *Clara Shortridge Foltz: Pioneer in the Law*, 27 HASTINGS L. REV. 545. 561 (1976), citing official reports giving her vote as 3,570.

8. *See Clara S. Foltz, Shortridge's Sister, Passes*, S.F. CHRON., Sept. 3, 1934, at 3; *Mrs. Foltz's Life Closes; Pioneer Woman of Bar Dies*, L.A. TIMES, Sept. 3, 1934; *Obituary*, N.Y. TIMES, Sept. 3, 1934.

9. Jennie Allen, *The Fight for a Public Defender*, 13 W. COAST MAG. 43 (1912); subsequent paragraphs rely on this source.

Note on Documentation

This book has an online supplement, *Woman Lawyer: The Trials of Clara Foltz*, On-line Notes, which is part of the Women's Legal History website (http://womens legalhistory.stanford.edu). The online companion contains essays and bibliographic notes that extend the documentation in the printed book.

An initial section provides (1) biographical material about Clara Foltz as well as compilations of her publications and archival collections of documents related to her life; (2) bibliographic essays on such topics as the legal status of women in the nineteenth century, the use of the term "feminism" in relation to pre-twentieth-century women's rights movements, and feminist biographies in particular and biographies of major figures in the suffrage movement in general; (3) brief biographical sketches and bibliographic sources for several other nineteenth-century women lawyers; and (4) timelines of the important events in Foltz's life.

After the introductory section, the online notes are arranged in chapter-by-chapter outlines, following the organization of *Woman Lawyer* and assuming familiarity with the text. The reader will find layered, detailed information on a wide range of topics pertaining to not only Clara Foltz's life but also her times.

Index

The index can be found on the Women's Legal History website (http://womenslegal history.stanford.edu). In addition to the standard book index, an expanded index includes links to the website content. See page 371 (Note on Documentation) for a brief description of the online supplement to *Woman Lawyer* and the website's main page for a detailed outline of the material.